MW00453842

Praise for *Excluded*

"In this brilliant book, Richard Kahlenberg deftly integrates quantitative and qualitative evidence to illuminate the basic theme of his career and one of the central controversies in contemporary America—how to reconcile the tension between class and race. More specifically, he shows how 'snob zoning' leads to segregation by both race and class and thus blocks opportunity for all Americans. Nevertheless, it is ultimately an optimistic book, showing necessary reforms are both technically feasible and politically possible. He eloquently evokes the final dream of both Martin Luther King and Bobby Kennedy, uniting working-class whites and people of color in a single coalition for reform."

—ROBERT D. PUTNAM, research professor, Harvard
Kennedy School, and author of *Bowling Alone* and *The Upswing*

"Kahlenberg, in his profound new book *Excluded*, exposes the hidden class injuries of exclusionary zoning. Once you see the terrible toll of this socially permissible form of discrimination, you won't be able to unsee it. It will change the way you think about your society and about the proper goals of a progressive politics."

—RUY TEIXEIRA, senior fellow, American Enterprise Institute

"Kahlenberg's in-depth exploration into the history of America's exclusionary housing policies is required reading for anyone interested in understanding the housing affordability crisis in the United States and its ripple effects throughout society. Our communities and citizens alike would be better off if every policymaker took the time to read through this exquisite undertaking, where Mr. Kahlenberg uses real-life examples and expert analysis to provide essential insight into one of the most important, complex challenges facing our nation."

—CONGRESSMAN EMANUEL CLEAVER II

"I loved reading *Excluded*. It addresses the great unfinished business of the civil rights movement: inequality in housing, which perpetuates inequality in schooling. Kahlenberg's practical proposals would give civil-rights lawyers the tools they need to fight persistent and deeply harmful practices that segregate Americans by race and class."

—JOHN BRITTAIN, former chief counsel,
Lawyers Committee for Civil Rights

"Richard Kahlenberg's assessment of the causes, implications, and cures for class-based residential segregation is must-reading for all those interested in urban policy and politics. His analysis is highly accessible and engaging, while rigorous and well-grounded in the latest research. Most importantly, he offers an unusually thorough and insightful prescription for breaking down the barriers posed by exclusionary zoning, not just to people of color, but to all lower income families."

—Vicki Been, NYU School of Law and former New York City
deputy mayor for Housing and Economic Development

"Persuasively addresses concerns from both the right and the left . . . a valuable guide to fixing one of America's most enduring social ills"

—*Publishers Weekly*

"A provocative study of how institutional measures reinforce inequality of opportunity in housing and other aspects of daily life. . . . A thoughtful, worthy argument for fair-housing reforms that are truly fair."

—*Kirkus Reviews*

EXCLUDED

HOW SNOB ZONING, NIMBYISM, AND CLASS BIAS BUILD THE WALLS WE DON'T SEE

RICHARD D. KAHLENBERG

PUBLICAFFAIRS
NEW YORK

PublicAffairs
Hachette Book Group
1290 Avenue of the Americas, New York, NY 10104
www.publicaffairsbooks.com
@Public_Affairs

Printed in the United States of America
First Edition: July 2023

Published by PublicAffairs, an imprint of Perseus Books, LLC, a subsidiary of Hachette Book Group, Inc. The PublicAffairs name and logo is a trademark of the Hachette Book Group.

The Hachette Speakers Bureau provides a wide range of authors for speaking events. To find out more, go to hachettespeakersbureau.com or email HachetteSpeakers@hbgusa.com.

PublicAffairs books may be purchased in bulk for business, educational, or promotional use. For information, please contact your local bookseller or Hachette Book Group Special Markets Department at special.markets@hbgusa.com.

The publisher is not responsible for websites (or their content) that are not owned by the publisher.

Print book interior design by Linda Mark

Library of Congress Cataloging-in-Publication Data
Names: Kahlenberg, Richard D., author.
Title: Excluded : how snob zoning, NIMBYism, and class bias build the walls we don't see / Richard D. Kahlenberg.
Description: First edition. | New York : PublicAffairs, [2023] | Includes bibliographical references and index.
Identifiers: LCCN 2022050375 | ISBN 9781541701465 (hardcover) | ISBN 9781541701489 (ebook)
Subjects: LCSH: Zoning—United States. | Social classes—United States. | Social status—United States. | NIMBY syndrome—United States. | Selfishness—United States. | Housing policy—United States.
Classification: LCC HD260 .K69 2023 | DDC 333.73/170973—dc23/eng/20230306
LC record available at https://lccn.loc.gov/2022050375

ISBNs: 9781541701465 (hardcover), 9781541701489 (ebook)

LSC-C

Printing 1, 2023

To Adam, Hailey, and David

ALSO BY RICHARD D. KAHLENBERG

A Smarter Charter: Finding What Works for Charter Schools and Public Education (with Halley Potter)

Why Labor Organizing Should Be a Civil Right: Rebuilding a Middle-Class Democracy by Enhancing Worker Voice (with Moshe Marvit)

Tough Liberal: Albert Shanker and the Battles Over Schools, Unions, Race, and Democracy

All Together Now: Creating Middle-Class Schools Through Public School Choice

The Remedy: Class, Race, and Affirmative Action

Broken Contract: A Memoir of Harvard Law School

Contents

Prologue

In November 2016, I was attending a school board meeting in Charlotte, North Carolina, when my thoughts ran to housing.

I had traveled to Charlotte, along with my colleagues, education planner Michael Alves and civil rights lawyer John Brittain, to answer any questions that the school board might have about a plan we had helped the district devise to improve student achievement.

I had spent the previous twenty years writing about education and published numerous articles and books about how to capitalize on an important but underappreciated social science finding. One of the very best predictors of academic success is not the per pupil spending in a school district but, instead, whether students have a chance to attend schools with an economically mixed group of classmates rather than schools where most of the classmates are poor.

Charlotte, which is highly segregated by race and class, and which ranks at the bottom nationally on social mobility, was poised that evening to adopt a groundbreaking plan that would create a healthy mix of low-, medium-, and high-income students at a small subset of public schools that families choose to attend—those with "magnet" themes such as science and engineering or the visual arts. As the roll call of Charlotte board members provided unanimous support to create economically mixed schools, something I'd championed for decades, a big part of me was elated.

But when Michael, John, and I went to celebrate after the vote, I couldn't help thinking about the vast majority of students in the Charlotte system who would still be assigned to segregated neighborhood schools. In the end, I increasingly recognized, the education issues that I'd grappled with for years often were indelibly shaped by housing policy as well. In particular, educational opportunity too frequently was determined by the largely invisible zoning rules towns used to dictate which economic groups can live where.

The idea that housing policy was driving school policy had been nagging at me for some time. Six years earlier, I edited a landmark study by Heather Schwartz of the RAND Corporation on housing and schooling. Schwartz studied two policies that Montgomery County, Maryland, a suburb of Washington, DC, implemented to improve the lives of low-income students.

On the one hand, Montgomery County Public Schools spent $2,000 extra per pupil in low-income schools. On the other hand, Montgomery County's housing policy provided that builders must set aside a portion of new developments for affordable housing. Schwartz's study found that low-income students who lived in middle-class neighborhoods and attended middle-class schools under the "inclusionary zoning" housing policy benefited far more than low-income students attending schools with extra funding. What the housing authority did was more consequential for students than what the school board had done.

The importance of housing policy to educational opportunity was not the only lure that drew me to write a book about exclusionary zoning. For me, the other compelling thread, which dates back to my college days in the 1980s, has been my growing recognition that liberalism—the political ideology I was raised in and still am most generally attracted to—has a serious elitism problem that needs correcting.

In the 1960s and 1970s, I was raised in an upper-middle-class, white, educated household. My father, a liberal minister and then classics teacher, and my mother, a leader of a local good-government group, taught me to care about fairness and civil rights. My senior year of college, I added a twist on that version of liberalism when I wrote my senior honors thesis on Bobby Kennedy's 1968 campaign for president.

Kennedy's key insight, as he told reporter Jack Newfield, was that "I've come to the conclusion that poverty is closer to the root of the problem than color." He said, "We have to convince the Negroes and the poor whites that they have common interests."

And, for a brief thrilling moment in an otherwise tumultuous year, Bobby Kennedy did just that. He campaigned on what I call a "liberalism without elitism and a populism without racism." His 1968 campaign managed to build a coalition of working-class Black, Hispanic, and white voters at a time when these groups were at each other's throats. Since then, Democrats have largely failed to reassemble that multiracial working-class coalition, as Richard Nixon, Ronald Reagan, and especially Donald Trump won over working-class white voters.

Bobby Kennedy's insights about the need to tackle the fundamental class divide in America have driven virtually all my professional research and writing since I graduated from college and then law school in the 1980s. In 1996, I wrote a book suggesting that affirmative action programs in higher education should not ignore the neglected injuries of class that students of all races face. Five years later, I published a book suggesting that it was important to integrate schools not just by race but also by socioeconomic status, because racially integrated but all-poor schools rarely educate kids well.

In 2010, I edited a book on the unfairness of legacy preferences in college admissions, a blatant form of class discrimination that provides affirmative action for the rich. And two years later, I coauthored a book making the case that, just as it is wrong to discriminate in employment on the basis of race, so it is wrong for employers to discriminate against people who are trying to organize a union in order to join the middle class.

When I began to investigate housing, it became clear to me that exclusionary zoning is one of America's most damaging and pervasive forms of class discrimination. Especially troubling for me is the research that finds that liberal communities actually engage in higher rates of exclusionary zoning than conservative ones. Highly educated liberals who are admirably concerned with inequality by race, gender, and sexual orientation nevertheless often support policies that tell working people that they are unwelcome in a neighborhood unless they can afford a single-family home, sometimes on a half-acre lot. People who support racial diversity, and oppose building a wall on the Mexican border, nonetheless support, or at least tolerate, laws that segregate their communities by income.

This book is intended to help people learn about the walls we don't see—and then do something to bring them tumbling down.

Richard D. Kahlenberg

Rockville, Maryland

INTRODUCTION

The Walls We Don't See

KiAra Cornelius felt trapped. A single mother who works as a claims analyst at UnitedHealth, Cornelius was living a few years ago in a tough neighborhood in South Columbus, Ohio, with her two school-age children, a daughter, KiMarra, and a son, Senoj.

Cornelius had grown up in South Columbus but says the community deteriorated over time. "It's definitely not the same anymore," she says. "It can be dangerous," with "gang-related activity." Trash littered the sidewalks. For a time, Cornelius would drive her children to her mother's home a few blocks away because she worried that if they walked there, they might "get crossed up" if something happened on the street.

Then the family suffered a couple of difficult setbacks. The basement in their home flooded, spawning a major mold problem. Then she and her children were in a car accident, which sent Cornelius to the hospital. The kids were fine, she says, but the bills started piling up, so she moved in with her mother, her mother's fiancé, and Cornelius's siblings.[1]

Quarters were tight, and Cornelius also was worried about her kids' education. The local public schools were struggling. At Siebert Elementary School, where almost all of the students come from low-income households, only about a quarter are proficient in reading or math, and even fewer in science.[2] So Cornelius opted to send her kids to a charter school, but students perform only somewhat better there. In particular, she wanted more academic challenges for her son, Senoj, a straight A student.[3]

Cornelius would have jumped at the chance to live in one of Columbus's suburban neighborhoods, with their high-performing public schools, but moving there was a distant dream. She was stuck, even if she couldn't clearly see what was trapping her.

Had she been a generation or two younger, Cornelius's racial identity as a Black American would have been the primary obstacle. As Richard Rothstein, Ta-Nehisi Coates, and others have painstakingly documented, for much of the twentieth century, federal, state, and local governments systematically engineered racial segregation through racial zoning laws, court enforcement of racially restrictive covenants, redlining of federally backed bank loans, and the deliberate placement of public housing projects in poor Black areas.[4]

But the tale that Rothstein and others have outlined is not the only story, or even the most important one today. For low-wage workers like Cornelius, the biggest obstacle, increasingly, is state-sponsored economic discrimination. In most American cities, on three-quarters of residential land, zoning laws prohibit the construction of multifamily units—duplexes, triplexes, and apartment buildings—that might be affordable to people like Cornelius.[5] In some suburbs, it is illegal to build multifamily housing on nearly 100 percent of the residential land.[6] Only single-family homes are permitted—sometimes with a minimum lot size requirement added in. Some local laws provide that when multifamily units are allowed, they must have expensive features, such as special trims or facades. All of these requirements are designed to keep families like Cornelius's out.

These laws are not part of a distant, disgraceful past. They are, says, one researcher, "a central organizing feature in American metropolitan life."[7] Indeed, following passage of the Fair Housing Act of 1968, which outlawed racial discrimination, communities doubled down on economically discriminatory zoning—and other discriminatory land-use policies (such as growth moratoria)—which disproportionately hurts people of color like Cornelius and also hurts working-class white people.[8]

The new economic discrimination is harder to see because it is more subtle than raw racism. Residents of rich communities aren't hurling bricks at buses carrying Black schoolchildren or assembling in threatening mobs, as was the case in years past in white working-class communities in places such as Boston and Little Rock. Instead, government-sponsored economic discrimination takes the form of arcane zoning laws that cannot be vividly captured by TV cameras. Laws that ban the construction of multifamily housing and require a minimum lot size to keep families like Cornelius's out constitute what I call "the walls we don't see."

And so, in recent decades, we've seen a paradoxical set of trends: as racial housing discrimination has declined, racial segregation has fallen; but at the same time, increasing income discrimination has spawned rising economic segregation. The good news is that the 1968 Fair Housing Act cleared the way for many middle-class Black people to escape ghettos. The Black–white dissimilarity index (in which zero is perfect integration and 100 is absolute segregation) has shrunk from a high of 79 in 1970 to 55 in 2020—a decline of roughly 30 percent.[9] Though still too high, researchers conclude, with respect to race, "residential segregation has declined markedly in recent decades."[10]

The bad news, as Robert D. Putnam, a political scientist at Harvard, notes, is that "while race-based segregation has been slowly declining, class-based segregation has been increasing." In fact, Putnam says, "a kind of incipient class apartheid" has been sweeping across the country.[11] In 2015, in a panel discussion with Putnam, President Barack Obama observed that "what used to be racial segregation now mirrors itself in class segregation."[12] Despite the existence of a small set of high-profile gentrifying, mixed-income urban communities, the number of families living in economically segregated neighborhoods has more than doubled since 1970, and indexes of economic dissimilarity are on the rise.[13]

This book will shine a bright light on economically discriminatory government policies. It will expose the insidious ways in which American meritocracy, which officially denounces prejudice based on race and gender, has nevertheless spawned a new form of bias against those with less education and income.[14] On a more hopeful note, it will also detail the growing movement in different parts of the country to tear down the walls that inflict so much damage on the lives of millions of Americans.

Zoning seems like a technical topic, but it touches many of the issues Americans care about most deeply. As I will explain in the chapters that follow, if you are concerned about equal opportunity, housing affordability, the environment, racial justice, the growing economic divide, and the survival of the American Dream, you have to care about zoning rules that dictate who gets to live where.

Simply put, snob zoning blocks opportunity. Government-sponsored economic discrimination matters a great deal, as Chapter 1 outlines, because where you live in America dramatically shapes your opportunities and those of your children. Neighborhoods determine one's access to transportation, employment opportunities, decent health care, and good schools.

We have known for decades that low-income children raised in more affluent neighborhoods typically fare better than low-income children in high-poverty neighborhoods. Until recently, though, it was hard to know how much of the difference was the result of varying neighborhood opportunities as compared to differences in families—the fact that particularly motivated low-income families may be more likely to seek out better neighborhoods.

In a much-discussed 2015 study, Raj Chetty of Harvard University and his colleagues looked at how children who relocated from high-poverty to low-poverty areas through the federal Moving to Opportunity program fared as adults. They found that compared with a control group that wanted to move but could not because of the program's limited number of spaces, children who moved before age thirteen significantly improved their chances of attending college and earned a third more as adults.[15]

KiAra Cornelius and her kids experienced firsthand what a difference a change in neighborhood can make. In 2018, Cornelius applied to take part in a program called Move to PROSPER, which provides temporary housing aid to single mothers. The program provided three years of financial support and counseling to ten single mothers, whose annual incomes ranged from $23,000 to $37,500. At first, the program's organizers weren't sure if anyone would apply, given the probability that families who moved would have less contact with their existing social networks and might well face discrimination in the suburbs. But by June 2018, more than three hundred single mothers had applied. Cornelius was lucky enough to get one of the ten spots.[16] Experience in other cities where counseling has been provided to low-income families, says one researcher, debunks "the myth that poor people live in poor areas merely out of preference."[17]

With Move to PROSPER's support, Cornelius moved to an apartment in Gahanna, a suburban neighborhood where the kids are free to walk around without fear. In particular, the schools are better. Senoj, Cornelius said, is receiving the challenge he needs at Goshen Lane Elementary, where 69 percent of students are proficient in reading, 73 percent in math, and 79 percent in science.[18] Cornelius's daughter, KiMarra, has also benefited from attending the high-performing Gahanna South Middle School, where the level of performance is similar to that of her brother's school.[19] The teachers push her "the extra step" in a way they didn't at her charter school, Cornelius says.[20]

Gahanna schools have more resources and smaller classes and give students the freedom to bring laptops home from school. And Gahanna parents are actively involved. Parents organized, for example, to get an app that allowed families to know when school buses would be arriving.

Teachers are also very diligent about reaching out. "I swear I get email every day" from teachers, Cornelius says. "They really keep you in the loop about what's going on."

Cornelius also likes the student diversity. At the Columbus charter school, 78 percent of students were African American like her daughter, but at Gahanna South Middle School, the Black population constitutes 26 percent of the student body, so KiMarra is stretched to go beyond "her comfort zone" and meet students of many different races and ethnicities. "I'm proud of her for stepping outside the box, hanging with different people . . . just to learn different things about how other cultures work," Cornelius said. "The Gahanna school has definitely given her a more diverse world."[21]

Cornelius says of the new schooling opportunities for her kids: "It is much, much better." Considering all the possibilities available in Gahanna, Cornelius says, "it's just a total difference" from South Columbus.

Cornelius's ability to move because of a special mobility program both shows what is possible and underlines the unfairness of government zoning policies that systematically thwart opportunity for most low-income and working-class families. Many people think that the free market essentially determines where people live. But the fact is that economically discriminatory zoning is just as responsible for today's economic segregation in housing.[22]

Exclusionary zoning not only blocks the chance of families to live in neighborhoods rich with opportunity but also stacks the deck against working families by making housing in entire metropolitan areas less affordable. As Chapter 2 explains, when a community says that available land can only be used for single-family homes on large lots, we see the face of snob zoning and how it makes housing unaffordable. It artificially limits the supply of housing and increases housing costs just as surely as OPEC increases the price of oil when it limits production. By contrast, if homeowners were allowed to subdivide their houses into two-family or three-family buildings, a community could potentially double or triple the supply of housing available to families, making housing more affordable for everyone. Exclusionary zoning is, as the *New York Times* editorial board has noted, "one area of American life where government really is the problem."[23]

Allowing government to drive up home prices makes little sense when the United States is facing what the Urban Institute has called "the worst affordable housing crisis in decades."[24] Going back to passage of the United States National Housing Act of 1937, public policy has suggested that families should spend no more than 30 percent of their pretax income on housing. Yet, today, nearly half of all renters (twenty million Americans) spend more than that—double the proportion than in the 1960s.[25] In 2022, homes became less affordable than at any time in the past thirty-three years.[26] Although some of this affordability crisis can be chalked up to wage stagnation, it is also true that rents have been rising faster than other costs for decades.[27] At its extreme, the housing affordability crisis leads to eviction and homelessness.

Government policies that limit housing supply and thus increase housing costs have made life miserable for people like Janet Williams, a single mother of two in Ohio whose modest income as a community health worker requires her to make agonizing decisions each month about whether to pay the rent in full or pay the electric and gas bills.[28] And the affordability issue also affects many college-educated middle-class millennials, who simply can't afford to live in coastal parts of the country.[29] At a time when consumers are facing the highest rates of inflation seen in four decades, and policymakers are racking their brains about how to control costs for families, it makes no sense that local governments are employing practices that actively inflate housing costs.

In addition, the unaffordability of housing is keeping many American workers from moving to highly productive cities like New York and San Francisco, which in turn reduces US economic growth and the wages of workers. In the twentieth century, Black people took part in the Great Migration from the South, and poor white Okies moved west to California for opportunity, but today high housing prices thwart that type of movement. Workers make twice as much in San Jose as in Orlando, but housing costs are four times as high.[30] Because workers can't easily move to places where wages are higher, research finds that average worker wages in the United States are several thousand dollars lower than they could be if zoning in high-growth areas was relaxed.[31]

By increasing the price of housing artificially, exclusionary zoning also pushes families farther out to the periphery of metropolitan areas in search of an affordable home. This sprawl, in turn, increases automobile emissions and damages the environment. Moreover, by banning multifamily units, exclusionary zoning prohibits, by government fiat, the construction of the types of housing that are easier to heat and cool than single-family homes are, further harming the planet.[32]

If exclusionary zoning and economic discrimination in housing hurt people of all races, it is also true that the sting of class bias is especially sharp for Black Americans, as outlined in Chapter 3. Decades ago, Dr. Martin Luther King Jr. recognized that four hundred years of racial oppression left a terrible economic legacy that needed addressing before Black people would be truly free. "What does it profit a man to be able to eat at an integrated lunch counter if he doesn't have enough money to buy a hamburger?" King asked.[33] The work of the civil rights movement will not be complete, King argued, until economic barriers to Black advancement—and the advancement of all people—are removed.

When it comes to housing, Black people are disproportionately hurt by today's economic housing discrimination not only because they have lower annual incomes than white people on average; more importantly, generations of discrimination—and contemporary housing inequities— mean that Black wealth (accumulated savings over time) is stunningly low. Whereas white people typically make 1.6 times as much as Black people in income, white median household wealth is eight times as high as median Black household wealth.[34]

Having little wealth makes it hard to come up with a down payment for a single-family home, even for middle-income Black people. Today middle-income Black families live in neighborhoods with higher concentrations of poverty than do low-income white families.[35] The fact that economic discrimination by government zoning perpetuates both economic and racial segregation puts many African Americans at a terrible disadvantage.

Indeed, historians have documented the ways in which single-family exclusive zoning laws were originally designed specifically to provide a legal way of perpetuating racial segregation. In the early twentieth century, explicit racial zoning laws prohibited Black people from buying in majority white areas, from Baltimore to Atlanta and from St. Louis to Louisville. The US Supreme Court struck down such laws as a violation of the Constitution in the 1917 decision of *Buchanan v. Warley*, but single-family zoning soon became a convenient workaround to the decision.[36]

A 2022 study found that those cities that had the highest rates of Black migration from the South from 1940 to 1970 have the most exclusionary forms of zoning.[37] In Milpitas, California, a suburb of San Jose, for example, the town adopted a policy of banning apartments and allowing only single-family homes in the 1950s, shortly after 250 African Americans were transferred to work in a new Ford auto plant in town. Because federal mortgages were not generally available to Black people and apartments were illegal, Black Ford employees had to choose between living in apartments in segregated neighborhoods in San Jose and putting up with long commutes from more distant neighborhoods.[38]

Tackling housing segregation remains the biggest piece of unfinished business of the civil rights movement. Dr. King, who faced high levels of vitriol when he campaigned for voting rights and nondiscrimination in employment, said he had never seen the full measure of white hatred until he joined a 1966 campaign for fair housing in Chicago and he and his fellow marchers were pelted with rocks and bottles.[39]

Over the past fifty years, we have made considerable strides reducing discrimination in restaurants, hotels, transportation, voting, and employment, writes Richard Rothstein in his compelling book *The Color of Law*, but progress on housing integration has not kept pace.[40] Although Black people have been integrated into the nation's political life and military over the past several decades, Harvard's Orlando Patterson notes, "the civil rights movement failed to integrate Black Americans into the private domain of American life."[41] No policy limits African American income, wealth, and education as thoroughly as housing segregation.[42]

Even though race is important to the history of exclusionary zoning, Rothstein's focus on racial animus largely misses the biggest piece of the story today: pervasive class bias and elitism. As Chapter 4 explains, race does not explain why wealthy white people have resisted integration with lower-income white families in places like La Crosse, Wisconsin, or why upper-middle-class Black families have resisted housing for lower-income residents in Prince George's County, Maryland.[43]

Indeed, if race was the only driving factor behind exclusionary zoning, one would expect to see such policies most extensively promoted in communities where racial intolerance is highest, but in fact the most restrictive zoning is found in politically liberal cities such as San Francisco, where racial views are more progressive.[44]

Harvard philosopher Michael Sandel argues that prejudice in America is evolving. The prevailing American ethos of meritocracy—which appropriately disavows racism and sexism—has also given rise to what he calls "the last acceptable prejudice," a disdain for the less-educated people.[45] Meritocracy's winners, Sandel says, "inhale too deeply of their success."[46] Indeed, social scientists have found that highly educated elites "may denounce racism and sexism but are unapologetic about their negative attitudes toward the less educated."[47] A 2018 study by five psychologists, for example, concluded that well-educated elites in the United States are no less biased than those who are less educated; "it is rather that [their] targets of prejudice are different."[48]

Our laws reflect and reinforce this cultural distinction: racial zoning is unconstitutional, but economic zoning is perfectly legal, indeed pervasive. A landlord who discriminates against a low-income Black person because of her race is in violation of federal law; a landlord who discriminates against the same individual instead because of her source of income—a Section 8 Housing Choice Voucher—faces no legal jeopardy under federal law.

For important historical reasons, being a class snob is not held in the same disrepute in America as is being a racist. But in the context of exclusionary zoning laws, the messages of the racist and the class snob are cut from the same cloth: Black families and working-class families of all races are held in such low regard that the state is somehow justified in sponsoring laws to make it illegal to build the types of housing they can afford.[49]

Some Not in My Back Yard (NIMBY) forces may say opposition to multifamily units has nothing to do with either race or class. As we note in Chapter 5, proponents of this argument advance several concerns: that zoning protects families from rapacious developers who will bulldoze quiet neighborhoods, add traffic, and overcrowd schools. And, though it is wrong to discriminate by race, the NIMBYs say, it is different excluding poor people, who are more likely to commit crimes, and change could reduce property values, robbing families of their hard-earned money for retirement. From the left, some argue that making space for more private-market housing won't make housing much more affordable or neighborhoods more integrated and that, in some cases, changes to zoning could lead to more gentrification and displacement.

Although some of these concerns are more reasonable than others, Chapter 5 provides evidence that it is possible to liberalize zoning for "missing middle" housing (duplexes, triplexes, and small garden apartments) that can enhance neighborhoods and that, as an empirical matter, concerns about low-income families bringing crime and lower property values are overblown and have unfortunate resonance with the arguments advanced in the twentieth century about the presence of Black people.[50] Just as it was unfair to paint Black people with a broad brush, so it is unfair to stereotype poorer people, when in fact most violent crime is committed by a very small group of individuals.[51] Importantly, it is not poverty, per se, but concentrations of poverty that can accelerate social ills such as crime.[52]

Fifty years ago, our fair housing laws recognized that even if a white family could provide statistical evidence that selling a house to a Black family might reduce property values, public policy should not honor that prejudice. By the same token, if KiAra Cornelius and her kids want to move into a neighborhood to escape a high-crime area, our public policies should not look at the size of her bank account as a justification for enacting laws to effectively bar her from moving.

The concerns on the left contain a kernel of truth. It is true that reform to zoning alone cannot solve all of our housing problems; more support should be provided for subsidized housing. But zoning reform is an important piece of the overall puzzle, because if we don't expand housing supply, government subsidies of housing will go less far. Likewise, the displacement that comes from gentrification is a real concern. But the evidence suggests that liberalizing zoning to allow more housing *reduces* the chances of displacement in most cases. When new housing is capped, it's not as if wealthy newcomers decide to forgo taking a coveted job. Instead, gentrifiers simply outbid existing residents in a zero-sum competition for a limited number of homes. By contrast, when new housing is built, space is created for new, wealthier gentrifiers to live alongside longtime less-affluent residents.[53]

If exclusionary zoning is a fountainhead of economic and racial inequality, artificially drives up prices, and is bad for the environment, why does it persist? The short answer is that, for generations, politicians have been terrified to address the issue. With solid support for exclusionary zoning among both wealthy conservatives and wealthy liberals, a political consensus has emerged that reform is virtually impossible. Until recently, that pessimism was well earned, as outlined in Chapter 6.

Shortly after the passage of the 1968 Fair Housing Act, for example, Richard Nixon's secretary of housing and urban development George Romney, the father of Senator Mitt Romney, tried to use a provision of the newly passed legislation to help loosen what he called the "high-income white noose" around Black inner-city neighborhoods. As journalist Nikole Hannah-Jones notes, Romney's "Open Communities" project would have withheld federal infrastructure aid from states and wealthy localities unless they agreed to "build more affordable housing and end discriminatory zoning practices" and open up suburbs to "the lower, middle-income and the poor, white, black, and brown family." When Nixon received complaints from politicians representing the suburbs, however, he immediately killed the program. "Stop this one," he wrote curtly on a memo provided by domestic policy chief John Ehrlichman.[54]

Seeing little path for change through the political process, reformers turned to litigation. In New Jersey, for example, supporters of equal opportunity won an important legal victory in 1975 in *Southern Burlington County NAACP v. Mount Laurel*, which required wealthy communities in New Jersey to provide their "fair share" of moderate and low-income housing. But politics again intervened. Although *Mount Laurel* has produced some meaningful reforms for the placement of affordable housing, the political branches of government have been recalcitrant, with some New Jersey governors openly hostile to reforms envisioned by the courts. Likewise, in the 1990s, when the federal government created the Moving to Opportunity program to open up suburbs to small numbers of low-income families, conservatives were joined by liberals like Senator Barbara Mikulski (D-MD) in curtailing the experiment.[55]

For all these reasons, observers were stunned in 2018 when the city of Minneapolis voted to do something long considered impossible in American politics: end single-family exclusive zoning in an entire city. In Minneapolis, housing advocates succeeded in part by shifting the focus of attention away from loud NIMBY voices of wealthy white homeowners toward the victims of exclusionary zoning.

The change was dramatic. Previously, Minneapolis had banned duplexes, triplexes, and larger apartment buildings from almost three-quarters of its residential land. The new plan, named Minneapolis 2040, allowed two- and three-family buildings on what had been single-family lots, tripling the potential number of housing units in the city.

Advocates made racial justice central to their message and also emphasized the ways in which single-family exclusive zoning, by constraining housing supply, made housing less affordable. Although unions traditionally focus on wages and benefits for members, SEIU Healthcare Minnesota—an offshoot of the Service Employees International Union—became a key part of the coalition for zoning reform in Minneapolis. Citing the ways in which single-family exclusive zoning put housing out of the reach of working people, the union drove home the idea that strict local land use rules have real-world consequences. Advocates of change also allied with environmentalists, who explained how exclusionary zoning contributes to climate change by pushing development farther and farther out, which puts cars on the road for longer commutes.

In Minneapolis, advocates for reform made sure that changes to exclusionary zoning would not inadvertently increase gentrification and displacement of low-income families. Some community members argued that zoning reform could pave the way for new construction, which can attract wealthier residents who are willing to pay more precisely because the units are new. To reduce any displacement, reformers insisted on writing into the plan new funding for affordable housing as well as "inclusionary zoning" requirements to compel developers to set aside some new units for low-income and working-class people.

To avoid the debate being dominated by NIMBY voices, city planners and advocates sought direct input from those hurt by exclusionary zoning. City staff went to street fairs, festivals, and churches to gather input on zoning reform from people in low-income and minority communities. They didn't speak in jargon-laden terms about "increasing housing density," but instead asked big questions such as, "Are you satisfied with the housing options available to you right now?" and "What does your ideal Minneapolis look like in 2040?"[56]

Once Minneapolis broke the logjam, other major victories followed. In 2019, a bipartisan group of legislators in Oregon passed the nation's first statewide ban on single-family exclusive zoning.[57] The provision applied to all cities with a population of at least ten thousand residents and overcame the strong opposition of the League of Oregon Cities.[58] In June 2021, Charlotte, North Carolina, became the first southern city to abolish single-family exclusive zoning.[59] In the fall of 2021, the largest state in the country, California, eliminated such zoning statewide.[60] The California legislation was signed by Governor Gavin Newsom over the objections of more than 260 city leaders.[61] And in 2022, a bipartisan group of Maine legislators legalized accessory dwelling units ("granny flats") on lots that had been restricted to one single-family home, over the opposition of the Maine Municipal Association.[62]

In yet another sign of changing winds, Chapter 7 notes that at the federal level several 2020 Democratic presidential candidates, including Joe Biden, elevated the issue of exclusionary zoning to the national stage—and beat Donald Trump's attempt to demagogue the issue.

One of the early presidential aspirants to advocate zoning reform was New Jersey senator Cory Booker, who introduced federal legislation to discourage exclusionary zoning in 2018. For Booker, the issue was personal. The Fair Housing Act made it possible for Booker's parents, African American executives, to move to Harrington Park, New Jersey, outside of Newark. The strong public schools there helped launch Booker to Stanford, Oxford, Yale Law, and beyond.[63]

But as a child, Booker saw that for his less-affluent Black friends and colleagues, outlawing racial discrimination was not sufficient; exclusionary zoning kept places like Harrington Park out of reach. In an exclusive interview before his legislation was introduced, Booker told me that he visited relatives living in predominantly Black communities and "clearly saw that something was wrong."[64] As a young adult, he learned about the *Mount Laurel* litigation in New Jersey, which exposed the way in which municipal zoning laws were employed to "segregate our state by income as well as race."[65]

Booker introduced the Housing, Opportunity, Mobility, and Equity (HOME) Act, cosponsored by South Carolina's Rep. James Clyburn, to require states, cities, and counties receiving federal funding for public infrastructure and housing to develop strategies to reduce barriers to housing development and increase the supply of housing. Plans could include authorizing more high-density and multifamily zoning and relaxing lot size restrictions. In 2020, Democratic presidential nominee Joe Biden endorsed the HOME Act and declared that he would "eliminate local and state housing regulations that perpetuate discrimination."[66]

As part of Biden's jobs bill in 2021, he included the Unlocking Possibilities program to provide $1.75 billion for the first-ever Race to the Top program to reduce exclusionary zoning. But, as noted in Chapter 7, these types of carrots to encourage states and localities to do the right thing should be supplemented by sticks. In that chapter, I outline a proposal for a new Economic Fair Housing Act to give plaintiffs who are hurt by exclusionary zoning laws the chance to sue municipalities for income discrimination, the way people of color can currently sue for race discrimination.[67]

To be sure, the politics of reform remain tricky, and in the 2020 campaign, Donald Trump sought to win over suburban voters by saying he would protect them from Biden's attempt to "eliminate single-family zoning."[68] In repealing an Obama-era Fair Housing Act rule that aimed to promote racial and economic inclusion, Trump tweeted, "I am happy to inform all of the people living in their Suburban Lifestyle Dream that you will no longer be bothered or financially hurt by having low income housing built in your neighborhood."[69]

Nonetheless, there is reason for optimism about reform. Trump's attempt to use unsubstantiated fears about increased crime and reduced property values to win over "suburban housewives of America"—at a time when many people were rejecting racism in the wake of George Floyd's murder—fell flat.[70] Biden actually saw a nine-point gain in white suburban voters compared to Hillary Clinton in 2016.[71] And though the single-family *home* has a prized place in American culture as a symbol of success, single-family exclusive *zoning*, which involves a government fiat that bans people from building anything else, is much less popular.[72] Indeed, exclusionary zoning is at odds with two deeply held American beliefs: democratic egalitarianism, on the one hand, and the liberty to be free from government interference, on the other. Typically, those values are in tension with one another, but in the case of exclusionary zoning, they point in the same direction.

Today, both Republicans and Democrats say they believe in democratic egalitarianism, though in recent years each party has emphasized a different aspect of this tenet. Democrats have pointed out the ways in which white people have wrongly declared themselves to be better than people of color, and Republicans have pointed to ways in which coastal elites have improperly looked down upon working-class white people who lack educational credentials.

The movement to eliminate exclusionary zoning unites those two populist threads—it is anti-racist and anti-elitist. The notion that working-class people should be excluded from entire communities is deeply insulting both to Democratic-leaning working-class people of color and to the non-college-educated white people who flocked to Donald Trump in part because they felt looked down upon by coastal Democrats. Meanwhile, opponents of exclusionary zoning can also tap into the American belief in liberty. Ending economically discriminatory zoning can be seen as a form of government "deregulation" that will appeal to small-government conservatives. Uniting egalitarian and libertarian views—which normally work at cross purposes—can constitute a powerful combination in American politics.

As I note in the epilogue, it is possible to imagine a brighter future. Tearing down invisible walls of exclusion can reduce segregation, foster social cohesion, and make housing more affordable—and it can do so without the enormous commitment of treasure often associated with promoting those goals. The first step is to see the walls we've built, and the second is to take action to remove these barriers to the American Dream so that all families have a chance to move up the economic ladder.

ONE

THE WALLS THAT BLOCK OPPORTUNITY

PATRICIA MCGEE WAS LIVING IN THE MANDALAY PALMS APARTments in a rough section of Dallas a few years ago when one day her ten-year-old son said, "Momma, look." McGee peered out the window and saw a sex worker hanging out at the bus stop in front of the apartment "doing some things she shouldn't be doing." McGee was horrified. "Your kids, they pay attention to everything," she says. They begin "talking about stuff they ain't got no business talking about."

McGee was deeply discouraged at the time. "Living in Mandalay," she explains, "was one of the worst areas I have ever lived in. It was prostitution at the bus stop. It was drug-smoking in my breezeway where my door was. . . . Every time you turned around, there was some crime."[1]

McGee was upset that her children were experiencing a version of the difficult childhood she herself had endured. McGee's mother had struggled with drug addiction and alcoholism, so at a young age, McGee shuffled back and forth between an aunt in Dallas (who favored her own kids over McGee) and a foster home in Longview, an oil town located two hours east of Dallas, near the Louisiana border.[2]

McGee dropped out of high school and over an extended period of time gave birth to her four children, two daughters (who in 2021 were in twelfth grade and tenth grade) and two sons (then in seventh grade and third grade). (McGee asked that the names of her children not be used.) Without a high school degree, she worked various jobs but struggled financially. She tried to take classes to get her GED, but it's been difficult. "My main priority was to make sure that I had a roof over my head and my kids' heads." That, too, was tough, and for a time, she and her family became homeless and had to stay in a shelter or sleep in a car "because we had nowhere else to go."[3]

With support from a program called Under One Roof, McGee was able to move to the Mandalay Palms Apartments, which provides affordable units in the Oak Cliff section of Dallas. But McGee says the environment was unbearable. "I actually stayed in Mandalay Palms Apartments for a year, dealt with all that drama, trafficking, prostitution, drugs, gunshots, all that." In addition, the apartment itself was unhealthy, she says. Her unit had a water leak, which created mildew, McGee says, but "they wouldn't do nothing about it."

McGee says she has high expectations for her kids and tries to teach them that "regardless where you came from, if you do what you're supposed to do, you can go wherever you want to go." She says she tells her kids, "It's up to you to get that education. It's up to you to ask your teacher for the information. If you don't understand or you want to get ahead in class, you ask for extra work." She continues: "I stay on my kids," she says. "I tell them every single morning before they go out the door to schools, 'Pay attention, make sure you're focused, make sure you keep them grades up because you're going to need it. Yeah, you going to be a boss, you're going to run your own business. . . . You going to have people looking up to you.' That's what I'm trying to put in my kids' head. You're going to have people working for you."

McGee encourages her kids to watch inspiring movies, and in a comment that is painful to hear, she tells them, "You ain't got to be nothing like me, and I hope you don't want to be nothing like me. I want y'all to be better than me and y'all daddies." She tells her daughters, "It's easy to get sidetracked and then you'll be sitting at home drawing food stamps 'cause you can't work 'cause you're pregnant."

But living in the Oak Cliff section of Dallas, McGee says, she felt as though the local public schools were holding her kids back. "The school, to me, was a hot mess," she says. T. W. Browne Middle School was particularly problematic. The school, where 97 percent of students are low-income, and 96 percent are Black or Hispanic, has low levels of achievement. Just 23 percent of students are proficient in math, 23 percent in reading, and 19 percent in science.[4]

There were also issues of safety. One of McGee's daughters, she says, "was jumped by two girls walking home from school and just because she didn't want to be their friend." McGee complained to the school in order to resolve the issue, but, like the problem with her apartment, the powers that be "didn't do nothing about it."

The elementary school, Ronald E. McNair, was also problematic, McGee says. In a school that is 94 percent Black or Hispanic and 98 percent low-income, just 50 percent of students are proficient in math, 32 percent in reading, and 21 percent in science.[5] The teachers were disrespectful, McGee says. One of McGee's sons was grabbed by the collar by one of the teachers, she says. McGee complained to the principal in what she described as a forceful fashion. "I actually went off, I had to be 'ghetto' myself that particular day." But the staff never updated her on what, if anything, was done.

McGee also says she didn't like the way her older son was held to low expectations and passed along, even though he struggled with his reading. It wasn't until later, when he went to a more challenging school, that the problem was discovered. "That's something that should have been taken care of" earlier, she says. In Oak Cliff, McGee says, "you got some teachers that feel like, 'hey, I'm just here for a paycheck.'"

The situation became so difficult that McGee moved three of her children to KIPP Destiny Middle School, a charter school with a better reputation.[6] "They was okay there," McGee says. But student proficiency remained low.[7]

McGee wanted something better for her children. But she felt discouraged. The safer neighborhoods with good schools were completely off-limits to her.

Many think someone like Patricia McGee can't afford to live in the suburbs because, under the free market system, some communities just have bigger houses that cost more money. Indeed, people often think where you live is basically a reflection of individual merit, and that "poor life choices" and "drugs/alcohol" are bigger causes of poverty than factors such as "lack of job opportunities" or "discrimination."[8] There is often an underlying cultural assumption that people live where they deserve to, as one commentator noted, "that affluent space is earned and hood living is the deserved consequence of individual behavior."[9]

Emblematic of this thinking is the way the term *ghetto* has morphed from a noun to an adjective. Whereas *ghetto* once connoted an enforced separation of a people, whether Jews in sixteenth-century Venice or Black people in modern America, today it is also "a pejorative" used to describe "dress, speech, and social codes" that are rejected by middle-class Americans.[10]

It is true, of course, that in desirable communities, with attractive amenities like good schools and low crime rates, the free market in housing drives up land prices, with or without zoning. What this misses, however, researchers find, is that "even if land is expensive, developers can still satisfy the demand for housing from lower-class households by using it more intensively," that is, by building multifamily housing and amortizing the land's cost "over a larger number of buyers or renters." In a truly free market, they say, "developers—especially non-profit developers—could buy land in affluent desirable areas and erect apartment buildings containing affordable units for lower-income families."[11] With rents skyrocketing in affluent communities, developers find it profitable to build multifamily units even in places where land is expensive, such as Greenwich, Connecticut, and even when builders are required to set aside 30 percent of units below market rate. "The density allows the math to work," says one developer.[12]

But local governments in wealthy communities literally outlaw that possibility. "Government gatekeepers," says one author, "dictate which buildings can be built and how they should look," which, in turn, determines who can live where.[13] Poor and rich neighborhoods, then, are not the natural result of sorting by merit; to the contrary, they have been socially engineered by government.

Growing income and wealth inequality is part of the reason we see growing income segregation. The bottom 90 percent of Americans now own just 10 percent of the nation's wealth.[14] But housing policy matters a lot as well. As one researcher notes, "Our highly dispersed and profoundly unequal distribution of housing is not inevitable; indeed, it is not the norm around the world."[15] Japan, Germany, and France, for example, have very different zoning regimes and far less segregated housing.[16]

Just how important is exclusionary zoning to explaining current American levels of economic and racial segregation? Some of the best evidence compares jurisdictions with more-intense and less-intense levels of exclusionary zoning. An important 2010 study of fifty metropolitan areas found that "a change in permitted zoning from the most restrictive to the least would close 50 percent of the observed gap between the most unequal metropolitan area and the least, in terms of neighborhood inequality."[17] The study employed a model that allowed the researchers to conclude that land use regulations *caused* income segregation rather than the other way around.[18]

Likewise, a 2016 study examining ninety-five big metropolitan areas found that those with more restrictive zoning and land use regulation had higher levels of income segregation. The researchers found that greater "density restrictions" (such as minimum lot sizes) increased income segregation by segregating the wealthy from the middle class. In addition, the authors found that "the complexity of the municipal review process, measured by the number of approvals that local governments require for new housing developments, is strongly related to the segregation of low-income households."[19]

Restrictive zoning is also associated with increased racial segregation. A 2014 study found that metro areas with less-restrictive zoning tend to have less racial segregation. The authors concluded: "The more restrictive the density zoning regime [the stricter the limits on residential density], the higher the level of racial segregation and the less the shift toward integration over time."[20]

This was the case in Dallas, where—as in other parts of the country—a series of deliberate public policy choices was made throughout the city's history to place barriers in the paths of low-income families and families of color like McGee's who sought out better places to live. These barriers have not disappeared but rather have evolved over time.

As we shall discuss in Chapter 3, in the early and mid-twentieth century, Dallas-area officials were complicit in a series of racially discriminatory policies and practices in housing and schooling. Officials enacted racial zoning laws, enforced racially restrictive covenants, refused to back mortgages in Black communities that were redlined, tolerated white terrorism when Black people tried to move into white communities, and enforced de jure segregation of schools. Following the enactment of the Fair Housing Act of 1968, many of these policies and practices were deemed illegal, so discrimination took on new forms.

In essence, Dallas's efforts morphed over time to replace explicitly racist policies with economically discriminatory ones. In Dallas, and other parts of the country, economic discrimination in the post–civil rights era has taken on three central forms:

- Exclusionary zoning laws that prohibit the construction of multi-family housing or require minimum lot sizes, effectively screening out low- and moderate-income families
- Government policies that concentrate low-income housing in high-poverty (mostly Black) communities
- And state-sanctioned source-of-income discrimination by landlords against those with Section 8 Housing Choice Vouchers

In the early twentieth century, Dallas, like Baltimore before it, adopted a racial zoning law to forbid Black people from living in white neighborhoods.[21] After the US Supreme Court declared such laws illegal in the 1917 case of *Buchanan v. Warley*, white officials in Dallas (as in other parts of the country) quickly switched to economic zoning, which banned multifamily housing that might be affordable to Black people.

"Such economic zoning was rare in the United States before World War I," author Richard Rothstein notes, "but the *Buchanan* decision provoked urgent interest in zoning as a way to circumvent the ruling."[22]

Economically exclusionary zoning remains a widespread problem in the Dallas region.[23] Within Dallas itself, 65 percent of residential land is dedicated to single-family homes.[24] In the suburbs, the problem can be even worse. Says one former Dallas school board member: "It's like the Wall of Troy around some of these communities of privilege."[25]

Consider the zoning laws in Highland Park, Texas. Home to Southern Methodist University, Highland Park is a "donut hole" carved out of the middle of Dallas. As one Dallas official observes: "It's nearly all rich white people, a separate [school] district, separate town council, separate police surrounded on all sides by the city of Dallas."[26] The district was created in the early twentieth century, as the Highland Park town website itself notes, "as a refuge from an increasingly diverse city."[27]

Today, the school district—which has five elementary schools, one middle school, and one high school (along with two alternative schools)—has a student population that is 82 percent white, 7 percent Asian or Pacific Islander, 5 percent Hispanic, 2 percent two or more races, and less than 1 percent Black, Native American, and Native Hawaiian. A remarkable 0 percent of students are reported to be from low-income families.[28] By contrast, in the surrounding Dallas district, 69 percent of students are Hispanic, 21 percent Black, 5 percent white, and 1 percent Asian or Pacific Islander—and 86 percent of students are from low-income families.[29] "Highland Park," says one local observer, "is only five minutes away from the deepest concentrations of poverty."[30]

How does Highland Park maintain its segregated status? Historically, the town segregated its students explicitly by race. In the 1950s, Highland Park sent the small number of Black students residing in the area to Dallas public schools.[31] Today, Highland Park uses exclusionary zoning. In the vast majority of Highland Park, it is illegal to build anything but a single-family home. The second biggest area of land in the community is set aside for the country club. Only tiny slivers on the outskirts of the community are designated for multifamily housing.[32]

Another quintessential example of exclusionary zoning in the Dallas area is the suburban town of Sunnyvale, which has been the subject of extensive litigation over its zoning rules.[33] Sunnyvale is an affluent community located twelve miles east of Dallas's central business district—"just a hop, skip, and jump," fair housing attorney Demetria McCain has noted.[34] Nestled on the shores of Lake Ray Hubbard, it had a median household income of $132,488 in 2019, more than twice the median household income of Texas residents as a whole.[35]

For many years, Sunnyvale had a complete ban on townhouses and apartment buildings and a minimum lot size for single-family housing of a whopping one acre. A pamphlet aimed at businesses that might want to locate in Sunnyvale, a federal judge noted, "made clear that the only type of housing allowed in Sunnyvale is low-density, single family housing. The apartments, presumably for the workers, are in other cities," such as "Garland, Mesquite, and Northeast Dallas." In 1985, Sunnydale refused to permit any Section 8 housing as requested by the Dallas Housing Authority, claiming such housing would pose challenges to providing sewer and water services. Around that time, Sunnyvale was 94 percent white and just 1 percent Black.[36]

The roadblocks holding economic inequality in place and the decades it takes to remove them can be seen in a lawsuit Mary Dews, a counselor for the Dallas Tenants' Association, filed in 1988 against Sunnyvale for its exclusionary zoning laws. The lawsuit was soon joined by a real estate development corporation that wanted to build affordable multifamily housing in the town by 1995. In 2000, a federal district court found Sunnyvale's exclusionary zoning laws both intended to discriminate and had the effect of discriminating on the basis of race in violation of the Fair Housing Act. The federal district court found that the ban on multifamily housing and the one-acre lot minimum had "imposed a barrier that cannot be overcome except by a token number of black households."[37]

Sunnyvale argued that its exclusionary zoning was justified "for the purpose of protecting the public health with septic tanks" and promoting "environmental protection." But the court rejected these arguments as pretexts for discrimination and noted, in any event, that less-discriminatory alternatives exist for furthering those goals. The court enjoined Sunnyvale from implementing its zoning practices and required the town to take steps to encourage the development of multi-family housing.[38]

In 2005, an agreement was reached between the parties to make some units available for low- and moderate-income families.[39] But even after the court order, the city resisted, said McCain. The litigation dragged on and on for years, and it was not until 2014, some twenty-six years after the lawsuit began, that a set of affordable multifamily units opened its doors. Even then, said McCain, the town put the homes "on the outskirts of Sunnyvale, as far on the boundary as possible."[40]

Low-income families didn't know about the opportunity to live in the homes, so a nonprofit housing group advertised it to Section 8 Housing Choice Voucher holders. It was unknown how many low-income families would apply. In the end, said McCain, "they responded at a level that was so great that the property manager had to rent a hotel room to take applicants."[41]

Sunnyvale represents a rare modest victory amid a depressing national picture. Today, Sunnyvale's Black population has grown to 9 percent, and its Hispanic population is 12 percent.[42] But very few courts have ruled in ways similar to the decision of the judge in the Sunnyvale case. And since the 1970s, the nationwide growth in exclusionary zoning has increased the economic barriers to people like Patricia McGee and KiAra Cornelius.[43]

A second driver of economic and racial segregation is government decisions about where to place public housing—decisions that are themselves influenced heavily by exclusionary zoning.

In recent decades, the federal government has supported public housing mainly through two types of public–private partnerships: the Section 8 Housing Choice Voucher program, and the Low-Income Housing Tax Credit (LIHTC). In principle, both types of programs could facilitate desegregation because housing vouchers can theoretically be used in any community and LIHTC housing can be built in more affluent, high-opportunity areas as well as in communities of concentrated poverty. But in Texas, as in many parts of the country, upper-middle-class communities have fought Section 8 and LIHTC-supported housing and sought to exclude low-income families. This income discrimination disproportionately hurts Black people, especially in Dallas, where 86 percent of the Dallas Housing Authority's clients are African American.[44]

In a lawsuit challenging the concentration of Section 8 vouchers, a federal district court noted in 1989 that "suburbs of the City of Dallas were refusing to participate in DHA Section 8 assistance program," thereby preventing those with housing assistance from using that support *anywhere* in the Dallas suburbs.[45] As part of a 1990 consent decree, an organization, eventually called the Inclusive Communities Project (ICP), was founded to promote integration through a program that allows a relatively small number of voucher holders (about 1 percent) to live in high-opportunity neighborhoods.[46]

Texas also concentrated poverty after Congress created the LIHTC in 1986. For years, Housing and Urban Development (HUD) and the Texas Department of Housing and Community Affairs have concentrated tax-credit-supported low-income housing in high-poverty, predominantly Black areas in Dallas rather than in whiter and more affluent areas in the suburbs. In 2008, ICP sued, charging that the LIHTC policies in Texas had a negative "disparate impact" on Black people and furthered racial segregation in violation of the 1968 Fair Housing Act.[47] It won a victory in the US Supreme Court, where, in 2015, the court ruled that disparate impact cases are valid under the Fair Housing Act, but after the court remanded the case to the lower courts for final determination on the facts in Dallas, a US District Court ruled against ICP in 2016 for failing to specify precisely the cause of the racial exclusion.[48]

Government officials in Texas employ a third tool to keep families like Patricia McGee's out of more affluent white communities: source-of-income discrimination, such as refusing to take Section 8 Housing Choice Voucher holders. In the Dallas area, this is the "primary defense to enforce segregation," a local journalist notes.[49] Whereas it is illegal for a landlord to openly discriminate based on race, Texas communities do not protect Section 8 voucher holders like Patricia McGee against source-of-income discrimination.

Worse, the state of Texas actually made it illegal for local communities to pass laws protecting against income discrimination. In seventeen states, such as New York, California, Washington, Maryland, and Massachusetts, it is illegal for a landlord to discriminate on the basis of a renter's source of income.[50] But after Austin, Texas, passed such an ordinance, the Texas legislature voted in 2014 to preempt all local source-of-income discrimination laws, removing source-of-income discrimination protection in the state.[51] Texas and Indiana are the only two states that have taken such a draconian step.[52]

As a result, source-of-income discrimination is rampant in the Dallas area. According to a 2020 Inclusive Communities Project survey of landlords in Collin, Dallas, Denton, and Rockwall Counties, 93 percent said that they would not accept voucher holders.[53] The areas where the most white people live—such as Fairview, Prosper, Flower Mound, and Rockwall—were the most likely to refuse vouchers.[54] If you have a voucher and are looking for an apartment in a high-opportunity neighborhood, one local official says, "you'd have to call so many landlords to find the magical one who actually accepts the voucher."[55]

———

One day, while searching for ways she could get assistance putting together a rental security deposit, Patricia McGee came across the housing mobility program sponsored by the Inclusive Communities Project.[56] ICP's Mobility Assistance Program provides housing search assistance and counseling annually to 350 families who want to move to higher-opportunity neighborhoods. These neighborhoods include those that are in the attendance area of "an elementary school that is ranked as high performing."[57]

Fair housing attorney Demetria McCain, president of ICP from 2016 to 2020, sees its work as the latest stage in the fight for civil rights to break free of limits imposed by wealthy white interests. In the eighteenth and nineteenth centuries, she says, in the face of enslavement by advantaged white landowners, Black people courageously risked their lives to escape slavery. In the twentieth century, millions of resilient Black people living in the South uprooted their lives to free themselves from the tyranny of Jim Crow laws as part of the Great Migration. To-day, many wealthy white people continue trying to exclude Black fam-ilies from their communities. Many Black people stuck in dangerous neighborhoods with struggling schools are seeking help from ICP so they can take the risk to move to wealthier areas—where they may face discrimination—because these areas nevertheless offer a better chance for their children.[58]

Patricia McGee is a member of that third wave of resilient Black people seeking better opportunity through migration—in her case, within a metropolitan area to a safer neighborhood with strong schools. With ICP's support, McGee was able to move to Forney, Texas, in May 2019. A city of twenty-four thousand, Forney has a median household income of about $93,000, and a population that is 64 percent white, 19 percent Hispanic, 14 percent Black, and 2 percent Asian. In Forney, "it's mostly a mixture of colors," McGee says.

Families in Forney reached out to make sure McGee's kids were okay. "It's been a great move for me and my kids because when we was in Dallas, you really didn't get the support," McGee said in a 2020 in-terview. "Since we've been out here, I have had people call and ask if it's okay to donate this to you and your children."

McGee says the schools in Forney are much stronger than they were in Dallas. In 2020, the four children attended four different schools. Her first-grade son was at Lewis Elementary, her fifth-grade son was at Smith Elementary, her eighth-grade daughter was at Brown Middle, and her tenth-grade daughter was at Forney North.[59]

Student achievement levels are much higher in Forney than in Oak Cliff schools or the charter school McGee's children attended in Dal-las. At Brown Middle School, for example, 50 percent are proficient in reading and 42 percent in math—roughly double the rates in Oak Cliff.[60]

One big difference is the teachers' level of engagement, McGee says. In Forney, she says, if teachers "see your kid struggling, they gonna call you. . . . They're gonna stay on top of your kids and make sure you're able to stay on top of them." She continued, "They're more on it than [the teachers in] Oak Cliff."

At Smith Elementary, for example, where McGee's son was in fifth grade, he was having some problems, but she went in and met with the teachers. "We came up with a solution and since then I haven't had no problems." Likewise, after McGee became homeless a number of years ago, her oldest daughter lost a lot of education credits; but in Forney, the school system put her in a credit recovery program that enabled her to be placed back in her original grade.

Another difference is the level of parental involvement. "A lot of these people are involved, you'd be surprised," McGee says. The parents chaperone field trips, volunteer in class, and help out in the lunchroom, she says.

McGee says she is very grateful to ICP for supporting her move. "If it wasn't for them, I wouldn't be where I am today. I would probably be still somewhere in Oak Cliff or Pleasant Grove, areas that I really wouldn't want to stay in because of the high violence." She says, "I'm very thankful I was able to take my kids out." McGee says she knows lots of people who were unable to access assistance as she did. "Everybody don't want to stay in the hood," she says. "Everyone wants an opportunity to have a nice home, a nice area where people come to visit and don't have to worry about ducking and rolling. . . . It's so peaceful out here. It's quiet. . . . You don't hear no gunshots. You don't hear no loud music rolling through your neighborhood. You don't hear fighting." McGee says, "I love it out here."[61]

For a time, McGee took a job as an Amazon warehouse worker, where she earned fifteen dollars an hour. She often worked the graveyard shift, 7:00 p.m. to 5:00 a.m., but didn't complain about the hours. "Well, I thank God that I got me a job," she says. Her work, she says, has given her a sense of dignity. "In order to get what you want, you got to work," she says. "All these programs that they put out here are supposed to be a stepping-stone. You not supposed to stay on it forever." She says she chastises her cousin who, she says, is "dependent on the system way too much." In return, her cousin calls McGee "Ms. Boughie." But McGee says she wants to set an example of self-reliance for her children. "Go to work. Show your kids," she says. She tells her children, "Don't get on these programs unless you really, really, really, really need it."[62]

After COVID-19 swept the country in the spring of 2020, McGee left her Amazon job and went to work for Maximus, a contractor that provides support for IRS call centers. In the fall of 2020, McGee's life was upended again, when the home she was renting in Forney was sold. With support from ICP for her rental deposit, she relocated to Rockwall County, east of Dallas. She says Rockwall is "pretty nice. It's quiet." There is "less of all the drama" than she had in Oak Cliff.[63]

In 2021, McGee's children were attending the local public schools, including Rowlett Elementary and Rockwall High School. Both are high-achieving schools. But at the high school, which is 67 percent white, 17 percent Hispanic, 7 percent Black, and 3 percent Asian, her daughters are sometimes the only Black students in their class, and "someone may say something that they shouldn't," McGee says. "But I tell them to look over it and keep doing what they supposed to do." McGee says her youngest is doing well and likes Rockwall schools better than the schools in Forney.[64]

Unfortunately, Patricia McGee's experience is very much an exception in Texas, where there is a rising tide of economic segregation and most people don't enjoy the catapult that ICP provides over exclusionary walls. The 350 families per year that ICP helps move to higher-opportunity neighborhoods represent about 1 percent of the 26,257 families in Dallas who use Section 8 Housing Choice Vouchers.[65] They represent an even tinier slice of the Dallas region's 7.6 million residents, many of whom are low-income wage earners like McGee.[66]

Exclusionary practices that discriminate by income—and indirectly, by race—continue to take a significant toll on the vast majority of low-income Dallas residents. A 2015 study found that Dallas–Fort Worth was the seventh most economically segregated large metropolitan region in the entire country (after Austin, Columbus, San Antonio, Houston, Los Angeles, and New York).[67] A September 2020 Urban Institute study ranking major cities on three measures of inclusion found that Dallas was among the worst. The study compared 274 cities on "economic inclusion" (measured by "income segregation, housing affordability, the share of working poor residents, and the high school dropout rate"), "racial inclusion" (measured by "racial segregation; racial gaps in homeownership, poverty, and educational attainment; and the share of the city's population who are people of color"), and "overall inclusion" (which is a combination of the economic and racial inclusion scores). Dallas, the Urban Institute found, was near the bottom of the barrel for all categories. The city "ranked 272nd out of 274 cities on overall inclusion, 270th on economic inclusion, and 246th on racial inclusion."[68] (Smaller cities were among the most inclusive. Among the top ten in Urban's rankings were Naperville, Illinois; Bellevue, Washington; and eight California cities, including Freemont, Daly City, Torrance, and Santa Clara.)[69]

The combination of economic and racial exclusion is deeply troubling. In an assessment of Dallas's housing equity, the Dallas Housing Authority's Myriam Igoufe was particularly alarmed to find that since 1990 the number of racially or ethnically concentrated areas of poverty (R/ECAPs) doubled from eighteen to thirty-six and that many Section 8 Housing Choice Voucher holders were residing in these areas.[70]

TEHANI (COLUMBUS, OHIO)

Exclusion is hardly just a southern phenomenon. One thousand miles northeast of Dallas, Tehani (who asked that her last name not be used) faced some of the same issues that confronted Patricia McGee.

A divorced Hispanic mother of three, Tehani lives in the Columbus, Ohio, region, as does KiAra Cornelius. When I spoke with Tehani in 2020, her daughter Brandy was fourteen; her son, Beau, was twelve; and her daughter Natasha was four. As a child, Tehani attended Columbus Public Schools (now known as Columbus City Schools), and when she and her husband had children, she knew she wanted something better for her kids. They lived in Reynoldsburg, a Columbus suburb, but after six years, Tehani and her husband divorced. She suffered a major financial setback and was evicted from her home. She and her kids became homeless and eventually had to take an apartment in Columbus.[71]

The apartment was infested with bugs, the stairs were broken, and the front door did not lock properly. With drugs dealt on the block, Tehani worried for the safety of her children. A small outdoor swing set for the baby was stolen from her front porch, which prompted Tehani to ask, "Who does that?"[72] The unsafe housing made it hard for her to take on more work opportunities because she worried about her kids getting on the bus by themselves in the morning.

The Columbus public school system had an overall D rating on the state report card and an F rating for academic achievement, a miserable set of marks that underlines the desperate state of the schools.[73] At Forest Park Elementary School, located close by Tehani's home, 100 percent of students were from low-income backgrounds and only 36 percent were proficient in reading, 40 percent in math, and 30 percent in science.[74]

Because Tehani had lived in suburban Reynoldsburg and because she had been homeless, her children were permitted under a provision of federal law to stay in Reynoldsburg public schools. Reynoldsburg had a C rating as a school district, an improvement over Columbus's D rating. But Tehani was not satisfied. In particular, she was concerned that Reynoldsburg schools did not provide her daughter Brandy, who loved choir and drama, with programs in either. "They've lost a lot of arts programs over in Reynoldsburg," Tehani says.[75] In any event, she needed a safer and better living situation than that found in Columbus.

Tehani, like Patricia McGee, felt trapped. The public policies of Columbus, Ohio's capital city, made things much worse, especially the area's long history of state-sponsored racial and economic exclusion and segregation.

In the twentieth century, white Columbus-area residents enforced segregation of people of color through multiple means, including racially restrictive covenants, redlining, and purposeful segregation of schools. Although racially restrictive covenants were struck down by the US Supreme Court, redlining was outlawed by the US Congress, and de jure school segregation was prohibited by *Brown v. Board of Education*, economic discrimination continued unabated in Columbus.

One Ohio State University researcher noted, "We have a Fair Housing Act, but if they're not caught discriminating by race . . . they can still discriminate by class. We've learned that if they do that with zoning, they get the same effect."[76] Economically restrictive covenants and economic zoning are among the most common weapons employed against people like Tehani in Central Ohio.

As one scholar painstakingly documented, after racially restrictive covenants were struck down by the US Supreme Court in 1948, Columbus-area developers doubled down on socioeconomically "restrictive covenants" that prohibited land from being used to build houses below a certain price or size. In the Columbus area, "If land developers did not directly control by race who used the land, they could and did attempt to control by socioeconomic status who used it, as well as how it could be used." Two out of every three subdivisions studied were reserved for single-family homes. Moreover, "subdivisions aimed at the upper middle class" imposed minimum square footage requirements and often banned one-story homes.[77]

Zoning laws in the Columbus region later codified these restrictive covenants. Zoning ordinances are justified to promote "public health, safety, and welfare," but too often they were used instead to keep Black and lower-income individuals out of wealthy neighborhoods.[78] Zoning laws in Columbus, the scholar wrote, often "protected rich from poor and white from black."[79] Today, says one Columbus-area developer, "One of the reasons why there's not affordable housing units in suburbs like Dublin and Hilliard and New Albany is exclusionary zoning."[80]

Limiting areas to single-family homes is only the most blatant mechanism for excluding families of modest means. Some communities require that apartments have brick facades, which are more expensive than, say, vinyl siding, and which make the apartment unaffordable.[81] Indeed, sometimes politicians welcome townhomes so long as they are designed to be expensive and attract a wealthy clientele.[82] Just as Southerners kept people out of voting booths with literacy tests, so the "brick facade" requirement becomes a more sophisticated way of keeping low-income families out of suburban apartments.

Many communities in the Columbus area and throughout the country engage in what is known as "fiscal zoning"—approving only the types of development that will generate more in revenue than the occupants consume in public services. Amy Klaben, an attorney and the former president of Homeport, a nonprofit housing developer, says some

Columbus suburbs, for example, reject proposed developments where the majority of the units are three- or four-bedroom apartments because they don't want units that will accommodate working-class parents with children who will use the public schools.[83] In essence, these suburbs will only approve housing units that are expensive enough so that "the property taxes generated cover the cost of the children in schools."[84] One housing lawyer notes that this is a common problem across the country: "People are not threatened by seniors. [They] are worried about demand on schools."[85]

Developers understand the political dynamics, which is why they often conduct an explicit economic impact analysis to say why the community will benefit—an analysis that often hinges on the economic status of the would-be homeowners and renters. One developer notes: an impact analysis might show that if you build an expensive single-family home, "it will essentially pay for itself." That is, through property taxes, each single-family home will support the schools, library, police, and fire. Because people owning homes have more disposable income to spend, their presence will also be a "net positive economic driver" and produce an economic "multiplier" in the community. By contrast, occupants of a less-expensive townhouse may consume the same level of services but pay fewer property taxes, which might be a "net loss" for the community from a fiscal standpoint.[86]

Finally, in the Columbus area, like Dallas, it is typically legal to discriminate based on source of income. Although the federal Fair Housing Act makes it illegal for a landlord to discriminate against Tehani for her ethnicity, in Central Ohio, Klaben says, landlords can generally discriminate based on source of income, refusing to take any Section 8 Housing Choice Voucher recipients.[87]

Given all these impediments, Tehani, like KiAra Cornelius, was thrilled to hear about the small Move to PROSPER program for single mothers who needed a way to surmount the exclusionary walls built by Columbus suburbs with safe neighborhoods and high-performing schools, such as Dublin, Hilliard, Gahanna, and Olentangy.[88] Beginning in 2018, Move to PROSPER provided Tehani, Cornelius, and eight other low-income single mothers the opportunity to live in such high-opportunity suburbs. Move to PROSPER (which stands for Providing Relocation Opportunities to Stable Positive Environments) has a particular focus on improving the life chances of kids. "It all started with the children," says Amy Klaben, who is now Move to PROSPER's project facilitator.[89]

Through the program, Tehani obtained housing in the Dublin School District, which received a B rating from the state of Ohio, a big improvement over other districts.[90] Tehani's two oldest children, Brandy and Beau, attended Ann Simpson Davis Middle School in 2020. In the school, 61 percent of students are proficient in reading, 66 percent in math, and 78 percent in science. There is a healthy economic and racial mix, with 38 percent of students from low-income backgrounds and no one racial group consisting of a majority.[91] Tehani says her kids haven't faced discrimination in Dublin.

The Dublin schools are well resourced: at the beginning of the year, Tehani says, her kids "came home with brand new Chromebooks that they keep for the entire year." Importantly, Dublin has the resources to offer the drama and choir programs that Brandy craves.

Tehani, who worked her way up to being a human resources manager at Scotts Miracle-Gro Company, marvels at the change in her life since she and her family were homeless—the quality of the housing, the schools, the neighborhood, and even more basic things. "One of the things we don't have to worry about is consistent housing and that's something that's a big deal." For the moment, she is happy. Her kids are challenged at school. And her youngest has a small swing set outside that sits undisturbed. "It makes a big difference," she says.[92]

But Move to PROSPER's initial program was both small (ten recipients) and designed to be temporary (a three-year duration). For most low-income residents, Columbus's exclusionary policies—the economically restrictive covenants, the economic zoning, and the failure to protect against source-of-income discrimination—impose a terrible burden. A 2015 study found Columbus to be the second most economically segregated large metropolitan region in the United States (after Austin, Texas).[93] Another 2015 study, by Harvard University professor Raj Chetty and colleagues, found that of the fifty largest metro areas in the

United States, Columbus ranked near the very bottom—forty-fifth—in social mobility. (By contrast, cities like San Jose, Seattle, and Salt Lake City had double the rates of mobility found in Columbus.)[94]

THE NATIONAL PICTURE

Nationally, the stories of Patricia McGee in Dallas and KiAra Cornelius and Tehani in Columbus are typical in some ways and completely atypical in others. The exclusionary policies these families faced are pervasive throughout the country. The fact that neighborhoods had such a powerful impact on their lives is also borne out by national research. On the other hand, the ability of these mothers to draw upon programs to surmount the obstacles placed by government is highly unusual.

Indeed, most voucher holders are stuck in high-poverty neighborhoods, with no access to special programs like those provided by the Inclusive Communities Project or Move to PROSPER. A 2019 study of the nation's fifty largest metropolitan areas found that only 5 percent of Housing Choice Voucher families live in high-opportunity neighborhoods.[95] Similarly, according to a 2012 study, students in public housing generally have nearby public schools that are poor performers. Among Section 8 Housing Choice Voucher households nationally, the median performance of the nearest school was roughly in the bottom quarter in math and English language arts performance.[96] This matters because talented low-income students in these schools are less likely to get the education they deserve.

The paucity of voucher holders in high-opportunity neighborhoods is not for lack of demand. In Columbus, thirty mothers applied for every spot available in Move to PROSPER. In Dallas, a program called Children First North Texas, which is designed to relocate families living in high-poverty segregated neighborhoods to higher-opportunity environments, surveyed two hundred families to see whether they wanted to move. Only three did not. "Overwhelmingly, they all want to move," says one Dallas Housing Authority official.[97] In meetings, when families heard about the possibility of moving to better neighborhoods, she says, "a lot of folks actually cried because they were like, 'this is something I never thought would come to me.'" One grandmother, the official recalls, was tearful about the prospect of getting her grandson away from local gangs. Overall, of those polled, the number one desire was for safe neighborhoods, then good schools, and third was access to grocery stores, a major concern given the large number of food deserts in the Dallas area.[98]

Yet in many parts of the country, exclusionary zoning is rampant. Dallas and Columbus are both located in "red" states, but as we shall see further in Chapter 4, exclusionary zoning and related practices are, if anything, more common in coastal "blue" states.[99] The essential tools of exclusion have become more pronounced in the past fifty years and include single-family exclusive zoning, minimum lot size requirements, bans on small homes and mobile homes, bans on accessory dwelling units, and minimum parking requirements.

The paradigmatic forms of exclusionary zoning are bans on duplexes, triplexes, and any other form of multifamily housing. In most US cities, zoning laws prohibit multifamily units on at least three-quarters of available land.[100] Such policies effectively say that people are not welcome in a community unless they can afford a single-family home.

This practice is exclusionary because single-family homes are typically less affordable than multifamily homes. Multifamily homes are generally cheaper because the cost of a plot of land can be partitioned among several homeowners. Multifamily housing has fewer exterior walls, keeping construction costs lower. Compact developments also reduce per unit infrastructure costs for gas, electric, water treatment, and internet. As community planners have observed, "Not all dense housing is affordable, but all affordable housing is dense."[101]

In the 2019 American Housing Survey conducted by the Census Bureau and HUD, detached single-family homes were generally the most expensive type of housing within regions, followed by attached single-family homes, then multifamily homes, with mobile homes being the least expensive. In metropolitan areas with more than one million residents, for example, the median total monthly housing costs were 25 percent higher for detached single-family homes than for duplexes, triplexes, and quads, and 78 percent higher than for mobile homes.[102]

In Montgomery County, Maryland, a suburb of Washington, DC, the average price of a detached home ($775,000) was more than twice that for attached homes, such as townhomes ($370,000).[103] In Arlington, Virginia, the minimum household income needed to purchase a unit in a sixplex or eightplex is estimated to be $118,000, compared with a $430,000 income required for a single-family home.[104]

Moreover, in the American Housing Survey, when a detached suburban single-family home was located in a neighborhood where 90 percent or more of neighbors had single-family homes—that is, an area that likely has exclusionary zoning—the price was 33 percent higher than when the detached single-family suburban home was in a neighborhood where fewer than 90 percent of neighbors had single-family homes.[105]

Some exclusive communities go further and require that single-family homes be built on minimum lot sizes, ensuring that those homes are even more expensive. In Connecticut, an astounding 81 percent of residential land requires one-acre lots.[106] These requirements screen out less-advantaged families. High-amenity neighborhoods with strict minimum lot sizes are less economically diverse; on average, incomes are 30 percent higher than in high-amenity Connecticut neighborhoods without strict minimum lot sizes.[107] In the state, the average median income of sixty-eight towns with very large minimum lot sizes is 24 percent higher than the median income of Connecticut as a whole, and these towns have a 36 percent greater white population than the state as a whole.[108] Unless you are at the high end of the income scale, these policies work against you.

Zoning that prohibits the construction of small homes is another common technique of exclusion. Calhoun, Georgia, for example, requires that new single-family dwellings be at least 1,150 square feet. When Tiny Homes Hands Up Inc. proposed building smaller homes, one community member made clear what the regulation was really about, objecting that without the zoning laws, low-income people might move in. "You think of low-income, how are they going to keep up with everything [like] trash pickup and this and that." She suggested small homes would bring "more riffraff than we're already dealing with."[109]

Similarly, throughout America, communities have banned trailer homes or mobile homes (now referred to as manufactured homes), which constitute a less-expensive form of housing.[110] Setting aside property costs, the average cost of building a single-family home on site was $309,000 in 2020, compared with a cost of $87,000 to build a manufactured home.[111] Manufactured homes used to be common; indeed, in 1972, manufactured housing accounted for 60 percent of all new single-family homes. But manufactured housing has since declined dramatically, in part because bans are common.[112] In Gloucester Township, New Jersey, for example, officials banned the construction of a mobile home park anywhere in the community.[113] In Yorba Linda, California, residents permitted a trailer park, but only after a developer agreed to erect a five-foot wall around the complex. One city administrator noted: "We don't even know they're there." The Biden administration is hoping to change zoning laws restricting manufactured housing, which now accounts for about 9 percent of all new single-family homes.[114]

Other forms of class discrimination abound. Single-room-occupancy living, in which individuals have a private bedroom but share a kitchen and bathroom, used to be commonplace but is illegal in many communities.[115] And homeowners' associations increasingly restrict the ability of owners to rent properties because, as one analyst notes, "there is a pretty deep and pervasive social stigma against renters," who tend to make less money than owners.[116]

Many communities also ban the creation of garage and attic apartments or small backyard homes, also known variously as "in-law suites," "granny flats," and "accessory dwelling units" (ADUs). These bans severely restrict relatively affordable units in higher-opportunity neighborhoods.[117]

The pent-up demand for this more affordable housing can be seen in California. After the California legislature adopted changes to allow single-family homes to add ADUs, activists said it was "like opening a floodgate." In 2018, Los Angeles permitted more than four thousand units, "an astonishing figure when one considers that municipal authorities tend to add just a few hundred affordable housing units per year," one observer noted. The potential is enormous: converted garages or backyard cottages could add up to five hundred thousand housing units in Los Angeles.[118] Statewide in 2020, ADUs constituted more than 10 percent of new housing. That figure is up from less than 1 percent eight years earlier.[119] Between 2016 and 2021, the number of ADUs permitted increased by a whopping 1,421 percent.[120]

Another trick used by communities to exclude new neighbors is the excessive use of off-street parking requirements, which considerably jack up the prices of housing. One researcher found that some zoning codes in wealthy Connecticut communities "would require three units of parking for one studio apartment," an absurd condition that was employed to make new development economically infeasible.[121] Off-street parking requirements can increase costs and serve as "a poison pill for low-cost housing."[122] Jurisdictions from Buffalo to Hartford to St. Paul have eliminated off-street parking requirements entirely, and research found that developers, weighing consumer demand, decreased the amount of parking built below what had previously been required by law, suggesting the government requirements had been artificially high.[123] Market forces provide incentives for builders to provide enough parking; if they don't, no one will buy those units.[124]

Exclusionary tactics—which are manifold and numerous—have been increasingly employed over time. Boston University researchers, for example, observed that "land use restrictions have become notably more restrictive in many regions of the United States over the past four decades."[125] After the first wave of exclusionary zoning was adopted in the early twentieth century, communities doubled down beginning in the 1970s. As we will discuss further in Chapter 3, the passage of the Fair Housing Act of 1968, which outlawed racial discrimination, combined with the shift in American assets toward housing, led to the new wave of exclusionary practices.[126]

As one measure of growing regulation, researchers have found that the number of court cases mentioning "land use" has risen dramatically over time, controlling for population growth.[127] Manhattan, for example, has tightened regulations so much that 40 percent of existing housing in Manhattan would not comply with new, more stringent zoning policies if a builder attempted to construct it today.[128] Meanwhile, as regulations have tightened nationally, the proportion of new homes that are attached has declined by half over the past thirty years, from 20 percent to 10 percent.[129]

———

State-sponsored exclusionary tactics have grown even though they are strangling the American Dream by keeping low-income and working-class families out of more advantaged neighborhoods. In decades past, skeptics could suggest that poor people are poor mostly because of bad choices, so allowing some to move to better neighborhoods wouldn't do much for their life chances. But following William Julius Wilson's groundbreaking work, *The Truly Disadvantaged* (1987), which found that neighborhood environment could have a profound impact on families, researchers have provided the evidence that the prospects of adults and children are shaped dramatically by the neighborhoods in which they are allowed to live.

Where you live in America matters greatly to your quality of life and the life chances of your children. It determines your odds of being safe, of getting a job, of accessing good health care and enrolling your children in strong public schools. Poor families who live (often because of government zoning) in low-opportunity neighborhoods with poor schools and high crime rates face very different odds than poor families who live in higher-opportunity neighborhoods where schools are stronger and streets safer. The authors of *American Apartheid* note: "Where one lives—especially where one grows up—exerts a profound effect on one's life chances. Identical individuals with similar family backgrounds and personal characteristics will lead very different lives and achieve different rates of socioeconomic success depending on where they reside."[130]

Adults in high-poverty neighborhoods are often cut off from transportation and jobs, which can have a crippling effect on families. If a parent does not live in a neighborhood with good transportation options, it can take up to two hours to commute. That can mean less time to help nurture a child when home after work.[131] Miss one bus exchange, and a worker can get fired for showing up late, with devastating effects on the whole family.

Families in poor neighborhoods are also often cut off from health care. To take one example, Bethesda, Maryland, an affluent suburb of Washington, DC, has one pediatrician for every four hundred children, compared to poor and predominantly Black Southeast DC, where there is one pediatrician for every thirty-seven hundred children.[132] Poor neighborhoods are also more likely to have environmental hazards such as lead paint that can lead to lower IQ for children.[133]

Overall, the cumulative lifetime impact of neighborhood on opportunity can be enormous. A 2014 study estimated that "the lifetime household income would be $910,000 greater if people born into the bottom quartile of the neighborhood income distribution had instead grown up in a top-quartile neighborhood."[134]

HOUSING POLICY IS SCHOOL POLICY

Education has long been viewed in American society as "the great equalizer." But in practice, American schools are highly segregated by race and socioeconomic status, which defeats the equality goal. Research dating back five decades shows one of the most powerful ways to improve the life chances of disadvantaged students is giving them the opportunity to attend high-quality schools that educate rich and poor students under a single roof.[135]

Residential segregation, not gerrymandered school boundary lines, is the fundamental driver of school segregation. Indeed, recent research found that if students were all assigned to the very closest school, racial school segregation would actually be 5 percent worse than it is today. Given that school boundary lines have a small ameliorative effect, the evidence suggests "residential segregation explains more than 100 percent of school segregation in the US."[136]

Some students attend school outside their neighborhoods, but in a country where 71 percent of students attend neighborhood schools—that is, are simply assigned to the public school nearby their homes—school integration efforts need to include housing integration.[137] Policymakers, researchers, and advocates have long noted that it is important to pursue a parallel set of housing strategies that, if successful, could help integrate neighborhood schools. As one scholar has put it, "Housing policy is school policy."[138]

Low-income students stuck in schools located in high-poverty areas are surrounded by peers who, because they have had less opportunity, are typically less academically engaged and more likely to act out than those in schools in higher-income neighborhoods. Adding to the challenge is a community of parents who are less actively involved in school affairs, in part because they may have less flexible work schedules and lack transportation to get to school easily. Finally, high-poverty schools on average have weaker teachers who have less experience and lower expectations for students.[139]

High-poverty schools are twenty-two times less likely to be as high-achieving as middle-class schools.[140] On the 2017 National Assessment of Educational Progress (NAEP) given to fourth graders in math, low-income students who attended schools that were more affluent were almost two years of learning ahead of low-income students in high-poverty schools.[141] Likewise, a 2008 study found that growing up in high-poverty neighborhoods had the effect for African American children of reducing verbal ability later in life on the order of one year of schooling.[142] And controlling carefully for students' family background, a different 2008 study found that students in mixed-income schools showed 30 percent more growth in test scores over their four years in high school than peers with similar socioeconomic backgrounds in schools with concentrated poverty.[143]

Being isolated in a high-poverty school also reduces the chances that low-income students will befriend wealthier classmates, a phenomenon that new research finds can significantly boost one's adult earnings. A 2022 study by Raj Chetty and colleagues of 21 billion friendships among 72.2 million users of Facebook found that having cross-class friendships was "the single strongest predictor of upward mobility identified to date." It is more important to social mobility than any other factor studied—

including the median household income of the family a child grows up in, the degree of racial segregation in a neighborhood, and the share of single-parent households there.[144]

A number of local programs have demonstrated the importance of where children grow up and go to school. In 1974, for example, Montgomery County, Maryland, a Washington, DC, suburb, adopted a groundbreaking inclusionary zoning program that years later was shown to have dramatic effects on the academic achievement of low-income students. Under the policy, when a developer builds more than a certain number of units, 12.5 percent to 15 percent of the new housing stock must be affordable for low-income and working-class families. Between 1976 and 2010, the program produced more than twelve thousand moderately priced homes, of which the housing authority has the right to purchase one-third for public housing.[145] Children in a subset of these units had the chance to attend middle-class schools.

More recently, Montgomery County implemented a second intervention: the school board allocated an additional $2,000 per pupil to schools in higher-poverty areas to allow for reduced class size in the early grades, extended learning time, and better teacher development.

In 2010, a RAND Corporation researcher compared the effects of the inclusionary zoning and the compensatory spending programs on the academic outcomes of elementary school students.[146] She examined 858 children who had been randomly assigned to subsidized housing units scattered throughout Montgomery County and who were enrolled in Montgomery County public elementary schools between 2001 and 2007 and asked: Who performed better—subsidized housing students in higher-poverty neighborhoods where schools have extra financial resources or similar students in lower-poverty schools that spend less?

Over time, the researcher found, the effects of neighborhood and the poverty level of classmates trumped per pupil spending. Low-income public housing students in low-poverty ("green zone") schools performed far better in math than low-income public housing students in higher-poverty ("red zone") schools with more resources. Low-income students in green zone schools cut their large initial math gap with middle-class students in half. The reading gap was cut by one-third.

She estimates that most of the effect (two-thirds) was due to attending low-poverty schools, and some (one-third) was due to living in low-poverty neighborhoods.

New Jersey provides another example. As noted earlier, in 1975, the New Jersey Supreme Court ruled in *Southern Burlington County NAACP v. Mount Laurel* that zoning laws that have the effect of excluding low-income families violate the state constitution. The court ruled that localities have an affirmative obligation to provide their "fair share" of moderate and low-income housing.[147] Although implementation of the *Mount Laurel* decision has often proven difficult because of political opposition (see discussion in Chapter 6), thousands of low-income families have been able to move to low-poverty neighborhoods as a result of the decision.[148]

Researchers set out to compare the outcomes of families in subsidized housing who moved to Mount Laurel with those who applied but could not be accommodated because of space constraints.[149] In *Climbing Mount Laurel: The Struggle for Affordable Housing and Social Mobility in an American Suburb*, they reported finding "significant improvements in mental health, economic independence, and children's educational outcomes as a result of moving into the project."[150]

The impact on families was very large. The people who moved, the study found, saw "a 428 percent increase in economic independence (e.g., working for pay, share of income from work)," and "a 303 percent increase in school quality (as assessed by class size, test scores, attendance rates etc.)."[151] Poor children benefited. Children who moved to Mount Laurel have "fared better. They study twice as many hours and spend more time reading. That extra effort is paying off—even though their schools are more academically rigorous, they earn slightly better grades."[152] (The researchers did not have access to test scores.)[153]

A third housing intervention involved a program to give inner-city Chicago families a chance to move to low-poverty Chicago suburbs as part of a housing desegregation remedy. In the case of *Gautreaux et al. v. Chicago Housing Authority*, Dorothy Gautreaux charged the Chicago Housing Authority and the US Department of Housing and Urban Development with purposely segregating ten thousand public housing units in Black neighborhoods in violation of the US Constitution and the 1964 Civil Rights Act. Gautreaux won in the lower-level courts, and in 1976, the US Supreme Court upheld a remedy that would go on to help twenty-five thousand public housing participants choose voluntarily to live in low-poverty neighborhoods in one hundred communities throughout the metropolitan Chicago area.[154]

Researchers found that inner-city students whose families moved to publicly subsidized housing in the affluent suburbs were much more likely to succeed than similar students whose families moved instead to other parts of Chicago. The students who moved to the suburbs were four times less likely to drop out of high school (5 percent versus 20 percent), almost twice as likely to take college preparatory courses (40 percent versus 24 percent), twice as likely to attend college (54 percent versus 21 percent), and almost eight times as likely to attend a four-year college (27 percent versus 4 percent). Because 95 percent of movers chose the first available placement, whether in the city or in the suburb, the greater success of suburban movers is unlikely to be heavily influenced by self-selection. Indeed, researchers have lauded the *Gautreaux* finding as particularly reliable because the study involves a "natural experiment" of virtually random placement.[155]

In part on the basis of the successful results stemming from Chicago's *Gautreaux* program, in the 1990s, the Clinton administration supported a new program called Moving to Opportunity (MTO) in five major cities to deconcentrate poverty and rigorously study the results. The experiment, run by the US Department of Housing and Urban Development between 1994 and 1998, randomly assigned 4,604 families living in high-poverty housing projects in the five cities to one of three groups: those receiving a Section 8 housing voucher to move to a census tract with a poverty rate below 10 percent, those receiving a voucher to live anywhere, and a control group that was not offered a voucher to move.[156]

As noted in the introduction, a 2015 follow-up study of the Moving to Opportunity program found that the adult outcomes of moving to a low-poverty neighborhood were significant for those who moved as children before the age of thirteen. The total mean income as adults for early movers was 31 percent higher than for the control group.[157] The expected lifetime earnings benefit was estimated at $302,000.[158]

Although much of the research has focused on the ways in which low-income families benefit when exclusionary barriers are torn down, it is important to note (as we will discuss further in Chapter 5) that the benefits of diversity flow in all directions. Students and adults in middle-class neighborhoods also benefit when children and adults who bring different life experiences are able to enrich classroom discussions and neighborhood gatherings. Research finds that novel ideas and different points of view can make people think more creatively and deeper in solving problems than when participants all come from very similar backgrounds.[159]

Likewise, entire communities benefit when the harms of segregation are avoided and a region can tap into the talents of all its members. A 2017 study found that bringing down Chicago's level of segregation to the median for the nation's largest one hundred metropolitan areas would raise the number of bachelor's degrees earned in the Chicago area by eighty-three thousand, boost worker income by $4.4 billion, and increase Chicago's gross domestic product by $8 billion. The lifetime earnings of Chicago's workers would rise by $90 billion.[160]

Fighting exclusionary zoning is a particularly promising way to open up and desegregate schools for two reasons. To begin with, zoning reform can address the thorny challenges around "interdistrict" school integration. To the extent American school districts have plans in place to integrate, they are almost always limited to within a district's boundaries. The problem is that about two-thirds of racial segregation in metropolitan areas is between districts rather than within them.[161] Because school integration plans almost never reach across districts, housing integration efforts are a key way to effectively combat interdistrict segregation.[162]

In addition, housing integration efforts avoid a major problem associated with school integration efforts: many Americans dislike the idea of long bus rides for kids. A 2021 study found that longer commutes significantly weaken support for school integration. Americans support racially diverse schools in principle by 2:1 but by 2:1 oppose creating such schools when it requires that students be transported to schools farther away.[163]

At the end of the day, zoning laws, coupled with school attendance boundaries, conspire to shut millions of working-class families out of high-performing public schools. Under one set of housing laws, it is illegal to build multifamily housing, and under another set of school rules, it is illegal to travel from outside the district to attend schools that are in theory "public." As one author wryly notes, the Palo Alto Unified School District in California is "free and open to the public. All the public has to do is buy a home in a neighborhood where the median home value was $2.8 million in 2020."[164]

Trying to get around this system, in which educational opportunity is essentially allocated by wealth, can land a parent in jail. Ask Kelley Williams-Bolar, an Akron mother who wanted better schools for her kids. Her father lived in the sought-after Copley-Fairlawn City School District, so Williams-Bolar tried to enroll her kids using his address. When a private investigator documented the arrangement, Williams-Bolar was charged with larceny and served nine days in jail. Hers was, one commentator said, "a Rosa Parks moment for education."[165]

Exclusionary zoning and assignment to public school by neighborhood are the twin linchpins in the architectural design that keeps opportunity in America grossly unequal. Patricia McGee, Tehani, and KiAra Cornelius all know what it is like to live outside the exclusionary walls, and then to be allowed to catapult over them. Millions of others, like Williams-Bolar, are not so fortunate.

TWO

KEEPING HOUSING UNAFFORDABLE

JANET WILLIAMS, A BLACK SINGLE MOTHER OF TWO, WORKS AT A community health center and frequently faces a tough dilemma when her meager paycheck arrives. On several occasions, it's gotten "to the point," she says, "where I had to choose to pay for groceries, pay rent, pay gas and electric or . . . pay childcare."[1] Sometimes her hand is forced. "I've had times where, if I didn't pay my rent, the next day I was going to have eviction filed." On those occasions, "the whole check goes to my rent," and while she waits for the next paycheck to arrive, she may have to tell her kids, we will "not have hot water and not have the electric working."[2]

With a college education, Williams didn't expect to be in this position. She grew up on the north and west side of Columbus, Ohio, as the youngest, and the only girl, in a large family. She has five brothers, one half brother, and four step brothers. After graduating from Groveport Madison Ohio Public Schools, she attended community college and then earned a bachelor's degree in human services from Ohio Christian University in 2019.[3]

With two kids and loans from college, Williams says her job as a community mental health worker and substance abuse case manager for a nonprofit doesn't provide enough. She lives on the east side of Columbus in a neighborhood with a fair amount of police activity, and she often has trouble making ends meet. "I've never been homeless," she says, but she is often "behind on my rent."[4]

Williams did what society asked her to do by working hard and getting a college degree. But she took on $70,000 of debt in the process. Her income is just above what would qualify for food stamps, she says, so "it's on me to put groceries in the house." She hates owing money, so when she gets a windfall, like a COVID-19 stimulus check, she uses it to pay down her credit card debt. But she's frustrated that high housing costs mean she is constrained to a neighborhood where her kids don't feel safe. "I can't tell you how many times we've seen the police outside of our window," she says. To avoid dangers in the neighborhood, she says, "we pretty much keep to ourselves. We don't really do too much."[5] What really aggravates her is that even in her crime-ridden East Columbus neighborhood, the rent is so high that "every month is deciding what's going to get paid."[6]

WHY HOUSING IS SO EXPENSIVE: THE ROLE OF ZONING

The solution, when many people think about Williams's dilemma, involves finding ways to raise wages or increase government housing subsidies. Both approaches make good sense and are necessary.[7] But equally, perhaps more, important is doing something about the "supply side" and addressing the question: What is driving housing prices so high? To what degree do hidden government policies, such as exclusionary zoning, help *create* the housing affordability crisis in the first place?

There is near-universal agreement among economists that since the 1970s, the rise of zoning laws that forbid the construction of multifamily housing has prevented housing supply from keeping up with demand. The 1970s were a turning point, in part, because they were an era of growing inflation, and home equity became an increasing proportion of the financial portfolio of most families.[8] The share of owner-occupied housing as a proportion of net worth rose from an average of 21 percent in 1970 to 30 percent in 1979.[9] Capital income from housing sales tripled as a share of total capital income between 1950 and 2010.[10] As homeownership was transformed from a consumer commodity to an investment, homeowners became increasingly anxious about how new development might affect their property values—and demanded new zoning constraints.[11]

Government policies that forbid multifamily housing *generated* a housing shortage. If homeowners were allowed to subdivide their houses into duplexes or triplexes, or if more multifamily housing could be built near transit, for example, a community would increase the supply of housing available. But single-family exclusive zoning prohibits that possibility. The fundamental problem is that local government policies are preventing builders from creating the housing people need where they need it.[12] One recent study found that between 2012 and 2019, the shortfall in housing nationally doubled in size.[13] In 2021, Freddie Mac economists estimated that we need to build another 3.8 million homes to satisfy demand.[14]

Economists point out that zoning laws that limit development artificially drive up prices.[15] "Imagine," one writer says, "if there were a law that only 1,000 cars could be sold per year in all of New York. Those 1,000 cars would go to whoever could pay the most money for them, and chances are you and everyone you know would be out of luck."[16] This doesn't happen, as one expert observes, because "Ford and General Motors don't have to ask government permission to increase the number of cars or SUVs that their factories produce." By contrast, "all changes to housing supply require explicit approval from local governments."[17]

Just how much do zoning and other land use regulations contribute to the affordability crisis? A 2003 study estimated the "regulatory tax" as a percentage of median home price varied from 53.1 percent in San Francisco and 46.9 percent in San Jose to 1.8 percent in Baltimore.[18] In other words, a $1 million home in San Francisco would have cost around $654,000 in the absence of a $346,000 "zoning tax."[19]

An updated 2021 study found that in San Francisco, the "zoning tax" was estimated at $409,706 for a home on a quarter acre, while in Los Angeles, New York City, and Seattle it ranged from $150,000 to $200,000, and in the Boston area, the tax was estimated at $45,000.[20]

Finding affordable housing has always been a challenge for some families, but as exclusionary zoning has increased, it has helped produce a terrible affordable housing crisis.[21] Today, about a quarter of renters in the United States (about 10.5 million families) spend more than *half* of their income on housing needs.[22] "There is not a county in America," says Senator Cory Booker, "where you can make the minimum wage and afford a two-bedroom apartment."[23] And in 2021, average rents increased 14 percent across the country, and home prices rose nearly 20 percent.[24]

Purchasing a home has become more difficult. US homeownership in late 2017 was near a fifty-year low, at just 63.9 percent.[25] Overall, home prices have been rising twice as fast as wages.[26] Whereas in 1970, the typical American home cost 1.7 times the median household income, by 2020, that median American home cost 4.4 times the typical income.[27] Median home prices continue to rise, having increased by 23 percent in July 2021 from the year before.[28] Taking homeowners and renters together, nearly thirty-eight million Americans are "cost burdened," meaning they pay more than 30 percent of their income for rent or mortgages.[29]

Vulnerable people, like Janet Williams, are hit particularly hard and endure tremendous stress in deciding which expenses to prioritize and in facing the possibility of eviction and homelessness. When housing is too expensive, that has an enormous impact on a family's overall budget because housing is the biggest single monthly expense for most families.[30]

Consider the choices faced by Wisconsin resident Larraine Jenkins, a fifty-four-year-old white mother of two adult children. As Matthew Desmond recounts in his book *Evicted*, Jenkins faced a difficult decision each month about how to allocate her income of $714—the amount she received through the federal Supplemental Security Income (SSI) program for a learning disability she has suffered with from childhood. Jenkins's rent, for a manufactured home in a rundown trailer park on the south side of Milwaukee that hosted prostitutes and drug dealers, was $550 a month. That left $164 for food, medicine, utilities, and other necessities. To make ends meet, Jenkins had in the past chosen not to pay her gas bill. As a result, the gas company had cut her off and she couldn't take a hot shower. But when she was tired of smelling bad, knowing the hot water from the shower would make her fibromyalgia more bearable, she decided to pay the utility and run short on rent. Her landlord sent an eviction notice soon after.[31]

When government zoning policies curtail housing supply in a metropolitan area and increase competition for housing, including in trailer parks, rents rise and millions of Americans suffer. According to the Urban Institute, "Nearly 4 in 10 nonelderly adults reported that in 2018, their families had trouble paying or were unable to pay for housing, utilities, food, or medical care at some point during the year."[32] In 2017, a year of relatively low unemployment, the Urban Institute notes, "one in eight" Americans said "they must turn to high interest rate payday loans, auto title loans, or pawn shops to tide them over."[33] In 2020, one survey found that 17 percent of Americans missed or delayed paying major bills to ensure a household member had enough to eat, and 16 percent reported having serious problems affording food. Some 19 percent reported serious problems paying the mortgage or rent, and 18 percent reported serious problems paying utilities.[34] A 2021 report, vividly entitled "The Rent Eats First," found that "nearly a quarter of renter households were spending more than half of their incomes on rent each month, leaving little income to cover other expenses."[35] A September 2020 study found that twenty-three million Americans (about 10 percent of all adults) "reported that their household sometimes or often had 'not enough to eat' in the last seven days."[36] Making housing more affordable, one author writes, "is literally a lifesaver. People who spend less on housing costs have more money to spend on food and medical care."[37]

In the years that government-sponsored exclusionary zoning has increased, squeezing housing supply and driving prices up for homes and for rents, eviction has become more prevalent. As Matthew Desmond notes, evictions used to be rare, and when they did occur, sometimes outraged neighbors and friends of those being evicted would stage protests. Today,

evictions have soared into the millions, and "there are sheriff squads whose
full time job is to carry out eviction and foreclosure orders." He says: "There
are moving companies specializing in evictions, their crews working all
day, every weekday." And this doesn't count the informal evictions which
occur when landlords simply take the front door off a home.[38]

In poor Black neighborhoods, eviction is the female counterpart
to mass incarceration, Desmond says. Too often "poor black men were
locked up. Poor black women were locked out." In poor white trailer
parks, evictions can be common as well. In one eviction in the Milwaukee area, as a white woman was forced out, "the neighbors began to
gather. Some grabbed beers and positioned lawn chairs as if watching a
NASCAR race."[39]

The toll of eviction is immeasurable. As Desmond shrewdly observed, although poverty often causes housing instability, the converse
is true as well. "We have failed to fully appreciate how deeply housing is
implicated in the creation of poverty." When someone is evicted, their
life falls apart. When you need to spend time finding a new home, and
you are poor, you are less likely to be able to show up to work regularly
and you risk getting fired.[40] Eviction is also enormously disruptive to
children, who often must change schools.

Eviction causes not only material pain but also deep psychic pain:
you lose the place where you can relax and let down your guard. As
Desmond writes: "The home is the center of life. It is a refuge from the
grind of work, the pressure of school, and the menace of the streets. We
say that at home, we can 'be ourselves.' Everywhere else, we are someone
else. At home, we remove our masks."[41] Taking that away is devastating.

Finally, because zoning artificially limits the supply of housing and
increases rents, homelessness is rising. A 2012 study, for example, estimated when median rents increase $100, homelessness rises 15 percent.[42]
Likewise, a 2017 report found that "homelessness is especially high in
more expensive rental markets."[43] Plotting a graph with the percentage
of people who are homeless and median rents shows, says one scholar,
"a direct correlation between median rents and the size of the homeless
population."[44] Although many people blame homelessness on substance
abuse and mental illness, these undeniable contributors to homelessness

don't explain the recent rise in tent cities. "We have had substance abuse problems in this country for centuries," one analyst notes. "What we have not had is modern homelessness," which she says is related to the precipitous drop in housing supply.[45] Los Angeles tried to fix its homelessness problem with Proposition HHH to increase funds for affordable housing, she says, which is a positive thing, but unless one also deals with the way that zoning artificially constrains the supply of housing, the problem will fester.[46]

HOUSING AFFORDABILITY AND THE MIDDLE CLASS

The affordability crisis in housing hits low-income populations hardest, but today middle-class people also feel the aggravation that comes from rising prices in places where demand outstrips housing supply. In 74 percent of markets in the United States, the *median* worker cannot afford the median house price.[47] In California, the median price of a single-family home is more than $800,000.[48] Affordability has become such a crisis in Milpitas, California, that the school district in 2022 sent a note to parents asking them to allow teachers to move in and rent a room.[49]

In July 2021, the *Wall Street Journal* noted that a broad swath of millennials is being shut out of buying starter homes. "This is a big deal," Sam Khater, chief economist at Freddie Mac, told the *Journal*. Affordability issues are not only affecting low-income and middle-class people. "It's now going up into the upper-middle-income stratum."[50] Developers like building modest starter homes because they are less risky and the profit margins aren't generally higher on large homes. But when exclusionary zoning drives up the price of land and forbids creating anything but a single-family home, builders have little choice but to erect large homes to recoup the cost of land. Today, only 8 percent of new homes are 1,400 square feet or less, compared with nearly 70 percent in the 1940s.[51] With few starter homes available, new buyers are often shut out. According to a 2022 report of the National Association of Realtors, first-time home buyers, who used to account for 40 percent of the market, now account for just 26 percent, the lowest level since the association began tracking the information forty-one years ago.[52]

According to one study, 48.3 percent of baby boomers were home-owners by age thirty, but that proportion has declined to 35.8 percent among early millennials (those born between 1980 and 1984).[53] The median age of a first-time homeowner has risen to age thirty-six, the oldest such age recorded since 1981.[54] "It just feels like every little thing keeps getting put on hold," Samantha Berrafato, a young person looking for a house in the Chicago area, told the *Wall Street Journal*. "I've been putting having kids on hold, and I had to put having a wedding on hold because we just couldn't afford it. Now it's like [that with] the house buying."[55]

As we shall discuss further in Chapter 8, public opinion polls reflect the frustration. In a 2017 survey of mayors, high housing costs were cited as the most likely reason residents leave their cities, outranking lack of jobs, school quality, public safety, and taxes.[56] Sarah and Robbie Tripp, for example, moved to San Francisco in 2016 with high hopes of making connections and succeeding in their work as social media influencers but in their search for housing could only find "places for $1 million that looked like rundown shacks and needed a remodel." They soon decamped to Phoenix.[57]

Mayors directly tied high housing prices to a lack of housing supply: only 13 percent said "their cities' housing stock was a good match for the needs of their constituents."[58] Almost two-thirds of mayors complained that housing policy was driven by a vocal minority—NIMBY homeowners—in contrast to other issues like education and policing, where only one in five mayors said the vocal minority held sway.[59]

The stress and hardship that the housing affordability crisis imposes on families also affect health, the ability to migrate to opportunity, and the environment.

The high cost of housing spurred on by exclusionary zoning directly exacerbates health problems, scholars find. Zoning that makes housing unaffordable often pushes multifamily housing closer to highways, which increases health risks associated with air pollutants. The irony, researchers note, is that, although zoning was originally meant to promote health and safety, it can sometimes do the opposite.[60]

Likewise, the affordability crisis causes families to double up or triple up in apartments, resulting in overcrowding that promotes the spread of disease as we saw in the COVID-19 pandemic. Although some early re-porting focused on the false idea that housing *density* spreads COVID-19, in fact, studies show that it's overcrowding—too many people living in the same apartment or home—that presents the largest health concerns. Some small towns in Georgia and Louisiana had high infection rates be-cause individual housing units were crowded, with three or four families living in a single home.[61] Some very dense cities, such as Seoul and Sin-gapore, were relatively successful in containing the spread of COVID-19 because units themselves were not overcrowded.[62]

THWARTING INTERNAL MIGRATION

Exclusionary zoning and the high housing prices it causes also thwart internal migration within the United States, which has historically al-lowed lower-income people to move to wealthier regions of the country where there are better, higher-paying jobs.

The United States for years had fairly high mobility because even higher-opportunity metropolitan areas were affordable. In the 1950s and 1960s, for example, one economist notes, "housing prices throughout the United States were fairly similar among regions." Housing in Cali-fornia was not more expensive than that in comparable communities in the Midwest or Northeast.[63] In 1960, the median price for a home was about the same in Illinois and Nevada as in California.[64]

Over the years, migration was the rule. Poor white families, like those depicted in *The Grapes of Wrath*, moved from Oklahoma to Cali-fornia during the Great Depression seeking better opportunities. Low-income Black people left poor southern states to escape the oppression of Jim Crow for wealthier industrial cities with more job opportunities.[65] Theirs was a "double migration," seeking relief not only from racial bru-tality but also from economic impoverishment.[66] As Isabel Wilkerson details in *The Warmth of Other Suns*, the Great Migration helped trans-form the lives of millions of Black people, such as Ida Mae Gladney, who fled Mississippi for Chicago in 1937, trading a life of sharecropping to become a solidly middle-class blue-collar worker, or Robert Foster, who became a successful doctor after leaving Louisiana in 1953.[67] Altogether,

between 1915 and 1970, the proportion of Black Americans living outside the South more than quadrupled, from 10 percent to 47 percent.[68]

The large expansion of exclusionary zoning that began in the 1970s
changed all of that and tended to make areas of high economic vitality
much more expensive, because the growth of home building in these
regions could not keep up with demand. The "paradox of land," says
Richard Florida, is that "there are seemingly endless amounts of land
across the world, but not nearly enough of it where it is needed most."[69]
In more than one hundred zip codes in the New York, Los Angeles, and
San Francisco metropolitan areas, he reported in 2017, the median home
price exceeded $1 million. The composition of cities and towns changed,
as economically diverse communities became the province of the relatively well-off. In the SoHo neighborhood in Manhattan, for example,
the median value of an apartment could be used to purchase fifty homes
in parts of Toledo, Ohio, or seventy homes in parts of Detroit.[70]

As a result, migration levels fell, and lower-income and working-
class people could no longer pursue their dreams because housing in
economically dynamic areas became prohibitively expensive. Economists note that "before 1960, Americans followed the money, finding
opportunity by moving to states with higher incomes. Between 1990
and 2010, however, poorer states added population more quickly than
rich states."[71] High-income states like Massachusetts and New Jersey
had slower population growth than relatively lower-income states such
as Texas and South Carolina.[72]

One scholar has noted, "For the first time in American history, it
makes sense to talk about whole regions of the country 'gentrifying'—
whole metropolitan areas whose high housing costs have rendered them
inhospitable" to many low-income and middle-class families.[73] This is
particularly true on the West Coast, says economist Paul Krugman.
Restrictive zoning has driven up housing prices to the point where
"California as a whole is suffering from gentrification." The wealthy are
moving in, but the poor have to move out of state. As a result, in recent
years, Krugman says, "more Americans have moved out of California
than have moved in." Even though California is bound by an ocean,
Krugman says, "there is plenty of scope for building up."[74]

Parts of the East Coast suffer the same problem. Says Sam Khater of Freddie Mac, "In the past, Americans used to move for opportunity. But in recent years, they've been moving for affordability."[75] Between 2010 and 2020, Silicon Valley, which is rich in jobs, grew by a modest 6.5 percent, while Harris County, Texas, which includes Houston and has less land but cheaper housing, grew 175 percent faster.[76] During that decade, California, with its high-paying jobs, grew so little that it lost a congressional seat for the first time in its more than 170-year history.[77]

A Yale University scholar has documented the degree to which working people living outside the coasts are "stuck."[78] Moving to New York or Los Angeles or Washington or San Francisco simply became just too expensive. From this perspective, exclusionary zoning is not only snobbish, it's incredibly selfish. The practical consequences, one journalist notes, is that "working class people can't live where the wages are highest," and, in some cases, women can't afford to live in states that guarantee the right to choose to have an abortion.[79] One writer says to NIMBY forces in those cities: "We cannot sacrifice the lives, the futures and the dreams of every other American because you don't want to see an apartment building."[80] Indeed, if exclusionary zoning had existed in the early twentieth century to the same extent that it does today, it is doubtful that the Great Migration of Black Americans could have happened on the scale that it did.

Richard Florida calls this development "the New Urban Crisis." The old urban crisis of the 1960s involved race riots and rising crime, urban decline and white flight. The new urban crisis, he says, is different: dynamic cities with great opportunities are off-limits to many working-class Americans because of skyrocketing housing prices. And when these families do manage to find housing that is affordable in a region, it's often at great distances from where they work, economically segregated from where the knowledge class resides.[81] "The crux of the problem," Florida says, is that "land is scarce precisely where it is needed most" in part because restrictive zoning and building codes "limit the market's ability to build as needed."[82]

During the COVID-19 pandemic, as many office workers engaged in remote work, some of the most expensive cities saw outmigration.[83]

But this phenomenon hardly solved the housing crisis. Many workers—such as bus drivers, teachers, factory workers, grocery clerks, and health-care professionals—cannot generally work remotely and must still live in proximity to their jobs. And as white-collar employers have increasingly settled on a "hybrid" approach to remote work (some days in the office, others working from home), the need to live in the community where your office is located did not disappear.

Economists say that it's not only individual dreams that are crushed; the American economy as a whole suffers to a staggering degree. The American economy requires dynamism—so that when jobs are created in a certain area, Americans can move to meet the labor demands. Economists are very worried that exclusionary zoning in highly dynamic areas thwarts this response—and keeps productive workers from moving. NIMBYs, Richard Florida notes, "put a brake on the very clustering that drives innovation and economic growth."[84]

The system of artificially limiting housing supply benefits a small number of homeowners who can afford these areas and see their home values increase, but the overall effect is to reduce productivity for the larger society. NIMBYs are what economists call "rent seekers"—those who receive "an extraordinary return that comes about through little or no real effort"[85] (unless, of course, one counts the effort of showing up at neighborhood zoning meetings to block development). This "winner take all" approach, says Florida, drives wealth inequality.[86]

The economic cost to American society of government regulations that jack up housing prices in high-productivity cities, such as New York, San Jose, and San Francisco, is staggering. One study found that if these cities relaxed restrictions on housing supply by, for example, allowing more multifamily housing, workers could move to high-wage areas and average wages nationally would rise an astounding $8,775.[87]

Another study estimates that "a *lower bound* cost of restrictive residential land use regulation is at least 2 percent of national output."[88] As Susan Rice, director of the Domestic Policy Council, noted, 2 percent would constitute more than $400 billion in GDP growth.[89] Government zoning policies that have the effect of preventing workers from moving to high-wage areas constitute an extraordinary drain on the American economy.

People in highly productive regions often resent tech workers and others whose presence drives up home values. In Oakland, for example, protesters directed anger at private buses that transported tech workers from a gentrifying community to Silicon Valley. But Richard Florida argues that such ire is misplaced. Having knowledge workers in a community means more economic growth, better services, and more restaurant options, which are beneficial to everyone; the culprit isn't tech workers, it's NIMBYs who are driving up prices by artificially constraining the supply of housing available.[90]

In China, explicit laws exist to keep rural workers from moving to cities where there are jobs. It is called the "household registration system," which requires rural residents to have internal passports in order to work in growing urban areas. Wealthy urban residents, who don't want low-income internal migrants coming into their communities and schools, push to strictly limit the number of internal passports and require migrants to return home to educate their kids and access social welfare benefits. This artificial system keeps China's economy much less productive—and much more unequal—than it would be with freer movement.[91]

America's system of exclusionary zoning is a more indirect but perhaps no less effective version of China's household registration: it effectively bars many would-be migrants from seeking good jobs and pursuing the American Dream by keeping housing unaffordable in high-growth regions, at a terrible cost to individuals and society.

DAMAGING THE PLANET

By making housing less affordable, exclusionary zoning also pushes families out on the periphery of metropolitan areas, which imposes hardships on those families and is bad for the environment. In Washington, DC, some area blue-collar workers can commute from as far away as Pennsylvania or West Virginia.

By artificially propping up housing prices and forcing metropolitan areas to "build out" rather than "build up," exclusionary zoning makes lives miserable for many Americans. It is unsustainable, Richard Florida notes, when "teachers, nurses, hospital workers, police officers, fire-fighters, and restaurant and service workers can no longer afford to live within reasonable commuting distances to their workplaces."[92] In 2019, 4.6 million people lived at least ninety minutes from work. The most expensive regions of the country had the most such "super-commuters."[93]

Consider the Dallas region, for example, where population has been exploding. Between 2010 and 2020, Dallas was one of only three cities in the country to add at least 1.2 million residents. With a metropolitan population of 7.6 million, Dallas–Fort Worth is the nation's fourth-largest metropolitan area.[94] The *Dallas Morning News* reports that "planners foresee a day when development reaches out 100 miles from Dallas."[95] These long commutes impose a severe hardship on these workers. Long-distance commuters have more headaches and backaches. They have higher blood pressure and more sleep disturbances. They are also more likely to neglect friends and family and have little time for hobbies.[96] All of this increases the likelihood of divorce.[97]

Long commutes also produce more greenhouse gases, damaging the planet for everyone.[98] Scientists estimate that transportation accounts for 29 percent of greenhouse gas emission in the United States, the largest single contributor.[99] And the problem is getting worse. The number of vehicle miles traveled increased 48 percent between 1990 and 2019, according to the EPA.[100]

The sprawl that results from exclusionary zoning also leads to habitat destruction, which is a major factor in threatening the extinction of animals. According to the EPA, "Habitat destruction is the main factor threatening 80 percent or more of the species listed under the federal Endangered Species Act."[101]

Among scholars, there is widespread agreement that laws banning the construction of multifamily housing promote damage to the earth for other reasons as well.[102] Multifamily units have a smaller carbon footprint than does housing the same number of residents in detached single-family homes, because apartments have fewer exterior walls, making them easier to heat and cool and thus more energy efficient than single-family homes.[103] Residential buildings account for an estimated 16 percent of greenhouse gas admissions.[104] Families should always have the freedom to make personal choices about their living arrangements, but as the planet heats up, it is odd that government—which is fighting in all sorts of arenas to reduce greenhouse gases—would explicitly *prohibit* construction of the most environmentally friendly options.

Taking the issues of commuting time and home efficiency together, researchers have found that "the average carbon footprint of households living in the center of large, population-dense urban cities is about 50 percent below average, while households in distant suburbs are up to twice the average."[105] Likewise, studies find emissions in low-density developments were 3.7 times higher than those found in high-density developments.[106] Doubling urban density would reduce carbon emissions from travel by 48 percent and reduce residential energy use by 35 percent.[107]

Change will not occur, however, until people connect the dots between exclusionary zoning and the environment in the way they have between automobiles and climate change. Many liberal San Francisco residents have "solar panels on their roofs and compost bins at their driveways, flanked by hybrid and electric cars," note two journalists, yet at the same time they fiercely resist greater density that could bring about even more sizable environmental benefits than installing solar panels on all new construction.[108]

—⧫—

The costs of the housing affordability crisis are manifold: it adds unnecessary stress and anguish to the lives of working people like Janet Williams; it causes overcrowding and its attendant health problems; it curbs the internal migration that has provided opportunities for families for generations; and it pushes people out to the periphery of metropolitan areas, where their long commutes damage the planet. All in all, the toll on America is terrible. Astonishingly, the crisis is made profoundly worse by the government's own zoning laws that make it illegal for builders to provide the housing that Americans need.

THREE

HOW CLASS BIAS BECAME THE PRIMARY OBSTACLE TO HOUSING ADVANCEMENT FOR BLACK PEOPLE

FOR MUCH OF AMERICAN HISTORY, THE PRIMARY IMPEDIMENT to Black advancement in housing was strictly racial in character. In the late nineteenth century, working-class white and Black people were reasonably integrated in the city of Baltimore, Maryland. In the early twentieth century, however, when George W. F. McMechen, a Black Yale Law graduate, moved into a white upper-middle-class neighborhood, white families reacted with violence and legislation. "Whites threw stones and bricks into the McMechens' new home," Georgetown University professor Sheryll Cashin writes, and Baltimore's mayor, J. Barry Mahool, championed the nation's first racial zoning legislation, which banned Black people from moving into white neighborhoods.

Mahool did not mince words. "Blacks should be quarantined in isolated slums in order to reduce the incidents of civil disturbance, to prevent the spread of communicable disease into the nearby white neighborhoods and to protect property values among the white majority," he declared. The *New York Times* article about the ordinance, Cashin notes, "featured an image of the handsome, dapper, and presumably disease-free McMechen."[1]

Mahool's idea that racial zoning would protect white people from disease sounds bizarre to the modern ear, but in the late nineteenth and early twentieth centuries, developers of upper-middle-class white suburbs widely propagated the argument that living in an environment free of Black and low-income people was the "healthy" option. The developer of Roland Park, then an all-white suburb of Baltimore, placed an advertisement in 1895 that suggested: "In buying a home, a location should be chosen which is protected from unhealthful surroundings and undesirable neighbors." The message from the Roland Park developers, says one researcher, was that "undesirable neighbors were more likely to be disease vectors, based on their class, race or place of birth."[2]

Racial segregation—in Baltimore or wherever it occurs—is sometimes thought of as a naturally occurring phenomenon that reflects an almost innate desire of people of similar backgrounds to congregate. In fact, however, segregation was deliberately created, mostly during the twentieth century, through a series of government policies.[3] Indeed, those policies would help racial segregation to double between 1880 and 1940.[4]

In 1910, after Baltimore pioneered racial zoning by prohibiting Black families from buying in majority white areas, or white people in majority Black areas, similar racial zoning policies spread throughout the country, Richard Rothstein notes, to include "Atlanta, Birmingham, Dade County (Miami), Charleston, Dallas, Louisville, New Orleans, Oklahoma City, Richmond (Virginia), St. Louis and others."[5]

In the 1917 *Buchanan* decision, the US Supreme Court ruled that Louisville's racial zoning ordinance violated the Fourteenth Amendment and related statutes, which "entitle a colored man to acquire property without state legislation discriminating against him solely because of color."[6] Some white homeowners, who opposed zoning limitations because they wanted to be free to sell or rent to the highest bidder, irrespective of race, allied with the National Association for the Advancement of Colored People (NAACP) in the case.[7]

Fifty-one years later, Congress passed, and President Lyndon Johnson signed, the 1968 Fair Housing Act. Today, a Black Yale Law graduate can purchase a home in a white neighborhood without facing the intense, naked racial discrimination that George W. F. McMechen did. But that does not mean that Black people, on the whole, are free to live wherever they want. Systemic racial discrimination in the twentieth century (much of it well known to readers) conspires with twenty-first-century economic discrimination in zoning (that is less well recognized) to hurt Black families especially, even those with middle-class incomes. Black Americans face a one-two punch. As I detail in this chapter, the intense racial discrimination in the last century robbed Black people of wealth; and intense economic discrimination today—which is perfectly legal—cripples the ability of low-wealth families (many of them Black) to live in high-opportunity neighborhoods.

RACE AND HOUSING: PROGRESS AND DISAPPOINTMENT

Today, progress on reducing racial residential discrimination and levels of racial segregation in housing is a mixed bag, neither as promising as some optimists might suggest nor as dire as others might posit.

On the one hand, research suggests that the combination of the Civil Rights Act and the Fair Housing Act has generated important successes for middle-class African Americans. With passage of civil rights laws, the Black middle class grew. As Harvard's Henry Louis Gates noted in 2020, "One of the most dramatic shifts to the structure of the African-American community has been the doubling of the Black middle class and the quadrupling of the Black upper middle class since 1970."[8] Sheryll Cashin finds that antidiscrimination laws helped a subset of the Black population to move up economically. "Before the movement, the majority of Blacks were poor. Today, a large majority of Black Americans are not poor," she says.[9] Indeed, as William Julius Wilson has observed, income inequality within the Black community is greater than within any other racial or ethnic group (white, Hispanic, or Asian).[10]

The Fair Housing Act has also had some considerable successes, particularly in reducing blatant racial discrimination. Four national audit studies conducted by the Urban Institute over the course of thirty-five years found that racial discrimination in housing has been declining.[11] In 1977, Black people faced discrimination 27 percent of the time when attempting to buy or rent a home; by 2012, they faced discrimination 10 percent of the time, and the type of discrimination is also less severe in the sense that families are very rarely turned away entirely, as they were in the past.[12] The Urban Institute's 2012 study found that "when well-qualified minority home seekers contact housing providers to inquire about recently advertised housing units, they generally are just as likely as equally qualified white home seekers to get an appointment and learn about at least one available housing unit."[13]

As a result, a growing Black middle class has been able to move out of highly segregated Black slums, as Wilson has documented.[14] Between 1970 and 1995, the percentage of the Black population living in the suburbs shot up from less than one-sixth to almost one-third.[15] Indeed, says Cashin, the seven million Black people who moved to the suburbs during those years far exceeds the number of Black people who participated in the Great Migration out of the South from 1940 to 1970.[16] Progress has continued in the years since 1995. Between 2000 and 2020, the proportion of Black residents living in the suburbs increased from 43 percent to 54 percent in the largest one hundred metropolitan areas. Truck driver Chris Calhoun, for example, moved in 2014 from the tough Roseland section of Chicago to suburban South Hill, Illinois, after asking himself: "Where can I live where my kids can go outside and ride their bikes, or we can take a walk around the block as a family without looking over my shoulder?"[17]

The change has helped transform America's suburbs. In 1980, 80 percent of suburban metropolitan areas were predominantly white. But by 2010, of people living in the fifty largest metro areas, 31 percent lived in diverse suburbs and only 18 percent in predominantly white suburbs (those that are more than 80 percent white).[18] By 2020, less than half of white households lived in predominantly white areas, marking the first time in modern American history that most white people lived in mixed-race neighborhoods.[19] Suburbs like Winnetka, Illinois (92 percent non-Hispanic white in 2022), are mostly a thing of the past in large metropolitan areas.[20]

Reflecting on the transformation in 2018, former US senator Walter F. Mondale (D-MN), who championed the 1968 Fair Housing Act in Congress, remarked: "Because of the Fair Housing Act, more than half of African Americans, Latinos and Asians live in the suburbs today. Almost 45 percent of suburban residents in the largest metropolitan areas live in racially diverse suburbs. These suburbs—the children of the Fair Housing Act—are some of the nation's most wonderful places."[21]

These changes help explain why Black–white racial segregation has fallen by about 30 percent since 1970.[22] In addition, the proportion of metropolitan-area Black people living in hypersegregated environments was cut roughly in half, from 61 percent to 32 percent, between 1970 and 2010.[23] Indeed, says Cashin, between 1970 and 2009, "the percentage of middle-class or affluent Blacks who lived in islands of advantage grew from 12 percent to 34 percent."[24]

The bad news is that despite all this progress for middle-class Black people, many low-income Black people remain stuck in high-poverty, highly segregated environments. Analyzing data over time, one researcher writes of African Americans: "Few groups in American history have ever experienced such high levels of segregation, let alone sustained them over decades."[25] The dissimilarity index for Black–white segregation (0.526; in which 1 is apartheid and 0 is complete integration) remains higher than it is for segregation between non-Hispanic white people and Asian people (0.467) or for segregation between non-Hispanic white people and Hispanic people (0.407).[26] If current trends continue, Black people will not reach more moderate levels of segregation for another thirty years.[27]

Moreover, even though middle-class Black households have a greater chance of living in integrated neighborhoods than do low-income Black families, middle-class Black families still face substantial obstacles. Middle-class Black families earning $100,000 or more per year live in neighborhoods with the same disadvantages as the average white household earning less than $30,000 per year.[28] Equally astonishingly, *middle-income* Black people live in neighborhoods with higher poverty rates than *low-income* white people.[29] Likewise, the average nonpoor Black person lives in a neighborhood with a higher violent crime rate than the average poor white person.[30] The disparity in neighborhoods among Black and white people of the same income was most stark in places like Milwaukee and Newark, where the median white family making $50,000 a year had neighbors with a median income 1.8 times the size of a typical Black family making $50,000.[31] One researcher notes that "about half of middle-class African Americans are raised in neighborhoods with poverty rates of 20 percent or more, compared with just 1 percent of their white peers."[32]

WHY DOES SEGREGATION REMAIN SO HIGH?

There are three big explanations for why Black–white segregation levels remain high: personal preference, persistent racial discrimination, and class barriers that disproportionately affect people of color. These explanations intertwine and are not mutually exclusive.[33]

The idea that groups self-segregate because birds of a feather flock together provides, at best, only a partial explanation. Although African Americans, and people of color in general, may have an understandable desire to live in a neighborhood that is a haven where they do not have to face discrimination, the data indicate that most members of minority groups want to live in more integrated neighborhoods than they currently do.

Researchers note, "Compared to whites, blacks express considerably greater tolerance for integration, preferring neighborhoods with considerably more non-blacks than the neighborhoods blacks reside in."[34] A poll of Long Island Black residents found that 69 percent preferred integrated neighborhoods, while just 1 percent wanted to live in all-Black neighborhoods.[35] And yet Long Island's Meadowbrook Parkway creates a stark dividing line in community after community: on one side is mostly white Merrick, North Merrick, and East Meadow, while on the other is mostly minority Freeport, Roosevelt, and Uniondale. Some communities on one side of the parkway are as little as 1 percent white, and others on the other side are as little as 2 percent Black—a level of virtual apartheid that has little to do with the preferences of Black families.[36]

National data show the same phenomenon. For example, a recent Pew Survey found that Black people are much more supportive of integrated schools than are white people, particularly when that integration necessitates children going to schools outside their neighborhoods. Sixty-eight percent of Black people say that "students should go to schools that are racially and ethnically mixed, even if it means some students don't go to school in their local community," compared to just 35 percent of white people.[37]

Given the finding that Black people as a group want more integrated settings than they in fact live in, it might be natural to conclude that racial discrimination remains the major culprit for high levels of segregation. But though there is some distressing evidence that landlords and real estate agents continue to engage in discrimination by race,[38] national audit studies find discrimination has fallen sharply. As researchers note, the discrimination paradigm can "no longer explain, [in] the face of substantial declines in discrimination rates, persistently high levels of segregation."[39]

Alongside choice and racial discrimination, something else is going on to sustain racial segregation. Considerable evidence finds the prime culprit today is economic zoning to maintain low levels of density by banning multifamily housing. Noting that "the degree of discrimination has fallen substantially over time on federally sponsored audit studies," researchers find that "one factor in the mix of segregation-producing arrangements clearly stands out: restrictive density zoning in the suburbs."[40] Evidence shows: "Density zoning is now *the most important mechanism* promoting class and racial segregation" in the United States.[41] The effect of density zoning on segregation is not just associational; it is "causal."[42]

THE SUSPICIOUS HISTORY OF THE GROWTH OF ECONOMIC ZONING

If economic zoning causes racial (and economic) segregation, there is very strong evidence to demonstrate that the spread of such zoning was often motivated by that very purpose. Economically exclusionary zoning saw two great waves of expansion that were spurred at least in part as a backlash against racial progress: in the early twentieth century, following the Supreme Court's decision to ban racial zoning; and again in the early 1970s, shortly after passage of the Fair Housing Act.

As noted earlier, many cities that employed racial zoning quickly shifted to economic zoning after the 1917 *Buchanan v. Warley* decision.[43] And the federal government got into the act as well.[44] President Warren G. Harding's secretary of commerce, Herbert Hoover, created an Advisory Board on Zoning, which included members who wanted to use zoning to segregate and "keep low-income families out of middle-class neighborhoods."[45]

In 1924, Hoover's commission drafted the Standard State Zoning Enabling Act, which had an enormous influence on the state authorization of local zoning. According to one economist, "Nearly every state adopted legislation that was either taken verbatim from this model statute or was heavily influenced by it."[46]

In 1916, just eight cities had zoning ordinances; by 1936, that number was 1,246.[47] Today, every major city has zoning policies with the exception of Houston, Texas.[48] And even Houston has a number of ways to create obstacles for low-income families who want to live in middle-class areas—including economically restrictive covenants that require homeowners not to develop multifamily units (enforceable in court), minimum parking requirements, minimum lot size requirements, and policies that place virtually all subsidized housing in a few areas that are predominantly poor and populated by people of color.[49]

To be sure, racial animus was only one reason for the growth of these policies. As we shall see in Chapter 4, economic snobbery coupled with concerns about property values has also played a role.[50] But it hardly seems a coincidence that cities that experienced the highest rates of Black migration have the most restrictive zoning or that exclusionary policies were sometimes timed to an influx of Black families.[51] Because African Americans were (and are) disproportionately low-income, economically exclusionary zoning accomplished much of the same end result as explicit racial zoning did.[52]

Although exclusionary zoning was often motivated by racism and snobbery, the Supreme Court in 1926 upheld such laws. Contrasting with the explicit discrimination by race, which was struck down in *Buchanan*, the US Supreme Court upheld discrimination by class in the landmark ruling *Euclid v. Ambler* (1926).[53] The court held that just as it was permissible for a community to exclude industrial facilities from residential areas in order to promote health and safety, barring multifamily housing, which brings more people and traffic, is similarly justified.

Half a century later, America saw its second great wave of exclusionary zoning laws adopted, this time shortly after passage of the 1968 Fair Housing Act. In the 1970s, suburbs adopted new exclusionary zoning and growth management rules, which were at least in part a response to efforts by civil rights lawyers to open up the suburbs.[54] Although explicit racial efforts were no longer tolerated, one observer notes, "zoning could, however, be used to reduce potential contact between races, or between high- and low-income people, by the superficially neutral expedient of insisting on large lots and single-family homes in residential districts."[55] By barring racial discrimination, experts at UC Berkeley note, "the Fair Housing Act may have contributed to the enactment of restrictions based on class, and helped set in motion developments that led to greater economic segregation." They continue: "Resistance to the Fair Housing Act was channeled into class-based exclusionary land use policies."[56]

As noted in Chapter 2, the 1970s rise in exclusionary zoning was also related to the fact that housing was becoming a larger piece of the financial portfolio of average Americans, and these two concerns—property values and the prospect of racial and class integration—combined to create a climate of fear. As home values became more important to families, the concern that opening up the suburbs to racial and class diversity could detrimentally affect property values merged to produce a major increase in zoning laws that made it exceedingly difficult to build new housing in many exclusive suburbs.

Bans on multifamily housing in exclusive neighborhoods screen out low-wage Black families like Patricia McGee's and KiAra Cornelius's in a straightforward fashion. But how do such zoning policies work also to exclude middle- and upper-middle-income Black people? One answer is that zoning policies create large barriers related to wealth, not just income.

To purchase a single-family home, especially one in a neighborhood where exclusionary zoning creates scarcity that artificially raises prices, a would-be buyer must put down a much more substantial down payment than if she were purchasing a smaller unit of housing or even a single-family home in a neighborhood without zoning-induced artificial scarcity. The sizable down payment requires the accumulation of wealth.

But for decades, white policymakers have created housing rules that had the effect of denying Black families the chance to accumulate such wealth. As a result, even middle-class and upper-middle-class Black families often lack the accumulated assets necessary to overcome exclusionary barriers. While white people typically make 1.6 times as much as Black people in annual income, the wealth gap is much larger. White median household wealth is eight times as high as median Black household wealth.[57] Stunningly, African American households headed by an individual *with a bachelor's degree* have just two-thirds of the wealth, on average, of white households headed by an individual who *lacks a high school degree.*[58] Not surprisingly, HUD secretary Marcia Fudge has identified the challenge Black buyers have in coming up with down payments as the biggest impediment to Black homeownership.[59]

The Black–white wealth gap is largely the result of government policies, enacted by white people, which robbed Black people of the opportunity to accumulate wealth. This social engineering began, of course, with slavery, when enslaved Black people were not paid for their hard work, but it continued on through the twentieth century, especially through housing policy.

Consider, for example, how social engineering in the Dallas area affected the ability of families like Patricia McGee's to inherit wealth to purchase a home. The big way for the parents and grandparents of people like McGee to begin accumulating wealth was to purchase a starter home and then see that home appreciate in value. A piece of that wealth can then be handed down to the next generation.

For many white families in America, this process has been straightforward. But for Black families, two sets of government-sponsored impediments were put in place. For one thing, the process of "redlining," which denied government-backed mortgage assistance to people in neighborhoods based on race and socioeconomic status, cheated Black families of the chance to purchase a home and begin the process of wealth accumulation. In addition, a series of government policies—racial zoning, judicial enforcement of racially restrictive covenants, school segregation, and government indifference toward white violence—all conspired to create residential racial segregation. This, too, inhibited Black wealth accumulation. Even if a Black family could manage to scrape together money to purchase a home without a government-backed mortgage, the fact that the home was likely located in a segregated community meant it would appreciate at much slower rates than homes in predominantly white communities.

As part of the New Deal, the federal government—in Dallas and elsewhere—sought to expand homeownership by guaranteeing mortgages, broadening the group of people who could buy homes. Instead of having to save up enough money to purchase a home outright, the government allowed would-be homeowners to pay just 20 percent down and then the government would insure the mortgage on the remaining 80 percent of the price of the property, which families could pay back over time.[60]

The federal Home Owners Loan Corporation (HOLC) and its successor, the Federal Housing Administration (FHA), cruelly instructed appraisers to focus this aid on economically homogenous and all-white communities. The HOLC created "residential security maps" that assessed risk based on racist and classist assumptions about the safety of investments. Red lines were drawn around neighborhoods deemed hazardous, and green lines around areas deemed safe for investment. The FHA used the HOLC maps to guarantee mortgages for developers and families, often on the condition that white neighborhoods include racially restrictive covenants to prevent homeowners from later selling to Black people.[61]

The whole enterprise was designed around the recurring theme of "property values"—to which we will return in Chapter 5. HOLC, and then the FHA, was concerned about the financial safety of government-backed loans and deemed it too "risky" to guarantee loans in certain areas. FHA's principal economist, Homer Hoyt, came up with an elaborate ranking of races and nationalities on their perceived "beneficial effect on land values," in which "those with the most favorable come first in the list and those exerting the most detrimental effect appear last." His list reads as follows:

1. English, Germans, Scotch, Irish, Scandinavians
2. North Italians
3. Bohemians or Czechoslovakians
4. Poles
5. Lithuanians
6. Greeks
7. Russian Jews of the lower class
8. South Italians
9. Negroes
10. Mexicans[62]

An FHA manual suggested the best financial bets were those with safeguards, such as highways separating communities to prevent "the infiltration of . . . lower class occupancy, and inharmonious racial groups."[63] As Ta-Nehisi Coates notes, the FHA provided the strongest financial support to green-zoned areas that, as one appraiser noted, lacked "a single foreigner or Negro." All-Black areas were coded red and received no federal support.[64] In 1940, the FHA actually denied insurance for a white development located near an African American community in Detroit until the builder agreed to construct a half-mile concrete wall, six feet high, to separate the two neighborhoods.[65] The official position of the FHA—which underwrote $120 billion in new housing construction between 1934 and 1962—was that Black people were an adverse influence on property values.[66]

In Patricia McGee's Dallas, the federal government "redlined" predominantly Black communities to cheat Black families out of government-backed mortgages. As a result, most Black families couldn't partake in the grand opportunity to move from renter to homeowner and lost the ability to create the associated wealth. The FHA loans helped enable homeownership nationally to rise by 50 percent between 1930 and 1960 (from 40 percent to 60 percent).[67] But nonwhite people were mostly shut out: they received less than 2 percent of home mortgage loans.[68] Millions of Black people had to keep paying rent and missed the chance to reap the financial benefits of homeownership. One housing expert notes, "African Americans lost almost 40 years of equity growth" because of redlining.[69]

The effects of redlining on the Black–white wealth gap are staggering. According to a 2020 study by the Federal Reserve Bank of Chicago, redlining in Chicago "is responsible for as much as half of the current disparities between Black and white homeownership and for the gaps between the housing values of Black and white homes in those communities."[70]

Even when Black families could manage to put together enough money to purchase a home without the help of government-backed mortgages that white families routinely received, government-sponsored tools to segregate Black people ensured that those homes would appreciate at slower rates than homes in predominantly white communities.

Economists have long found that homeownership does not provide equal returns across neighborhoods. Even when one takes other housing characteristics into account, neighborhoods with large Black populations appreciate at slower rates than those in predominately white neighborhoods.[71] A 2021 study found that between 1980 and 2015, homes in communities of color appreciated at just half the rate of those in predominantly white neighborhoods. In dollar terms, the homes in predominately white neighborhoods appreciated in value nearly $200,000 more during that time period than "comparable homes in neighborhoods of color."[72] Paula Campbell, a resident of the predominantly Black Memphis neighborhood of Orange Bound, says if you took her four-thousand-square-foot home and moved it to predominately white suburbs, it would double in value.[73]

Why do homes appreciate at slower rates in Black neighborhoods? Most evidence suggests it can be attributed to anti-Black attitudes on the part of white and other home seekers.[74] Research finds that otherwise identical homes in Black neighborhoods with the same amenities as

white neighborhoods are worth $48,000 less on average.[75] Buyers get a
"discount" when they purchase a property in a Black neighborhood, but
when it comes time to sell, they ultimately lose out because their homes
appreciated more slowly.[76] The fact that many home seekers place a value
on being separate from Black people—*combined* with the fact that white
families have more wealth to spend on homes than Black families—
means that there is more competition for homes in white areas, and so
prices are continually bid up.[77]

The segregation of Black people that results in lower rates of return
on homes has, in turn, been socially engineered by government over
decades. In Patricia McGee's Dallas, for example, the tools to segregate Black people were plentiful. In the early twentieth century, Dallas used the most straightforward mechanism: explicit racial zoning of
neighborhoods.

When the US Supreme Court struck down such laws, white people
in Dallas and throughout the country adopted racially restrictive covenants, which required home purchasers to agree not to later resell the
property to Black people or others considered "undesirable." The ugly
logic was that selling to a Black family would degrade the neighborhood
in the same way that selling property for industrial use would. One such
provision, for example, forbade the buyer from reselling the home to
someone who would construct "any slaughter house, smith shop, forge
furnace" or "for any structure other than a dwelling of people of the
Caucasian race."[78]

These racially restrictive provisions were initially upheld by the US
Supreme Court in a 1926 decision in *Corrigan v. Buckley* on the theory
that the covenants were private contracts not subject to the Constitution.[79] The decision applied faulty reasoning, however, because contracts
do not have force without the power of the state. Chillingly, in city after city, for more than two decades, courts and sheriffs evicted African
American families from homes they had rightly paid for to enforce racially restrictive covenants. For example, in Oakland, California, a Black
doctor and World War II veteran, DeWitt Buckingham, was ordered by
a state court to vacate a property he had purchased in 1945 because it
had a racially restrictive covenant.[80] In 1948, civil rights activists won

a victory when the US Supreme Court reversed its earlier ruling and unanimously struck down racially restrictive covenants as a violation of the Constitution in the case of *Shelley v. Kraemer.*[81] The opinion only involved six justices because three—Stanley Reed, Robert Jackson, and Wiley Rutledge—had to recuse themselves, presumably on the grounds that their own homes contained such covenants.[82]

In addition, real estate agents in Dallas and elsewhere often steered Black customers away from white communities. Real estate agents were actually taught that integrating a neighborhood by race was wrong because it would lower property values. Indeed, the 1924 National Association of Real Estate Boards' code of ethics prohibited real estate agents from "introducing into a neighborhood a character of property or occupancy, members of any race or nationality, or any individuals whose presence will clearly be detrimental to property values in that neighborhood."[83]

The local government in Dallas also conspired to keep Black people in segregated communities by looking the other way while white supremacists physically attacked Black families trying to move into white neighborhoods. In the 1940s and 1950s, white people committed "a wave of bombings of homes of middle-class Black families," writes one journalist. In early February 1950, for example, Horace Bonner, a fifty-seven-year-old Black employee of a printing company, was asleep in his home in a white neighborhood when a bomb exploded. Although Bonner escaped without injury, the front of his beautiful home, for which he had worked so hard, was reduced to rubble and char. Dynamite was the tool used by white people, who organized through their churches to bomb the homes of Black families who had the temerity to live outside carefully circumscribed Black areas.[84]

Dallas authorities had yet another tool to create housing segregation: de jure segregation of the public schools. Families often prefer to send their children to a nearby school, so when the state created separate Black and white schools, families had an incentive to purchase a home in an area near their race-assigned school.

As in much of the South, schools in the Dallas Independent School District (DISD) were segregated by law before the 1954 Supreme Court decision in *Brown v. Board of Education*; and for many years following the Supreme Court ruling, the Dallas school board balked at taking action to meaningfully desegregate.[85] Likewise, predominantly white suburban towns around Dallas routinely told the few Black students who might be living there that they needed to attend Dallas schools rather than local schools.[86]

Sixteen long years after *Brown*, Black civil rights activist Sam Tasby sued the Dallas Independent School District for violating the requirements of *Brown*, and in 1971, a federal district court judge found DISD guilty of continuing to maintain a dual system of education. In the case *Tasby v. Estes*, Judge William M. Taylor Jr. noted that although the school district's student population was 59 percent Anglo, 33 percent Black, and 8 percent Mexican American, 70 of the district's 180 schools had 90 percent or more Anglo students, and 49 had 90 percent or more minority students. Among Black students, the judge noted, 91 percent attended schools that were 90 percent or more minority, and only 3 percent attended majority-Anglo schools.[87]

Judge Taylor ordered desegregation with the goal that individual schools more closely mirror the district-wide racial representation.[88] White resistance to the decision was fierce. In an August 1971 *Dallas Morning News* poll, Anglos opposed the desegregation plan 89 percent to 6 percent, whereas Black people favored it by 50 percent to 36 percent, and the Hispanic population disfavored the plan 55 percent to 37 percent.[89] When the program was implemented, white families fled to the suburbs in large numbers. During the height of large-scale busing, in the early 1970s, DISD lost forty thousand (or 43 percent) of its Anglo students. Although the district had been losing Anglo students prior to busing, there was a fivefold increase in loss at the time of busing.[90]

Some integration was achieved for a time, however, and one study found that between 1980 and 1989, the achievement gap between Black and white students was reduced by more than half (from 35 percentage points to 16).[91] But the federal court eventually released the school district from having to take further steps to desegregate, which reduced levels of integration, and in any event, white flight continued to take its toll.[92] Today the district's schools are just 5 percent white.[93] The desegregation plan, wrote Dana Goldstein in the *New York Times* in 2017, ultimately "replaced one form of segregation with another."[94]

The use of redlining, racially restrictive covenants, and school segregation to create and reinforce housing segregation was by no means just a southern phenomenon confined to places like Dallas. In Columbus, Ohio, where KiAra Cornelius grew up, Black people and other people of color were similarly denied the ability to accumulate wealth.[95]

The ripple effects of being deprived of the same ability to accumulate assets as white people are still felt today and will likely be perpetuated in the future. US Census data shows that 74 percent of white people were homeowners in 2021, but just 44 percent of Black people owned their own home.[96]

Racial segregation has allowed government to overinvest in white communities and starve Black ones. The underinvestment has bred desperation and social ills among residents, which exacerbates white fear. As Cashin explains, "Segregation begat disinvestment. Disinvestment begat whites' biased attitudes, which in turn contributed to segregation."[97]

This phenomenon perpetuates a whole host of racial disparities in America. There are "many small answers" to explain why the Black–white income gap, academic achievement disparities, and wealth disparities persist decades after the civil rights movement, say experts, but "there is one giant answer: housing segregation."[98]

African Americans in moderately segregated metropolitan areas have much better employment levels, earnings, and mortality rates than do African Americans in metropolitan areas with very high segregation levels—both in absolute terms and when compared with non-Hispanic white Americans living in the same regions.[99]

The unemployment rate for Black men ages twenty-five to thirty-four, for example, was 17.4 percent in highly segregated areas, such as New York, Milwaukee, and Chicago in 2015. By contrast, the unemployment rate for Black men ages twenty-five to thirty-four was 10.1 percent in moderately segregated areas such as Phoenix, San Diego, and Nashville. Unemployment of these young Black men was 3.48 times the level of unemployment of non-Hispanic white men of the same age in highly segregated areas like New York, but 1.44 times the unemployment

level of non-Hispanic white men of the same age in moderately segregated areas like Phoenix. Earnings for Black men ages twenty-five
to thirty-four were $4,000 higher in moderately segregated areas like
Nashville than in highly segregated areas like Milwaukee. The earnings of young Black men were 69 percent of young non-Hispanic white
males in moderately segregated areas compared with 48 percent of non-
Hispanic white males in highly segregated areas. Likewise, for all Black
people, age-adjusted mortality (relative to that of non-Hispanic white
people) was better in moderately segregated regions (1.14) than in highly
segregated areas (1.42).[100]

In a separate analysis, economists found that if the Black–white dissimilarity index were reduced by just eight points, "as much as a third of
the black/white difference on key outcomes in education, employment
and earnings" could be eliminated.[101]

Racial segregation—driven in part by exclusionary zoning—also
hurts the life chances of Black children and other children of color by
increasing their likelihood of living in high-poverty neighborhoods. Researchers find that Black people are more likely to live in concentrated
poverty in metropolitan areas with high levels of racial segregation than
in those with moderate levels of racial segregation. Some 17 percent of
low-income Black people living in moderately segregated metro areas
reside in concentrated poverty; by contrast, 33 percent of low-income
Black people living in highly segregated areas reside in communities of
concentrated poverty.[102]

Nationally, poor people of color disproportionately live in concentrated poverty compared with poor white people. As one researcher found
in 2015: "More than one in four of the black poor and nearly one in six of
the Hispanic poor lives in a neighborhood of extreme poverty, compared
to one in thirteen of the white poor."[103] Overall, African American children are eleven times as likely to grow up in poor neighborhoods as white
children (66 percent versus 6 percent).[104]

Because of racial residential segregation, low-income African Americans are much less likely to be afforded the opportunity to attend socioeconomically integrated schools, where students tend to learn more.
According to a 2017 study, 81.1 percent of poor Black children attended

high-poverty schools in 2013, compared with just 53.5 percent of poor white children who attended high-poverty schools.[105] That is to say, fewer than one in five poor Black children had access to a predominantly middle-class school, whereas almost half of poor white children attended middle-class schools.

When racial segregation concentrates poverty for students of color, it condemns them to settings that are on the whole detrimental to educational growth. As discussed in Chapter 1, low-income students attending socioeconomically integrated schools perform as much as two grade levels higher than low-income students in high-poverty schools.[106] Low-income kids can perform well if given the right environment, but concentrated poverty significantly reduces their chances of doing so.

WHAT IS TO BE DONE?

In Chapter 7, we will discuss in some detail a menu of ideas for what to do about economic and racial segregation of neighborhoods. Some of those ideas will be race specific—such as enforcing the Fair Housing Act's Affirmatively Furthering Fair Housing rule aimed at dismantling racial segregation, devoting more resources to "testers" who ferret out racial discrimination among landlords and open them up to prosecution, and bringing more "disparate impact" lawsuits that seek to curtail policies that have the effect, if not necessarily the intent, of discriminating against communities of color.

But as this chapter explains, addressing economically discriminatory housing policy head-on must be part of the strategy as well. Following Dr. King's admonition that we must take on economic inequalities that frustrate racial advancement, we need new tools to fight government-sponsored economic discrimination that—because of our terrible legacy of racist housing policies—perpetuates racial inequality today.

FOUR

HOW MERITOCRATIC ELITISM
SUSTAINS THE WALLS

In Springfield, Massachusetts, Samantha encountered many of the same obstacles faced by KiAra Cornelius and Tehani in Columbus and Patricia McGee in Dallas. Samantha (who asked that her last name not be used) grew up in public housing in Springfield, one of the poorest cities in the state.[1] A single mother of three children, she worried, like Cornelius, McGee, and Tehani, about raising her kids in a tough area with a high crime rate and weak schools. She dreamed about living in one of the more affluent nearby suburbs such as Longmeadow. As a child, she had trick-or-treated there for Halloween and looked at the broad lawns and safe streets with longing. But as a second-generation public housing resident, she believed living in a place like Longwood was a fantasy.

Springfield has struggled economically. Its median household income of $39,432 in 2019 was less than half the state's median income.[2] The schools have the second-highest concentration of low-income students in

Massachusetts (after Holyoke).[3] Samantha says the neighborhood where she was raising her kids saw shootings and drug activity and "the street was a little dangerous. People were just flying down the road."[4] FBI statistics for 2019 found there were 91 violent crimes per 10,000 people in Springfield, compared with 6 per 10,000 in nearby Longmeadow.[5] As a result, she says, "I always kept my kids home."[6]

Having grown up in Springfield, Samantha, who works with stroke patients in a rehabilitation hospital, had some idea of what was in store for her kids if they stayed in Massachusetts's third-largest city.[7] Samantha's father, a mechanic, died when she was age ten, and her mother was disabled and couldn't work, so after her father's passing, they moved into public housing. "In Springfield, it was difficult," she says. Samantha attended Springfield public schools, including Springfield's High School of Commerce, but did not have a good experience. "I got up to eleventh grade," she says, but dropped out because of rowdiness in the school.

Samantha's own three children were struggling in the Springfield public schools. Desmond in tenth grade in 2021, Zivianna in fifth, and Adrian in the fourth all faced educational challenges. Her oldest son, Desmond, is severely autistic, and her daughter, Zivianna, has a more modest form of autism.[8]

The three schools the children attended are predominantly low-income and perform considerably below the state average on standardized test scores. At Frank H. Freedman Elementary, 78 percent of students are low-income with 36 percent proficient in math, 37 percent in English, and 19 percent in science;[9] at Elian Brookings Elementary, 86 percent of students are low-income, and 22 percent are proficient in math, 28 percent in English, and 19 percent in science;[10] and at Springfield Public Day Middle School, 90 percent of students are low-income, and virtually none of the students are proficient in math, English, or science.[11] Samantha was deeply distressed with the education that her children were receiving.

Springfield Day Public Middle School was an especially bad fit for her son Desmond. Samantha says it is the district's school of last resort for unruly students, and it wasn't resourced to serve students who have special needs such as autism. "He was in crisis every day. I had to get him. He was in altercations or just having a bad day, which was because they put autistic children with other kids that just have bad behaviors, that didn't like to go to school. So it didn't mix."[12]

Like Cornelius, McGee, and Tehani, Samantha was blocked from living in a safer area with stronger schools by something more than free market housing forces. Exclusionary zoning played a big role in keeping her trapped in Springfield. Kristin Haas of the Massachusetts Department of Housing and Community Development notes that across the state, "exclusionary zoning continues to be a huge, huge problem."[13] She says, "We have lots of communities that are primarily zoned for single-family homes, and it's really hard" for low-income families "to have any opportunities in those types of communities." There are so few multi-family units available and those that do become available have rents that "are just astronomical."[14] Indeed, the Metropolitan Area Planning Council found that in the decade between 2007 and 2017, 200 of the state's 351 cities and towns did not build *any* new multifamily housing.[15]

Like Cornelius, McGee, and Tehani, Samantha was trapped. Unlike them, she is white. (Her kids, she says, are "mixed. They're Spanish and white.")[16] Although in the public imagination, fed by media reports, the typical low-income American may be envisioned as Black or Hispanic, white people outnumber Black people in the SNAP (Supplemental Nutrition Assistance Program) food aid program, and white people constitute the plurality (49 percent) of those in project-based Section 8 housing and 35 percent of those in the Housing Choice Voucher program.[17]

DEPLORABLE?

Samantha, Cornelius, McGee, and Tehani may face similar predicaments, but the dominant media narrative paints them very differently. As Americans, we are familiar with the idea that it is working-class white people, like Samantha, who are most likely to hold "deplorable" views on issues of race. That it's working-class white people, not highly educated white people, who show up at Donald Trump rallies, filled with racial invective. (Trump returned the favor by saying, "I love the poorly educated.")[18]

In fiction, working-class and poor white people are often depicted as racist villains. As Nancy Isenberg, the author of *White Trash*, notes, the beloved novel *To Kill a Mockingbird* contains a disturbing stereotype about which group of white people is racist. The educated white lawyer Atticus Finch is the principled opponent of racism who defends an innocent Black worker, Tom Robinson, against false charges of rape. The racist scoundrels are the poor white family members who level the false accusations—Mayella Ewell and her father, Bob Ewell, who are, says Isenberg, unmistakably "white trash." Harper Lee, the book's author, describes the Ewells in this way: "No truant officer could keep their numerous offspring in school; no public health officer could keep them free from congenital defects, various worms, and diseases indigenous to filthy surroundings." The family lived near the town dump in a shack that was "once a Negro cabin."[19]

This familiar narrative of good whites and bad whites played out on the other side of Samantha's home state in the 1970s when Boston's working-class white people violently resisted school desegregation efforts. But one thoughtful analyst saw it a little differently.

In October 1974, Harvard child psychiatrist Robert Coles, like many people, watched with horror as working-class white Boston residents shouted ugly epithets and used bottles and bricks to pelt school buses carrying young Black children. For Coles, the images recalled an angry white mob he had seen more than a decade earlier in New Orleans. In the early 1960s, Coles had been stationed in the South as an air force doctor and was appalled when he observed groups of angry white people showing up daily at a New Orleans elementary school to scream at a six-year-old Black girl, Ruby Bridges. Coles befriended the Bridges family and sought to provide psychological support for young Ruby, who endured a hellish walk to school each morning as a racist mob yelled at her. One woman even repeatedly threatened to poison her. One day, Coles saw Ruby mumbling words to herself just before she entered the school and asked her about what she was saying. He was astounded to learn that Ruby was praying for her tormentors.[20]

Coles wrote about Bridges in the *Atlantic* and later in *The Story of Ruby Bridges*.[21] Norman Rockwell famously painted the scene of a diminutive Ruby, escorted by giant FBI agents, in an iconic piece of art, *The Problem We Live With*, that later hung outside of President Barack Obama's Oval Office. The experience was as clear a drama of good and evil, and right and wrong, as one gets, pitting an innocent Black girl against a hateful white mob who objected to her presence solely based on the color of her skin.

Coles was disgusted by the northern white mobs in Boston showing the same hatred. But as he watched his Harvard colleagues shower disdain on working-class white people of Boston for their resistance to school integration, Coles also began to think about the invisible walls—the bans on multifamily housing and the minimum lot size requirements for single-family homes—that kept most Black people, and most working-class white people as well, out of the neighborhoods and schools in the sorts of suburbs where many educated white liberals resided.[22]

Even the federal judge who ordered desegregation, W. Arthur Garrity Jr., lived in Wellesley, a wealthy and mostly white Boston suburb, which, almost fifty years later, remains just 2.9 percent Black and 5.1 percent Hispanic and has a median household income of $197,132.[23]

In an extensive October 1974 interview with the *Boston Globe*'s Mike Barnicle, Coles noted that although the busing crisis pitted Black and white low-income families against each other, it ignored the larger reality that "people in the suburbs are being protected by a wall around the city of Boston." He noted, "All the laws are being written for the wealthy and powerful. The tax laws, the zoning laws, the laws that have to do with protecting their housing and their education."[24] Of the wealthy people living in suburbs who condemned working-class white people, Coles said: "Their lives are clean and their minds are clean and their hands are clean. And they can afford this long, charitable, calm view. And if people don't know that this is a class privilege, then, by golly, they don't know anything."[25]

For a number of reasons, the exclusionary zoning barriers Coles identified were less obvious than the barriers thrown up against school desegregation. One difference is the means employed. Wealthy white people, for the most part, are not violent in their exclusionary tactics and don't hurl stones or bottles. What they do hurl are obscure zoning ordinances that keep people out just the same. The exclusion doesn't take place in widely televised violent confrontations on the streets; it happens in the little-noticed confines of zoning or planning board meetings.

Another difference has to do with the nature of the exclusion. Americans, particularly those who are well educated, are now deeply familiar with terrible stories of racial exclusion and of white oppression of Black people. Ibram X. Kendi's *How to Be an Anti-Racist* and Robin DiAngelo's *White Fragility* have sat atop the best-seller lists. By contrast, American elites are less attuned to the very real existence of class exclusion that discriminates against people not by skin color, per se, but rather based on the size of their wallets. But Coles pointed out, in inversion of the familiar *Mockingbird* narrative, that wealthy white Americans use zoning laws to discriminate against Black and working-class white people all the time.

Indeed, researchers have recognized the liberal Boston region as having relatively high levels of exclusionary zoning when compared with other big cities nationally.[26] The wealthier the suburb, the more likely it is to engage in the practice of exclusionary zoning. Compare, for example, the Boston suburbs of Waltham (median income of $96,000) and Lexington (median income of $186,000). If a developer wants to build a triplex, she would face a far different set of rules in the two municipalities. In Waltham, a three-family home requires a minimum 6,000-square-foot lot; for Lexington, the same three-family home would need a minimum lot of 15,500 square feet, thus driving up the price of any such development, perhaps even beyond affordable rates. In Waltham, building a triplex requires no special permit; in Lexington, all multifamily developments require a special permit.

Overall, a builder in Waltham must comply with seventeen regulations, while in Lexington, a builder faces thirty-four regulations. These regulations govern everything from the use of septic tanks to the shape of a parcel of land. The greater number of regulations give NIMBY Lexington residents far more tools to delay or stop a proposed project in its tracks. The bottom-line result: "In relatively unregulated Waltham, 65 percent of permitted units between 2000 and 2015 were for multifamily housing, and 35 percent were for single-family homes. Over the same time period, 94 percent of permitted units in Lexington were for single-family homes, and only 6 percent were for units in multifamily buildings."[27]

Likewise, the affluent outer-ring Boston suburb of Weston (median household income of $207,702 in 2019) engages in much more exclusionary zoning than the comparatively diverse city of Cambridge (median household income of $103,154).[28] For example, the two municipalities, located just fifteen miles apart, have wildly different lot size requirements for multifamily homes. In Cambridge, the minimum lot size is 900 square feet, while in Weston, it is 240,000 square feet, some *267 times higher.*[29]

Affluent and white families are particularly likely to exploit zoning laws to kill projects. Looking at the minutes from zoning and planning meetings in ninety-seven Massachusetts municipalities, researchers found that older, male, white homeowners tended to dominate discussions. In Lawrence, Massachusetts, where the population is 75 percent Hispanic, for example, over a three-year period, only one resident with a Hispanic surname ever spoke at planning and zoning meetings.[30] Those who show up, the researchers find, are unrepresentative in two ways: "Relative to their broader communities, they are socioeconomically advantaged and overwhelmingly opposed to the construction of new housing."[31]

Exclusion is a slippery process, fair housing advocates note, and can occur even in communities that permit multifamily housing. In such cases when multifamily housing is allowed, says Dana LeWinter of the Citizens' Housing and Planning Association (CHAPA), a nonprofit organization that supports affordable housing, municipalities often seek to limit the number of bedrooms in apartments in order to reduce the presence of children. The issue "comes up all the time," she says.[32]

Those who wish to exclude and stop or modify projects also know that requiring additional studies that mean a delay is a powerful weapon in their arsenal. Researchers explain, "Such delay requires developer to pay additional property taxes and maintenance costs on the property," thereby enhancing the bargaining position of opponents to exact, at the very least, major modifications.[33]

In addition to government-sponsored exclusionary zoning, low-income people like Samantha face source-of-income discrimination from private landlords and real estate agents in Massachusetts, even though such conduct has technically been illegal in the state since 1971.[34] Although landlords are guaranteed Section 8 payment by the government, some landlords don't like the government inspections that come with taking Section 8 funds, and others hold negative stereotypes that lower-income families will do damage to the property.[35]

A 2020 study sought to test the degree to which real estate brokers and landlords discriminate on the basis of race and of source of income in Boston and nine area suburbs. The researchers tried to disentangle race and source-of-income discrimination by placing two hundred fictional renters into four groups of fifty each: white people who could pay market rent; Black people who could pay market rent; white people with a Section 8 Housing Choice Voucher; and Black people with a Section 8 Housing Choice Voucher.

The researchers found an unconscionable amount of racial discrimination: white renters paying market rate were shown apartments 80 percent of the time, whereas Black renters paying market rate were shown apartments only 48 percent of the time. But the impact of class was even stronger. Black voucher holders were shown apartments just 18 percent of the time, and white voucher holders fared the worst, being shown apartments only 12 percent of the time.

In all, the researchers found, voucher holders were ultimately turned away from apartments nine times out of ten. The authors note, "People should not have to contact ten housing providers in order to see one unit." Voucher-based discrimination was "more explicit" than racial discrimination, the researchers found. "About 40 percent of the time, the housing provider stopped communicating with testers altogether after the testers revealed they intended to use vouchers."[36] This finding is consistent with research in Chicago that found that source-of-income discrimination is more than twice as prevalent as racial discrimination.[37]

Haas of the Massachusetts Department of Housing and Community Development says that in her experience working with Section 8 Housing Choice Voucher holders, source-of-income discrimination "is often overt," such as "a listing that says 'No Section 8.'"[38] She says online applications are also troubling. They will often ask renters to list their income but include no place for applicants to note that payments will include a Section 8 housing subsidy. As a result, applicants are summarily dismissed because it looks "like they in no way can afford the rent," Haas says.[39]

Even when source-of-income discrimination is blatant, Haas notes, Section 8 voucher holders often decide not to file a complaint. Voucher holders "are really focused on their housing search. They have a lot of other things going on, typically, and are not necessarily going to take the time or feel comfortable reporting something to some authorities."[40] Voucher holders have a limited amount of time to use their voucher, so participants often "just want to move on to the next potential apartment and not get bogged down pursuing something that probably is not going to get them an apartment immediately."[41] Department of Housing and Community Development staff typically don't file complaints on voucher holders' behalf, so if the voucher holders choose not to file a complaint, the discrimination may go unreported, she says.[42]

Dana LeWinter of the Boston-area nonprofit CHAPA says the issues of exclusionary zoning and source-of-income discrimination are connected. "When there is not enough housing supply, landlords may feel more confident to discriminate as they know there is ample demand for their apartments."[43]

The results of income discrimination in zoning combined with source-of-income discrimination by landlords in the Boston area are completely predictable. According to 2016 research, the number of families in Boston and surrounding suburbs who live in mixed-income neighborhoods declined from 7 in 10 families in 1970 to 4 in 10 families in recent years. The percentage living in the very highest poverty neighborhoods rose from 8 percent to 20 percent during that time period, while the proportion living in the most concentrated wealth increased from 6 percent to 16 percent. North Andover, for example, used to be home to factory workers and farmers but is now among Massachusetts's wealthiest towns. Nearby Lawrence, meanwhile, used to have a solidly lower-middle-class population but has since sunk into much deeper poverty.[44]

SAMANTHA CATCHES A BREAK

In 2019, recognizing the numerous barriers that people like Samantha face, Massachusetts created a new housing mobility program, SNO Mass (Supporting Neighborhood Opportunity in Massachusetts), to help families get around the walls built by local governments and live in high-opportunity areas.[45] Haas says there was "a recognition that our voucher holders were disproportionately concentrated in high-poverty neighborhoods," which was a violation of the "choice" principle of the Housing Choice Voucher program.[46]

When Samantha heard that the SNO Mass program would allow her to move to a home in Longmeadow, which has a median household income triple that of Springfield, she was thrilled.[47] She says: "I always wanted to live in a better area than Springfield." Recalling her days as a child trick-or-treating in areas like Longmeadow, she said, "I always wished I could live out here." Unlike Springfield, where Samantha kept her kids mostly in the house, now that her family is in Longmeadow, she says, "they're happier. They can explore, they can do much more than they ever did before." She continues, "There's so many parks. It's really not crowded. And . . . the people are very friendly." Through SNO Mass, Samantha is able to rent a single-family home with an aboveground pool and provide her kids with a type of experience she never had growing up.

The education provided in Longmeadow is also much better, she says. "The schools have the number one ratings out here," and they are well designed to address students with special needs.[48] Zivianna and Adrian have been able to attend Wolf Swamp Road Elementary School, where 7 percent of students are low-income and 58 percent are proficient in math, 72 percent in English, and 69 percent in science.[49] Desmond attends Longmeadow High School, where 6 percent of students are low-income and 79 percent are proficient in math, 80 percent in English, 52 percent in science, and 49 percent in biology—all far above the state average. The contrast between student performance in Wolf Swamp Elementary and the kids' previous school, Frank H. Freedman Elementary in Springfield, is striking.[50]

Samantha senses that the teachers in Longmeadow are much more interested in her kids, particularly Desmond. The teachers, she told me in August 2021, "keep in touch, on a daily basis, even right now in the summer, the teachers are emailing me, like, 'How's your son? Are you doing okay?'" Whereas some of the teachers in Springfield "didn't care, honestly." Samantha is struck that, in Longmeadow, "even though the teachers are off the clock, they still communicate with the moms that have children with special needs." She is impressed by their dedication. Even during summer break, she says, "They will gladly do a Zoom call" with Desmond. "And that's awesome."

The transformation for Desmond has been dramatic. In Longmeadow, Samantha says, he stopped acting out. She marvels: "My son, actually, for the first time ever, when we moved here, he actually looked forward to going to school, even during the pandemic." He would ask Samantha, when schooling was online-only to reduce the spread of COVID-19: "Why can't I just go to school? I want to go to school. I miss my teachers." She says: "You would never have had that if we lived back in Springfield. . . . It's totally different. I don't have to really worry." Since the move, Samantha says, "He's toned down, like, a lot. Friends and family even said [that they see] a dramatic change in his behavior, his mood, and it's honestly the school."

In moving to Longmeadow, Samantha's big worry was that because she is a person with low income, and because her children have a Hispanic father, they might be poorly treated by neighbors and school classmates. "I was scared about that," she says. The fear was legitimate. But in her case, as it turned out, she says, "the neighbors are great. They're not judgmental to other kids. They play with my kids perfectly fine." Overall, she concludes: "Longmeadow is like one of the greatest moves that I ever did."[51]

While SNO Mass provides a vital catapult for people like Samantha to move to communities such as Longmeadow, the walls surrounding exclusionary communities remain. Only forty-five families were benefiting from SNO Mass statewide in the fall of 2021, and hundreds of thousands of low-wage families in the state remain cut off from opportunity.[52]

A big limiting factor to the program is exclusionary zoning. In western Massachusetts, where Samantha lives, Springfield has "tons of apartments," says Haas, but "as soon as you get outside of Springfield, it's almost entirely single-family homes."[53] Haas, who directs the SNO Mass housing mobility program, says, "We've struggled mightily in the Springfield area in western Massachusetts to find apartments" in high-opportunity areas.[54] Over a two-year period, only six families have been able to move in the area. "That's a very small number given that we have two staff that are 100 percent dedicated to SNO Mass," she says. "We're just kind of floored how few families were finding anything."[55]

THE RISING SIGNIFICANCE OF CLASS BIAS IN AMERICAN HOUSING

Samantha's story highlights an important reality in America. Although the dominant story of racial exclusion is very real, as discussed in Chapter 3, race is not the only basis for discrimination. Indeed, increasingly today, it is class discrimination that explains America's growing inequality.

Upper-class Americans have long held their fellow lower-income citizens in low regard. And this disdain is actually felt within all racial groups. To begin with, middle- and upper-class white people have a long history of looking down on poor white people, whom they tellingly refer to as "white trash." This important part of the American experience helps explain the staying power of songs like Dolly Parton's "Coat of Many Colors." Parton tells of growing up in Tennessee as a poor white girl who is proud of the coat her mother lovingly stitched together from different-colored rags, only to be ridiculed by school classmates for her poverty.[56]

Class bias also surfaces in the job market. Many readers may know of the appalling finding that applicants with "Black-sounding names" on their résumés are less likely to be recruited. Less well known is that in a study comparing candidates with otherwise identical résumés, men who gave clues to having a lower-class social background (e.g., an interest in country music) were thirteen times less likely to get an interview with a prestigious law firm than those who gave clues of a high-class social background (e.g., an interest in classical music). (Research finds that only 24 percent of country music fans have a college degree and that classical music is much more popular among college-educated Americans than those with less education.)[57] Those who participated in upper-class sports like polo were deemed to be a "better fit" for legal clients than those who were first-generation college students who had served as peer tutors for other first-generation college students, according to follow-up interviews.[58]

In the housing market, white professional zoning officials have long targeted poor white as well as Black people as disfavored groups. The FHA's underwriter's manual, which was first issued in 1935, noted the importance of both race and class to property values. "If a neighborhood is to retain stability, it is necessary that properties shall continue to be occupied by the same *social and* racial classes."[59] An FHA manual recommended investments be made only where barriers—such as highways—would prevent "the infiltration of . . . *lower class occupancy*" as well as "inharmonious racial groups."[60] (The reference to "inharmonious racial groups" was deleted in 1947.)[61] In Los Angeles, Nancy Isenberg notes, "suburbs were appraised by the Federal Housing Authority along class lines: high marks were given to places where gardening was a popular hobby, and low marks to places where poor whites raised food in their backyards."[62] The FHA penalized homes that did not have sufficient setbacks, another researcher found, which "functioned as class restrictions."[63]

Upper-middle-class white people have also resisted school integration with lower-income white students. Consider the case of La Crosse, Wisconsin, an overwhelmingly white community that encountered strong opposition to an effort to integrate the public schools by economic status in the late 1970s and again in the early 1990s. Historically, La Crosse's North Side was home to white brewery workers, railroad workers, and other laborers, whereas the South Side included white-collar employees at the University of Wisconsin and two major medical facilities. A marsh separates the two sides.

In the late 1970s, the school superintendent Richard Swantz sought to socioeconomically integrate Logan High School on the North Side (which was considered the blue-collar vocational school) and Central

High School on the South Side (which was the wealthier, college preparatory school). The move was hugely controversial. "That marsh was like
a Mason-Dixon Line," Swantz recalled. A University of Wisconsin professor recalls that "a lot of older people in La Crosse had a fit about this."
Some moved to avoid being in the new district; others rented houses to
stay in the Central district.[64]

The new boundaries eventually were accepted by the community,
but when Swantz sought to socioeconomically integrate the elementary
schools, he created another uproar. The board's January 1992 vote to
change boundaries to integrate by economic status sent shock waves
through La Crosse. In a regularly scheduled April 1992 election, three
challengers replaced three incumbents who had supported the economic
integration plan. In a special recall election held in July 1992, four more
incumbents were replaced by opponents of the integration plan, giving anti-integration forces a seven-to-two majority on the board.[65] One
journalist wrote that "La Crosse is encountering the same sort of resistance that accompanied busing for racial integration."[66] Although La
Crosse eventually made peace with its plan after the recall board was
exposed as dysfunctional, the extraordinary reaction of La Crosse voters suggests that socioeconomic integration can engender strong opposition from upper-income white residents even in overwhelmingly white
communities.

Socioeconomic housing integration can also arouse strong resistance
when race is not at issue. Across the country, town after town has enacted bans on mobile homes occupied by low-income white people. In
a Levittown community in Bucks County, Pennsylvania, for example,
new homeowners in the 1950s passed an ordinance to bar local construction workers from living in trailer parks. These "transients," residents said, should be "gotten rid of as soon as possible."[67]

Judges have supported such laws. In the 1962 case of *Vickers v.
Township Committee of Gloucester Township*, for example, the New Jersey
Supreme Court upheld by 5–2 a Gloucester Township, New Jersey, ordinance that barred a trailer park even though it was to be located in an industrial area of the township. The court held that "trailer camps, because
of their particular nature and relation to the public health, safety, morals

and general welfare, present a municipality with a host of problems, and these problems persist wherever such camps are located." These camps, the court said, could "be detrimental to property values" in part because "a trailer park is not an attractive appearance." A majority of the court rejected the dissent's view that "trailer living is a perfectly respectable, healthy and useful kind of housing, adopted by choice by several million people in this country today."[68]

Reviewing a number of such cases, Nancy Isenberg notes in *White Trash* that the trailer park can be America's "most controversial housing option." She writes: "Segregation, then, was more than simply a racial issue. Zoning laws made it inevitable that housing would adhere to class-delineated geography."[69]

Experimental research finds that college students are more likely to view a fictitious family negatively if the students are told the family lived in a trailer park. The college students, most of whom were upper middle class, viewed an otherwise identical family as more foolish, dirty, lazy, and dumb when given the detail that the family resided in a trailer park.[70] Although Black poverty is more concentrated than white poverty, the fastest growth in poverty concentrations since 2000 has come among non-Hispanic white people, who saw a 145 percent increase in those living in high-poverty neighborhoods.[71] Consider Beattyville, Kentucky, an impoverished Appalachian community that is 98 percent white. In 2015, when the *Guardian* sought to identify the four poorest towns in America based on median household income, Beattyville was among the group, along with one that was predominantly Black, one predominantly Hispanic, and another predominantly Native American. After the coal mines shuttered around Beattyville, median household income dropped to $14,871. The town, where a third of adults have dropped out of high school and just 4 percent have bachelor's degrees, has been overrun by opioid addiction. The locals in Appalachia call it "hillbilly heroin."[72]

So, too, some middle-class Black communities—from New York to Chicago—have shown a strong resistance to low-income housing, opposition rooted in class rather than race.[73] For decades, says Sheryll Cashin, "Black elites" engaged in "social distancing" from Black people from the agrarian South by "trying to live apart" from them.[74] One Black resident of a high-income community in Westchester County, New York, for example, opposed the Obama administration's legal efforts to promote low-income housing, arguing, "I am appalled at this decision to reward those individuals who . . . chose the easy way out instead of dedicating oneself to hard work."[75] In a Massachusetts study on zoning, Boston University researchers found that, among those who made public comments, "majorities of all racial groups—including black people—oppose the construction of new housing."[76]

Prince George's County, Maryland, a Washington, DC, suburb, is illustrative. Prince George's is one of the rare communities that has actually grown wealthier as its Black population has increased in size.[77] When Jack Johnson served as the Prince George's County executive from 2002 to 2010, he created policies, developers say, to discourage the construction of more townhomes because the county wanted to become even more upscale like its neighbor, Montgomery County.[78] Matt Murphy, who has worked in real estate development in the metropolitan Washington, DC, region since the mid-1980s, says because Prince George's County wanted to attract high-end retailers, "the politicians didn't want to have any more inexpensive townhomes."[79]

Beginning in the 1980s, Murphy says, Prince George's County public officials made clear to developers: "We want luxury single-family homes. . . . We want to improve our image, so bring in the high-end builders."[80] Jack Johnson, Murphy says, imposed "a de facto moratorium" on affordable townhouses. The "economic redlining" in Prince George's County, Murphy says, was "not because of racism, it's more because 'we don't want the low-income folks here.'"[81]

Policies like these help explain why economic segregation within the Black community increased by 41 percent between 1970 and 1990 and why, between 1990 and 2007–2011, segregation between poor Black people and nonpoor Black people continued to climb.[82] In a 2014 analysis, one researcher found that the level of segregation between poor Black and affluent Black families was actually greater than that between Black families and white families.[83] The separation of Black and white families is more visible to the naked eye, but the separation of the affluent Black lawyer and the poor Black sanitation worker is more pronounced.

The reality, notes Sheryll Cashin, is that "the truly disadvantaged descendants of slaves are Black Americans stuck in neighborhoods that higher-income Blacks have fled."[84] Those left behind, as William Julius Wilson has observed, have become worse off after "the exit of middle-class and professional Blacks from poor neighborhoods."[85] Those who remained lost the "middle-class buffer"—the Black doctor or executive who provided the connections to job networks—that had in the past been provided to working-class Black families.[86]

If race were the only driving factor behind exclusionary zoning, one would also expect to see such policies most extensively promoted in conservative communities where racial intolerance is highest.[87] But, in fact, numerous studies find that most restrictive zoning is found in the most politically liberal cities and regions of the country, where racial views are more progressive and voters are, on average, more highly educated.[88]

Two major national surveys—one from Brookings in 2006, the other from Wharton in 2008—examine the stringency of zoning in different regions of the country. Both found it is more strict in politically liberal parts of the United States and less strict in conservative areas such as the South.[89] Writing in 2022, a Brookings Institution researcher observed that "decades of painstaking research of zoning by economists and urban planners have produced a high degree of consensus on which places in the United States have tight land use regulations, regardless of the method used to measure zoning." It is clear, this scholar writes, that "overly restrictive zoning is most prevalent and problematic along the West Coast and the Northeast corridor from Washington D.C. to Boston."[90] These areas "lean heavily Democratic in national, state and local elections."[91] And studies that examine the stringency of zoning within states—for example, California—find that the most restrictive zoning is found in the more politically liberal cities.[92]

Consider, for example, liberal Palo Alto, home to Stanford University. In November 2013, the city council voted to relax its zoning to increase density and allow a sixty-unit affordable housing complex for elderly people. An outcry ensued and voters passed "Measure D" by 56 percent to 44 percent, voting to reverse the decision and forbid the construction of anything other than single-family homes.[93] Or consider

Connecticut, a politically dark-blue state. The nonprofit Desegregate Connecticut created a "Zoning Atlas" for the state and concluded that two-thirds of Connecticut is zoned exclusively for single-family houses. Eight towns do not permit any multifamily housing whatsoever, and in six additional towns only 2 percent of housing is multifamily. For example, in Weston, Connecticut, where only 1.7 percent of residents are Black, an astonishing 99.6 percent of residences are single-family.[94] Statewide, 91 percent of zoned land allows single-family homes "as of right" (requiring no public hearing). By comparison, only 29 percent of zoned land allows duplexes as of right, and 2 percent allows triplexes, quads, or more units as of right.[95]

And then there is deep-blue San Francisco, where opposition takes a more subtle but no less resistant stance on new multifamily and affordable housing development. Single-family homeowners in San Francisco's Sunset District on the west side of town have managed to oppose affordable housing developments while appearing to the untutored eye to sound eminently reasonable, says Don Falk, who recently stepped down as CEO of the nonprofit Tenderloin Neighborhood Development Corporation (TNDC).[96] "You can't say in San Francisco, 'we don't want low-income people around us,'" he says.[97] And sometimes, it may be considered bad form to oppose an affordable housing development outright. Instead, opponents will call for projects to be downsized, which effectively kills them by making them economically infeasible, Falk says.[98] A seven-story apartment building may require a local government subsidy of $250,000 per unit, but cutting it to five stories drives the subsidy up to $300,000 per unit. A city like San Francisco is unlikely to be willing to invest the extra $50,000 per unit, so opponents can effectively kill a proposal while claiming to be good-hearted supporters of inclusion.[99]

Greater exclusionary zoning means more economic segregation—a problem that is also more prevalent in highly educated politically liberal areas. Richard Florida finds that "the Overall Economic Segregation Index is positively associated with political liberalism and negatively associated with political conservatism."[100] Florida finds that the highest levels of economic segregation are found in places like Boston, New

York, Washington, Los Angeles, San Francisco, and Austin.[101] Florida concludes that "the central contradiction" is that "the places that are the most productive and offer the highest wages . . . and that are the most liberal in their political leanings nonetheless face the harshest levels of economic inequality and economic segregation."

Why is exclusionary zoning and economic segregation worse in liberal parts of the country and in liberal cities than in conservative areas? The most benign explanation is that liberals—for good reason—created a series of rules to protect the environment, preserve historic sites, and allow for public input into decisions through open meeting laws than did conservative communities. But whatever the original intent of these laws, the evidence suggests that NIMBYs have today twisted and exploited these very rules, not to promote those goals but to exclude and drive up housing prices.[102] A second explanation is that when it comes down to their own property values, liberals are just as self-interested as conservatives and perceive low growth to be in their interest. Some research supports this idea, but that doesn't explain why exclusionary practices are *worse* in liberal areas than in conservative ones.[103] Perhaps, despite their stated views, highly educated white liberals are just as racist as conservatives, and exclusionary zoning is driven by a desire to keep Black people out of their community. But again, there is little evidence that liberals are secretly *more racist* than conservatives; some educated liberals appear to even take special pride in the fact that some neighbors are Black or Hispanic.

Instead, the most likely explanation for the prevalence of exclusionary zoning in liberal communities is different. As commentator Fareed Zakaria has noted, if the cardinal sin of the political right is racism, the primary sin of the left is elitism.[104]

Over the years, the Democratic Party, once the champion of the blue-collar worker, has increasingly become the party of the highly educated.[105] *New York Times* chief political analyst Nate Cohn explains the astonishing transformation over time. In 1960, John Kennedy won working-class white voters but lost white college graduates by two to one. In 2020, "the numbers were almost exactly reversed for Mr. Biden, who lost white voters without a degree by a two-to-one margin while winning white college graduates."[106] Thomas Piketty, likewise, has found that in the years following World War II, the top income decile favored Republican by 12 percent or more, but in 2016, Hillary Clinton beat Donald Trump in the top decile by close to twenty points (60 percent–40 percent).[107] In that year, Clinton won 76 percent of PhDs, 70 percent of those with master's degrees, and 51 percent of those with college degrees.[108]

In 2020, Joe Biden won one-sixth of the nation's counties, but they were among the wealthiest and most economically productive and accounted for 71 percent of the nation's GDP.[109] Between 2012 and 2020, the Democratic Party's support among college-educated white people rose by sixteen points, while its advantage among nonwhite working-class supporters declined by nineteen points.[110] In 2021, one Minnesota official complained that his state's political party, known as the Democratic-Farmer-Labor (DFL) Party, has a problem because "The F's and the L'ers aren't voting for us."[111] In 2022, for the first time, Democrats were receiving a larger share of their support from college-educated white voters than from nonwhite voters.[112]

Typically, greater education is thought to bring greater tolerance and understanding, but it turns out that highly educated people have their own biases. In a fascinating study, researcher Toon Kuppens and colleagues conducted a number of experiments to examine the effect of educational attainment on bias.[113] Under the standard "moral enlightenment hypothesis," education reduces bias.[114] The researchers verified the hypothesis with respect to bias against what in the United States is the "classic target of prejudice," Black people. The more education, the less bias.[115] But the researchers also found a highly disturbing *increase* in bias among highly educated people toward less-educated individuals. Highly educated people not only viewed those with less education as less competent, they also actively *disliked* otherwise identical individuals who had less education.[116]

The authors conclude: "Thus, although the least educated appear to be more prejudiced toward the classic targets of prejudice compared to those who are more highly educated, a noteworthy point is that for the higher educated, prejudice toward the lower educated seems to be acceptable, whereas it is not for the classical targets. In short, it seems that the claim that the lower educated are more prejudiced is only part of the story. It is rather that the targets of prejudice are different."[117]

Other research has found that higher-income families are more likely than low-income families to blame poverty on lack of effort by poor people (as opposed to societal barriers).[118] Hollywood often projects these classist attitudes. Shows like *Duck Dynasty* and *Here Comes Honey Boo Boo* play on stereotypes, Nancy Isenberg writes, that poor white people are "hopelessly ill bred."[119] Or consider how *Saturday Night Live* unfairly mocked those without a college degree in November 2021 after Republican Glenn Youngkin won the Virginia governor's race. "My win in Virginia proves that people are deeply concerned about education," Youngkin's character notes. When asked, "And who are most of your voters?" Youngkin replies, "People who didn't go to college." The studio audience found this condescending joke hilarious, laughing at the two-thirds of Americans without a college degree, incorrectly assuming that non-college-educated adults do not care about their kids' education.[120]

THE CULTURAL ACCEPTANCE OF ECONOMIC DISCRIMINATION IN HOUSING

Americans are often accepting of economic discrimination and exclusion in housing. Sometimes we even celebrate it. Although American society has made considerable progress in recognizing that discriminating by race is shameful, a neighborhood that excludes by class can actually be seen as desirable, a place to be coveted. Consider the language used in a brochure from the Philadelphia Visitors Bureau. It describes the city's Rittenhouse Square area as "the heart of City Center's most expensive and exclusive neighborhood."[121] The *New York Times*, America's newspaper of record, noted in passing in 2017 that President Obama was purchasing a home in Washington, DC's Kalorama, "an exclusive neighborhood."[122] An Airbnb advertisement boasts of "Beautiful Home in Exclusive Neighborhood."[123]

Indeed, even as open racial discrimination became less acceptable, the nation has seen a rise in the "gated communities" phenomenon in which private guards and extensive fences literally exclude less-advantaged

Americans.[124] What one researcher has termed "secession of the success-ful" has, if anything, accelerated during the same era in which racial exclusion has become delegitimized.[125]

Upper-middle-class liberals will strenuously argue, on the one hand, that people should never be denied an opportunity to live in a neigh-borhood because of race or ethnic origin. On the other, though, many may have no problem with government policies that effectively exclude those who are less educationally and financially successful. As politi-cal scientist Omar Wasow (formerly of Princeton, now at UC Berkeley) acerbically notes, "There are people in the town of Princeton who will have a Black Lives Matter sign on their front lawn and a sign saying 'We love our Muslim neighbors,' but oppose changing zoning policies that say you have to have an acre and a half per house." He continues: "That means, 'We love our Muslim neighbors, as long as they're million-aires.'"[126] Having a modest number of wealthy neighbors who are people of color can actually be affirming to privileged white people because it suggests the system is just.[127]

Likewise, some white liberals living in exclusive neighborhoods may have fervently opposed Donald Trump's wall on the Mexican bor-der as racist but still support zoning walls that make it unlikely that any recent immigrants will be able to afford to live in their neighbor-hoods. A California Yes in My Backyard (YIMBY) activist notes that progressives are rightfully proud of their openness to immigrants, so why, he asks, are some standing by exclusionary zoning that says "we welcome outsiders—but you've got to have a $2 million entrance fee to live here"?[128] As one Brookings scholar has noted, "Walking around my own rich, liberal suburban cocoon, I pass many signs declaring that 'Hate Has No Home Here.' In my more cynical moments, I fantasize about putting up some new signs next to them: 'But Restrictive Zon-ing Does!'"[129]

Consider Lexington and Weston, the exclusionary Boston suburbs discussed earlier. They are not havens for intolerant right-wingers who embrace racist politicians. In 2020, Lexington voters supported Biden over Trump by 82 percent to 17 percent. And exclusionary Weston delivered three-quarters of its votes to the Democratic candidate.[130] Class exclusion and liberal politics coincide readily in America.

It is telling that even Donald Trump himself, widely considered the most racist president in modern American history, understood the cultural limits were different for denigrating potential neighbors by race than they are for denigrating them based on class.[131] After Trump began his campaign to win over "suburban housewives of America" by saying Biden would eliminate single-family zoning, critics (appropriately) accused him of race-baiting. Trump responded by explaining that he wanted to exclude by class rather than by race. In an August 2020 press conference, he was asked about a tweet in which he warned of an "invasion" of the suburbs if Biden's zoning reforms went through. Trump (correctly) noted that the suburbs were already racially diverse, that "30 percent plus of the people living in suburbia are minorities, African-American, Asian American, Hispanic American." Trump knew that explicitly saying "I want to keep Black people out of the suburbs" was culturally untenable. But in the very next sentence, he signaled that he also knew it was completely permissible to say something else: that he was strongly opposed to plans "to change zoning so that you have lots of problems where they want to build low-income housing."[132]

As we shall see in Chapter 5, in my own advancement of ideas around addressing class discrimination in zoning, it speaks volumes that *New York Times* readers who commented on my arguments in an op-ed would go out of their way to suggest their opposition to zoning reform had nothing to do with race but felt no compunction about stereotyping low-income residents of all races as being loud and unpleasant neighbors who wouldn't keep up their lawns, who argue a lot, and whose dogs even bark louder than the dogs of wealthy people.[133] Alice from Berkeley, for example, was frank in commenting on my article that she did not want to be around poor people. "I don't want to live in a neighborhood populated with high-school dropouts, ex-cons, and multi-generational 'family units' with ten cars amongst them," she wrote. Substitute "Black" or "Hispanic" for Alice's signifiers of class and it is unlikely that the *New York Times* would have published the comment.

THE CULTURAL CONSENSUS IS WRITTEN INTO AMERICAN LAW

The cultural consensus that racial discrimination is wrong but class discrimination is broadly acceptable is mirrored in American laws. It is found in the Supreme Court's interpretation of the US Constitution's requirement for "equal protection" and in our statutes on housing. Notably, as outlined below, this legal and cultural posture on discrimination by race and class is an international outlier.

To begin with, it is significant that in interpreting the broad language of the Fourteenth Amendment—that Americans deserve "equal protection"—the US Supreme Court has treated discrimination by government based on race very differently from discrimination based on class. The language of the equal protection clause of the Fourteenth Amendment to the Constitution is broad: "No State shall . . . deny any person within its jurisdiction the equal protection of the law."[134] In a series of cases, the Supreme Court has held that distinctions based on race are subject to "strict scrutiny," which forbids government distinctions unless they serve a "compelling government purpose" and the means used are "narrowly tailored." Strict scrutiny is not always fatal to legislation, but it typically is. By contrast, government distinctions based on economic status are subject to a "relaxed" form of scrutiny under which the government must merely have a "rational basis" for the classification, and there must be a "rational relationship" between the economic distinction and the ends sought. As a result, in the housing arena, the justices have held that states and localities may not discriminate against racial minorities but may discriminate against poor people. Consider two examples: the differential treatment of zoning by race and class, and how the court treats popular referenda that discriminate based on those two different criteria.

As noted earlier, the US Supreme Court appropriately struck down zoning laws that discriminate by race in the 1917 *Buchanan* case. Less than a decade later, it upheld zoning laws that discriminate by income in the 1926 *Euclid* case.[135] The district court judge noted that the decision of Euclid, Ohio, to ban multifamily housing in certain areas was economically discriminatory: "The result to be accomplished is to classify the population and to segregate them according to their income or situation in life."[136] But when the case reached the Supreme Court, the justices declared that exclusionary zoning presented no constitutional problem. In a landmark decision, the Supreme Court said that just as excluding industrial uses in a residential neighborhood was clearly justified to promote the health and welfare of residents, excluding apartments was also appropriate. In language laden with class bias, the court said that an apartment house can be "a mere parasite, constructed in order to take advantage of the open spaces and attractive surroundings created by the residential character of the district." Apartment houses would bring more people and traffic, "depriving children of the privilege of quiet and open spaces for play, enjoyed by those in more favored localities—until, finally, the residential character of the neighborhood and its desirability as a place of detached residences are utterly destroyed. Under these circumstances, apartment houses . . . come very near to being nuisances."[137] The court argued: "A nuisance may be merely a right thing in the wrong place—like a pig in the parlor instead of the barnyard."[138]

The court gave no consideration to the people, of all races, who could not afford single-family houses and were thus, by government edict, excluded from entire neighborhoods—and the public school districts associated with those neighborhoods. One supposes that in the court's view, working-class Americans could live in the human equivalent of the pig's barnyard, far from the parlors found in fancy neighborhoods.

Some forty years later, the Supreme Court continued to look much more favorably upon the legality of discrimination by class than by race, this time in the context of reviewing anti–fair housing referenda. In *Hunter v. Erickson* (1969), the Supreme Court struck down an Akron, Ohio, law that said any ordinance prohibiting race discrimination in housing could not take effect unless a majority of voters approved the law, thereby placing "special burdens on racial minorities."[139] However, the court was far more tolerant of income discrimination. In *James v. Valtierra* (1971), the court took up the constitutionality of a provision in California law that provided that no low-income housing could be constructed without a local community first providing majority support in a referendum. In the case, a San Jose city councilwoman claimed poor

people can "drag the whole neighborhood down," bringing "piles of gar-
bage" and "undisciplined children." But the court ruled the California
provision was perfectly legal. The difference between the *Hunter* and
James cases, the court said, was that the Akron law singled out minorities,
whereas the California law applied to "any low-rent public housing project, not only for projects which will be occupied by a racial minority."[140]

The Supreme Court's comparative willingness to tolerate explicit
economic discrimination is mirrored in American public policy and the
1968 Fair Housing Act. In outlawing racial discrimination, passage of
the Fair Housing Act was a monumental advance for human dignity and
freedom.[141] The Fair Housing Act makes it illegal to "refuse to sell or
rent . . . or otherwise make unavailable or deny, a dwelling to any person
because of race, color, religion, sex, familial status or national origin."
The legislation covers about 80 percent of the nation's housing supply.[142]
The law applies to private landlords who discriminate on these bases,
but it also applies to local governments. Although local governments
don't typically rent or sell apartments, zoning laws can run afoul of the
prohibition to "otherwise make unavailable or deny" dwellings on the
basis of race.[143]

The 1968 Fair Housing Act's focus on racial discrimination, on one
level, made enormous sense. The 1968 Kerner Commission report on
recent urban riots was right to find that "our nation is moving toward
two societies—one black, one white—separate and unequal." After Dr.
Martin Luther King Jr.'s tragic assassination in April 1968, Congress's
passage of the Fair Housing Act within days was a fitting tribute to
King's fight for civil rights and racial justice. But King also believed
in economic justice, and the Fair Housing Act's failure to protect low-
income people against government discrimination is unfortunate.

Private-sector discrimination is held to the same double standard depending on whether discrimination is based on race or income. As noted
earlier, for more than fifty years it has been illegal for private landlords
to discriminate based on race in the sale or rental of housing, yet there is
no federal protection for discrimination based on "source of income." A
landlord who discriminates against a low-income Black person because
of her race is in violation of federal law; a landlord who discriminates

against the same individual instead because of her source of income—a Section 8 housing voucher—faces no legal jeopardy under federal law.

Some supporters of the 1968 Fair Housing Act actually pushed this limitation of the bill as a feature rather than a bug. The late Senator Edward Brooke (R-MA), for example, noted the bill would allow only "those who have resources" to escape the ghetto.[144] Likewise, says Harvard's Alexander von Hoffman, Senator Walter F. Mondale (D-MN) assured critics that "under the Act's prohibition of housing discrimination, only middle-class Blacks would escape impoverished central-city neighborhoods."[145] As von Hoffman notes, "Ironically, some fair housing supporters seemed willing to consign the poor to the dreadful ghettoes they described to allay the fear of white suburbanites and their representatives of an invasion by low-income city dwellers."[146]

Senator William Proxmire (D-WI) was a lonely voice arguing that HUD should withhold money from government jurisdictions that discriminated on the basis of class (as well as race) when they used large-lot zoning and other devices to inhibit "the development of housing for people of low and moderate incomes." But as von Hoffman notes, "Congress had little appetite for a sweeping approach that imposed penalties on communities."[147]

Some states and localities have taken action to protect against source-of-income discrimination, but according to a 2022 analysis by the Poverty & Race Research Action Council, nearly half of voucher holders nationwide lack such protection.[148] And, as noted earlier in this chapter, even in states like Massachusetts, which technically outlaw source-of-income discrimination, the practice remains widespread. Likewise, a few state courts have interpreted state constitutions to disfavor zoning laws that discriminate by income, but under federal law, only racial discrimination triggers the ability to challenge zoning laws.[149]

It is important to recognize that US public policy is an outlier in failing to protect against income discrimination. In a 2016 comparative analysis of nondiscrimination protections in Europe, researchers noted that numerous countries, including Austria, Belgium, Bulgaria, Croatia, Cyprus, Estonia, Hungary, Iceland, Italy, Latvia, Lithuania, Portugal, Romania, Serbia, Slovenia, Spain, and Turkey, protect against various forms of economic discrimination.[150] Moreover, many countries have specialized bodies that are designed to enforce protections based on economic status.[151]

Likewise, the United States is unusual in not providing socioeconomic rights in its federal Constitution.[152] Citing the constitutions of nations from Norway to Peru to South Africa, Harvard Law School's Cass Sunstein concludes that "the constitutions of most nations create social and economic rights," making the American Constitution's failure to create such rights "distinctive." Austria's Article 7, for example, provides that "All nationals are equal before the law. Privileges based upon birth, sex, estate, *class* or religion are excluded."[153] In the 1960s and 1970s, the US Supreme Court came close to interpreting the Fourteenth Amendment's Equal Protection Clause to include economic rights, Sunstein says, but "a modest shift in personnel" on the court, precipitated by President Nixon, foreclosed that option.[154]

On one level, there is very good reason that discrimination based on race is especially disfavored: American history is saturated with it, from slavery to Jim Crow to policing today. Anti-Black bias is a particularly virulent strain in the American story that fully deserves special condemnation. But having said that, why does America turn such a blind eye to class discrimination?

To begin with, class is less visible to the naked eye than race, so when economic discrimination promotes economic segregation, it is less immediately vivid to the observer than when racial discrimination produces racial segregation. So, too, long-standing reputable organizations, like the NAACP and NAACP Legal Defense and Education Fund, with strong middle-class supporters, help keep people focused on discrimination by race, as they should. Fewer organized groups representing low-income families of all races exist to draw attention to income and class discrimination.

And because class is less visible than race and has weaker constituencies, we don't teach class discrimination in our schools in the same way we teach the history of other forms of discrimination. We have Black History Month, Hispanic Heritage Month, and Women's History Month—once again, as we well should—but we don't have a month dedicated to talking about the contributions of poor and working-class people in America. Students are taught much more about King's fight for racial justice than his subsequent Poor People's Campaign for economic justice.

Louisiana State University professor Nancy Isenberg argues the omission in the curriculum is glaring. Isenberg says, "Popular American history is most commonly told—dramatized—without much reference to the existence of social classes."[155] Our history books do not highlight the fact, for example, that when Thomas Jefferson admirably proposed public funding for education, he employed a demeaning metaphor for poor white children. Jefferson wrote that through public education, "twenty of the best geniuses will be raked from the *rubbish* annually, and be instructed at the public expense, so far as grammar school goes."[156] Nor do history books emphasize that the eugenics movement of the early twentieth century targeted not only Black people but also poor white women.[157]

But the biggest underlying reason we don't talk about economic discrimination and segregation is America's deep belief that, in a system of meritocracy, poverty is essentially the fault of the poor person. Any system of subjugation—whether based on race or class—requires a story to provide a rationale. For generations, author Heather McGhee notes, racists relied on ludicrous theories of white supremacy. As white Americans stole the labor of enslaved Black people and stole the lands of Indigenous people, these "atrocities needed justifications." White supremacy is not a reflection of tribalism dating back thousands of years; it is a fairly modern concept that was invented as a means to buttress the worst kinds of economic exploitation.[158] As Ibram X. Kendi writes, "For roughly two hundred thousand years, before race and racism were constructed in the fifteenth century, humans saw color but did not group the colors into continental races, did not commonly attach negative and positive characteristics to those colors and rank the races to justify racial inequality, to reinforce racist power and policy."[159]

Today's believers in meritocracy admirably reject racism and sexism as both shameful and inefficient because such bias interferes with identifying who is most hardworking and talented. Immutable characteristics are rejected as an irrational basis for consideration of who should advance in a meritocracy. One can't change one's race, it is often noted, the way one can change one's class.

By the same token, however, once those atavistic race and sex considerations are eliminated or at least greatly reduced, in the meritocratic logic, growing inequalities can be morally justified as a basis for rewarding those who work hard to develop their talents.[160] Indeed, the modest amount of racial diversity among the upper-middle class, says one writer, is "central to our collective self-image" and belief that the system is fair.[161]

The meritocratic ethos may help explain why some highly educated elites are simultaneously liberal on issues like racial and gender equality but are in fact more punitive in their views of economic inequality and poverty. A study of law students who attended Yale University in 2007, 2010, and 2013, for example, found that, although students identified themselves as Democrats rather than Republicans by a factor of more than ten to one, they were far less likely than ordinary Americans to favor economic equality.[162] Though social liberalism has become part of the ethos of well-educated people, it appears to be difficult for many of these young liberal winners in the meritocratic race to simultaneously acknowledge that, on economic issues, their own success may be partly a matter of luck, as is the misfortune of those less economically well-off.

In sum, while the prevailing American ethos appropriately recognizes that racism is a terrible deviation from meritocracy, class bigotry is in many ways a natural outgrowth of it. The logic, Michael Sandel says, is that "if my success is my own doing, their failure must be their fault."[163] To a believer in meritocracy, exclusionary zoning extends the logic. People who have talents deserve greater rewards and the ability to live in certain neighborhoods as an incentive to develop those talents; and if government recognizes that extra value by writing laws to allow meritocratic winners to congregate (and exclude others), the incentive of the talented to work hard becomes even greater. So long as the exclusion is not based on an immutable factor like race, what's the harm?

There is, to be sure, much to be said for the fundamental system of meritocracy as a way of allocating jobs and opportunities. At its best, one analyst notes, merit is "the opposite of corruption."[164] Indeed, we very much want the most talented and highly trained to fill positions that require great skill. There is no good alternative to meritocracy in America.

But the *hubris* that goes along with the meritocratic logic, especially the idea that losers in the race are so degraded as to justify government laws that keep them separated, is appallingly wrong for several reasons.

To begin with, though it is commonly argued that race is different from class because race is immutable and class is not, this way of thinking minimizes the extent to which class status is often less a reflection of hard work and character than it is good luck or bad luck. So much of adult socioeconomic status today is a reflection of the family one happens to have been born into. With social mobility levels in the United States low and getting lower, the class status of your parents has an enormous impact on your life chances; in that sense, the distinct line traditionally drawn between inheritance of race and inheritance of class has blurred.[165] Among Americans born in the 1940s, 90 percent did better than their parents, but among those born in the 1980s, only 50 percent did better.[166]

And being born with talent itself is a matter of luck. From a moral perspective, it is the hard work that shows character, not whether that hard work is accompanied by the good fortune of the "genetic lottery" of being good at math or reading or having other endowments.[167] That is why we speak of students being "gifted" or having "God-given talents." There is also a large element of fortune in being born into a society at a time when your particular talents (developed through hard work) are valued. As Sandel points out, if LeBron James worked hard to be a superb arm wrestler rather than a phenomenal basketball player, he would not be making tens of millions of dollars.[168]

Finally, a stroke of bad luck (or good luck) can have a profound impact on one's economic status. For KiAra Cornelius in Columbus, the bad luck came in the form of a car accident followed by a flood in her house. For many, it is a health setback or death of a parent that sends one on an unexpected trajectory in life.[169]

Because of the role of luck (the family one is born into, the talents one inherits through the genetic lottery, and the like), progressives used to emphasize the value of hard work per se.

Dr. Martin Luther King Jr. recognized that "all labor has dignity" and told striking sanitation workers in Memphis that their labor was as important as a physician's because if they didn't do their job, disease would become rampant.[170] Laws that fence out sanitation workers and other hardworking people humiliate them as unworthy of living in a community. As a matter of basic human dignity, these laws send a terrible signal, just as racial zoning laws did: that some people are so beneath others that the government is justified in setting up rules to keep them apart. Excluding fellow humans who make less money from living anywhere in a community betrays ugly sentiments, even if there is no underlying racial animus.

It is one thing for a market to discriminate by income; markets function by providing incentives and rewards. It is an entirely different thing for a government to put its heavy thumb on the scale in favor of the wealthy and to say that those who cannot afford to live in single-family dwellings should be banned from entire communities—that their presence would be, in essence, a "nuisance" to be kept out, akin to an industrial factory or slaughterhouse.

It is especially humiliating to tell people they are welcome to *work* in a community, so long as they don't *live* there. Every day, wealthy families ask low-wage workers to travel into their communities to provide vital child and elderly care or to landscape their lawns and to clean their homes—while effectively zoning them out from living anywhere in the community. Instead, we should adopt the ethos, one commentator has noted, "anyone good enough to work here is good enough to live here."[171]

While government-sponsored exclusion humiliates those who are denied entry, it also falsely inflates the egos and self-regard of the privileged. Heather McGhee shrewdly observes that class is about much more than the size of someone's wallet; it is associated with feelings of status and superiority that flow from having resources. She writes: "The being matters more than the having. Often, what we have (a nice home, cash in the bank, a good car) is a simple way of telling ourselves and others who we are."[172] One writer observes that "the right home in the right neighborhood" can be "an exercise in self-branding." An important aspect of owning a home in an exclusive neighborhood is "what the address on the title says about you."[173] Public laws that exclude based on income put the government's imprimatur on the effort to elevate the status of some over others in our democracy.

Finally, government markers of status via zoning laws seem especially cruel for the children of low-wage workers. Even if one somehow believes it is appropriate to exclude low-income and working-class people from neighborhoods because their economic status is their own fault, in what moral universe is it acceptable to exclude a five-year-old child from a good neighborhood and its good public school because they "chose the wrong parents"?

And this is especially true because snob zoning not only puts the government in the business of delineating lines between the worthy and the unworthy but also stacks the deck with resources for the fortunate. Research finds that the top 20 percent of households by income are about three times as likely to live near very high-performing public schools as households from the bottom 40 percent by income.[174] As such, zoning helps perpetuate a system where meritocracy's winners in one generation build a quasi-aristocracy in which privileges can be handed down to their children. Children of less-educated families are kept out of high-opportunity neighborhoods and schools not only because they are disdained but also because the wealthy want to rig the game against them to reduce competition.[175] The unfair advantage provided by exclusionary zoning is a form of "incumbent protection."[176]

DECLINING RACIAL SEGREGATION AND RISING INCOME SEGREGATION IN A MERITOCRACY

The logic of the meritocracy as applied to residential real estate helps explain both the good news (declining racial segregation) and the bad news (increasing income segregation). As noted earlier, Black–white segregation declined 30 percent between 1970 and 2020.[177]

By contrast, income segregation, as Robert Putnam notes, "was significantly higher in 2010 than it was in 1970."[178] In a 2013 study, researchers found that income segregation has grown significantly, for both low-income and, particularly, for high-income families. Looking at the segregation of families (households where children and guardians are present) over the past four decades in 117 metro areas that had a population of at least five hundred thousand, the authors found that family income segregation has steadily grown in every decade from 1970 to 2009, with the growth from 2000 to 2009 being the most significant.[179] A 2016 study found that the proportion of families living in rich or poor (as opposed to middle-class) neighborhoods increased from 15 percent in 1970 to 34 percent in 2012.[180] A 2015 report found that "the number of people living in high-poverty ghettos, barrios, and slums has nearly doubled since 2000, from 7.2 million to 13.8 million."[181] And a 2016 study found that income segregation grew primarily among families with children compared with those without children between 1990 and 2010.[182]

In a 2022 report examining the very latest data, researchers found that economic segregation increased by 13.1 percent from 2000 to 2015–2019. In addition, using better techniques to measure income segregation shows that the levels are "far greater than previously believed."[183] Another 2022 analysis found that the proportion of families living in middle-income neighborhoods declined by almost one-fifth from 1990 to 2020 (from 62 percent to half).[184]

Taking the income and racial trends in tandem, one researcher argues that "we are substituting Jim Crow by race with Jim Crow by income."[185] In truth, income and racial segregation both remain high and whether one is higher than the other depends on how one defines income groups. A direct comparison is hard to make, researchers note, because, though choosing two racial groups for dissimilarity measures (e.g., Black and white people) is fairly straightforward, income "is continuous," so judgment calls must be made. A comparison of poor and nonpoor people shows income segregation substantially below racial segregation. But this measure may not be appropriate, one scholar suggests, because someone "just above the poverty line is hardly distinguishable from someone just below it."[186] But if we look at segregation levels between the top and bottom income brackets in the Census data (roughly the top and bottom 6–7 percent nationally) or the top and bottom two brackets (roughly the top and bottom 12 percent by income), then income segregation is actually higher than Black–white segregation.[187]

The blame for rising income segregation lies in part with larger rises in income inequality in the US economy. But research finds that neighborhood inequality has risen faster than household-level inequality since 1970. One scholar notes, "Not only have neighborhoods become more unequal over the past four decades, they have become more unequal at a faster rate than households have."[188] This rising income segregation coincides with the explosion in new zoning laws that slowed growth beginning in the 1970s, particularly in exclusive communities.[189]

Given these trends, it is time for new policies to address income discrimination in zoning and the income segregation it spawns. We will discuss these policies in much greater detail in Chapters 6 and 7, but we briefly sketch them here before we entertain some objections to reform in the next chapter.

To begin with, states, which have the constitutional authority to direct zoning, should eliminate single-family exclusive zoning to allow duplexes and triplexes statewide, similar to legislation already adopted in Oregon and California. Municipalities should do so as well, following the lead of cities such as Minneapolis and Charlotte. Reasonably sized apartments should also be legalized along major mass transit corridors.

In addition, the federal government should create an Economic Fair Housing Act to allow plaintiffs to sue when municipalities discriminate against them on the basis of income when government cannot offer a sufficient justification. Just as the 1968 Fair Housing Act has made a dent in racial segregation, an Economic Fair Housing Act that makes it illegal for governments to engage in unjustified income discrimination would likely reduce economic segregation (and also aid in the Fair Housing Act's efforts to reduce racial segregation). Class discrimination is real in America, and it is time we stop turning a blind eye to it.

FIVE

RECOGNIZING AND RESPONDING TO EIGHT CONCERNS

As I RESEARCHED AND BEGAN WRITING THIS BOOK, I SURFACED some of the themes and ideas in articles in the *New York Times*, *Atlantic*, and *American Prospect*. People who support the current system of zoning raised concerns and objections—sometimes in quite spirited language—which have helped inform my thinking. In April 2021, for example, when I advanced a version of the argument in this book in a *New York Times* op-ed, the paper received 766 comments, some of which I discuss below.[1]

From this, and other responses, it became clear to me that complaints about zoning reform and new housing run the gamut from entirely legitimate to completely illegitimate. Nearby buildings indisputably affect the character and quality of life in a neighborhood. A high-rise apartment in the middle of a community of single-family homes could cast a large dark shadow on virtually everyone else. A very large new development might legitimately be a threat to wetlands or—if poorly planned—impose impossible competition for parking.[2] Scale matters. But sometimes the concerns raised have to do less with *the number* of new residents than with *who* is coming in. For some, the presence of a smaller home in a neighborhood of large houses is troubling because the social status of neighbors would change. For some, the presence of a plumber's or landscaper's van parked in the driveway overnight is somehow unsettling.[3] For others, the presence of Black or Muslim neighbors in a mostly white and Christian community is upsetting.

In discussions about zoning reform, eight sets of concerns repeatedly arise from individuals across the political spectrum. The first five often come from the political center and right, the last three from the political left. These objections suggest the following:

(1) Opposition to zoning reform has nothing to do with class or race bias. It is, instead, about protecting families from rapacious developers who would like to build high-rise towers that will increase traffic, create parking headaches, overcrowd schools, and change the character of neighborhoods.

(2) Whereas it is wrong to discriminate by race, hardworking people have a right to separate from poorer people, who are more likely to bring crime and disorder to a neighborhood and reduce school quality.

(3) By changing the level of density or the demographics of neighbors, zoning reform will reduce the value of residents' single biggest investment needed for their retirement.

(4) Reform represents typical liberal overreach, telling people they can't have things they want, like single-family homes. In pursuing reform, liberals are just trying to homogenize communities and make them all the same.

(5) Reformers are pushing untested ideas. No one knows whether proposed changes will actually result in making housing more affordable and less racially and economically segregated.

From the left, there are those who say they agree with the goals of reformers but think changes to zoning laws are not the right path.

(6) Changing zoning laws to increase density is not enough to increase affordability or reduce racial and economic segregation. The real solution is to build more government-supported housing, not to "deregulate" zoning.

(7) Zoning reform will actually lead to *less* affordability. Developers will simply build more luxury condos, which leads to neighborhood gentrification and displacement of low-income residents, especially residents of color.

(8) Zoning reform—and a focus on income discrimination—is a distraction from the centrality of race in the fight for fair housing.

We take each in turn.

RAPACIOUS DEVELOPERS

One of the strongest responses to zoning reform is that it is a giveaway to rapacious developers. They will use their power to bulldoze quiet residential areas in pursuit of profits and build high-rises that destroy the aesthetic appeal of neighborhoods. The result will be traffic, parking headaches, and overcrowded schools, the argument runs.

The most highly recommended comment to my *Times* article came from "Larry from Richmond," who argued: "Single-family zoning may have its downsides, but it is typically the only defense homeowners have in conflicts with developers, who otherwise hold all the cards and will not rest until every square foot of every metropolitan area in the country is paved over with apartments, big box stores and parking lots."[4] Larry reframed the power struggle: it is not between relatively advantaged single-family homeowners trying to exclude the less wealthy, he said, but between regular homeowners and greedy developers. "Without single family zoning," Larry argued, "ordinary families wouldn't have a chance."

In this way of thinking, the issue is density. Racism and classism have nothing to do with opposition to new housing; people just don't want more neighbors of any race or income level. In Chevy Chase, Maryland, residents opposed allowing duplexes and triplexes because it would mean more on-street parking difficulties and congestion.[5] School overcrowding is a perennial concern raised by opponents of new housing. In Katy, Texas, a city west of Houston, for example, residents opposed to the construction of low-income apartments cited concerns "about potential overcrowding at Sundown Elementary School, where some pupils attend classes in seven portable buildings."[6] A private consulting firm that seeks to provide support for local communities opposing new housing has an entire web page articulating the reasons why development will cause school overcrowding, and why that is harmful to children.[7]

Larry is right to say developers generally want more units per plot of land because they can make more money. But existing homeowners are looking out for their own economic self-interest, too, by limiting supply—and in the vast majority of cases, homeowners have won. If there is a balance to be struck between too much development and not enough, Americans have clearly built too little. As discussed in Chapter 2, we have a housing shortage of 3.8 million homes, which has spawned an affordability crisis.[8] In areas with growing populations, the political process has generally yielded underdevelopment, not overdevelopment.

Moreover, the choice is not between single-family exclusive zoning and allowing, as Larry put it, a "big box store" next door. Just because today's exclusionary laws impose one extreme—nothing but detached single-family homes—doesn't mean that reforms involve swinging to the other extreme, whereby a developer could erect a shopping mall or a skyscraper smack in the middle of a residential neighborhood that currently contains single-family homes.

Most of the reforms discussed in this book seek a middle ground. Minneapolis and Oregon, for example, focus mostly on legalizing duplexes and triplexes—so-called "missing middle" housing. Oftentimes, such housing appears from the street view to be very similar to single-family homes.

Missing middle housing can also include accessory dwelling units (ADUs), "cottage courts" (several houses on relatively small lots that sit around a common shared lawn), and garden apartments (two- to three-story apartments with lots of green space).[9] This type of housing is particularly common in cities like Chicago, Illinois, and Madison, Wisconsin.[10] Low-rise or higher-rise apartments make more sense near major mass transit corridors.

In addition, many NIMBYs raise concerns about traffic in their neighborhood; however, these legitimate worries must be weighed against regional traffic concerns. People have to live somewhere. A little more traffic and parking competition in one community, for example, will usually mean less urban sprawl and a large overall reduction in traffic in the region.

The argument that new neighbors will overcrowd schools is also problematic. It is true, of course, that overcrowded schools present real challenges for teaching and learning; but the answer, in a wealthy society, isn't to arbitrarily cap who can move into a community but to find space for every child. This can be accomplished by building more schools, by adding capacity to existing schools, or by making more efficient use of school space. In some communities, certain schools may be overcrowded while others are underenrolled and have extra room. A system of universal public school choice, like that employed in Cambridge, Massachusetts, gives parents the option of sending their child to a less crowded school a bit farther away, which can free up space at overcrowded schools.[11]

A free democratic society should not forbid people from moving into a community because there is no space for their kids in the public schools. Even when not a single new unit of housing is built, neighborhoods naturally change over, as older couples with grown children move out, and new families with young children move in. In such cases, we don't stop the sale to a young family on the grounds that new children will "overcrowd" the schools—we make room for them by expanding existing schools or building new ones. It becomes problematic, therefore, to suggest that we can never expand the housing supply because "other people's kids" will overcrowd "our" public schools.

Finally, the concern that new housing—perhaps duplexes or triplexes—will be aesthetically unpleasing and change the "character" of the neighborhood because they fail to "fit in" is a weak plank on which to base exclusion of new neighbors. There is no accounting for taste, but typically, some diversity in architecture is seen as a sought-after quality. Some homogenous neighborhoods, in fact, are derided for their "cookie-cutter" homes that all look very similar.

UNPLEASANT NEIGHBORS

Whereas it is wrong to discriminate on the basis of race, a second argument suggests, hardworking people have the right to avoid unpleasant neighbors who are poor, since they bring crime and disorder to a community and reduce school quality. Unlike the first concern, which focused on the number of new people coming in, the emphasis here is on who the new neighbors will be.

One *New York Times* reader, for example, wrote, "I wouldn't care if my neighbors were Black, Asian, white or Martian," but living among apartment dwellers in "a not-so-great section of a city . . . stinks." The neighbors are messy and fight "with some regularity."[12] Another reader from Texas was equally blunt: "My wife is half Black. My closest friend is of Asian descent. But there's no chance you'll ever convince me to live among the poor again."

In particular, some readers said that low-income neighbors would be criminals. "Mick from New Mexico" argued, "Unfortunately the reality is crime follows low income housing as day follows night." The fear that economic diversity will bring crime to wealthy neighborhoods is sometimes stoked by the media. In 2008, for example, Hanna Rosin published a widely read piece in the *Atlantic* suggesting that after the demolition of a high-rise housing project in Memphis, Tennessee, former residents used housing vouchers to move to surrounding suburbs, and crime spiked in these areas as a result. Rosin wrote that when researchers overlaid the presence of Section 8 voucher holders with crime statistics, the pattern was clear: "On the merged map, dense violent-crime areas are shaded dark blue, and Section 8 addresses are represented by little red dots. All of the dark-blue areas are covered in little red dots, like bursts of gunfire."[13]

Relatedly, some argue that because the free market discriminates based on income, it is appropriate for the government to do so as well. "Zoning may discriminate against some economically, but so does Mercedes and BMW," "Robert from Princeton New Jersey" argued. Others suggested that because they had worked hard, they had earned the right to avoid low-income neighbors. Larry wrote: "I know that living in a single-family neighborhood is a privilege and not something everyone can afford, but it is something I worked very hard for, and that I and my parents made sacrifices in other areas in order to achieve. It is, after my family, the most important thing in my life."

Finally, some argue that if lower-income families are not zoned out by law, the presence of their children would cause the local public schools to deteriorate. In St. Charles County, Missouri, for example, one mother suggested that an influx of low-income Black schoolchildren into St. Charles would inevitably mean violence and require the installation of metal detectors and drug-sniffing dogs.[14]

There is no doubt that crime is higher in poor neighborhoods. People living in poor urban areas had violence victimization rates of 43.9 per 1,000, and in poor rural areas of 38.8 compared with 16.9 per 1,000 in high-income areas.[15]

But it is profoundly inaccurate and unfair to paint all low-income people as likely criminals. Most violent crime, researchers find, is committed by "a tiny group of people who are linked together in a tight network of victims and offenders."[16] For example, in Boston, young gang members represent only 3 percent of the youth population in high-risk neighborhoods.[17] In Richmond, California, which is "one of the most violent cities in the country," one author notes, just 28 of more than 100,000 residents caused 70 percent of the city's gun violence.[18]

Moreover, there is an important difference between the effects of concentrated poverty and poverty. Because high-poverty neighborhoods produce pathologies does not mean individuals living in those neighborhoods are somehow destined to be pathological.[19] Indeed, the Moving to Opportunity research suggests that low-income children, when given opportunities and the right environment, can be placed on very different trajectories in life.

In a 2013 analysis, one scholar reviewed more than a dozen studies on crime and subsidized housing and concluded that "concentrated disadvantage is the chief culprit when subsidized housing affects crime." Scattered-site public housing, by contrast, has little or no effect on neighborhood crime, he found.[20] Likewise, in a detailed study of the effects of a 140-unit low-income housing project in the affluent community of

Mount Laurel, New Jersey, researchers found that the project did not negatively affect crime rates in the community. When they compared crime trends in Mount Laurel and three surrounding communities before and after the housing project opened in 2000, they found "no evidence" that it "had any influence at all on crime rates in Mount Laurel, which were falling before 2001 and continued to fall afterward."[21]

Indeed, a host of researchers have debunked Hanna Rosin's *Atlantic* magazine article about Memphis. In 2011, researchers from New York University and UCLA analyzed Rosin's hypothesis by looking at longitudinal, neighborhood-level crime and voucher utilization data in ten large US cities. They found that areas with more voucher holders did have more crime, but that the causal relationship ran in reverse of what Rosin suggested. Because many landlords won't accept Section 8 vouchers, voucher holders are more likely to move to neighborhoods where crime is high and rising and apartments are available. They found: "More crime predicts more voucher holders in the future."[22]

Moreover, basing decisions about whether to exclude groups of people on statistical associations fundamentally robs individuals of their dignity. Most people would acknowledge that finding a statistical association between crime and race is an appalling reason to discriminate against all Black people, and the same logic applies to excluding all economically disadvantaged families.

Indeed, it seems particularly cruel to trap law-abiding low-income people like KiAra Cornelius, Patricia McGee, Samantha, and Tehani in high-poverty neighborhoods when, far from being criminals themselves, they express a strong desire to move in order to *avoid* crime. Their experience is typical. Surveys find that far from being a threat to public safety, large numbers of low-income families want to move in order to avoid neighborhood crime that is associated with concentrated poverty.[23]

Relatedly, the fact that the private marketplace discriminates based on income—not everyone can buy a Mercedes, "Robert from Princeton" says—does nothing to justify *government* discrimination against low-income people. When the government declares that it must pass laws to quarantine low-income people and keep them out of more affluent neighborhoods because of a perceived threat to public safety, the ugly logic is not too far from that invoked by Baltimore officials a century ago to quarantine Black people. We should, as Sheryll Cashin puts it, change policy and culture "to transform the lens through which society sees residents of poor Black neighborhoods, from presumed thug to presumed citizen."[24]

Larry may say that because he "worked very hard," he deserves the right to pass laws that exclude those with less income, but this line of argument fails to recognize that because someone earns less money does not mean they work less hard. KiAra Cornelius works hard too. So does Patricia McGee, who worked the graveyard shift at Amazon, from 7:00 p.m. to 5:00 a.m. So do sanitation workers and grocery clerks and restaurant workers, few of whom earn large salaries. And so do the hospital workers who clean the bedpans and "catch the early bus" to do so.[25]

Finally, Larry's argument misses the possibility—indeed, the fact—that allowing a richer diversity of neighbors can *enhance* the lives of people in exclusive neighborhoods. Increases in economic and racial diversity open the possibility of meeting people who will enrich one's understanding of the world and lead to a more interesting life than one experiences in a homogenous neighborhood. In more ethnically and racially diverse communities, one is likely to experience a wider variety of food offerings, live music possibilities, and artistic experiences. More *pupuserias*, Ethiopian groceries, and sushi restaurants. Economically mixed communities may offer a greater assortment of businesses: thrift shops and laundromats alongside higher-end restaurants and shops. And mixed-income communities may also offer a greater diversity of young and old people than wealthy communities, which tend to exclude younger families.[26]

In denser neighborhoods, meanwhile, people are more likely to run into one another and converse than when they are isolated by large lots.[27] The combination of greater density and diversity can yield more innovation and creativity.[28] "By its nature, the metropolis provides what otherwise could be given only by traveling; namely, the strange," Jane Jacobs famously wrote.[29] And it is from experiencing things novel and different—in travel and in diverse, denser communities—that we learn and grow.

Many people are recognizing these attractions. As the *Wall Street Journal* has noted, some developers are now catering to those who "are seeking out economically, racially and culturally diverse communities." For example, Jeff Travers, a middle-aged white nonprofit executive, recently moved from suburban (and racially and economically homogenous) Chevy Chase, Maryland, to a mixed-income community in Washington, DC, explaining, "I don't want to live in a cookie-cutter place anymore. Here, there will be more of a mix, not everyone looking the same with their dog. I'm excited about being part of something different."[30]

Relatedly, there is a growing body of evidence to suggest that in public schools the benefits of diversity by race and class run in all directions—to middle-class and white students as well as minority and low-income students. Researchers find growing evidence that "diversity makes us smarter." As one set of scholars put it: "Students' exposure to other students who are different from themselves and the novel ideas and challenges that such exposure brings leads to improved cognitive skills, including critical thinking and problem solving."[31] A classroom discussion of the role of racism in American society takes on a very different life when some of the students can talk from personal experience about having been unfairly treated by police. By the same token, a liberal white student might think differently about immigration policy if she is in a class with a Mexican immigrant who says her family waited patiently to emigrate and is opposed to lax border enforcement.

Apart from the cognitive benefits, there are additional reasons increasing numbers of middle-class families now want to send their children to diverse schools. Middle-class and white millennials realize that their children are growing up in a very different country, demographically, than did previous generations. For the first time since the founding of the republic, a majority of public school K–12 pupils in the United States are students of color. Students can learn better how to navigate adulthood in an increasingly diverse society—a skill that employers value—if they attend diverse schools. Ninety-six percent of major employers say it is "important" that employees be "comfortable working with colleagues, customers, and/or clients from diverse cultural backgrounds."[32] Business leaders have advocated for school integration because, they told teachers, "people have to be able to work together. . . . The number one problem in the workplace is not not knowing your job or not knowing the skills for your job. . . . It is people with skills not being able to get along with coworkers."[33]

Although it is common for middle-class parents to worry that academic standards will decline in schools as socioeconomic diversity increases, studies show that integration is not a zero-sum game in which gains for low-income students are offset by declines in middle-class achievement.[34] The research on racial integration found similar results: test scores of Black students increased and the scores of white students did not decline.[35] In Boston, for example, the cross-district choice program, under which Black students could attend white suburban schools, showed positive effects for Black students and no test score decline among white students. The same experience was true in a Texas study.[36]

"GOODBYE TO MY SINGLE BIGGEST INVESTMENT"

No small matter for many homeowners is the fear that opening up their neighborhoods through zoning reform will reduce the value of their property by increasing the number of neighbors or increasing the economic and racial diversity of neighbors. Perhaps both. "Benjamin from San Francisco" noted, "My home is my retirement account" and claimed that "zoning keeps my single most important investment safe." For a large group of people, he argues, "this issue is economically existential."

The stakes are high because homeowners have a lot of money tied up in housing. In 2021, owner-occupied housing in the United States was worth a staggering $24.1 trillion, according to the National Association of Realtors.[37] Owner-occupied homes constitute the majority of wealth for most people.[38]

Unlike stock portfolios, which can be diversified to minimize risk, money in housing is usually concentrated in a single home—something government has sought to encourage through tax policy. If one invests in a stock and later sells it, one pays a tax on the entire capital gain (albeit at a lower rate than on ordinary income). For homes, the rule is different. A married couple investing in a home will pay no capital gains tax whatsoever on the first $500,000 in gains.[39] Likewise, the tax code includes an incentive to spend disposable income on a larger house rather than other consumer goods such as a nicer car or new boat. For those who itemize their deductions, it is possible to write off interest on a home mortgage of up to $750,000, but it is not normally possible to deduct interest from something like an auto loan.[40]

Propping up property values is at the heart of why exclusionary zoning programs were created in the first place and why they endure to this day. As noted earlier, local governments doubled down on exclusionary zoning policies in the 1970s in part because, as home values increased as a portion of the financial portfolio of American families, the sensitivity to anything that might harm that nest egg increased.[41]

If property values are the preeminent driving force behind zoning—and have been since the days of racial zoning and redlining—what are we to make of the argument today? There are three different property-value-related concerns that should be treated differently on the merits. The first issue is how the *scale and tastefulness* of new development might affect property values. Second is how changes in *racial and economic diversity* might affect property values. And third is how an *increase in the supply* of housing in a region might affect property values. The first is legitimate; the second and third, in my view, are not. (Setting aside the arguments on the merits, in Chapter 8, I discuss a way to alleviate property owners' concerns as a practical political matter by offering home equity insurance.)

First, to the extent that property values are threatened by the construction of new buildings on an enormous scale, the objection may be completely legitimate and can and should be addressed in any legislative proposals that are designed to curb abuses of zoning. Scale matters: in a particular community, building one hundred units may not negatively affect property values, but building one thousand units—with the prospect of thousands more—might.[42]

The evidence suggests that when a proposed plan is tasteful and scaled appropriately, it will likely not reduce property values. Typically, a rezoning that allows for more housing will involve market-rate homes, which will open neighborhoods to the next-adjacent economic rung of residents—those, who, for example, can afford a duplex but not a single-family home. But even when the publicly subsidized units for low-income families are built, if they are tasteful and appropriately scaled, property values are not negatively affected, research finds.

A 2013 study, for example, examined the effects on local property values of an affordable housing development built in the affluent Philadelphia suburb of Mount Laurel, New Jersey, which has a population of forty-five thousand.[43] In Mount Laurel, the scale was reasonable (140 units), and the property was well maintained and aesthetically similar to the surrounding area homes.

Under these circumstances, what was the effect? The study took advantage of a quasi-experiment that compared property values in Mount Laurel with similar townships that "did not experience the sudden opening of a 100 percent affordable housing project" of 140 units, with a population that was 90 percent Black and Hispanic. The authors found no statistically significant differences between property value trends in Mount Laurel and the control townships. This was true both for neighborhoods adjacent to the project and the town as a whole.[44]

Other studies on programs that introduce affordable housing to neighborhoods generally find small effects on property values when the projects are well designed. One overview of seventeen studies found negative effects on property values were small and could have been mitigated by making sure the architecture was compatible with the neighborhood's existing architecture and public housing was not concentrated.[45]

Concerns about property values that focus on the appropriate appearance and scale of new developments provide room for legitimate debate. Arguments that invoke property values to justify perpetuating two unfair practices—limiting housing supply to drive up prices and limiting racial and socioeconomic integration to preserve values—are unpersuasive. Preserving future outsized gains that are attributable to government policies that rig the system in order to create artificial scarcity and perpetuate segregation should not be used to justify continuing those unfair practices.

As noted in Chapter 2, there is widespread agreement among economists that exclusionary zoning artificially props up property values by creating scarcity.

Using zoning laws to keep out competition in housing is a classic example of "rent seeking," which occurs when the homeowner does not do much to improve her land but "extracts unearned income by virtue of having a kind of monopoly over a particular point in space."[46] In San Francisco, for example, the median house appreciated at $60.13 an hour during any given workweek in 2018, and in San Jose, the appreciation was an astounding $99.81 an hour.[47]

This rent seeking has already paid off very nicely for exclusive neighborhoods compared with the average one. In 1980, homes at the ninetieth percentile in value were worth about six times as much as those in the tenth percentile. By 2012, the ratio had grown to ten to one.[48] A 2022 study from the National Association of Realtors found that between 2010 and 2020, about 71 percent of the $8.2 trillion increase in overall home values went to high-income households. High-income homeowners increased their share of total housing wealth from 28 percent in 2010 to 43 percent in 2020.[49] Notably, the key way to drive up values in exclusive neighborhoods, one author says sardonically, is to "work to keep density low and squeeze every undesirable person out to some other, undisclosed location."[50]

The flip side of existing homeowners wanting very high returns on their investment is that it makes housing unaffordable for everyone else—not a particularly agreeable trade-off. "Benjamin from San Francisco" may think that maintaining government policies that inflate market prices is necessary and that reforming unfair policies presents an "existential" threat to the economic well-being of retirees, but what about the truly pressing threat to people like Janet Williams, who live in a world where housing scarcity means having to choose between paying the rent and buying medicine? What about the family that would like to move to a high-wage, high-growth region of the country to improve their lot in life but can't because zoning policies have helped make housing unaffordable?

Rigging zoning policies to inflate property values, just because many existing homeowners want to keep it that way, cannot be the final word. The logic, such as it is, would be analogous to a shareholder in a company that was engaged in anticompetitive behavior complaining that his stock didn't appreciate as quickly after the Justice Department cracked down on unfair competition.

Eliminating exclusionary zoning would not bring property values below market value; it would bring them to the market level by reducing a government distortion of the market. Millions of Americans who are now shut out of the housing market by artificially high prices would benefit from this form of government deregulation.

As we have seen, the second way that exclusionary zoning unfairly produces outsized gains is by facilitating segregation. Recall from Chapter 3 that American families are willing to pay $48,000 extra for a similar home with similar amenities that is located in a predominantly white rather than a predominantly Black neighborhood.[51] Other researchers analyzed the same data and concluded that Americans are paying the extra $48,000 to avoid being near low-income and working-class people, rather than Black people, per se.[52] Either way, it appears wealthy (mostly white) Americans will pay to avoid either race or class integration. And because this group has the most money—and because income inequality is growing in America—houses generally appreciate faster in wealthy white communities than in other areas.[53]

Should we really be concerned that removing artificial barriers to racial and economic integration of housing means that some property owners will no longer reap outsized appreciation gains related to the financial premium wealthy homeowners will pay for segregated settings?

There is, after all, a very long, ugly, and now deeply discredited history in America of invoking "property values" as a reason to exclude. Baltimore's Mayor Mahool justified racial zoning in part "to protect property values among the White majority."[54] In 1924, the reason the National Association of Real Estate Boards said it was "unethical" to integrate neighborhoods was that property values might suffer.[55] The guidance said, "A realtor should never be instrumental in introducing into a neighborhood . . . members of any race or nationality . . . whose presence will clearly be detrimental to property values in the neighborhood."[56] In a 1928 federal report, officials justified exclusionary policies as a way of protecting against "the deteriorating influence of undesirable neighbors."[57] And in the 1930s, federal redlining maps were drawn to withhold much-needed mortgage insurance from would-be home buyers in Black neighborhoods because doing so would allegedly be financially "hazardous" for the federal government. The Federal Housing Administration economist Homer Hoyt's creepy ranking of races and nationalities was based on people's perceived "beneficial effect on land values."[58]

For today's homeowners to complain about removing unfair government-sponsored barriers to people of color and low-income people on the basis of how it might affect the homeowners' property values is a bit like a white person in 1964 complaining that passage of the Civil Rights Act would subject her to new competition from Black people in the job market and thereby hurt her pocketbook.

"THERE THEY GO AGAIN"

A fourth defense of exclusionary zoning invokes the sanctity of the single-family home in the American ideal. Unlike Europe, the United States is a place of wide-open spaces and single-family homes, not crowded, European-style apartments. "There they go again," this line of reasoning suggests. "It's typical liberal overreach, telling people they can't have nice things they enjoy and that all communities need to look alike."

People want single-family homes, which represent the iconic image of the American Dream, the argument runs. Indeed, there are more than a hundred million single-family homes in the United States (compared with forty million multifamily homes).[59] Banning single-family exclusive zoning, critics charge, constitutes typical liberal puritanism, telling people they can't enjoy what they have worked hard for because of supposed social ills it causes. Americans don't want environmentalists telling them they can't have a single-family home because they think it is bad for the planet. In this line of thinking, opposition to single-family exclusive zoning is part of a deeply off-putting strain of judgmental progressivism akin to a vegetarian college student haranguing his parents for eating beef.

We should resist a puritanical uniformity, "Mick from New Mexico" commented in the *New York Times,* and allow communities to exclude through zoning because doing so creates a diversity of neighborhood types. "Forcing every place to be the same would create a bland monoculture. It is similar to forcing every restaurant to be a Burger King." Liberals, this argument suggests, are trying to homogenize communities and make them all the same.

It goes without saying there is nothing wrong with people wanting to enjoy life, including their single-family home. When ill-humored Marxists took the view that it is immoral to relish in the arts and nature in a world where poor people are suffering, declaring that "roses are bourgeois," George Orwell responded appropriately: "Is it politically reprehensible . . . to point out that life is frequently more worth living because of a blackbird's song [or] a yellow elm in October?"[60]

But reforming single-family exclusive zoning will not require a single individual in America to modify or subdivide her home if she does not want to. Quite the opposite: it is the advocate of exclusionary zoning who is supporting a policy that dictates that homeowners can build only one type of housing—a detached single-family home—on their land. Reform doesn't require people to change their homes to improve the environment; it is current policy that forbids an environmentally conscious family from erecting a multifamily unit that is better for the planet.

Mick's concern that reform will make all types of neighborhoods the same is also misplaced. Relaxing zoning prohibitions will not result in every neighborhood looking like Greenwich Village. Neighborhoods are so different to begin with and evolve slowly, so it is inconceivable that every neighborhood would take on the same uniformity as a franchised restaurant. More to the point, if one's concern is with promoting "bland monoculture," isn't that precisely what current laws do—dictate that all the homes of a neighborhood be of a single type, on a single size of lot, all but ensuring a certain level of homogeneity that lacks spice?

AN UNTESTED IDEA

Because the United States has a long history of single-family exclusive zoning going back to the early twentieth century, some argue that radical calls for reform in places like Minneapolis, Charlotte, Oregon, and California are plunging us into an untested set of experiments that could have disastrous results. The truth is, this line of argument suggests, we have no idea whether reforms will lead to greater affordability or increased integration, as proponents suggest. Indeed, the policies could lead to serious unintended consequences.

In fact, however, zoning reforms that bring about greater density— more neighbors—are not radical; we have lots of experience with less-restrictive zoning, both in the United States and abroad.

Parts of the United States have had "missing middle" housing for generations. Historically, many municipalities developed an array of housing options. For example, in Cook County, Illinois, which includes Chicago and its nearby suburbs, fully one-quarter of the housing stock is made up of two- and four-flat buildings.[61] And recall that in New York City, the tightening of zoning codes is a relatively recent phenomenon. Close to half of existing stock in New York City would not comply with new stricter regulations if it were built today. These existing units, many of which are treasured, couldn't be built now because they would be considered to have too many dwelling units for the lot size, cover too much of their lot, or not set aside enough parking spaces.[62]

Many Americans choose to live in mixed-income communities. One researcher has identified thirteen hundred neighborhoods, housing about seven million Americans, that are racially diverse and mixed income, across forty-four of the nation's fifty-two largest metro areas. The Hillcrest community in the New York City borough of Queens, for example, which is home to St. John's University, has a diverse mix of Asian, Russian, Hispanic, Black, and Jewish families, coming from all income groups and divided evenly between those living in apartments and those living in single-family homes.[63]

Nor is the idea of more liberal zoning untested in the rest of the world. Indeed, the United States is actually very much the outlier in giving localities such power to exclude and segregate. One researcher goes so far as to say: "The discretion given to localities to place restrictions on the use of land is unique to the United States, and it has given local communities enormous power to engineer economically exclusive communities."[64]

Indeed, US inattention to the ways zoning can segregate stands in contrast to many other developed nations. According to an international comparison of zoning practices, "the issues of spatial segregation and social exclusion generally are taken more seriously at all levels of government in western Europe and by the European Union than in all but a handful of states in the United States."[65] Consider Japan, Germany, and France.

Whereas zoning in the United States is highly localized, allowing small affluent communities to erect barriers to exclude, in Japan, land use policies are mostly set at the national level.[66] In principle, national policymakers can prioritize the national interest in making housing affordable and less economically segregated rather than local governments, which cater to parochial interests that seek to drive up home values and exclude lower-income families. The theory has played out in practice: Japan is "the clear frontrunner" among ten leading industrial nations in providing "housing plentiful enough so that it is broadly affordable and has stable rents and prices," says one housing expert.[67] One observer marvels: "Japan zoning doesn't have anything resembling single-family zoning."[68] Since 1990, two scholars note, "Tokyo has experienced a huge expansion of its housing stock with little run-up in prices, while similar 'superstar' cities in the U.S. and other industrialized countries have experienced huge price increases but little housing-stock growth."[69] Research also finds that socioeconomic segregation in Japan is relatively low. Japan's largest city, Tokyo, for example, has lower levels of economic segregation than many US and European cities.[70]

Germany, like Japan, has a land use regime that tilts more toward federal control than does the United States. Moreover, Germany provides major federal incentives for localities to adopt zoning that is inclusive.[71] One author writes: "Germany does not mandate that its cities welcome homebuilding. It makes doing so worth their while, by tethering their revenue directly to how many residents they have."[72] In addition, Germany's zoning categories are much more likely to contemplate different types of housing. The concept of single-family exclusive zoning does not exist there.[73] Germany also has no mortgage interest deduction for owner-occupied homes, so people have less incentive to overinvest in housing and then defend that investment zealously with exclusionary zoning.[74]

Some German cities have high housing prices, but for the most part, says one researcher, "Housing is dramatically more affordable in Germany than in hot housing markets elsewhere in Europe or North America."[75] Likewise, in an international comparison, researchers have found that residential segregation in Berlin was considered "moderate to low."[76]

Historically, France has not always had the most progressive housing policies.[77] Its income segregation levels are more like those found in the United States than those in more integrated nations like the Netherlands.[78] But in 2000, France adopted an Urban Solidarity and Renewal (SRU) law to require that most urban municipalities ensure that they have their fair share of social housing—homes that are subsidized but include middle-class as well as low-income families—because that housing historically was concentrated in the suburbs. By 2025, most urban municipalities are supposed to ensure that 25 percent of their housing is publicly supported. (Spain's Catalonia region set a similar goal to ensure that every municipality include social housing as at least 15 percent of its overall housing stock.)[79]

In France, the government imposes tough penalties for failure to accomplish the goal, and many communities are making significant progress. One researcher found: "Between 1999 and 2017, the number of exclusionary municipalities in the Paris region—those with relatively low levels of social housing—declined, from 86 cities with less than 7 percent social housing to just 45."[80] France built 1.8 million public housing units between 2001 and 2019, mostly in desirable locations.[81]

As a result of various efforts abroad, most other wealthy countries are less economically and racially segregated than the United States. In a 2016 analysis of twenty highly developed Organisation for Economic Co-operation and Development (OECD) nations, the United States had the highest level of income segregation among schools.[82] Other researchers have found the United States has higher levels of concentrated ethnic disadvantage than other countries.[83]

DENSITY IS NOT ENOUGH

Progressives raise concerns about zoning reform that are different from those of people in the center and to the right. First, they say, market-based reforms in places like Minneapolis to open up wealthy single-family-zoned neighborhoods to duplexes and triplexes and ADUs are unlikely to lead to big advances in affordability or integration for the lowest-income families. The new units in highly desirable areas are still likely to be out of reach for low-income households. What is really needed, these advocates suggest, is government programs—like the inclusionary zoning for publicly subsidized housing in Montgomery County, Maryland—not deregulation of restrictive zoning. Indeed, some regulations that drive up prices in housing—such as Occupational Safety and Health Administration (OSHA) rules to protect workers, environmental regulations to protect water and air, and safety regulations to ensure that the home is structurally sound—are all wholly legitimate, progressives say.[84]

The critique is half-right. Some zoning regulations are essential, and zoning reform by itself is not sufficient to solve our problems. Having said that, it is equally important not to underestimate the degree to which reform of overly restrictive exclusionary laws and regulations can make an enormous difference in the lives of even the most vulnerable Americans. The fact that reform takes a market-based approach, which can sometimes win support from moderates and libertarians, is a plus, not a reason to shrink from it in horror.

Building safety codes and environmental and worker safety regulations are critical, so long as they are not twisted as a means of exclusion. And reforming zoning laws is not a silver bullet. Because density by itself does not equal affordability, government support for affordable housing is also necessary. If we want to help more people like KiAra Cornelius, we need both to break down zoning barriers that keep them out *and* provide greater financial support for affordable housing.

To begin with, the Section 8 Housing Choice Voucher program that people like McGee and Samantha rely upon is critical. Housing vouchers make an enormous difference in the lives of tenants because the amount they must contribute to rent is capped at 30 percent of their income.[85] But according to the Center for Budget and Policy Priorities, "due to inadequate funding, just 1 in 4 voucher-eligible families received any type of federal rental assistance program."[86] Only 10.2 million Americans—about 3 percent of the total US population—currently receive such assistance.[87]

It is an indefensible shortfall, one researcher argues. "Imagine if we didn't provide unemployment insurance or Social Security to most families who needed these benefits. Imagine if the vast majority of families who applied for food stamps were turned away hungry. And yet this is exactly how we treat most poor families seeking shelter."[88]

Stunningly, more funding is provided in the form of homeownership tax benefits that often benefit wealthier homeowners than direct assistance to poor people. According to a 2022 study, total federal rental assistance programs to states was $48.5 billion in 2020. The scholars noted: "Despite the importance of rental assistance, more federal dollars go to homeownership subsidies like the mortgage interest deduction, which mainly benefit higher-income households, instead of families that struggle the most to afford housing."[89] To rectify this problem, Rep. Ritchie Torres (D-NY) has proposed making Section 8 vouchers a federal entitlement so everyone who needed one would get one.[90]

Likewise, to make sure that Section 8 voucher holders have actual choice, the federal government should pass a law forbidding source-of-income discrimination, which, as noted earlier, is a substantial problem. Among others, Senator Elizabeth Warren (D-MA) has called for making it illegal for landlords to discriminate against renters with federal housing vouchers, just as it currently is illegal to discriminate on the basis of race.[91]

In addition to fighting exclusionary zoning, liberal critics are right to say that policymakers should push for affirmative inclusionary zoning requirements in larger developments. As discussed earlier, communities like Montgomery County, Maryland, require developers to set aside a portion of new housing units to be affordable for low- and moderate-income residents. In exchange, the developer receives a "density bonus," allowing him to create a larger number of high-profit units than the area is zoned for. This benefit for developers has proven critical to the idea's political acceptance. Among the states most dedicated to inclusionary zoning are New Jersey, Massachusetts, Maryland, and California.[92] In all, about four hundred municipalities have inclusionary zoning programs.[93] Altogether, 11 percent of Americans now live in jurisdictions with inclusionary zoning policies.[94]

Reducing exclusionary zoning and promoting inclusionary zoning through a density bonus can be pursued simultaneously because builders will usually want to pursue some marginal amount of density in exchange for setting aside some units for lower-income families. If, for example, a single-family exclusive area is rezoned to allow duplexes, an inclusionary zoning policy could still provide a density bonus to permit small garden apartments so long as some units are available for lower-income families.

If zoning reform is not sufficient by itself, it is nevertheless an essential complement to traditional liberal approaches that focus on greater funding for affordable housing. Increasing the supply of housing (by building duplexes and triplexes or garden apartments rather than single-family homes) is a necessary complement to affordable housing funding. It attacks the problem from what economists call the supply side as well as the demand side. So long as local governments artificially constrain housing supply, affordable housing funding is always going to lag behind because prices will just keep rising.

Even if low-income people cannot themselves buy or rent a new duplex or triplex in an area previously barred from building such units, people like Janet Williams will benefit indirectly through what economists call "filtering." When a middle-class family can buy a new duplex that was previously unavailable, they don't compete to bid up the price of an existing unit of housing. Multiply that thousands of times throughout a metropolitan region and housing prices will stop skyrocketing.[95] By contrast, every time wealthy families block the construction of multifamily housing, they increase the pain felt by people like Williams, and one more family is pushed farther out to the periphery of metropolitan areas, with a long commute, increasing greenhouse gases.

By the same token, although building duplexes or triplexes in a wealthy community won't by itself make that community racially and economically integrated, it will still have a positive effect. Because duplexes and triplexes are somewhat less expensive than single-family homes, on average, a broader range of families will have a shot at living in a high-opportunity neighborhood. As one writer argues, developers are already tearing down large houses in affluent communities like those in Southwest Minneapolis and building even bigger ones. "What if some of those were instead torn down to build triplexes or fourplexes?"[96] Moreover, the creation of missing middle housing provides an opportunity for more moderate-income families to move from renter to homeowner so that they can begin building wealth.

Some question whether there is a market for multifamily housing in what had been a neighborhood of single-family homes. Matt Murphy, who has been developing housing in the Washington, DC, area since the 1980s, counters that skepticism with evidence that developers typically are better off with more density. The land cost is usually the driving force in development today—it accounts for 47 percent of US home values, up from less than 20 percent in the early 1960s.[97] So if someone can build more units on a given plot of land, there is more money to be made.[98] In high-demand areas, builders today often tear down smaller homes to build very large ones to recoup the cost of the land because it is illegal to build multifamily units. This shuts out those looking for starter homes. But builders could often make even more money by creating a duplex or fourplex, which families looking to buy their first home could more readily afford.[99]

The Sightline Institute, a nonprofit research institute based in the Pacific Northwest, has crunched the numbers and notes that whether multifamily development occurs depends in part on how multifamily units are developed and on rental rates in an area. It is costly to tear down existing houses and rebuild new ones, so a duplex that preserves an existing unit and includes an additional one that functions as a duplex is generally more profitable than a teardown. In addition, the more expensive the rent in an area, the more likely it is that builders will construct multifamily units because then they can easily recoup construction costs by taking in multiple rents. On the coast of California, Long Island, and north Seattle, where rents are high, multifamily redevelopment will make economic sense.[100] In other words, the places with the worst housing crises are the mostly likely to see real change.

Some progressives are ideologically reluctant to rely on "deregulation" to achieve the liberal ends of greater inclusion and more affordability. But finding common ground with free market conservatives is a plus politically, and as progressive housing expert Matt Hoffman notes, there are powerful advantages to relying on market-based approaches. Think of it like a "judo match," he says, where "you use your opponent's force and momentum against him or her, to your advantage." He suggests the market usually wins, so why not use market forces—which want to build—to progressive ends to break down exclusionary government barriers that keep prices artificially high and block families from high-opportunity neighborhoods?[101]

At the end of the day, liberals cannot neglect the centrality of zoning reform in making housing better and more equitable. While progressive critics are right that we also need more funding of Section 8 Housing Choice Vouchers and more inclusionary zoning, there can be no ignoring the critical role that zoning plays in the package of necessary reforms to improve the lives of people like Cornelius, McGee, Williams, Samantha, and Tehani. As Sara Bronin of Cornell University notes, "Zoning affects everything that is built in our society. . . . It dictates our economy. It dictates how we relate to each other. It dictates our personal choices, our employment opportunities, our educational opportunities, and so much more." She concludes, "While zoning reform will never, ever be the only solution, it is the root of the structural racism that is embedded in our overall land development laws."[102]

GENTRIFICATION AND DISPLACEMENT

Some critics worry that zoning reform as applied to lower-income neighborhoods will lead to less affordability, not more. Developers will seize on "upzoning" to tear down single-family homes in distressed communities and build luxury condos for the wealthy that will drive out existing residents, this argument suggests. For example, "Sam of Washington DC," responded to my *New York Times* op-ed by arguing that, though those calling for zoning reform in his neighborhood are "flying the banner of racial equity," in fact, "nearly all" the new units "that will be built will be luxury apartments for more lawyers." The reform movement, he said, is driven by developers who "have paid millions into the mayor's campaign."

The paradox of market-rate housing in vulnerable communities, one housing expert says, is that the YIMBYs are right that zoning reform will reduce rents regionally, but new housing could simultaneously "raise rents locally by 'signaling' to the marketplace that the neighborhood is a safe place to invest."[103] This line of argument notes that new dense housing might be of higher quality and therefore more expensive than existing less-dense housing stock. In this way, even if more housing is good for a region's prices, it may be bad for a particular neighborhood, where new development means rising rents. Families will be pushed out as a result.[104]

Gentrification has gotten a very bad name because in some circumstances, arrogant white gentrifiers have driven up prices, displaced long-term residents, and acted in a racist manner toward remaining residents—being quick to call the police over neighbors playing music, for example. When rich and poor people come in close contact with one another and the rich, mostly white residents bully and displace longtime low-income residents of color, the outrage is fully warranted.

Having said that, a number of leading progressive voices have pushed back on this caricature of gentrification and displacement and the role of zoning reform in the process. Four points stand out:

- It's important to distinguish between gentrification (which can be very beneficial to communities by bringing greater investment and improved outcomes for low-income families) and displacement (which can indeed be very harmful to vulnerable populations).
- In most cases, research finds that gentrification does not lead to widespread displacement.

- Zoning reform in wealthy areas and in low-income communities increases the chances that a community can experience the benefits of gentrification while minimizing the downside of displacement.
- And in circumstances where reforms to zoning are leading to displacement, it is critical that officials implement a host of additional reforms—such as inclusionary zoning and housing trusts.

To begin with, it is critical to distinguish between the benefits of gentrification and the harms of displacement. In cases where low-income families are not displaced (a big if, to be sure), those families on the whole report being better off in gentrifying communities.[105] One expert notes, "Homeowners stand to gain a windfall as the value of their property appreciates. Increased retail activity brings more goods and services to once-forlorn areas. With gentrification, residents may no longer find it necessary to travel outside their neighborhood to have a sit-down meal or avail themselves of fresh produce."[106]

More importantly, gentrification (for those who can stay) improves life outcomes. A recent Federal Reserve Bank of Philadelphia study found that "long-term residents and children who are able to stay in gentrifying neighborhoods benefit as opportunity moves to them and poverty declines."[107] Most gentrification—which involves Hispanic, not white, people moving into Black neighborhoods in cities like Los Angeles and New York—improves the life chances of Black youth substantially.[108] One study that paired young Black people growing up in neighborhoods seeing gentrification and those that did not concluded that Black families in gentrifying neighborhoods saw a 28 percent rise in family income, from $30,104 to $38,545. It concluded, "There is strong evidence that when neighborhood disadvantage declines, the economic fortunes of black youth improve, and improve rather substantially."[109] The differences in outcomes "are not attributable to characteristics of the children themselves or to characteristics of their families. They are attributable exclusively to changes in the neighborhood environments surrounding the youth."[110]

The low-income neighborhoods that are in real trouble are the vast majority that remain segregated and untouched by gentrification, such as in parts of the Bronx. One journalist argues, "Segregation and concentrated poverty are the true blights of urban life, despite our fascination with gentrification."[111] While the press focuses an inordinate amount of attention on a small number of gentrifying areas, Cashin observes, in places like Baltimore, "four people lived in a neighborhood that was declining for each person who lived in a reviving or gentrifying area."[112] Isolated Black communities in parts of East and West Baltimore have struggled, particularly after a proposed mass transit line that would connect them to downtown was canceled.[113]

Of course, low-income residents who are pushed out by rising rents are not able to enjoy any of the benefits of gentrification, and their lives are made much worse off. Gentrification can lead to two types of displacement. The first is direct displacement, when zoning reform allows dense luxury housing in places like Silicon Valley.[114] When zoning changes pave the way for new construction, this can attract wealthier residents who are willing to pay more precisely because the units are new. In addition, gentrification can lead to indirect displacement when the influx of wealthy residents down the street brings amenities (such as restaurants and shops) that make a community more desirable to wealthy residents who bid up the rents of nearby properties.[115]

In the worst-case scenario, as one author notes, an influx of white professionals into a distressed neighborhood "culminates in the wholesale displacement and re-segregation."[116] Under these circumstances, communities go from one type of segregation (concentrated poverty) to another (concentrated wealth). In Silicon Valley, the Black population declined by 46 percent between 1990 and 2010, while the population of the region as a whole grew 16 percent.[117] In the Navy Yard and Shaw neighborhoods in Washington, DC, the poverty rates have dropped dramatically.[118] The disruption to families can inflict considerable pain and anguish.

In much of the media narrative, this nightmare scenario is commonplace: gentrification inexorably leads to displacement; rich people move in and poor people move out. But researchers have found this zero-sum game almost never plays out in practice.

One researcher, for example, finds that "longtime residents aren't more likely to move when their neighborhood gentrifies; sometimes they're actually less likely to leave (in part because of the improvements gentrification can bring)." He says, "In one study, I found that the probability that a household would be displaced in a gentrifying neighborhood in New York was 1.3 percent. A 2015 study in Philadelphia found something similar—that neighborhood income gains did not significantly predict household exit rates."[119] In areas that gentrified between 2000 and 2013—such as neighborhoods near the University of Pennsylvania and Temple University—residents were "less than 1 percentage point more likely to move out than those in non-gentrifying ones."[120] A 2019 study examining New York City found "no evidence that gentrification is associated with meaningful changes in mobility rates."[121] The worst-case scenario of the big flip—from concentrated poverty to concentrated affluence and from mostly Black to mostly white—is rare. One analysis found that stories like that in Williamsburg, Brooklyn, where a gentrifying neighborhood went from 14 percent white in 1990 to 67 percent white in 2016, is quite unrepresentative. More typical is the story of New York's West Midtown, which was 38 percent white in 1990 and remained 37 percent white in 2016. Looking at national data, the study concluded: "The neighborhoods that have integrated through gentrification have remained racially integrated for longer periods of time than the conventional wisdom suggests. Many are seeing little change in their white population share in the decades following gentrification."[122]

The third powerful point progressive researchers and writers make is that zoning reform—far from causing displacement—*reduces* the chances that displacement will occur. This is true for zoning reform in both rich areas and poor areas.

To begin with, exclusionary zoning in wealthy areas drives displacement that comes from gentrification. One researcher explains: "If a high-demand, high-cost neighborhood won't build, developers and people looking for housing will be diverted to the nearest low-cost neighborhood."[123] Distressed neighborhoods are ripe choices for new development both because they have cheaper land and because residents are less likely to have the time and resources to mount powerful resistance to new building.[124]

Likewise, changing zoning laws to allow more housing in low-income areas decreases displacement because it reduces the competition between wealthy and low-income families over a fixed number of houses—a competition rich people usually win. In a market economy, if people try to halt displacement by banning new construction, that effort will backfire on low-income families. One observer explained: "When you tell young urban professionals who are moving into these neighborhoods that you are not going to build any housing for them . . . they're *not* going to just say, 'OK, I guess I won't take my Facebook job.'" Instead, "what they're going to do is, they're going to go find whatever housing currently exists and bid up the price of that, because they have to and want to live there for their own personal reasons."[125] In this way, "even new buildings that service higher-income people are an anti-displacement tool."[126]

Research confirms that more housing in low-income areas generally eases rather than accelerates displacement. One 2016 study, for example, found that between 2000 and 2013, displacement in the San Francisco Bay Area was "more than twice as likely" when there were low rates of market-rate housing construction than in areas where there were high rates of construction.[127] The study concluded: "Considerable evidence suggests that construction of market-rate housing reduces housing costs for low-income households, and, consequently, helps to mitigate displacement in many cases."[128] A 2004 study, likewise, found that "a neighborhood's poverty rate could drop from 30 percent to 12 percent in a decade with minimal displacement. That's because gentrification often leads to new construction or to investment in once-vacant properties."[129]

Zoning reform is not the only step that will help garner the benefits of gentrification and racial and economic integration while reducing the possibility of harmful displacement. A number of communities—from Philadelphia to San Francisco—have implemented promising practices that promote integration and minimize displacement.

Philadelphia's Longtime Owner Occupants Program (LOOP), for example, reduces the possibility that long-term homeowners will be displaced because of property tax hikes related to gentrification. LOOP assists those below 150 percent area median income (AMI) who have lived in their homes for over ten years and have experienced at least a threefold increase in assessed home values. The average LOOP participant is a senior citizen who purchased their home in the 1970s and 1980s.[130] An April 2018 report by the Federal Reserve Bank of Philadelphia found that LOOP had proven effective in both reducing tax delinquencies and reducing displacement in gentrifying areas.[131]

Affordable Housing Trust programs like the one used in Cambridge, Massachusetts, provide another good tool to make sure affordable housing remains available in gentrifying areas.[132] Housing trusts use a dedicated stream of revenue (such as from a real estate transfer tax) to build, or preserve, affordable housing options for families. If housing trusts purchase properties early in the gentrification process, they can preserve affordable housing at a more modest cost than if they wait until later, when properties are quite a bit more expensive.[133]

Another smart strategy would prioritize vouchers for families in danger of being displaced by gentrification to help them either stay in an existing property or find another one to their liking.[134] And inclusionary zoning requirements should be put into place to compel developers to set aside some new units in gentrifying areas for low-income and working-class families.[135]

These anti-displacement measures are important on the merits, and they are also important politically. The hard reality is that if zoning reformers do not address concerns about displacement, left-wing NIMBYs are likely to stop reform in its tracks—and communities will remain segregated.[136]

TAKING THE EYE OFF RACE

Finally, some progressive critics may see a focus on issues of income discrimination that are at the core of exclusionary zoning as a distraction from the centrality of race in fights for fair housing. In the United States, some civil rights advocates argue, we are forever trying to change the subject from race. This book's proposal to create an Economic Fair

Housing Act as a supplement to the 1968 Fair Housing Act would detract attention from the fundamental issue of race, this line of argument suggests.[137]

One researcher who supports the idea of an Economic Fair Housing Act also wants to make sure we don't lose sight of the fact that race "plays an outsize role in the housing market." She continues: "Expectation of racial comfort, of white dominance, may explain why most whites still state preferences for majority white neighborhoods." She observes: "Black people remain the group all non-Blacks are least interested in integrating with."[138]

Clearly, race remains a central and fundamental basis for discrimination and segregation in American society, and our housing markets are infused with anti-Black sentiments in particular. To back away from a commitment to opportunities for Black people—by, for example, *replacing* the Fair Housing Act with an Economic Fair Housing Act—would represent a deeply unwise step backward in the fight for racial equality.

Instead, we need to double down on the fight against racial discrimination. We should use all the tools at our disposal, each of which is further discussed in Chapter 7.

- Provide greater funding for audit testing to detect and punish racial discrimination by landlords.
- Dedicate more resources for the Justice Department and private groups to enforce the Fair Housing Act.
- Fully implement the Affirmatively Furthering Fair Housing rule to require jurisdictions receiving federal money to take steps to dismantle racial segregation.
- Step up enforcement of the disparate impact rule that allows plaintiffs to challenge policies that have the effect, even if not the intent, of discriminating by race.

Moreover, adding income discrimination by government zoning to the list of policies that can be attacked by plaintiffs takes nothing away from ongoing efforts to challenge policies that discriminate by race. Indeed, any government funding to enforce the Economic Fair Housing

Act should be provided in a separate appropriation line from funds to enforce the Fair Housing Act so that there is no dilution of the latter.

The civil rights community has long recognized that additions to the Fair Housing Act in no way subtract from the core focus of racial discrimination. Over the years, the circle of protected classes under the Fair Housing Act has widened. The original 1968 law protected against discrimination based on "race, color, religion, and national origin." In the 1970s, sex was added as a protected class. And in 1988, the circle of those categories protected was widened again to include people with disabilities and families with children.[139]

Wade Henderson of the Leadership Conference on Civil and Human Rights explains that members of the civil rights community now want to expand the Fair Housing Act again, to cover discrimination against "the LGBTQ community, families with housing subsidies, and people with criminal records."[140]

Finally, as a practical matter, by allowing plaintiffs of color to challenge exclusionary zoning as economically discriminatory—without going through the extra hurdle of providing statistical evidence that racial minorities are disproportionately impacted—the Economic Fair Housing Act would add a new tool to the arsenal of civil rights groups. Curbing economic zoning, in turn, will reduce racial segregation, as research cited in Chapter 3 found.[141] In that sense, the Economic Fair Housing Act can be seen as an important instrument to address some of the critical unfinished business of the civil rights movement.

SIX

TEARING DOWN THE WALLS
IN LOCAL COMMUNITIES

JANNE FLISRAND, A WHITE MIDDLE-CLASS LIBERAL ACTIVIST IN Minneapolis, came to the issue of housing through her work in education. In the late 1990s, she was running an after-school program tutoring kids from low-opportunity neighborhoods. She was frustrated that "the kids that we were working with and hanging out with kept disappearing." When she'd investigate, she says, the children invariably had "some sort of housing instability story." So Flisrand shifted her focus from education to work supporting subsidized housing for low-income families. After a decade, however, there, too, she felt, "we were continuing to lose ground . . . despite the hundreds of millions of dollars" invested. She began to investigate "these deeper root economic rules" and zoning laws that at the time many "people didn't know about" and that "nobody was talking about."[1]

A community of like-minded individuals in Minneapolis began forming to slowly chip away at exclusionary zoning policies that kept housing scarce and less affordable. In 2014, council member Lisa Bender backed a successful plan to allow residents in single-family-zoned communities to add small in-law flats or accessory dwelling units (ADUs).[2] At the time, one council member raised the specter of ADUs becoming houses of prostitution.[3] But when some 140 ADUs were added and fears were not borne out, Bender was ready for more reform.[4]

So were Flisrand and other activists. In February 2017, a couple of Flisrand's friends, John Edwards and Ryan Johnson, started an art campaign and an associated Twitter account to raise awareness of the ways in which exclusionary zoning hurt people. Edwards and Johnson called their Twitter account "Neighbors for More Neighbors."[5] The name was a brilliant reminder to people of the shared humanity of those who wanted to be included—they were people, too, who simply wanted to be neighbors.

Momentum for reform built when Jacob Frey, a young candidate for mayor of Minneapolis and himself a renter, made affordable housing "one of the centerpieces of his campaign."[6] In November 2017, activists were thrilled when Frey—just thirty-six years old—was elected mayor. Five new members were elected to the city council. The council as a whole now had twelve Democrats and one member of the Green Party.[7] In January 2018, the council elevated then-thirty-nine-year-old Lisa Bender—leader of the earlier ADU fight—to be council president.

The generational shift was important, Flisrand says. The split in Minneapolis over housing was not so much Republican versus Democrat, but older Democrats versus younger ones. The younger elected officials, she notes, "get how housing, racial justice, school success, school segregation, and climate and all these other issues fit together" in a way that some older Democrats did not.[8]

In March 2018, word leaked to the media that the city council was considering allowing duplexes, triplexes, and fourplexes in areas previously zoned exclusively for single-family homes.[9] Critics were especially contemptuous of the provision to allow fourplexes, which opponents labeled "freyplexes" after the mayor.[10] Council member Andrew Johnson in Ward 12 said the zoning reform proposal would be received "like a lead balloon" by his constituents.[11]

"Quite a few council members reacted negatively," Flisrand recalls, but the flip side was that advocates were also energized.[12] She teamed up with Edwards and Johnson to create a new grassroots umbrella organization, taking the name of the Neighbors for More Neighbors Twitter account, to support Frey and Bender to do something no major city had ever accomplished: legalize duplexes and triplexes throughout an entire city in one fell swoop.[13] Usually reforms to relax zoning laws are fought community by community. But Minneapolis wanted to legalize "missing middle" homes throughout the city.

People were beginning to wake up to the idea, Flisrand says, that "there aren't enough homes for all the people who want to live in a growing city and that that is harmful in a whole host of different ways."[14] Flisrand says the draft proposal "was clearly pushing us somewhere we hadn't been yet." For advocates of change, "it injected a lot of energy. It gave people something to show up for and fight for."[15] While in the past, council and zoning meetings had been dominated by folks saying, "I love my neighborhood and I don't want it to change," suddenly new voices were calling for housing that was more abundant and affordable. "That made it feel possible," she says.[16]

But the odds were still very long, and there was plenty of reason to be skeptical. The proposal represented a big political lift and would require a major culture change. A city of 425,000 residents, Minneapolis had at the time one of the most stringent zoning policies, having banned duplexes, triplexes, and larger apartment buildings from 70 percent of its residential land. In New York City, by comparison, just 15 percent of residential land is set aside for single-family homes.[17]

And there was the reality that no major city had ever done what Minneapolis was trying to do. Indeed, dating back to the 1960s, people who tried to make changes almost invariably failed. Although there has long been a consensus among researchers that single-family zoning is bad for housing affordability, bad for the environment, and bad for racial justice, there has been an equally durable political consensus that little could be done to change these policies.

Such policies have been ubiquitous—"practically gospel in America," says the *New York Times*—and have long been viewed as impossible to reform.[18] As one journalist noted, increasing the supply of housing by relaxing restrictions runs into a classic political problem: "a lot of the beneficiaries are really diffuse," because those who would be better off from more building don't even live in a given neighborhood. Meanwhile, "the people who view themselves as being harmed are really concentrated."[19]

A researcher at Dartmouth coined the idea of the "homevoter hypothesis"—that, because homeowners place most of their assets into their homes, they fiercely resist development. Increased supply, as cartels like OPEC know, threatens rising prices.[20] And homeowners often fear that development might bring changes to the neighborhood that could negatively affect property values in *their* neighborhoods, the national research on the issue notwithstanding. Accordingly, when proposals surface to liberalize exclusionary single-family zoning, wealthy, white homeowners often show up in force, and older, male, white homeowners tend to dominate meetings.[21]

THE LONG HISTORY OF FAILED ZONING REFORM ATTEMPTS

Tackling exclusion in housing has always been a dicey political issue for progressives, and potentially career-ending. In 1966, Senator Paul Douglas of Illinois and Governor Pat Brown of California both lost their seats because they championed fair housing.[22]

In 1970, as noted earlier, Richard Nixon's secretary of housing and urban development George Romney proposed the ill-fated Open Communities program that would have withheld federal infrastructure aid to jurisdictions that employed exclusionary zoning that discriminated against poor or minority families.[23] But Nixon, fearing a backlash, killed the program.[24]

Because the politics of zoning change were so tough, reformers turned to litigation. In 1975, the New Jersey Supreme Court granted a victory in the *Mount Laurel* decision requiring that each community provide a "fair share" of affordable housing, and it gave the decision further teeth in the 1983 *Mount Laurel II* decision. But backlash was fierce. Tom Kean, who was governor of New Jersey from 1982 to 1990 and who is today regarded as one of the last of the liberal Republicans, called the *Mount Laurel II* decision "communistic," and he sought a constitutional amendment to limit the state supreme court's ability to decide zoning cases.[25]

Chris Christie, New Jersey's pugnacious Republican governor from 2010 to 2018, was also a fierce critic of the *Mount Laurel* decisions and of the Council on Affordable Housing, which was created to enforce the "fair share" requirement. When running for governor, Christie promised to "gut the mandates, gut the quotas, and gut the fees" imposed by the Council on Affordable Housing.[26] As governor, Christie issued an executive order in 2010 that sought to abolish the Council on Affordable Housing and transfer its duties to an agency under his control, but the effort was blocked by the courts.[27] In 2015, after Christie continued to seek to weaken the implementation of *Mount Laurel*, the New Jersey Supreme Court itself abolished the Council on Affordable Housing and decided that lower courts themselves must review local compliance with the *Mount Laurel* decision.[28] In the Mount Laurel community itself, there was strong resistance, and it took thirty-one years of fighting and litigation before a one-hundred-unit affordable housing project finally opened its doors.[29]

So, too, in the liberal Baltimore, Maryland, region, one of the metropolitan areas that participated in the Moving to Opportunity program, the small-scale federal housing integration plan spawned major backlash from white residents in the early 1990s. In response, the normally liberal Maryland US senator Barbara Mikulski, who chaired the Senate Appropriations Subcommittee with jurisdiction over HUD, rescinded $171 million earmarked for expanding the program.[30]

If all this weren't discouraging enough, Minneapolis activists watched as zoning reform in deep-blue California crashed and burned in early 2018. California state senator Scott Wiener, a San Francisco Democrat, drafted SB 827 to eliminate zoning restrictions for developers who wish to build apartments up to eighty-five feet tall (about eight stories) within a half mile of train stations and a quarter mile of high-frequency bus stops.[31]

The bill had a lot going for it. In California, the unaffordability of housing is legendary. Silicon Valley employers were having trouble attracting employees given the price of homes. According to a 2016

McKinsey Institute report, California needed to build 2 million units to meet existing demand, and a total of 3.5 million units to meet expected growth in demand by between 2016 and 2025. McKinsey further found that if local governments rezoned areas within half a mile of transit stops, there would be room for California to potentially build an estimated 1.2 to 3 million new housing units by 2025.[32]

By focusing on development near transit, Wiener was seeking to merge the affordability and environmental concerns so pressing for many Californians in the service of curtailing exclusionary zoning. The bill received extravagant praise from some corners. For example, *Boston Globe* columnist Dante Ramos said SB 827 "may be the biggest environmental boon, the best job creator, and the greatest strike against inequality that anyone's proposed in the United States in decades."[33]

Wiener knew that rich suburbs like Beverly Hills would oppose reform. But in early 2018, a number of community groups and urban city councils also came out in opposition. By focusing on communities close to transit—rather than wealthy communities that were exclusionary—the bill's authors unwittingly united wealthy and low-income communities that did not want to see development.[34]

Some progressive social activists worried that new development alongside transit stops could accelerate displacement that can come with gentrification.[35] In February 2018, thirty-seven housing and tenant advocacy groups came out in opposition to SB 827 in part because its focus was market-based housing, not publicly subsidized homes.[36]

In March 2018, Los Angeles mayor Eric Garcetti and the Los Angeles City Council came out in unanimous opposition to the legislation, arguing that many of the city's neighborhoods of single-family homes would lose their character if the bill were enacted.[37] (The bill would have affected almost 50 percent of single-family homes in Los Angeles.)[38] The opposition would ultimately prove lethal. One local housing advocate noted, "The California Legislature is not going to pass a land use bill unanimously opposed by the Los Angeles City Council and the city's mayor."[39]

YIMBY activists, who were mostly highly educated white people, grew frustrated and some acted obnoxiously. In early April 2018, at a

YIMBY rally in San Francisco, supporters shouted down protesters of color, lecturing them to "read the bill."[40] The legislation ultimately died on a 7–4 committee vote on April 17, 2018.[41] Boston University researchers note that a "fissure between relatively advantaged YIMBYs and affordable housing advocates was a key factor in the demise of SB 827."[42]

In the long run of attempted political reforms—from the late 1960s to the California debacle in 2018—zoning reform victories were few and far between. One limited exception was in Massachusetts, and even there, as we saw in Chapter 4, exclusion remains the rule. In 1969, the state did pass an anti–snob zoning law that empowered state officials to alter local zoning laws in communities where less than 10 percent of housing stock was deemed affordable and where developers proposed that at least 20 to 25 percent of new units be affordable. In 2010, an effort to overturn the law through a statewide referendum was opposed by 58 percent of voters.[43] But just as Massachusetts was the lone state to vote for George McGovern in 1972, its modest program was, in the spring of 2018, very much the outlier nationally. And even in Massachusetts, with its special law, single-family exclusive zoning in places like Weston and Wellesley remains entrenched.[44] If Minneapolis activists were looking for precedents, they didn't have much to go on.

THE MINNEAPOLIS MIRACLE

Janne Flisrand and other Minneapolis activists knew all of this history, but they set out to win, and to do things differently from how activists had in other places. Critically, Neighbors for More Neighbors adopted a strategy that included racial equity as a key theme and formed alliances with community groups to ensure that people not normally heard from—those hurt by exclusionary zoning—were a part of the conversation rather than just wealthier white NIMBY homeowners.

Supporters of reform also knew that in order to be successful, they needed to push a suite of comprehensive changes to supplement the signature issue of eliminating single-family exclusive zoning. Accordingly, the proposal also created the possibility of more housing density near

transit stops by allowing the construction of new three- to six-story
buildings. It proposed eliminating off-street minimum parking requirements, which can make development too costly. It provided for inclusionary zoning—requiring that new apartment developments set aside
10 percent of units for moderate-income households. And it proposed
increasing funding for affordable housing from $15 million to $40 million to combat homelessness and provide immediate relief to low-income
renters.[45] (Research would later show that some of these additional provisions had an even more immediate impact on improving housing affordability than did the elimination of single-family exclusive zoning,
which provoked so much controversy.)[46]

Neighbors for More Neighbors and their allies capitalized on the
fact that Minneapolis, by law, was required every ten years to go through
a major planning process. The community is forced to step back and
think big about the region's needs. In the larger framework, known as
"Minneapolis 2040," the city articulated several goals, but three in particular stood out: making the city's housing more affordable by building more of it; making the city fairer by reducing racial and economic
segregation; and combating climate change by reducing commutes and
making housing more environmentally friendly.

First, proponents of the 2040 plan argued, single-family exclusive zoning was driving a major affordability problem in Minneapolis.
Studies found that housing supply wasn't keeping up with growth. The
Metropolitan Council suggested that the city had built only sixty-four
thousand new homes since 2010 while adding eighty-three thousand
households.[47] With too many residents chasing too few housing options,
the city had an apartment vacancy rate as low as 2.2 percent.[48] (Economists suggest a 5 percent vacancy rate is one that will produce a healthy
environment in which rents don't exceed inflation.)[49] "When you have
demand that is sky-high, and you don't have the supply to keep up with
it, prices rise. Rents rise," noted Mayor Frey.[50]

More than half of Minneapolis's residents were renters, and half of
those renters were "cost burdened," meaning they were spending more
than 30 percent of their income on rent.[51] Moreover, the problem was
projected to persist in the future. The Family Housing Fund estimated

that Minneapolis was only on pace to build about three-quarters of the needed housing in coming decades.[52] Building more units, supporters said, would put supply and demand back in balance and reduce unhealthy upward pressure on housing prices.

Second, advocates of the 2040 plan argued that exclusionary single-family zoning should end because it fosters economic and racial segregation, which harms the community. "Large swaths of our city are exclusively zoned for single-family homes, so unless you have the ability to build a very large home on a very large lot, you can't live in the neighborhood," Mayor Frey told *Slate*.[53] As a result, families of different races and incomes often lived in different parts of the city—a problem common in American metropolitan areas with exclusionary zoning.

In 2018, Minneapolis's population was 60 percent white, 19 percent Black, 10 percent Hispanic, and 6 percent Asian, but this diverse population tended to live in very different parts of the community.[54] Many North Side households struggled economically, and 70 percent of its residents were people of color, whereas the South Side was more affluent and white.[55]

In the campaign for change, Flisrand and others put racial and economic justice front and center. Of fourteen goals outlined by supporters of the 2040 plan, eliminating racial, ethnic, and economic disparities was goal number one.[56] Proponents of 2040 pointed directly to the role of single-family zoning in fostering segregation.[57] Reformers explicitly pointed out the connection between local zoning and redlining. "Today's zoning is built on those old redlining maps," said the city's long-range planning director Heather Worthington.[58] Minneapolis City Council president Lisa Bender argued that Minneapolis had "codified racial exclusion through zoning."[59] Proponents of change highlighted the historical record. "That history," said Councilman Cam Gordon, "helped people realize that the way the city is set up right now is based on the government-endorsed and sanctioned racist system."[60] By owning up to its past, says *Slate*'s Henry Grabar, Minneapolis was "one of the rare U.S. metropolises to publicly confront the racist roots of single-family zoning."[61]

Advocates of zoning reform like Kyrra Rankine argued: "Zoning is the new redlining."[62] And supporters of change drew a direct line between the troublesome history of single-family zoning and contemporary racial disparities in Minneapolis. The 2040 plan noted that the gap in homeownership rates between white people (59 percent) and African Americans (21 percent) was enormous.[63] Indeed, it was the widest in any of the one hundred cities with sizable African American populations.[64]

Proponents of reform also connected zoning, race, and schools. The South Side of Minneapolis, which is primarily zoned for single-family homes, contained fourteen of the fifteen public schools that are rated as high performing.[65] The southwest quadrant of Minneapolis, which is particularly white and affluent, "is like the suburb in the city," says Rankine.[66] In theory, public school choice could equalize opportunities for low-income students living in high-poverty neighborhoods. But in Minneapolis, choice tended to exacerbate, rather than alleviate, segregation.[67] Although low-income Minneapolis students can theoretically request a transfer to a high-performing school outside their attendance area, affluent schools tend to be overcrowded already.[68] Even when low-income families know of the opportunities, those requests can be rejected on the basis of space constraints (which is typical). Moreover, families are required to provide their own transportation—a major hardship for those who are low-income.[69] Proponents of reform stressed that access to high-performing schools matters, because powerful evidence suggests that low-income students perform much better, on average, when given the opportunity to attend such schools.[70]

The third argument advanced by Neighbors for More Neighbors and other proponents of 2040's plan to eliminate single-family exclusive zoning and build more housing near transit stops was that it would be good for the environment. This argument had special resonance with young people. Single-family zoning, one observer noted in writing about Minneapolis, is "a policy that has done as much as any to entrench . . . sprawl."[71]

As expected, Neighbors for More Neighbors and other proponents of reform faced a strong backlash from wealthy white homeowners who didn't want change. Critics called the elimination of single-family zoning a gift to developers, who would change the "character" of neighborhoods by overbuilding. Red signs emblazoned with the slogan DON'T BULLDOZE OUR NEIGHBORHOOD proliferated, particularly in wealthy southwestern Minneapolis.[72] Town meetings became vitriolic.[73] Critics charged that developers would just tear down starter homes and build high-end duplexes and triplexes that would do nothing to actually help those seeking affordable housing—an argument that overlooked the basic rule of economics that increased supply of any kind reduces prices overall in a community.[74]

The Audubon Chapter of Minneapolis, ignoring the evidence cited by other environmentalists about how single-family zoning contributes to climate change, brought a lawsuit to stop the policy from moving forward. The suit argued that more housing development, and more people, in Minneapolis, would mean more pollution (something that is true but that also evades the obvious point that a growing population will require new housing *somewhere*).[75] According to the *Minneapolis Tribune*, "Defenders of single-family neighborhoods dominated the thousands of online comments submitted to the city."[76]

In many jurisdictions, this array of opposition might have ended any possible reform. But in Minneapolis, Neighbors for More Neighbors and other groups fought back, point by point. Reformers vehemently denied the idea that they were in the pocket of developers. Some developers, of course, have a strong interest in loosening rules on development and increasing density, but Flisrand says the story is more complex and developers were actually split on the 2040 proposal. Whereas some developers would benefit, other developers would lose their competitive edge that derives from their political access and ability to navigate the current complex web of regulations.[77]

Moreover, the specter of an army of new bulldozers taking over neighborhoods with single-family homes was ludicrous, supporters of the 2040 plan said, because people were of course free to keep their homes as is. In addition, neighbors were already tearing down starter homes to build McMansions. What was so wrong with a developer instead building three small units in a building of the same size?[78] In fact, supporters of the 2040 plan pointed out that a ringleader of the opposition, as it turned out, lived in a 4,500-square-foot house that had been erected after a smaller home was bulldozed.[79]

The "character" of neighborhoods might change with the addition of some duplexes and triplexes, supporters of the 2040 plan said, but wouldn't it be a step forward if a community's character came to include people from different walks of life? Likewise, it might be true that some builders would develop high-end units under the new rules, but even that would reduce overall housing costs in other units, supporters noted, by easing demand for existing homes.[80] Furthermore, the inclusionary zoning requirements for new apartment buildings erected under the 2040 plan meant that even high-end developments would have some units that were affordable.

Finally, to blunt criticisms about "freyplexes," supporters of the 2040 plan modestly scaled it back to allow duplexes and triplexes, but not fourplexes, in areas previously zoned for single-family homes.[81] General requirements about height and yard space remained unchanged in those zones, making duplexes and triplexes less daunting for neighbors.[82]

Flisrand and other activists knew that good arguments for zoning reform had been around forever. To get the proposal across the finish line, they also needed to build a new coalition that included new voices not normally heard in fights over zoning. Many of the core activists in Neighbors for More Neighbors were, like their YIMBY (Yes in My Backyard) movement counterparts in California, white, highly educated, and upper middle class.[83] Organizers recognized that, as such, they should only be part of a much larger, more socioeconomically and racially diverse coalition in favor of reform that included civil rights groups and labor (as well as environmentalists and seniors).[84] Minneapolis wanted to learn from the lessons of the spring 2018 failure in California: the importance of making alliances with more diverse community groups and the need to address displacement concerns.[85]

It was natural to ally with civil rights groups in Minneapolis given that civil rights groups nationally had been in the fight against exclusionary zoning long before YIMBY even existed. The NAACP had been the key plaintiff in the 1975 *Mount Laurel* case in New Jersey. And the NAACP Legal Defense Fund had been a leader in "disparate impact" litigation, under which exclusionary zoning can be struck down when it has the effect of discriminating by race, even if intent is not shown.[86]

Unlike in California, where the gentrification and displacement concerns drove community groups into an unholy alliance with wealthy towns, Minneapolis reformers wanted to address displacement concerns early on. That is why they insisted on writing inclusionary zoning requirements into the plan to compel developers to set aside some new units for low-income and working-class people. And the significant commitment to boost affordable housing funding made clear that YIMBY groups weren't advocating a purely market-based approach to reform.

Supporters of the 2040 plan also put a major emphasis on gathering authentic input from community groups in the engagement process, an important step too often ignored. The issue-based organization African Career, Education, and Resource, for example, supported the 2040 plan with extensive community engagement, at church meetings and community meetings, on the basis of the philosophy, says the group's program director Denise Butler, that "community members are the stakeholders and they are the true experts of their environment."[87] Activists wanted to reach out to constituencies in Minneapolis who could tell the story of how they were personally hurt by exclusionary zoning, the way KiAra Cornelius, Janet Williams, and Tehani did in Columbus, Patricia McGee did in Dallas, and Samantha did in Springfield.

Activists knew that wealthy white homeowners were going to make their voices heard.[88] It was critical that lower-income communities, immigrant communities, and communities of color have a seat at the table too. And so, says Flisrand, "The city made a point of creating an engagement pathway" for marginalized communities.[89] Indeed, if there was a secret ingredient in Minneapolis's success, it was community engagement, Flisrand said.[90] The city engaged in a multiyear effort to gain input.[91] The city's Long Range Planning Team within the Community Planning and Economic Development Department recognized explicitly that, "historically, people of color and indigenous communities (POCI), renters, and people from low-income backgrounds have been underrepresented in the civic process."[92] Going back to 2016, planners attended festivals and street fairs. The city also encouraged residents to hold "Meetings in a Box," whereby individuals were provided forms and surveys to seek input from community members at a time and place that was convenient.[93]

Running parallel to this process, Neighbors for More Neighbors helped community members attend the council meetings, heavily covered by the media, and encouraged people to wear purple so that supporters could find one another and feel comfortable.[94] The group also created purple lawn signs that said END THE SHORTAGE; BUILD HOMES NOW and NEIGHBORS FOR MORE NEIGHBORS that sent a positive signal that we "want a city that is growing and welcoming." In the end, says Flisrand, "Instead of hearing the same old powerful perspectives, we got to hear diverse perspectives."[95]

Neighbors for More Neighbors also worked closely with organized labor and tenant groups that were deeply affected by the ways in which single-family exclusive zoning drives up prices of housing for everyone in a community. Tenant groups, which in some cities have organized rent strikes and historically have been important instigators of housing reform, had good reason to support change.[96] Policy 41 in the package of Minneapolis 2040 reforms called for taking several steps to protect tenant rights. Among the provisions was one to "provide funding to community-based organizations that proactively help tenants understand and enforce their rights, and assist financially with emergency housing relocation."[97]

Labor unions—particularly those with low-income and minority membership—were also an important part of the push for the 2040 plan. The Service Employees International Union (SEIU) Healthcare Minnesota, which represents a large number of mostly low-income healthcare workers, provided critical political muscle for the coalition.[98] Rick Varco, political director of SEIU Healthcare Minnesota, explained that, though his union mostly focuses on statewide issues, his members convinced him that local housing issues were of critical concern. Members told Varco they couldn't afford to live in Minneapolis, near their jobs, and so many would have to take a "two and one half hour bus ride, with two transfers, to get to work." For many of SEIU's members, "housing is just an enormous cost for them," so the union realized "it was important for us to do and say something about it," he says.[99] In October 2018, Varco testified in favor of the 2040 plan before the City Planning Commission, noting the change in zoning would reduce housing costs without costing the city a penny. The current system of exclusionary zoning, he said, "simply elevates a few winners while depriving the large mass of workers the housing they need."[100] In a resolution, SEIU also noted that 2040 would help the economy and "promote union construction jobs."[101]

Most environmental groups (Audubon notwithstanding) also provided strong support for the 2040 plan. The Sierra Club and MN 350, a group fighting climate change, were both important in the 2040 plan effort.[102] As noted in Chapter 2, environmentalists generally favor density and smart growth and have for years decried urban sprawl, which causes longer driving commutes, as a "threat to our environment."[103] Density usually means more walkability and access to public transportation. Density also reduces the carbon footprint of housing because housing units that are closer together have lower heating and cooling costs.[104]

Faith groups, too, can be an important part of the coalition for change. Most major religious traditions emphasize the dignity of individuals, a principle that exclusionary zoning policies implicitly challenge by deeming some of our fellow human beings so degraded they should be excluded from entire jurisdictions. The Neighbors for More Neighbors slogan evoked the common humanity of God's children.

Many young people also supported the 2040 plan as a way of making Minneapolis neighborhoods more affordable, diverse, and walkable.[105] Millennials are less economically secure than their parents or grandparents were when they were the same ages, and they feel the housing affordability pinch acutely.[106] In addition, two-thirds of young people report being lonely (compared with one-third of all Americans).[107] So many are seeking housing that allows them to meet interesting people in walkable communities.[108] Part of the motivation is practical: because millennials change jobs frequently, they are looking to reside "in heavily networked urban spaces rather than isolated, sprawling suburban locations," research suggests.[109] Finally, progressive millennials are often more racially and environmentally conscious than their elders.[110] In many cities, young parents have fought for school integration and are natural allies in fighting for housing integration as a vehicle for integrating neighborhood schools.[111]

Paradoxically, some older Minneapolis residents also supported reform, often for very different reasons. Of course some older, wealthier residents resisted Minneapolis 2040, but others supported it, as did the American Association of Retired Persons (AARP). The group has pushed for more flexibility to build backyard cottages or to subdivide a home into multiple units as a way for elderly residents to "age in place" while bringing in extra income from tenants.[112] Other elderly individuals have backed efforts to legalize accessory dwelling units as a way for grandparents to live close to children and grandchildren (spawning the so-called PIMBY movement, "parents in my backyard").[113] Multifamily options can also be attractive to retirees who want to move out of a big, lonely house but who are not yet ready to move into assisted living.

Remarkably, the new coalition prevailed against once-invincible NIMBY forces.

On December 7, 2018, the Minneapolis City Council adopted what the *New York Times* called the "simple and brilliant" idea of ending single-family exclusive zoning citywide.[114] By a 12–1 vote, the city council legalized duplexes and triplexes on what had been single-family lots, which "effectively triples the housing capacity" in many neighborhoods.[115] (The one holdout was a council member from the wealthy southwestern section of Minneapolis, where schools are mostly white.)[116] The accomplishment was unprecedented. "No municipality has taken a more dramatic response to the housing gap than Minneapolis," one observer noted.[117]

Notably, supporters of the 2040 plan say its bold, sweeping scope may have made it easier to pass than more incremental reform. Traditionally, reformers have sought to "upzone" neighborhoods piece by piece, in part based on the theory that upzoning an entire city would consolidate opposition from disparate neighborhoods. But Minneapolis's director of long-range planning Heather Worthington says going big—citywide—turned out to be a political advantage. "If we were going to pick and choose, the fight I think would have been even bloodier."[118] When only some neighborhoods are chosen for change, locals can feel singled out.[119]

REFORM SPREADS TO OREGON, CHARLOTTE, AND CALIFORNIA

Was Minneapolis a one-off, a liberal unicorn in housing policy? Or could some of the strategies employed be applied successfully elsewhere? On one level, there was some reason for skepticism that the 2040 plan's success could be exported to other cities. *Forbes* magazine rated Minneapolis the sixth most liberal city in the United States.[120] Of the thirteen members of the city council, the only non-Democratic member was from the Green Party.[121] Would a more conservative jurisdiction provide tougher terrain for reform, critics wondered?

On the other hand, the politics of zoning reform are complicated. As noted in Chapter 4, politically liberal jurisdictions actually have *more* restrictive zoning and conservatives have their own reasons to oppose exclusionary zoning. In June 2019, President Trump's Housing and Urban Development (HUD) secretary Ben Carson—who otherwise has a troubling record on fair housing issues—visited Minneapolis and said he would like other cities to follow suit and eliminate single-family zoning.[122] "Look at some of the places that have the biggest homelessness problems, like Los Angeles, where 80 percent of the land is zoned for single-family housing, with a certain amount of property," he said. "The correlation seems very strong. The more zoning restrictions and regulations, the higher the prices and the more homeless people."[123] Also in June 2019, President Trump signed an executive order creating the White House Council on Eliminating Regulatory Barriers to Affordable Housing, headed by Carson, to study exclusionary zoning laws.[124]

As we shall discuss later, Trump and Carson subsequently reversed themselves during the 2020 presidential campaign.[125] But in general, right-leaning libertarians were enthusiastic about the Minneapolis plan. Christian Britschgi, writing in the libertarian *Reason* magazine, hailed Minneapolis's plan as "one of the most deregulatory housing reforms in the country," an embodiment of "libertarian policies." He wrote: "Free marketers should celebrate the vote."[126] Rick Varco, the SEIU political director in Minnesota, says he thinks some conservatives would support banning single-family zoning in other cities. "Small-government conservatives," who want to get "the government out of the business of telling people they can't build," along with "fiscal conservatives" who want "to grow the tax base," might support reform of single-family zoning, he says.[127]

Reform has indeed spread in several places, from Berkeley, California, to Gainesville, Florida; from Montgomery County, Maryland, to Raleigh, North Carolina; from Connecticut to Arkansas to Maine and Utah.[128] In addition, legislation to end single-family exclusive zoning has also been introduced in Nebraska, Virginia, New York, and Washington.[129] But the biggest victories to date have been in Oregon, in June 2019; Charlotte, in June 2021; and California, which overcame earlier opposition to pass bipartisan reform in the most populous state in the country in September 2021.

In Oregon, reformers were watching Minneapolis closely. "When Minneapolis took the bold step to address their crisis, it created a sense of momentum," said Oregon House Speaker Tina Kotek, the driving force behind reform in the state (and now the state's governor).[130] Remarkably, in 2019, Oregon actually upped Minneapolis's ante by taking zoning reform statewide and forming a bipartisan coalition in the process.[131]

In what's been called a historic development, on June 30, 2019, a bipartisan group of legislators passed House Bill 2001, a statewide ban on single-family exclusive zoning in cities with populations of at least ten thousand residents. In all those cities, parcels that had been reserved for single-family homes must allow duplexes; and in cities with populations larger than twenty-five thousand, lots that had been limited to single-family homes must also allow multifamily units up to fourplexes.[132] The law and subsequent state rulemaking also limited the ability of jurisdictions to impose onerous off-street parking requirements, "making HB 2001 the largest state-level parking reform law in U.S. history," according to the Sightline Institute.[133] The plan, which was signed by the governor in August 2019, has particular significance for Oregon's biggest city, Portland, in which 77 percent of residential land had been limited to single-family homes.[134]

For supporters of HB 2001 to prevail, they had to overcome opposition of the Oregon League of Cities, which, like organizations representing municipalities nationwide, jealously guarded its prerogative to set zoning rules on a local basis.[135] In addition, neighborhood associations in liberal cities such as Portland, Eugene, and Corvallis argued against reform, saying it would threaten the character of their neighborhoods.[136]

But supporters were able to overcome opposition through a combination of strong political leadership, reliance on a history of state involvement in zoning, the formation of a broad coalition, and the use of smart messaging.

To begin with, it was critical that House Speaker Tina Kotek, who represented Portland, and was the first openly lesbian Speaker of any state house in the country, led the effort.[137] As Speaker, she had the political savvy and muscle to see the idea to success. In addition, Oregon has a long history of asserting state authority over zoning and had already established the principle that all Oregon cities should be open to people of all incomes.[138] In 2017, Oregon passed Senate Bill 1051, which legalized accessory dwelling units (ADUs) in cities across the state, so legislators were familiar with the arguments for more housing.[139]

As in Minneapolis, a broad coalition of liberal groups joined in. Housing tenant organizations and labor unions emphasized the ways in which exclusionary zoning makes housing unaffordable. Racial justice activists were concerned about the way exclusionary zoning has been used to perpetuate racial segregation. Environmental activists knew how exclusionary zoning damages the planet. And groups representing elderly persons saw how older people could benefit. An umbrella group, 1,000 Friends of Oregon, coordinated efforts.[140]

Young people were also part of the coalition. Representative Julie Fahey, a Democrat from Eugene, emphasized the difficulty that families had in buying starter homes. Many people "might not be able to afford to buy a detached single-family home," she noted. "The prices of those starter homes are rising further and further out of reach. So to have duplexes, to have town homes, those sort of things . . . is really important."[141]

In Oregon, the Sightline Institute concluded that positive framing was also critical to success. Supporters of change emphasized to people not what they were giving up but rather what they were gaining. "Almost no one thinks 'single family zoning' is outrageous," write Sightline's Michael Andersen and Anna Fahey. "But when you tell people that duplexes are illegal to build in most of the United States and Canada, most people do actually find this outrageous."[142] Legalizing duplexes, triplexes, and apartments as the message is more popular than ending single-family zoning. As Speaker Kotek noted, "I grew up in a single-family home." She said: "This isn't about single-family homes. This is about choice. This is about the future, this is about allowing for different opportunities in neighborhoods that are currently extremely limited."[143]

Likewise, Sightline's messaging research suggests, when people say they worry about loss of "neighborhood character," advocates should point out that people matter more than buildings. "It's neighbors who give a community character. . . . When we allow only certain expensive building types, it determines who can or cannot afford to live in a community," say Fahey and Andersen.[144] In addition, they advise: be concrete about what's being proposed—use pictures of duplexes and triplexes, they say, so that people's minds do not erroneously go immediately to skyscrapers.

The passage of statewide legislation in Oregon was an enormously significant addition to Minneapolis's success in part because states need to be key actors in reform of zoning. As a matter of constitutional law, states possess the fundamental authority to zone, which they have generally delegated to localities. But when localities have abused their authority by excluding people and artificially increasing housing prices for everyone, the state has a responsibility to look out for all residents and provide some fairness guidelines to ensure that zoning promotes the public interest.

Political science 101 says statewide leaders will see the broader impact of local actions in a different way than local, parochial actors do. And empirical research backs up this finding. In a 2016 study examining ninety-five large metropolitan areas, Michael Lens and Paavo Monkkonen found that "more local pressure to regulate land use is linked to higher rates of income segregation" and that "income segregation is lower when state governments have more power over land use decision-making."[145]

The other feature that makes Oregon's reform stand out is its bipartisan nature. Unlike in Minneapolis, the Oregon coalition for reform extended beyond just liberals and Democrats. Speaker Kotek's staff led an intentionally bipartisan working group to design the legislation.[146] The coalition for reform included progressive groups, like Habitat for Humanity, AARP, and the NAACP.[147] But it also included groups like the Oregon Association of Realtors and Oregon Home Builders Association.[148] The support of both realtors and the homebuilders was said to be especially important to motivating Republican legislators.[149]

The support of realtors and homebuilders was not foreordained because interests can be divided within each of those communities and the politics of realtors and developer interest can be complicated. On the one hand, researchers note, "developers and realtors . . . stand to reap enormous profits from the construction of more housing."[150] Having said that, neither community is monolithic. "Large developers, for example, may actually benefit from a more complicated regulatory structure that prices out smaller operations." Meanwhile, "some realtors may favor a higher volume of sales, while others may actually prefer a tight real estate stock featuring many bidding wars and fast sales."[151] But in Oregon, both builders and realtor groups ultimately supported reform. The Oregon bill was also lauded by libertarians nationally.[152]

Bipartisan reform was also made possible in part because a fascinating populist coalition developed. One analyst noted: "There was an alliance of Oregon's urban and rural areas against the suburbs," which meant support from urban Democrats and rural Republican legislators, and opposition from some suburban legislators (both Democrats and Republicans).[153] For some Republicans, the anti-elitist message was attractive, Andersen says: "Two people familiar with legislative conversations said not to underestimate the appeal, to some rural Republicans, of passing laws that would annoy some well-off Portlanders." According to Jon Chandler, a former lobbyist for the Home Builders Association: "They [Republicans] didn't want to give Tina [Kotek] a win," but "what they liked was the pieces that slapped the cities around."[154]

As a result, whereas Minneapolis, a far-left-leaning city, included a coalition of Democrats and a Green Party member, in the statewide effort in Oregon, a much broader coalition emerged that included Republicans as well as Democrats in both the Senate, where the legislation passed 17–9; and in the House, where it passed 43–16.[155] In the House, 15 Republicans joined 28 Democrats.[156] The bipartisan support was particularly remarkable because Oregon is, says Andersen, "one of the most polarized states in a polarized country." Earlier in the 2019 session, Republican legislators had actually fled the state to prevent passage of tax increases on businesses and legislation to reduce carbon emissions.[157] The reform proved popular with voters. Andersen notes that 97 percent of backers of the legislation were subsequently reelected.[158]

Progress in Oregon continues. In August 2020, the Portland City Council went even further than HB 2001 required and adopted the Residential Infill Project, a program to allow more duplexes, triplexes, and fourplexes; allow new developments to be built without off-street parking; and allow up to six units on residential lots where at least half of the units are affordable—a boon to nonprofits who wish to build affordable housing.[159] Andersen called the Portland law "the most pro-housing reform to low-density zones in US history."[160]

Nationally, zoning reformers claimed a major southern victory in June 2021 when the Charlotte, North Carolina, city council voted to legalize duplexes and other multifamily units in areas previously reserved exclusively for single-family homes.[161]

The fight was not easy. The vote in the city council, led by council member Braxton Winston, was 6–5. And Republicans have pounced on the divided vote. Former Charlotte mayor and North Carolina governor Pat McCrory said, "This is Biden–Harris radicalism coming to a North Carolina town near you soon."[162]

Charlotte has grown a lot in recent years, and although its housing is still relatively inexpensive by national standards, wages are low, too, and Grabar says "the region's reputation for affordability is slipping away." But the big issue driving change was racial segregation. Researchers at Harvard found that Charlotte ranked dead last in social mobility out of fifty large US cities, and the city's racial segregation was seen as a prime culprit.

Winston and other critics of the status quo noted that exclusionary zoning was rampant in Charlotte. Just 16 percent of residential land was available for apartments, and Winston, who is Black, concluded that "single-family zoning is one of the chief weights put on the scale to ensure the de facto segregated city that we live in." In a tweet, he was more direct: "Single family zoning is a tool of segregation." For now, that argument has won the day in Charlotte.[163]

After three failed attempts—in 2018, 2019, and 2020—California reformers won a big victory in September 2021 when the state legislature passed SB 9, the California Housing Opportunity and More Efficiency (HOME) Act, to address the state's housing shortage, racial and economic segregation, and climate change.[164] The law legalized duplexes statewide and allowed people to subdivide lots, which could mean as many as four homes on what had been a single-family lot.[165] The law "has opened up entire communities that had been largely walled off," one expert said.[166] A companion piece of legislation, SB 10, also passed and requires localities to allow buildings with up to ten units near transit, a more modest version of the original Scott Wiener legislation.[167]

The California legislation was signed by Governor Gavin Newsom over the objections of more than 260 city leaders.[168] As in Oregon, California saw the emergence of an interesting urban–rural coalition, as crucial votes of support in the state assembly came not only from urban Democrats but also from seven Republicans, mostly representing rural areas, who provided the margin of victory.[169] As we will discuss further in Chapter 8, the alliance succeeded in part because California legislators in exurban areas, who represent constituents sick of long commutes, are angered by wealthy white liberals on the coast who say they are concerned about the environment and inequality but are unwilling to make room in their own neighborhoods for apartments.[170] The California Association of Realtors, an important constituency group, also supported reform.[171]

The prime driver of reform was intolerable housing prices in California, where the median home price exceeded $800,000, and some homes were selling for $1 million over the asking price; meanwhile, homelessness rose 40 percent in the past five years.[172] Even die-hard NIMBY constituencies—who may not be persuaded by moral arguments about racial segregation—appear somewhat receptive to the idea that exclusionary zoning negatively affects even their own families. Wiener says that older, upper-middle-class white homeowners were sometimes open to the argument that residents should work to avoid a situation in which their children were not "going to be able to afford to live in the community where they grew up."[173] Wiener says framing the stakes in those personal family terms was often "extremely powerful with people."[174]

SB 9, while remarkable for essentially legalizing duplexes, triplexes, and quads throughout the state, was less bold than the predecessor—SB 827, championed by Wiener. But Wiener makes the important point that legislators should advance bold proposals like SB 827 because doing so can change the conversation and make room for important, more modest reforms. In politics, Wiener says, there is "a tendency to want to start small."[175] But with respect to zoning, California's experience suggests the opposite can be true. When Wiener proposed sweeping legislation to require localities to open up transit corridors to apartment buildings, his dramatic proposal spurred alarm. "From the NIMBY perspective, it was like the Death Star was coming out," he says. The legislation started a conversation that "totally shifted the politics" so that more modest reforms became mainstream.[176] He concluded: "Even though that mega bill did not pass, it opened up enormous political space and shifted the goal posts in a positive way."[177]

In August 2022, California legislators went even further. They passed AB 2097 to reduce parking minimums near transit stops and AB 2011 to require by-right approval of affordable housing in commercially zoned lands. Unions and pro-housing advocates came together to get the legislation across the finish line.[178] State legislator Buffy Wicks (D) of Oakland said the political climate around housing had changed dramatically in the past few years. "When I ran in 2018, it was a vulnerability to be unapologetically pro-housing," she said. "Now it is absolutely an asset. I get up on the floor of the Assembly and say, 10 times a week, 'We have to build more housing in our communities, all of our communities need more housing, we need low-income, middle-income, market rate.' You couldn't do that in a comfortable way four years ago."[179]

NIMBYism, once thought to be an unalterable part of American politics, is beginning, here and there, to lose. As one writer put it, "If the NIMBY system is a mighty stone fortress, the YIMBY movement is like the ocean waves, calmly and relentlessly probing for cracks in the wall." As pieces of the stone begin to break off, "the edifice that has frozen our cities for half a century" could over time "come crumbling and crashing down."[180]

IMPLICATIONS FOR FEDERAL REFORM

State and local advancement of zoning reform suggests both that federal action may be possible, and also that it is probably necessary.

On the one hand, successes in Minneapolis, Oregon, Charlotte, and California eliminating single-family housing restrictions suggest that federal reform may be feasible, because we now have evidence that sometimes unlikely political coalitions of "groups that don't normally work together," as Wiener says, can coalesce to prevail over traditionally powerful NIMBY forces.[181] An unusual coalition of civil rights activists, labor unions, environmentalists, affordable housing activists, young people, seniors, employers, libertarians, builders, realtors, and rural white residents can achieve change despite the opposition of wealthy white homeowners.

By the same token, federal action is also necessary because states cannot do the work alone. Even the states with the most forward-looking efforts to curb exclusionary zoning need more support. Reviewing the effects of long-standing state statutes to curb exclusionary zoning in places such as Massachusetts and New Jersey, researchers find that though they've made progress, housing production has still been stymied and "those state statutes have not been able to prevent worse than average housing affordability problems in their states."[182]

Both necessary and possible, federal zoning reform would, for better and worse, become elevated to the presidential campaign in 2020.

SEVEN

MAKING ECONOMIC DISCRIMINATION VISIBLE NATIONALLY

FOR SENATOR CORY BOOKER (D-NJ), WHO WAS BORN IN 1969, the passage of the Fair Housing Act a year earlier was life changing. The law made it possible for Booker's parents in 1970 to become the first Black family to reside in Harrington Park, New Jersey, an affluent white community outside of Newark with strong public schools. The move wasn't easy, and the Booker family faced terrible resistance, but they had the law on their side.[1] Booker's family could take advantage of the Fair Housing Act because they had the financial resources to make the move. They could maneuver around the exclusionary zoning in Harrington Park.

Even as a child, though, Booker saw that for his less-affluent Black friends and colleagues, outlawing racial discrimination was not sufficient. He told me that less-well-off cousins were still stuck in high-poverty communities.[2] Harrington Park homeowners couldn't discriminate by race, but the town could erect economic barriers to keep most families of color out.

This meant Booker's relatives didn't have access to good schools, jobs, and health care. And it also meant they were subject to a very different style of policing, Booker says. He and his friends in affluent Harrington Park could act out and be fine. "But you have a very different criminal justice system in Harrington Park . . . than you do in Newark," where committing petty crimes can have catastrophic consequences for a young person.[3]

That experience led Booker, in advance of his 2020 presidential bid, to introduce federal legislation to discourage exclusionary zoning. His Housing, Opportunity, Mobility, and Equity (HOME) Act sought to do two things to make housing more affordable and equitable. The bill's first prong would provide a monthly tax credit for rent-burdened individuals to address the affordability problem immediately, and the second prong would increase the supply of housing by providing incentives for localities to make zoning less exclusionary.[4]

Booker's legislation, cosponsored by Rep. James Clyburn in 2019, would condition two types of federal funding—Surface Transportation Block Grants and Community Development Block Grants—on community efforts to reduce exclusionary practices.[5] The federal government currently doles out billions of dollars for infrastructure programs, so the legislation calls for recipients of those funds to take steps to curb exclusion.[6]

The legislation would provide a menu of options that communities could take to reduce exclusionary practices. They could authorize more high-density and multifamily zoning, relax lot size restrictions, or reduce parking requirements and restrictions on accessory dwelling units. Jurisdictions would also have incentives to allow "by-right development" so that projects that meet zoning requirements could be administratively approved rather than being subjected to lengthy hearings. Inclusionary zoning policies that allow developers to build more units when they agree to set aside some for affordable housing would also be encouraged. And jurisdictions would have an incentive to adopt prohibitions on "source of income discrimination." One provision in the bill—perhaps its most controversial one—would encourage jurisdictions to ban the practice of landlords asking potential renters about their criminal history.[7]

The goal of Booker's legislation was to ensure that affordable housing units would comprise not less than 20 percent of new housing stock.[8] But overall, "it is a light touch," Booker told me. "We're just basically saying, through our legislation, that you have to have a plan" for making zoning more inclusive. "And the components of the plan are on you."[9]

Although presidential candidates in the past didn't see taking on exclusionary zoning to address affordability and segregation as politically attractive, Booker was not the only Democratic candidate to do so in the 2020 primaries. Indeed, virtually all the presidential candidates on the Democratic side—including Bernie Sanders, Amy Klobuchar, Elizabeth Warren, Julian Castro, and Joe Biden—proposed making federal housing and transportation funding contingent on reducing stringent zoning, a discussion that fair housing scholars note was "largely absent from previous campaigns."[10]

In another small sign of progress, in March 2020, during the middle of the campaign, the House of Representatives passed the Yes in My Backyard (YIMBY) Act to require recipients of federal Community Development Block Grants to report on their efforts to reduce exclusionary zoning. (The bill did not pass the Senate.)[11]

THE ESTABLISHED FEDERAL ROLE IN ZONING

Although zoning decisions are typically made at the state and local levels, such powers have never been unlimited. The US Constitution has long provided federal courts and the US Congress with the authority to intervene in zoning questions when localities have abused their power. The federal government has a recognized role in regulating local zoning where it promotes racial discrimination, interferes with telecommunications, tramples on religious freedom, denies the rights of persons with disabilities, or leads to risky building in areas prone to flooding.[12]

Under the US Constitution, the Congress has two broad powers to regulate zoning: under the "Commerce Clause" and under the "Spending Clause." The power to regulate interstate commerce justifies, for example, federal laws preventing racial discrimination in housing (as well as other areas, such as employment) because these activities clearly affect interstate commerce.[13] There is broad authority under spending powers to place conditions on the use of funds to advance national goals, so long as those conditions are related to spending and are not unduly "coercive."[14] Because the federal government spends money to subsidize housing, it has a federal interest in reducing restrictive zoning that drives up housing prices and impedes the effectiveness of federal spending.[15]

Federal court intervention to prevent racial discrimination in zoning dates back to the 1917 *Buchanan v. Warley* decision of the US Supreme Court.[16] Congress's 1968 Fair Housing Act, likewise, has been used to strike down zoning policies that have a disparate impact on racial minorities.[17] And federal rules to protect people with disabilities through the Fair Housing Act and the Americans with Disabilities Act have trumped local zoning rules that prohibit group homes for disabled people.[18]

Congress has intervened in local zoning in other spheres as well. The Telecommunications Act of 1996, experts note, "allows the federal government to override local land-use regulations that impede the siting of cell phone towers."[19] The Religious Land Use and Institutionalized Persons Act of 2000, passed unanimously by Congress, came in response to an outcry from religious institutions that had faced discrimination when local governments denied zoning approval for places of worship. Under the federal law, religious institutions can bring suits and receive injunctive or declaratory relief.[20] And federal laws providing flood insurance have long allowed regulators to require appropriate local zoning to protect properties.[21]

EXCLUSIONARY ZONING IN THE 2020 GENERAL ELECTION CAMPAIGN

During the 2020 presidential campaign, Democratic candidate Joe Biden took two stances on zoning that captured the attention of Donald Trump. First, Biden supported the 2015 Obama administration rule implementing the 1968 Fair Housing Act's Affirmatively Furthering Fair Housing (AFFH) requirement that jurisdictions receiving federal funding take steps to dismantle racial segregation.[22] When legislators passed the 1968 law, they recognized that it was not enough to simply outlaw racial discrimination in the sale and rental of housing. Given the federal government's long history of creating segregated housing, and the entrenched nature of housing patterns, the law said that the Department of Housing and Urban Development (HUD) should take affirmative steps to dismantle the segregation it helped foster.[23]

The 2015 Obama-era rule required all municipalities receiving funding from HUD to complete a comprehensive assessment of fair housing and commit to taking specific steps to "overcome historic patterns of segregation."[24] The assessment would examine, among other things, the effect of exclusionary zoning laws.[25] The Obama AFFH rule stressed that the goal was that all racial groups should have access to communities with good jobs and high-performing schools, with transportation options, and with environmental health.[26] And the rule acknowledged the special harm that occurs when race and class segregation merge. The policy requires that data be collected on "racially or ethnically concentrated areas of poverty," which are generally defined as those with 50 percent or more minority populations *and* 40 percent or more poverty rates.[27]

In 2020, Joe Biden also endorsed the Booker/Clyburn HOME Act, declaring that he would "eliminate local and state housing regulations that perpetuate discrimination." The Biden campaign website explained: "Exclusionary zoning has for decades been strategically used to keep people of color and low-income families out of certain communities. As President, Biden will enact legislation requiring any state receiving federal dollars through the Community Development Block Grants or Surface Transportation Block Grants to develop a strategy for inclusionary zoning, as proposed in the HOME Act of 2019 by Majority Whip Clyburn and Senator Cory Booker."[28] (The legislation has not yet been enacted.)

Biden's support for the AFFH rule and the Booker/Clyburn HOME Act gave Donald Trump what he might have seen as a political opening. The Trump administration had long been critical of the AFFH rule. In 2018, the Trump administration postponed implementation of the rule; and in July 2020, Trump announced he was repealing it altogether.[29]

During the campaign, Trump told "suburban housewives of America" that his actions were going to protect them. With the AFFH rule, "your home will go down in value and crime rates will rise rapidly," he said. The rule "will totally destroy the beautiful suburbs. Suburbia will be no longer as we know it."[30] Trump said AFFH would be "bringing who knows what to your suburbs, so communities will be unsafe and your housing values will go down." He tweeted that "people have worked all their lives to get into a community, and now they're going to watch it go to hell. Not going to happen, not while I'm here." On another occasion, Trump tweeted, "I am happy to inform all the people living their Suburban Lifestyle Dream that you will no longer be bothered or financially hurt by having low income housing built in your neighborhood. . . . Your housing prices will go up based on the market, and crime will go down."[31]

Trump attacked the Booker legislation, too, and falsely claimed that Booker would become HUD secretary in a Biden administration and reimplement the AFFH rule "in a bigger form."[32] Biden's support of Booker's HOME Act drew the ire of *National Review* writer Stanley Kurtz, who said Booker's bill "goes much further than AFFH" and was part of a larger effort to "abolish the suburbs."[33] Trump seemed to love the phrase and adopted it as his own.[34]

In mid-August 2020, Trump teamed up with Ben Carson in a *Wall Street Journal* op-ed entitled "We'll Protect America's Suburbs."[35] The piece denounced the Minneapolis move to end exclusionary single-family zoning, even though Carson had applauded that very effort in Minneapolis months earlier.[36] In late August, the Republican National Convention featured a presentation by Mark and Patricia McCloskey, a white gun-brandishing couple from St. Louis, who had been charged for pointing guns at Black Lives Matter demonstrators.[37] They spoke in support of gun rights and the police, which was predictable. But then, seemingly out of the blue, Patricia McCloskey took the discussion in a different direction and warned that Biden's desire to end "single-family zoning" would bring "crime, lawlessness and low-quality apartments into now-thriving suburban neighborhoods."[38] It was terrible slander against people like KiAra Cornelius, Tehani, Patricia McGee, and Samantha, who themselves just want safe neighborhoods. But the architects of the Republican National Convention clearly thought they had a winning issue.

BIDEN'S VICTORY AND ACTIONS ON EXCLUSIONARY ZONING AS PRESIDENT

Donald Trump's relentless drumbeat in defense of exclusionary zoning and his attacks on Biden, Booker, and the Obama AFFH rule clearly did not swing the election. Biden actually performed nine points better among white suburban voters in 2020 than Hillary Clinton did in 2016.[39] Likewise, mainstream business groups, including the Business Roundtable, came out in support of AFFH's reinstatement in 2020.[40]

Once in office, Joe Biden followed through on his promise to restore the Affirmatively Furthering Fair Housing rule, and he also took two other steps to fight exclusionary zoning: strengthening the ability for racial minorities to sue when zoning practices have a "disparate impact" on them; and calling for the creation of a first-ever "race to the top" incentive program, which he called "Unlocking Possibilities," to encourage jurisdictions to curtail exclusionary zoning practices.[41]

Within days of taking office, Biden announced that he would reinstate a 2013 regulation articulating the Fair Housing Act rules governing so-called disparate impact litigation—a move HUD took in June 2021. Under disparate impact theory, unjustified rules with a racially discriminatory impact are illegal even absent discriminatory intent. Disparate impact lawsuits can be brought against unfair practices such as exclusionary zoning, but the Trump administration had rescinded the Obama rule.[42]

Under the 2013 rule, the burden shifted back and forth between plaintiff and defendant. First, the plaintiff "has the burden of proving that a challenged practice caused or predictably will cause a discriminatory effect."[43] For example, a plaintiff might show that single-family exclusive zoning disproportionately screened out Black families. If the plaintiff can make such a showing, then the defendant "has the burden of proving that the challenged practice is necessary to achieve one or more substantial, legitimate, nondiscriminatory interests."[44] Finally, if the defendant can make such a showing, the burden shifts back to the plaintiff. Under the rule, the plaintiff "may still prevail upon proving that the substantial, legitimate, nondiscriminatory interest supporting the challenged practice could be served by another practice that has a less discriminatory effect."[45]

As Biden sought to reformulate the rule, he had the support of a 2015 US Supreme Court decision in *Texas Department of Housing and Community Affairs v. The Inclusive Communities Project*, which, by a 5–4 vote, affirmed that disparate impact litigation is legitimate under the Fair Housing Act and noted that "zoning laws and other housing restrictions that function unfairly to exclude minorities from certain neighborhoods without any sufficient justification . . . reside at the heartland of" disparate impact jurisprudence.[46]

In *Inclusive Communities Project*, the Supreme Court specifically cited two cases as important precedents involving exclusionary zoning. The first was *United States v. City of Black Jack* (1974), in which the Eighth Circuit struck down the Black Jack, Missouri, ban on multifamily housing, which would have foreclosed 85 percent of Black people in the St. Louis, Missouri, metropolitan area from living in Black Jack.[47] Likewise, in the 1980s, the NAACP challenged the Huntington, New York, single-family exclusive zoning ordinance that channeled multifamily housing away from a section of town that was 98 percent white to an "urban renewal" zone populated by minorities.[48]

The Supreme Court in *Inclusive Communities Project* noted that not all government decisions that result in a disparate impact are illegal. "Valid government policies" can stand, but those that pose "artificial, arbitrary and unnecessary barriers" must fall.[49] When plaintiffs win disparate impact cases, they can seek injunctive relief, damages, and court-awarded attorneys' fees.[50]

In 2021, the Biden administration also proposed a $5 billion Race to the Top program to encourage localities to "eliminate exclusionary zoning and harmful land use policies." The Biden White House described the proposal as "an innovative, new competitive grant program that awards flexible and attractive funding to jurisdictions that take concrete steps to eliminate such needless barriers to producing affordable housing."[51] The proposal would reward localities that voluntarily agree to jettison such practices as "minimum lot sizes, mandatory parking requirements and prohibitions on multifamily housing."[52] Called Unlocking Possibilities, the proposed program constituted what, as Brian Deese, director of the National Economic Council, noted, would be the "first ever federal competitive grants program" to decrease exclusionary zoning.[53] A slimmed-down $1.75 billion version of the proposal passed the House of Representatives as part of the Build Back Better program, but that package of legislation ultimately failed in the Senate.[54]

Undeterred, in May 2022, Biden announced a Housing Supply Action Plan, which awards points in competitive grants under the Bipartisan Infrastructure Bill and other federal grant programs to jurisdictions that take steps to reduce exclusionary zoning. He pitched the effort as one that would make housing more affordable and bring down inflation.[55]

AN ECONOMIC FAIR HOUSING ACT?

Joe Biden's decision to elevate the issue of exclusionary zoning to a greater extent than previous presidents is not entirely surprising; in many ways, it is a natural issue for him. Biden ran on a campaign to "restore the soul of the nation." There are few steps more important in accomplishing this goal than addressing continued racial segregation of neighborhoods. As a candidate who explicitly distanced himself from elite coastal liberals by stressing his roots in Scranton, Pennsylvania, and his non–Ivy League education, Biden also understood the ways in which snob zoning is inherently offensive to working-class people of all races. And it made sense that Biden, as someone committed to uniting Americans of different backgrounds and outlooks, would seek to reduce the walls that divide and further polarize Americans.[56]

But to capture the imagination of the public and galvanize them for action, future presidents and state governors need to propose something even more dramatic than disparate impact rules and Race to the Top initiatives. Zoning can be seen as a technical and opaque issue, so policymakers need to advance a more powerful idea to provide moral clarity to the issue.

In August 2017, I proposed the idea of creating an Economic Fair Housing Act to make it illegal for government zoning to discriminate on the basis of income, just as the 1968 Fair Housing Act makes it illegal for parties to discriminate on the basis of race.[57] As I wrote in a *New York Times* op-ed on the topic, it is time, a century after the Supreme Court struck down racial zoning, to outlaw unjustified economically discriminatory zoning.[58] Although the private housing market would continue to function based on a consumer's ability to pay, the idea behind the Economic Fair Housing Act is that local governments (and homeowners' associations) should not themselves engage in economic discrimination by erecting artificial barriers to working-class people like Cornelius, McGee, Tehani, and Samantha, who wish to move with their families to higher-opportunity neighborhoods.[59] When local governments adopt snob zoning laws, which telegraph that less-advantaged families are unwelcome in a community, that government-sponsored income discrimination should be illegal.

In 2019, Thomas Loftus, president of the Equitable Housing Institute (EHI), a small nonprofit based in northern Virginia, contacted me about developing the concept of an Economic Fair Housing Act more fully into actual draft legislation.[60] Loftus, a good-natured retired government lawyer, became a cherished partner on this issue. He came by his social concern naturally. His maternal grandfather was Supreme Court Justice Robert Jackson, whom Loftus says has been "a terrific inspiration" and "a guiding star."[61] Jackson was part of the court that handed down *Brown v. Board of Education* and was a dissenter in *Korematsu v. United States*, which upheld the internment of Japanese American citizens during World War II.

When Loftus was born in March 1946, Jackson was in Nuremberg, Germany, serving as lead US prosecutor of Nazi war criminals, but the two came to know each other at Grandpa Jackson's McLean, Virginia, home Hickory Hill (later home to John, then Robert Kennedy).[62] In the years following Jackson's death in 1954, Loftus went off to Amherst and the Peace Corps, and while a student at George Washington University Law School focused on eviction problems and came to know "the trials and tribulations of low-income people trying to find housing."[63]

In 2008, Loftus created, with the help of Dartmouth economist William Fischel (who was a fraternity brother at Amherst College forty years earlier), what would become the Equitable Housing Institute to address a number of issues. At the top of the list, says Loftus, is exclusionary zoning, which he identifies as "the main structural problem as to why this country, with its vast land and natural and human resources, couldn't seem to build enough housing for people."[64]

In December 2020, after Joe Biden's election, I assembled a group of researchers, political figures, and civil rights leaders to talk about what Biden should do to address exclusionary zoning. The group, which included Loftus, discussed various options and provided good advice on how the Economic Fair Housing Act concept could be improved.[65]

In the draft legislation, the Economic Fair Housing Act would seek to "prohibit exclusionary housing practices comprehensively throughout the United States" by giving harmed individuals and Department of Justice officials the right to sue municipalities and homeowners' associations in federal court for engaging in exclusionary practices.[66]

The new law would draw upon the Fair Housing Act's "disparate impact" concept by prohibiting local governments or homeowners' associations from engaging in exclusionary housing practices that discriminate on the basis of income and "have the effect or intent of restricting housing opportunities without sufficient justification."[67] For example, a plaintiff might show that a policy that bans duplexes, triplexes, and apartment buildings has a disparate impact on low-income and working-class families. Then, as with racial disparate impact suits, the burden of proof would shift to the local government to prove—in the language of the *Inclusive Communities Project* case—that the policy "is necessary to achieve a valid interest."[68]

Under the Economic Fair Housing Act, remedies for plaintiffs who prevail in court would include those available under the Fair Housing Act: covering monetary losses to the victims, the cost associated with the work of attorneys to bring the lawsuit, and injunctions that would prevent municipalities from continuing to discriminate.[69] In addition, the Economic Fair Housing Act would ban source-of-income discrimination—the ability of landlords to discriminate against those using Section 8 housing vouchers, a practice that is currently legal in most states.[70]

The Fair Housing Act is a good model for the Economic Fair Housing Act because it has helped change American culture, helped foster a decline in racial discrimination in housing, and helped reduce racial segregation. As Wade Henderson of the Leadership Conference on Civil and Human Rights noted on the fiftieth anniversary of the law, "There is no doubt that the Fair Housing Act has been impactful"; it is, he said, a "powerful law."[71] The Fair Housing Act, which has evolved over time, became stronger in 1988, when the Congress amended it to remove a cap on punitive damages, allow HUD to initiate complaints, and if needed, order the Justice Department to proceed with litigation.[72]

To begin with, the Fair Housing Act helped transform American cultural views on the acceptability of racial discrimination in housing. Whereas we tend to think of culture shifts ushering in legal changes, the reverse can also be true. Just as the Supreme Court's decision to strike down laws against interracial marriage helped bring about positive changes in white attitudes, the Fair Housing Act helped delegitimize racial discrimination in housing.[73]

In 1963, for example, even though 85 percent of white people thought Black people should have an equal chance of getting a job, they showed "greater hostility to civil rights in housing," researchers note.[74] A majority of white people—56 percent—said they opposed laws that would allow Black people to "live wherever they want."[75] In 1964, California voters supported Lyndon Johnson by 59 percent to 40 percent over Barry Goldwater, but two-thirds also supported an effort to effectively repeal the state's fair housing law.[76] In the years since the passage of the Fair Housing Act, white support for laws barring homeowners from discriminating has skyrocketed, from 33 percent in 1973 to 72 percent in 2016.[77] In 1988, when the Fair Housing Act was amended to expand the circle of protected classes, the vote was 376–23 in the House and 94–3 in the Senate, and the legislation was signed by President Ronald Reagan.[78]

Along with the cultural change came a reduction in racial discrimination by landlords, as noted in Chapter 3. A 1977 study of housing found "a dramatic drop in discrimination rates from the 1960s, though plenty of discriminatory conduct remained."[79] In subsequent years, audit studies found continued declines. One housing expert observes: "The most blatant forms of housing discrimination have declined in recent decades as documented by four national studies conducted by the Urban Institute for HUD between 1977 and 2012."[80] The decline in discrimination, in turn, helped bring about a 30 percent reduction in racial segregation since 1970.[81] The job of eradicating racial residential discrimination is by no means complete, but the Fair Housing Act has had an important impact, so it could serve as a strong model for tackling rising income segregation.

An Economic Fair Housing Act could be even more effective than the Fair Housing Act in curbing the disparate impact of government-sponsored discrimination.[82] Not all discrimination is racial in nature, and an Economic Fair Housing Act would be broader and more inclusive by going after economic discrimination against poor and working-class people, including those who are white. And an Economic Fair Housing Act would also make it easier for low-income people of color to sue than is true under current law. Proving a disparate impact of exclusionary zoning on poor and working-class families should be easier than showing disparate impact on people of color because exclusionary zoning that bars more affordable types of housing from being built discriminates very directly on the basis of income and only indirectly on the basis of race. By their very nature, policies that drive up housing costs constitute government-sponsored income discrimination. Showing a racial impact is more like taking a "bank shot" in pool. It requires plaintiffs to prove that direct economic discrimination also indirectly hurts people of color, which adds a layer of complexity.

In racial disparate impact cases, plaintiffs must hire experts to conduct statistical studies to show the disproportionate impact on minority groups, which adds to the cost of litigation.[83] Thomas Loftus notes, "Courts routinely have dismissed 'disparate impact' lawsuits where the plaintiffs failed to prove that minority group members were affected disproportionately by economic discrimination."[84] Loftus points out that courts can be quite demanding on the standard for showing a disparate impact. For example, in *Gamble v. City of Escondido*, the Ninth Circuit found that the plaintiff, suing on behalf of physically disabled people, failed to show a disparate impact because a policy that banned *all* group living did not specifically target adult healthcare facilities. The court held: "The relevant comparison group to determine a discriminatory effect on the physically disabled is other groups of similar sizes living together. Otherwise, all that has been demonstrated is a discriminatory effect on group living. . . . No evidence has been presented suggesting that the City's permit denial practices disproportionately affect disabled group living as opposed to other kinds of group living."[85]

One of the most extensive studies of disparate impact litigation found that in the 2000s, plaintiffs prevailed on appeal in disparate impact cases just 8.3 percent of the time.[86] By removing an extra evidentiary hurdle, low-income plaintiffs of color suing under the Economic Fair Housing Act should have an easier time of prevailing than under the Fair Housing Act, and low-income white plaintiffs will have a new cause of action currently unavailable to them.

In addition, an Economic Fair Housing Act could and should add new guardrails not found in the Fair Housing Act to help distinguish between legitimate and illegitimate forms of zoning. Under an Economic Fair Housing Act, when plaintiffs make a showing that zoning policies negatively affect families with lower incomes, judges will have to decide whether or not local governments have then met the burden of providing a "sufficient justification," which means demonstrating that the policies are "necessary to achieve a valid interest."[87]

That broad language, drawn from the Supreme Court's decision in the *Inclusive Communities Project* case, is open to various interpretations. Is, for example, it really "necessary" to ban duplexes and triplexes to keep traffic congestion at a reasonable level? And is it really a "valid interest" (much less a "substantial" interest—a term also invoked in *Inclusive Communities*)[88] to minimize traffic in one community when the result is increased traffic for the metropolitan region as a whole? Is a requirement that new homes be equipped with solar panels a justified policy to fight climate change or an unjustified exclusionary practice that raises construction costs and keeps low-income families out?[89]

Given the leeway provided by the language, it would be prudent for an Economic Fair Housing Act to provide additional guidelines to federal judges to interpret what is a "sufficient justification" for zoning regulations that have an economically discriminatory impact.[90] The goal here is to strike a balance between honoring legitimate needs of government broadly (such as protecting the environment, worker safety, and building codes to ensure building safety) and seeing through pretexts in zoning laws for nonlegitimate objectives (such as segregating by income, keeping families out because they won't "pay their way," and limiting housing supply in order to jack up prices).

The guardrails should include guidance for the courts in two separate areas: what sorts of *policy designs* (e.g., bans on duplexes and triplexes and unreasonably large minimum lot sizes) are presumptively unjustified, and what sorts of *outcomes* (e.g., a tiny percentage of market-rate or subsidized housing that is affordable) mean policies are presumptively unjustified?

Other public policy proposals seeking to reduce exclusionary zoning have taken a similar two-pronged approach of examining both policy design and outcomes. For instance, some researchers have proposed directing infrastructure funding to states that adopt certain policies and achieve certain outcomes. A state that has eliminated single-family exclusive zoning, for example, would presumptively qualify for extra federal funding. The same would be the case for a state that created aggressive outcome measures for producing a certain amount of housing and ensuring that affordable housing was fairly distributed in different communities.[91]

The inclusion of outcome measures and policy design is based on the concern that if a law focuses solely on particular disfavored local policies, a community could remove one objectionable roadblock to the development of affordable housing (large lot sizes, for example) and then—quite easily—erect a new, less obvious barrier (unreasonable off-street parking requirements, for instance).[92] If you give localities a list of prohibited activities, such as single-family exclusive zoning, one researcher notes, "they will get around that in some way" by creating new barriers.[93] This scholar observes that "local governments have a nearly infinite range of land use tools that can effectively block unwanted development."[94]

But starting with a list of disfavored policy decisions would give judges—and localities—a clear sense of what constitutes unreasonable exclusionary tactics. The Economic Fair Housing Act could instruct judges that policies that result in an economic disparate impact are normally unjustified under three circumstances. One set of presumptively illegal laws are those that forbid the construction of duplexes or triplexes in a significant part of the community. A second involve those that impose unreasonably large minimum lot sizes. A third set would be having an excessive overall number of regulations, given research finding "a tight link between the number of regulations—even those not directly tied to multifamily housing—and the construction of new housing."[95]

As a matter of outcomes, the Economic Fair Housing Act could instruct courts that even where communities do not run afoul of a prescribed list of disfavored practices, a different set of practices may be unjustified when they result in the community failing "to provide its fair share of the regional housing needs"—in terms of both the supply of housing and the share of affordable housing.[96] In determining the "fair share" of affordable housing, judges could draw upon existing models that variously define affordable housing and set reasonable goals for a fair share: Massachusetts (10 percent), New Jersey (somewhat more than 10 percent), Catalonia (15 percent), and France (25 percent).[97] The outcomes measure used in judging whether an exclusionary policy is justified should look at overall housing production, as well as a fair share of affordable housing, to discourage communities from meeting their fair share and then completely ending all housing production.[98] Policies that restrict "all development, not just that for low-income people," should be disfavored because doing so drives prices artificially higher, which disproportionately harms low-income people.[99]

The guardrails are meant to provide guidance, not impose a straitjacket on judges. Local conditions are critical to zoning decisions, and the Economic Fair Housing Act, although administering a federal standard, is *in its application* highly localized.

Judges will listen to the individual justifications offered by local governments, in light of local conditions, to see whether they meet the standard of being "necessary" to meet a legitimate interest. This legislation does not provide a national mandate for a certain type of zoning, but it does allow judges to consider broad rules to prevent local abuse.

It should be made clear that an Economic Fair Housing Act would not authorize so-called reverse discrimination suits in which wealthy residents claim that zoning laws in low-income communities are discriminatory against the wealthy because they prevent gentrification. If a low-income community wished to slow gentrification and displacement, for example, by prohibiting the construction of luxury apartments, the Economic Fair Housing Act could not be invoked by rich people claiming economic discrimination. The draft bill specifically names "low-income" and "moderate-income" households as protected classes.[100]

The Economic Fair Housing Act's use of "sticks" that empower plaintiffs to sue municipalities that discriminate provides a critical supplement to the Unlocking Possibilities program, the AFFH rule, and the Booker/Clyburn HOME Act, which are all oriented toward providing "carrots" of federal dollars for communities that do the right thing. Seven advantages stand out.

First, the Economic Fair Housing Act would provide a comprehensive approach to exclusionary zoning. It would apply in every town and state in the country—not just those that want to participate in certain federal funding programs. Incentives only go so far. As the federal experience with Medicaid expansion found, some states will turn away what appears to be a sweet economic deal.[101] And many of the wealthiest suburbs that engage in the worst forms of exclusionary zoning don't receive much federal community development funding, so the Fair Housing Act's threat to cut off funds holds little leverage.[102] In 2016, for example, Douglas County, a suburb of Denver, Colorado, decided to give up community development funds rather than comply with the Fair Housing Act's Affirmatively Furthering Fair Housing requirements.[103]

Second, by giving plaintiffs the power to sue in federal court, the Economic Fair Housing Act seeks to minimize the ability of powerful political interests to neuter reforms—a constant concern when the issue is exclusionary zoning. As noted in Chapter 6, HUD secretary George Romney's Open Communities program to withhold federal funds from suburban jurisdictions that were not providing access for affordable housing was quickly killed after jurisdictions complained to Romney's boss, Richard Nixon.[104] More broadly, litigation also avoids the problem inherent in any strategy to condition federal funding. Officials whose job is to give away funds for important causes are loath to withhold them because they are in the business of providing support.[105] By contrast, the Economic Fair Housing Act "has a more robust enforcement framework," one law professor notes, because it bypasses the politicians and "anyone can bring a suit."[106]

Third, the Economic Fair Housing Act would put power in the hands of people who need it most: the direct victims of exclusionary zoning like Samantha, Tehani, KiAra Cornelius, and Patricia McGee. While other policies, such as those in New Jersey, empower builders to sue to address exclusionary zoning, the Economic Fair Housing Act would also empower the most direct victims—those excluded—to sue.[107] The provision that defendants must pay plaintiff attorneys' fees when plaintiffs prevail is critical because otherwise it often would be infeasible for low-income families to pay the necessary costs to contest unlawful housing practices.[108]

Fourth, by giving victims of income discrimination the same legal remedies as the Fair Housing Act provides to victims of racial discrimination, the proposed legislation has the potential to change American cultural attitudes about economically disadvantaged people and housing. Proposals to place conditions on funding for communities that exclude underlines the important point that exclusionary zoning *is bad policy* because it blocks opportunity, makes housing less affordable, and damages the planet. All of that is true, but creating Fair Housing Act–type penalties for state-sponsored income discrimination sends the more potent message that such discrimination is also *immoral*. Erecting government bans on housing to exclude and discriminate on the basis of income is a fundamental offense to human dignity. In the best-case scenario, the Economic Fair Housing Act will help change American culture about economic discrimination to make it shameful, just as racial discrimination is, by raising awareness about the walls we currently don't see.

Fifth, empowering litigants who are harmed by exclusionary zoning can aid state and local policymakers in their own attempts to make zoning more inclusive. Asked what federal action would most help his zoning reform efforts in California, state senator Scott Wiener replied: "broad fair housing standards." In pursuing state-level reforms, he said, it's very helpful to be able to say to localities, "You're going to get sued, [so] let's just fix this."[109]

Although litigation is time-consuming, the real power of a private right of action is the deterrence that comes from the threat of it being used. Wiener explains, "All of a sudden, you have cities getting advice from their attorneys saying, 'You have to approve this project or we're going to get sued and have to pay their attorneys' fees.' And all of a sudden, the projects start getting approved." A strong federal law, he says, "will provide enormous cover for people at the state and local level to say, 'I know you don't like to do this, but we have to do it because we're going to get sued under federal law, and that's going to be very expensive and costly.'"[110] The federal power to aid state reform should not be underestimated. One legal expert notes, "State level reforms, or in some cases, local level ones, may be the biggest opportunities for breakthroughs."[111]

Sixth, the Economic Fair Housing Act is less subject to constitutional challenge than programs like the Booker/Clyburn Act that condition federal funding on taking steps to reduce exclusionary zoning. The Economic Fair Housing Act is based on Congress's power to regulate interstate commerce, and as experts say, exclusionary zoning "clearly affects interstate commerce, including housing prices, mobility and aggregate economic productivity."[112] Exclusionary zoning has a pronounced negative impact on interstate commerce and economic growth in part because it raises housing prices and limits the ability of low-income families to migrate to metropolitan areas with good jobs.[113] In this sense, exclusionary zoning—by driving up the price of housing—also interferes with the constitutional right to travel, which includes the right to resettle in new communities in order to pursue new opportunities.[114] In sum, as one researcher observes, the Economic Fair Housing Act "seems to have the clearest sailing legally" of various federal approaches to exclusionary zoning.[115]

To be clear, the Booker/Clyburn Act, which is premised on Congress's ability to place conditions on federal spending, is basically on solid ground according to constitutional scholars.[116] But there is a bit more ambiguity. In recent decades, the US Supreme Court has placed greater constraints on Congress's ability to use its spending powers to shape state and local policy, requiring, among other things, that the condition on funding be "germane" to the underlying legislation and that the amount of money not be so large as to be unduly "coercive."[117] In 2012, for example, the Supreme Court struck down a requirement that states take new Medicaid expansion funding under the Affordable Care Act in order to continue receiving funding for the existing Medicaid program.[118]

A seventh and final advantage of the litigation approach is the modest requirement for federal investment. Some spending incentives—particularly the Race to the Top approach—require new funds to lure communities into doing what they should already be doing. Empowering plaintiffs, by contrast, requires communities to be more inclusive without having to pay them to do so.

The Economic Fair Housing Act also offers several key advantages over existing litigation tools to attack exclusionary zoning. Litigators can bring lawsuits against exclusionary jurisdictions where policies have a racially disparate impact—an important approach to which the federal government should devote greater resources.[119]

But as a supplement to this approach, the Economic Fair Housing Act offers four critical benefits.

First, conceptually, current disparate impact litigation is about racial discrimination, not class discrimination. These two categories often overlap because income discrimination in zoning very often results in a negative impact on people of color. But because race and class discrimination are distinct harms, the two do not coincide in all cases. Wealthy white people discriminate against poor white people in places like La Crosse, Wisconsin; and wealthy Black people discriminate against poor Black people in places like Prince George's County, Maryland.[120] Government-sponsored economic discrimination—which says to low-income and working-class people that they don't deserve to live in certain communities—is wrong, whether or not it results in a racially disparate impact.

Second, the contrasting trajectories of racial and economic segregation in the United States suggest new tools are needed. If the Fair Housing Act helped Black–white segregation decline by 30 percent, an Economic Fair Housing Act could help begin to reverse the trend of rising economic segregation, which has doubled since the 1970s.

Third, as we shall discuss in much greater detail in Chapter 8, a frontal assault on state-sponsored economic discrimination is likely to have broader political appeal than a narrow focus on racial discrimination and could strengthen alliances between working-class people of different races. Although right-wing politicians often pit working-class Black and white people against each other, the Economic Fair Housing Act could help to highlight an area of common ground between groups that are often at war with each other.

Fourth, a new statute explicitly affirming disparate impact litigation by income is less vulnerable to shifts in the makeup of the Supreme Court than is disparate impact litigation by race under the Fair Housing Act. Because the Fair Housing Act's disparate impact approach is implied rather than explicit, it almost failed to survive Supreme Court review in 2015. At that time, Justice Anthony Kennedy provided the crucial fifth vote in support of disparate impact litigation in the face of a vigorous dissent from four conservative justices. Since then Kennedy has been replaced by the more conservative Justice Brett Kavanaugh and Ruth Bader Ginsburg has been replaced by the more conservative Amy Coney Barrett. Although one can hope that disparate impact remains a strong tool to attack racial discrimination in housing for years to come, having additional legal avenues to curtail exclusionary zoning seems important.[121]

In May 2021, I met with the staff of Rep. Emmanuel Cleaver to discuss drafting and introducing an Economic Fair Housing Act. Cleaver, a veteran congressman, was chair of the House Financial Services Committee's Subcommittee on Housing, Community Development and Insurance. A minister and founder of the Southern Christian

Leadership's Kansas City chapter, Cleaver began his political career in the 1980s serving on the city council of Kansas City and in 1991 was elected the city's first Black mayor.[122] In October 2021, Chairman Cleaver invited me to testify at a House hearing on exclusionary zoning. He opened the hearing with an astute observation: zoning may sound like a technical issue, but sitting in on zoning discussions over the years, he said, you learn a lot about people, and about human nature.[123] I testified in favor of the Economic Fair Housing Act. At the hearing, both Republicans and Democrats on the subcommittee attacked exclusionary zoning (for different reasons) even as they disagreed on other issues, such as rent control.[124]

A few months later, Cleaver and I each spoke to Jerusalem Demsas, then a reporter at *Vox*, about the Economic Fair Housing Act for an article that was published on Dr. Martin Luther King Jr.'s birthday. Given King's commitment to racial and economic justice, Cleaver told Demsas, "I think one of the greatest tributes that we can make to Dr. King's legacy is for us, this year, to pass an Economic Fair Housing Act."[125]

In addition to pursuing federal efforts, Loftus and I also began working with activists to begin developing support for state-level economic fair housing acts in friendly political environments such as Maine.

An Economic Fair Housing Act would do a lot to improve the lives of Americans but would work best if envisioned as part of a larger package of reforms, not a stand-alone strategy. If the goal is to promote economic mobility, affordability, racial justice, and environmental sustainability in housing, the Economic Fair Housing Act should be part of a larger set of housing solutions, including the following:

- A Race to the Top/Unlocking Possibilities–type program to provide incentives for zoning reform
- Passage of the Booker/Clyburn HOME Act to require recipients of federal grants to reduce exclusionary zoning
- A reinvigorated Affirmatively Furthering Fair Housing rule to combat racial segregation
- A strengthened disparate impact regulation to combat racially discriminatory policies

- More funding of audit studies through the Fair Housing Initiatives Program (FHIP) to identify and punish racial discrimination by landlords
- Resources for lawsuits (like the *Gautreaux* litigation) to prevent the concentration of public housing in high-poverty racially segregated communities
- Passage of inclusionary zoning laws like the one used in Montgomery County, Maryland
- State-level lawsuits like New Jersey's *Mount Laurel* litigation to require wealthy jurisdictions to provide their fair share of affordable housing
- More support for housing mobility programs like Moving to Opportunity and the new $28 million bipartisan housing mobility competitive grants program[126]
- Full funding for Section 8 Housing Choice Vouchers as envisioned by Rep. Ritchie Torres
- State rules, like those used in Nevada, to target more of the Low Income Housing Tax Credit (LIHTC) to high-opportunity neighborhoods[127]
- Passage of state and local laws to legalize missing middle housing like the legislation passed in Minneapolis, Oregon, Charlotte, and California

Although there are multiple paths to reform, the Economic Fair Housing Act must be part of this larger package. No tool is more critical to educating the public and driving change than giving people harmed by government-sponsored policies of income discrimination the chance to vindicate themselves in any federal court in the country.

The question becomes: In a deeply divided country, can an Economic Fair Housing Act pass?

[EIGHT]

THE POLITICAL POSSIBILITIES
OF A BRIGHTER FUTURE

AFTER PASSAGE OF THE LANDMARK 1964 CIVIL RIGHTS ACT AND
the monumental 1965 Voting Rights Act, Dr. Martin Luther King Jr.
had critical decisions to make about what to tackle next. He made
two important choices. He decided to go to Chicago in 1966 to pursue fair housing. And he made a decision—highly controversial within
the civil rights movement—to launch his second great dream: a Poor
People's Campaign to unite disadvantaged people across racial lines.
In November 1967, he announced his plan to go "into the Southwest
after the Indians, into the West after the Chicanos, into Appalachia
after the poor whites, and into the ghettoes after Negroes and Puerto
Ricans."[1]

The key to making a multiracial coalition work, said Bayard Rustin, an adviser to King, was to recognize that lower-middle-class white
people are neither liberal nor conservative; they are both, and how they
vote depends on how issues are framed.[2] At Rustin's urging, King put
class at the center of his framing. In fact, he said any effort to address

the nation's terrible history of racial discrimination should also include low-income white people. He proposed a multiracial Bill of Rights for the Disadvantaged, rather than a Bill of Rights for Black people. In doing so, King wrote, "It is a simple matter of justice that America, in dealing with the task of raising the Negro from backwardness, should also be rescuing a large stratum of the forgotten white poor."[3] Then, on April 4, 1968, while King was in Memphis to support striking sanitation workers, his life was tragically cut short at the age of thirty-nine by a white assassin.

At King's funeral in Atlanta, as many of the nation's leaders followed the mule cart carrying King's body, cheers broke out for one politician in particular: the forty-two-year-old US senator from New York and candidate for president, Robert F. Kennedy. "Along the route, Kennedy became the star," David Halberstam of the *New York Times* noted; a friend told the reporter, "it's as if they're anointing him."[4] Kennedy was a strong champion of civil rights. In a May 1968 Harris survey regarding seven presidential candidates, Robert Kennedy was identified as the most likely to "speed up" racial progress (69 percent), whereas Alabama governor George Wallace was the least likely (5 percent).[5] And yet Kennedy wondered: Would it be possible to build a multiracial coalition that included Black and Hispanic voters alongside some of the working-class white voters who were tempted to support Wallace?

In May 1968, running in the Democratic presidential primary in Indiana, Kennedy participated in a nine-hour motorcade through the steel mill towns of Gary, Hammond, and Whiting. A year before, race had divided Gary's mayoral election, with 90 percent of white residents voting for a Republican over the Black Democratic candidate, Richard Hatcher. Yet as the motorcade drove through town, Hatcher sat on one side of Kennedy, and Tony Zale, a white boxer who was the native-son hero of Gary's Slavic steelworkers, sat on the other. "It was hard to escape the meaning of that kind of symbol," recalled speechwriter Jeff Greenfield.[6] In the Indiana primary, Kennedy swept the vote of Black Americans and also did well enough with working-class white voters to win the seven largest Indiana counties where George Wallace ran strongest in 1964.[7] In primary after primary, RFK brought working-class Black, Hispanic, and white constituencies together as he championed a liberalism without elitism and a populism without racism.[8] In June 1968, Kennedy, too, was struck down by an assassin's bullet.

Today, King and Kennedy's coalition is in shambles. In 2016, America elected as president someone I consider a twenty-first-century George Wallace, who sowed hatred and division and yet was idolized by many white working-class voters.[9] Democrats largely shifted to a new political coalition of people of color and college-educated white people, which means Democrats now need to tiptoe around a variety of economic issues that might offend the interests of those college-educated white people, including, perhaps more than any other, the issue of exclusionary zoning.

Which raises the pointed question: Can federal exclusionary zoning reform in general, and the Economic Fair Housing Act proposal in particular, become law under current political conditions? The received wisdom would suggest that a federal policy on exclusionary zoning like the Economic Fair Housing Act faces six converging headwinds:

- All powerful NIMBY property owners will rise up against reform.
- Deeply entrenched racism will prevent progress.
- America's commitment to local control will defeat federal efforts.
- The law will be caught up in the progressive civil war between affordable housing and fair housing advocates.
- The potential alliance between working-class white people and working-class people of color that King and Kennedy sought will prove a pipe dream on this issue (as it has on so many others).
- Bipartisan support for reform in a polarized country will prove elusive.

These perennial concerns constitute very real obstacles, to be sure; but recent reforms at the state and local levels suggest that under the right conditions even this considerable set of hurdles is not impossible to surmount.

OVERCOMING THE POLITICAL POWER OF PROPERTY OWNERS BY STRESSING AFFORDABILITY

The first piece of conventional wisdom is that NIMBY homeowners almost always prevail in politics. After all, they have a lot of money tied up in their property. They are counting on it for retirement. And they will therefore fight tooth and nail against any new development that they perceive (rightly or wrongly) will threaten future appreciation gains. Self-interested concerns about property values will trump idealist arguments about racial segregation and the environment in almost all cases, this line of thinking suggests.

For many years, one rarely lost by betting on NIMBY forces, but today, we have seen that the winds have shifted in a number of communities. This may be true in part for idealistic reasons (such as an enhanced sensitivity to racial inequality), but mostly things are changing because homeowners in wealthy areas are not the only people who have a material self-interest in the question of zoning. The flip side of one person's outsized property appreciation gains is another person's housing affordability crisis. In addition, as outlined below, practical steps can be taken to mitigate concerns of property owners in order to reduce their fierce political resistance.

Growing evidence suggests NIMBY forces are not what they once were. Although reducing exclusionary zoning has always been seen as a political third rail, homeowners in Minneapolis, Charlotte, California, Oregon, Maine, and elsewhere have come to recognize that their iron grip on politicians has eased. Advocates of affordable housing, civil rights, and the environment joined forces with labor unions, tenant activists, young people, older adults, realtors, some developers, and libertarians to bring down the invisible but durable wall of government-mandated single-family exclusive zoning.

At the federal level, there is also evidence that homeowners don't have the political power they once did. Homeowners took two major hits in 2017 federal tax legislation, which passed both houses of Congress and was signed by President Trump. The cap on the mortgage interest deduction was lowered from $1 million to $750,000; and the ability to deduct property taxes, previously unlimited, was capped at $10,000. These longtime subsidies for upper-middle-class homeowners, the *Washington Post* noted, were "once thought untouchable."[10]

One important reason the politics of zoning reform has shifted is that the housing affordability crisis has grown so severe in several parts of the country that renters, would-be homeowners, and those homeowners seeking to move up are all challenging NIMBY forces in exclusive communities. Among urban residents, housing affordability is the number one issue of concern nationally, according to an August 2021 Manhattan Institute poll. The issue ranked higher than COVID-19, public safety and crime, taxes, schools, and jobs.[11] In Washington, DC, seven in ten residents said it is difficult to afford housing in their neighborhood, according to a February 2022 *Washington Post* poll.[12] In Seattle, a government poll found that "three-quarters of survey respondents would be comfortable with increased density" if it made housing "more affordable."[13] And in California, affordability has become such a problem that by 2022 Governor Gavin Newsom was willing to declare publicly, "NIMBYism is destroying the state."[14]

If affordability was previously thought to be mainly the concern of subsidized housing advocates and tenant groups, today the political salience of affordability is greater because it affects a wider swath of Americans. In parts of California, for example, college-educated upper-middle-class millennials are complaining, says Brian Hanlon, president and CEO of California YIMBY: "I went to a good school and can't afford rent? WTF?"[15] Census figures show that one-third of California's renters pay more than half their monthly income for rent.[16]

Politically allied with these millennials are employers in the tech industry who are having trouble recruiting and retaining employees given astronomical housing prices.[17] In 2018, more than a hundred CEOs of technology companies wrote in support of state legislation to reduce exclusionary zoning, arguing: "The lack of homebuilding in California imperils our ability to hire employees and grow our companies," in part because "the housing shortage places a huge burden on workers, many of whom face punishingly long commutes and pay over half of their income on rent."[18]

Voters are drawing the connection between exclusionary zoning and affordability. A headline in literature from leading activists in California in 2018 suggested: "The Rent Is Too Damn High and Homes Are Too Expensive. SB 827 will end the shortage and create millions of homes."[19] Hanlon notes: "We have a housing crisis entirely of our own making."[20]

The political impact of housing prices is seen abroad as well. In New Zealand, liberals and conservatives, who are normally at odds, came together in 2021 to support legislation requiring triplexes be allowed in most places in the country's major cities. The driving force was a housing affordability crisis that was ranked the most acute among all OECD nations.[21]

Notably, within the United States, the housing affordability crisis used to be salient mostly in coastal communities, but that is changing. Affordability of homes has become a problem across the country, in places such as Springfield, Missouri; Naples, Florida; and Appleton, Wisconsin.[22] A 2022 report found housing production was not keeping up with population growth in forty-seven of fifty states (everywhere but North Dakota, Wyoming, and West Virginia).[23] Says Sam Khater of Freddie Mac: "It's like the cancer was limited to certain parts of our economic body. And now it's spreading." As the malignancy spreads, so does the political demand for reform.

Finally, there may be ways to tamp down the political opposition of NIMBYs concerned with their property values through scaling and providing innovative insurance programs. Scale matters a great deal in housing, and there is much less opposition to missing middle housing than there is to large apartment buildings. When voters were asked, "Would you support or oppose a policy to ensure smaller, lower-cost homes like duplexes, townhouses, and garden apartments can be built in middle- and upper-class neighborhoods?" supporters outnumbered opponents by two to one in a 2019 poll.[24] A 2022 poll in twenty-six metropolitan areas found 73 percent of homeowners would support allowing either ADUs or duplexes and triplexes in residential communities.[25]

Moreover, to tamp down opposition from die-hard opponents of development, government could make an accommodation to NIMBY homeowners. When societies make necessary adjustments for the greater good—whether it is reducing pollution to slow climate change or promoting free trade to benefit consumers—it is not unusual for policymakers to seek to compensate people (e.g., coal miners, textile workers) who are impacted by the necessary change.

To the extent that curtailing unfair exclusionary zoning policies creates financial uncertainty for some homeowners, it may be possible to mitigate any losses through a policy of home equity ownership insurance. Dartmouth economist William A. Fischel has argued that exclusionary zoning can be thought of as a kind of insurance for homeowners—a policy that reduces the risk that one's property value will decline because of the introduction of new residents. One way to address this anxiety, Fischel argues, is to offer homeowners insurance on their equity. This "home value" insurance could be offered by the federal government, as flood insurance currently is, or it could be offered by developers as a way of reducing opposition to new proposals.[26]

Fischel also says policymakers could reduce homeowner anxiety about zoning changes by discouraging individuals from overinvesting in homes as a single, undiversified asset. Fischel writes: "The most obvious policy to dampen demand for regulation is to reduce the federal income tax subsidy to owner-occupied housing."[27] In particular, Congress could limit the deductibility of mortgage interest (currently capped at $750,000 mortgages) to the mortgage needed for a starter home. Congress could also restore full capital gains taxes on the sale of a home (and allow losses) rather than taxing only gains above $500,000.[28] Fischel points out that the Swiss have many fewer tax incentives for homeownership and also have less NIMBYism.[29] More broadly, US policymakers could strengthen Social Security retirement benefits to match those found in countries such as the Netherlands, Denmark, and Israel so that families would not feel so much pressure to rely on rising home values in order to enjoy a financially secure retirement.[30]

OVERCOMING THE POLITICAL POWER OF RACISM BY BROADENING THE LENS TO CLASS

The second piece of received wisdom suggests that opponents of reform will activate racism among white Americans to defeat proposed changes.

Going back to Dr. Martin Luther King's march for fair housing in Cicero, Illinois, and the defeat of Senator Paul Douglas in the 1960s, racism has often defeated good housing reforms.

It is always a mistake to underestimate the role of white racism in shaping public policy, but considerable evidence suggests the power of racial opposition to open neighborhoods is not what it once was. As noted in Chapter 7, whereas large majorities of white Americans used to think that it was perfectly fine to refuse to sell a home to a Black person, the numbers on that question have shifted dramatically over time.[31]

And Donald Trump's racially charged efforts in 2020 to suggest that Biden would allow "low-income housing" to "invade" suburban neighborhoods—language reminiscent of Trump's fear-mongering over caravans of Central American immigrants in 2018—appear to have fallen flat, as Biden *gained* among suburban voters compared with Hillary Clinton.[32] Indeed, in places like Minneapolis, the slogan that zoning is "the new redlining" appears to have had resonance with people of color and with some good-willed white voters. "Despite backlash and fatigue," Sheryll Cashin writes, "Black Americans have more allies than they have ever had in US history."[33]

Finally, as discussed in much greater detail below, the Economic Fair Housing Act's racially universal framing could serve to blunt racist appeals by broadening the group of beneficiaries to include many of the white working-class voters to whom Donald Trump appealed. Although housing has long been an arena in which right-wing politicians sought to scare white voters about the possibility of nonwhite families moving in, the Economic Fair Housing Act flips that equation by highlighting the common predicament—condescension—faced by working-class constituencies of all races from wealthy white people in exclusive suburbs.

OVERCOMING AMERICA'S COMMITMENT TO LOCAL CONTROL LIKE EARLIER FEDERAL EFFORTS

In the conventional wisdom, a bold federal reform like the Economic Fair Housing Act is also likely to run into the buzz saw of beliefs around the importance of local control in American politics. Zoning rules are primarily constructed at the local level, so a federal law is likely to be seen as radical federal overreach, this argument runs. To the extent the federal government gets involved, it is better to promote modest interventions like the Booker/Clyburn HOME Act, the received wisdom says. Political science 101 would suggest low-key proposals are easier to enact, and that more aggressive programs will be a much heavier lift because they will arouse greater opposition.

Experience and logic, however, suggest this thinking is flawed and outdated. To begin with, the traditional right-wing talking point about "local control" doesn't work in the case of exclusionary zoning, even on its own terms. The Economic Fair Housing Act is an effort to deregulate local rules and to prioritize the *most local prerogative of all*: that of individual homeowners to do what they want with their own private property without government telling them what to do.

Moreover, although the more moderate Booker/Clyburn bill might normally stand a better chance than the bolder Economic Fair Housing Act, it is not clear that a moderate nature of zoning legislation provides any protection from right-wing attack. The HOME Act was designed, Booker said, to be "a light touch."[34] But as one researcher who worked for Senator Booker and helped develop the HOME Act notes, President Trump blew the modest bill out of proportion and "was tweeting about it constantly."[35] Shortly after Stanley Kurtz wrote an article in the *National Review* suggesting that Booker's bill sought to "abolish the suburbs," Donald Trump Jr. posted a link to the article, and later that day President Trump began tweeting about single-family zoning.[36] The Booker aide concluded that in terms of politics, "I personally don't think it matters what the actual content of the bill is. Anything that touches on this topic will be entirely vilified."[37]

Given that some on the Trump right may try to weaponize *anything* seeking to curb exclusionary zoning, there may be value in going bold in order to provide moral clarity around the conversation and galvanize action. The Economic Fair Housing Act proposal, which draws attention to the issue of economically discriminatory zoning and draws parallels to the issue of racial discrimination and the Fair Housing Act, raises the larger moral issues at stake more clearly than a more moderate approach that suggests exclusionary zoning is merely something to be discouraged rather than stamped out. Whereas milder reforms send the message that exclusionary zoning is not good public policy, the Economic Fair Housing Act makes clear that using zoning to exclude people like KiAra Cornelius, Patricia McGee, Samantha, and Tehani from entire communities is wrong—so wrong, in fact, that victims of this state-sponsored discrimination should have available to them the right to sue in federal court, just like victims of racial discrimination have under the 1968 Fair Housing Act.

In this way, an Economic Fair Housing Act would do a much better job of educating the public about the harms of exclusionary zoning than the Booker legislation. As one Brookings scholar notes, "It's really hard to motivate people to fix zoning when they don't think about zoning as a problem." She explains, "We are not at the point nationally where people say, 'single-family-exclusive zoning, that's bad.'"[38] The lesson from California, says state senator Scott Wiener, is that "starting really big and calling the question" is a critical way of "advancing the conversation."[39]

OVERCOMING THE PROGRESSIVE "CIVIL WAR" OVER AFFORDABILITY VS. FAIR HOUSING

Fair housing reforms have often run into pushback from fellow progressives over a philosophical disagreement: Is it better to invest in low-income communities (place-based strategies) or give low-income families a chance to move to higher-opportunity neighborhoods (mobility strategies)? Indeed, Obama administration officials called the formulation of the 2015 Affirmatively Furthering Fair Housing Rule "the Civil War Project" because it brought to the surface long-standing disputes between those liberals who push integration as the best path forward and those progressives who advocate investing more funds into creating educational and economic opportunities in high-poverty communities instead.[40]

The fight is particularly acute over the question of whether to place subsidized affordable housing in higher-poverty communities (where more units can be built per dollar because land prices are cheaper) or in wealthier communities (where public housing residents are likely to enjoy greater opportunities).[41]

Both sides agree, however, that exclusionary zoning in wealthy communities is wrong. "There is general agreement between fair housing and community development advocates," one researcher says, on "the elimination of land-use regulations that have the effect of excluding lower-income housing in suburban communities."[42] By increasing housing supply, reforming exclusionary zoning increases affordability, which community development advocates prioritize. And by opening up high-opportunity neighborhoods, reforms further the chance for fair housing as well, providing a rare moment of truce in the ongoing civil war.

BUILDING AN ALLIANCE BETWEEN WORKING-CLASS WHITE PEOPLE AND PEOPLE OF COLOR

Conventional wisdom would also suggest that trying to build cross-racial working-class support for an Economic Fair Housing Act is a pipe dream. Especially after the rise of Donald Trump, this thinking suggests, the old New Deal coalition of working people is dead, the casualty of virulent racism among America's white working class. The future, it is said, lies in a rising coalition of people of color and college-educated white people who are sympathetic to them. Giving working-class people of all races the right to sue exclusive rich white suburbs would divide today's prevailing Democratic coalition, this logic suggests. In a Twitter thread about the Economic Fair Housing Act, one University of California professor writes: "At a time when suburbs are politically up for grabs . . . it would be nuts for national Dems to launch a frontal attack on exclusionary zoning."[43]

It is certainly true that conservative wealthy white people have for decades sought to divide working-class people in America along racial lines, and with great success; indeed, divide and conquer is the story of American politics. It is also true that many wealthy white people, some of whom vote for Democrats, want to continue to be able to exclude others, so there could be a political cost to reducing exclusionary zoning with that subset of voters.

As set forth below, however, although divide and conquer is the rule, it is deeply nefarious and should not be accepted as an immutable reality. Indeed, when issues are properly framed, multiracial working-class coalitions have proven powerful, particularly around the housing issue.

Moreover, the Economic Fair Housing Act could highlight common economic concerns across racial lines without giving an inch to racist white people. Indeed, the act could help reverse the conventional thinking on race and expose the truly deplorable behavior of upper-class white people who are the excluders. Ultimately, a new coalition formed around an Economic Fair Housing Act—and other issues—could help bring greater social cohesion in a society where working-class people of different races have for far too long been at each other's throats.

Many Americans see racism as a white psychological disorder that particularly affects less-educated people, but other analysts emphasize the economic driver of racism in America. Writers such as author Heather McGhee and *New York Times* columnist Jamelle Bouie emphasize how, for generations, wealthy white interests have stoked white racism as a tool for advancing their own interests. Bouie is sympathetic to scholar Oliver Cromwell Cox's argument that "it is capitalist exploitation—and not some inborn tribalism—that drives racial prejudice and conflict."[44]

Using race to divide poor white and Black people is a constant in American history. As McGhee notes, going back to the late 1600s, white servants and enslaved Black people joined together in Bacon's Rebellion in Virginia, but soon after—to prevent such cross-racial alliances—"colonial governments began to separate the servant class based on skin color."[45] In 1848, the white supremacist US senator John C. Calhoun sought to rally white people around their racial identity in order to prevent cooperation among lower-income white and Black people. "With us the two great divisions of society are not the rich and poor, but white and black," he declared, "and all the former, the poor as well as the rich, belong to the upper class, and are respected and treated as equals."[46]

In the industrial era, as labor unions began to take root in the North, wealthy southerners once again used race to keep unions weak in the former Confederacy. McGhee writes: "In the two-hundred-year history of American industrial work, there's been no greater tool against collective bargaining than employers' ability to divide workers by gender, race, or origin, stoking suspicion and competition across groups."[47] The tactic has been highly effective. In his famous 1935 study of Reconstruction and the Black and white southern workforce, W. E. B. Du Bois wrote, "There probably are not today in the world two groups of workers with practically identical interests who hate and fear each other so deeply and persistently and who are kept so far apart that neither sees anything of common interest."[48] After World War II, when the AFL-CIO tried to organize southern workers in a campaign called "Operation Dixie," McGhee says, employers used racial division to make sure that the campaign "failed spectacularly."[49]

In 2016, Donald Trump employed unusually blatant racial appeals to divide America's working class, successfully winning enormous margins among non-college-educated white people.[50] Once elected, Trump promptly delivered large tax cuts to the wealthiest Americans.[51] In a familiar pattern, Trump used terrible means (stoking racism) to achieve terrible ends (promoting greater economic inequality and reduced opportunity).

Astonishingly, Trump managed to do something even worse: he convinced some progressives that working-class white people are, by and large, so inherently racist that their vote is no longer worth contesting. Elie Mystal of the *Nation*, for example, wrote in 2021 that "a majority of white voters are racist and will punish Democrats for being insufficiently so." Rather than appealing to "poorly educated whites," he urged Democrats to "turn out every white *college educated* voter who rejects bigotry."[52] The tragedy, then, is that Trump succeeded in convincing some Democrats to identify working-class white people—people without educational or financial advantages—as the primary problem in American society. Having fallen into the trap of thinking that divide and rule is foreordained and not even worth fighting, these Democrats focus on a coalition of voters of color and highly educated "enlightened" white people as the only path forward.

But if divide and conquer strategies usually work in the United States, it is also true that every once in a while, lower-income and working-class people of all races break free of this trap and come together and engage in "fusion politics."[53]

After the Civil War, during Reconstruction, one researcher observes, "multiracial working-class political alliances formed in North Carolina, Alabama, and Virginia."[54] The low-income white people who formed alliances with Black people were called "Hillbillies," a term now used to connote an "unsophisticated country person."[55] But, says McGhee, following the brief period of fusion politics, "the wealthy white power structure reacted to the threat of class solidarity by creating new rules to promote white supremacy"—Jim Crow.[56]

In the 1940s, Franklin Roosevelt forged a powerful New Deal coalition of working-class people across racial lines until Richard Nixon and Ronald Reagan, employing racial appeals, effectively ended it in the 1960s, 1970s, and 1980s. Efforts by Robert Kennedy and Martin Luther King Jr. in the late 1960s to build multiracial working-class coalitions were both cut short by assassinations.

Given the demise of the New Deal coalition, political observers in Texas were stunned in 1997 to watch fusion politics rally once again. Working-class white, Hispanic, and Black people came together to support Texas's Top 10 Percent Plan, which provided automatic admissions to the University of Texas (UT) at Austin for any students in the top of their high school class, regardless of SAT scores or other factors. Although race and ethnicity are powerful fault lines in Texas politics, the battle over the 10 Percent Plan fell along lines of class. Wealthy suburban families did not like the plan because it meant their high-scoring kids had to compete against one another for a limited number of slots in each high school. Meanwhile, working-class white, Black, and Hispanic parents rallied around the plan because high schools that had never sent someone to UT Austin were suddenly able to access the state's flagship. In 2009, when UT Austin tried to significantly curtail the number of seats that would be awarded through the Top 10 Percent Plan (so that the university would have greater discretion over admissions), a remarkable coalition of rural white conservative legislators representing working-class white people, and urban Black and Hispanic legislators representing working-class people of color, blocked the effort.[57]

Other examples abound. In recent years, for example, in Kansas City, Missouri, a tenants-rights group, KC Tenants, has organized across racial lines to fight for better housing opportunities for renters. Many of the organizers are Black, but they recently reached out to work with a group of mostly white trailer park residents—many with Trump stickers on their cars—to win better terms for tenants when the county sought to build a new jail on the site of the trailer park.[58]

Exclusionary zoning—which hurts working-class people of all races—has proved especially fertile ground for forming multiracial working-class alliances in a number of states, including Massachusetts, Texas, Oregon, and California.

In 1969, a diverse group of Massachusetts state legislators allied against wealthy suburbs to pass an anti–snob zoning law. As discussed in Chapter 6, the law provided that the state could override local zoning in communities where less than 10 percent of housing stock is affordable.[59] The law was motivated in part as payback for suburban support of a 1965 school desegregation law, known as the Racial Imbalance Act, that effectively exempted suburbs because they had so few minority students.[60] As one researcher explained, some urban legislators were prompted in part by "the opportunity for retaliation against the suburban 'armchair liberals' who had voted for the Racial Imbalance Act."[61] Forty-one years later, an effort by wealthy suburbs to repeal the anti–snob zoning provision, known as 40b, was turned back in a statewide referendum by 58 percent of voters who supported retaining the populist law.[62]

In Houston, Texas, a strong multiracial coalition of working-class voters has twice come together to defeat exclusionary zoning efforts. In 1962 and 1993, wealthy homeowners pushed for Houston to adopt zoning laws through voter referenda, but on both occasions, opponents argued that such laws would increase segregation and drive up housing prices. The zoning efforts were defeated with votes that "came principally from working class Houstonians of all races," one observer writes.[63]

Fast-forward to the 2019 Oregon fight over reforming single-family exclusionary zoning laws. Observers saw, as noted in Chapter 6, "an alliance of Oregon's urban and rural areas against the suburbs."[64] Conservative white working-class constituencies and people of color were both accustomed to being looked down upon—sometimes because of race, sometimes because of class and education level. Their representatives in the state legislature pushed back against those who did the condescending and changed the law to prohibit exclusionary single-family zoning.

And in 2021, California saw a version of the same coalition rise up against exclusionary suburbs. Just as support for the Texas Top 10 Percent Plan and Oregon's exclusionary zoning reform divided by class more than political party, so, too, says state senator Scott Wiener, fights over exclusionary zoning in California are divided not by Democrat versus Republican but by rich versus poor. Some left-wing Democrats and right-leaning Republicans supported efforts to reform exclusionary zoning, he says, and some of each group have been opposed, he says.[65] The opponents of reform had one thing in common, Wiener says—they represented wealthier constituents who "wanted to keep certain people out of their community."[66] Supporters of reform, by contrast, wanted an end to exclusion and an end to policies that artificially drive up rents and housing costs for everyone.[67]

The framing of the Economic Fair Housing Act as combating *economic discrimination* could capitalize on populist sentiments evident in the fights over exclusionary zoning at the state level. The act's focus on class discrimination across racial lines would tap into the profound insight of Heather McGhee's that practices rooted in racism often hurt working-class white people as well.

McGhee, in her brilliant book *The Sum of Us*, points out that after Black people, working-class white people are often the secondary casualties of racism. McGhee vividly illustrates the point by recounting the story of what happened in many southern communities after the US Supreme Court ordered the racial desegregation of public pools. In Montgomery, Alabama, for example, white people had long enjoyed the Oak Park pool, the crown jewel of the local Parks Department. When the courts said the pool had to be shared with Black residents, the town council decided to drain the pool and fill it in with dirt. "Uncomprehending white children cried as the city contractors poured dirt into the pool, paved it over, and seeded it with grass," McGhee writes.[68] Upper-middle-class families opted for private backyard pools or dues-paying suburban pool clubhouses. In Washington, DC, McGhee notes, "125 new private swim clubs were opened in less than a decade following pool desegregation in 1953. The classless utopia faded," and working-class people of all races were on the outside.[69]

McGhee, and others such as authors Nancy Isenberg and Sheryll Cashin, point out countless examples of the phenomenon in American history. While slavery's central harm was cruelly imposed on Black people, the institution also depressed the wages of poor white people. Poll taxes were used to exclude Black voters, but poor white voters, too, were "caught up in the dragnet," McGhee says. Redlining was used to withhold federal investment based on the racial demographics of a community, but it also withheld investment based on a community's class composition. Laws to ban the voting of convicted felons disproportionately harmed Black people but also blocked millions of white people from voting. And racist tactics to prevent union organizing meant both Black and white workers suffered.[70]

Economic zoning—used initially to exclude Black people—fits neatly into this pattern, McGhee notes. Bans on multifamily housing, she says, impact not only Black families but also "millions of struggling white families."[71] These poor white neighborhoods, Sheryll Cashin observes, are places where residents experience many of the same "social ills" as those who live in poor Black neighborhoods.[72]

Naming the ways in which white people are hurt by racism—even if they aren't the primary victims—is politically important, McGhee says. She contrasts two approaches: an unsuccessful effort to organize workers across racial lines in Canton, Mississippi; and a successful fight to raise wages in Kansas City. In Canton, the United Auto Workers spent ten years trying to organize workers at a Nissan plant but failed after a campaign that used the rhetoric of civil rights fell flat with more conservative white workers.[73] In the successful "Kansas City Fight for $15," by contrast, fast-food workers didn't shy away from talking about race but also called out how all workers—including white workers—would benefit. In Kansas City, one sign read BLACK, WHITE, BROWN: DEFEAT MCPOVERTY, DEFEAT HATE. McGhee writes: "I thought back to Canton: The UAW's message about race had invoked civil rights for Black workers, but the fast-food message explicitly included white people in the coalition and named division, not just racial oppression, as a common enemy."[74] McGhee concludes: "By inviting white workers to see how the powerful profited from selling them a racist story that cost everybody ('whether brown, Black or white' as workers so often said), the Fight for $15 had managed to win the support of whites as well."[75]

In the housing arena, some proposals ignore McGhee's insight. Rep. Maxine Waters, for instance, has proposed providing $25,000 in down payment assistance to first-generation home buyers but excluding low-income white people from the program.[76] By contrast, an Economic Fair Housing Act is explicitly inclusive of working-class people of all races. It would help Patricia McGee in Dallas and Tehani in Columbus, but also Samantha in Springfield.

Research consistently finds an economic framing of policies—including efforts to curtail exclusionary zoning—is more powerful than a strictly racial framing. Yale University scholars have found in experimental research that "despite leftward shifts in public attitudes toward issues of racial equality, racial framing *decreases* support for race-neutral progressive policies."[77]

In the realm of zoning, specifically, a 2021 poll found that the *economic* case for allowing more construction of multifamily housing has broader public support than the narrower *racial* argument. Americans favored multifamily zoning over single-family zoning by just one percentage point (44 percent to 43 percent) after hearing that "Supporters of this say that it's a matter of racial justice. Single-family-exclusive zoning requirements lock in America's system of racial segregation, blocking Black Americans from pursuing economic opportunity and the American dream of home ownership." By contrast, support grew to eleven percentage points (47 percent to 36 percent) when respondents were presented with an economic argument: "Supporters of this say that this will drive economic growth as more people will be able to move to high opportunity regions with good jobs and will allow more Americans the opportunity to get affordable housing on their own, making it easier to start families."[78] Even Democrats, who liked both arguments, favored the economic growth rationale over the racial justice argument, by twelve points.

Moreover, other research finds that appeals to fairness have an even stronger influence than the economic productivity argument raised in the *Vox* poll. A 2021 poll in New Hampshire found the most effective argument with voters was one that said: "New Hampshire's planning and zoning regulations are unfair to working families struggling to make ends meet. By limiting the new housing that can be built, these restrictions drive up rents and house prices, making housing completely unaffordable for more and more Granite Staters. Everyone knows that some towns in New Hampshire are much more expensive to buy in than others, and they tend to be the places with better schools. So poor families in New Hampshire get stuck in poverty, because they cannot afford to live where they can get a better education for their kids."[79]

Although some progressives, like *The Nation*'s Elie Mystal, write off white working-class voters as irredeemably racist, research finds that there is great variation among America's millions of working-class white people. About 9 percent of white Americans are hard-core racist who have a favorable view of the Ku Klux Klan and will never be part of a progressive coalition.[80] But research has also found that about 15 percent of white working-class voters are liberal, about half are conservative, and about 35 percent are somewhere in between.[81] This suggests there are many white working-class swing voters to whom progressives can appeal, at least when issues are framed broadly to include them.

Moreover, framing policies that explicitly include both voters of color and also white working-class voters is not only politically smart. The inclusions of working-class white voters can also *reduce* their racial resentment and racism. A key purpose of segregation, after all, was to reduce feelings of solidarity among white and Black workers.[82] Research evidence suggests the very act of forming coalitions with Black people—as white labor union members do—can make white people less racist.[83]

And the rejection of white working-class voters as desirable partners betrays an ugly elitism that is at odds with what Democrats are supposed to stand for. The disdain was made explicit in 2016 when Hillary Clinton described half of Trump supporters as "deplorables."[84] Although Clinton was certainly right to denounce racist, sexist, and homophobic attitudes as deplorable, her comments were troubling on several levels. She changed what is normally an adjective into a noun, suggesting that white working-class people with less education than her were completely defined by their attitudes on race. Clinton used the line while speaking to audiences whom she described as "successful people" at fundraisers in the Hamptons and Martha's Vineyard, where her audiences knowingly chuckled at America's benighted white working class.[85] And it did not go unnoticed, one journalist remarked, that *deplorables* is not a term Clinton ever applied to highly educated Wall Street bankers who brought about the Great Recession and threw millions of people out of work.[86]

In 2016, the philosopher Michael Sandel says, some working-class people were left with "the galling sense that those who stood astride the hierarchy of merit looked down with disdain on those they considered less accomplished than themselves."[87] Trump knew exactly what to do with this. A candidate "keenly alive to the politics of humiliation," Sandel says, Trump claimed he respected working-class people.[88] Hillary Clinton won more than 70 percent of voters with advanced degrees, but Trump won voters without a college degree—a much larger share of the electorate—by seven percentage points, and non-college-educated white voters by two to one.[89]

Hillary Clinton's attitude did not disappear with the 2016 defeat. Speaking in Mumbai in 2018, Clinton bragged that she "won the places that represent two-thirds of America's gross domestic product"—that is, the places that had been successful in the era of globalization. This, Sandel writes, "displayed the meritocratic hubris that contributed to her defeat." The Democratic Party "once stood for farmers and working people against the privileged. Now, in a meritocratic age, its defeated standard bearer boasted that the prosperous, enlightened parts of the country had voted for her."[90]

If looking down upon those with less education fundamentally conflicts with Democratic values, there is another reason Martin Luther King, Bobby Kennedy, and others saw an alliance of working-class people across racial lines as the holy grail. If you want genuine social change in the country, it is unwise to be harnessed to a coalition that includes large numbers of upper-income highly educated people who are essentially at peace with the prevailing economic hierarchy.

In the case of exclusionary zoning, better-off suburban voters often don't want reform; rather, it's working-class people and people of color who feel looked down upon and humiliated for various reasons—Black and Hispanic people because of their race and ethnicity; and working-class white people because of their low education levels. For them, exclusionary zoning is part of a larger system in which doctors and lawyers and journalists and professors "go to college with one another, intermarry, gravitate to desirable neighborhoods in large metropolitan areas, and do all they can to pass on their advantages to their children."[91] Government zoning laws aid and abet this process and leave working-class people shut out of the club. But the common feeling of exclusion creates exciting possibilities for change. J. Anthony Lukas, author of *Common Ground*, a book about the Boston busing crisis, asked: "What kind of alliance could be cobbled together from people who feel equally excluded by class, or by some combination of class and race?"[92]

Although many progressives today ask why one would want to build a coalition that includes working-class white "deplorables," the issue of exclusionary zoning is clarifying because it reverses that question. Reforming exclusionary zoning would improve opportunity, make housing more affordable, reduce racial segregation, and be good for the planet, but if the UC professor cited above is right—that it would be "nuts" for Democrats to venture into this space given their college-educated constituency—what does that say about the costs of the current makeup of the Democratic coalition?[93]

Framing exclusionary zoning in terms of class helps make clear who constitutes the good guys and the bad guys in this story. So long as exclusion is framed exclusively as an issue of race, highly educated white people are let off the hook, because many of them probably do genuinely value having a Black doctor as a neighbor, and they can feel superior to the working-class white people they see on television spewing hate at Donald Trump rallies. But the class lens makes plain that working-class white, Black, Asian, and Hispanic people are all victims of a system that excludes what Cashin notes is "the vast majority of people" from residential "bastions of affluence."[94]

If, on the issue of exclusionary zoning, Democrats were to reembrace the narrative from an earlier era—taking the side of average Americans of all races who are seeking a better life—they could send a much more welcoming message to working-class white voters than the current media narrative that paints less-educated voters as ignorant and narrow-minded. As McGhee notes, it's human nature that "we all like to see ourselves as on the side of the heroes in a story."[95]

The COVID-19 pandemic could be a catalyst for reform. The experience reminded Americans that the country's working class consists of everyday heroes: the grocery clerks and bus drivers and nurses who came through for everyone else. The experience of the pandemic appears to have awakened a fighting spirit among some workers. Union organizing has surged at Amazon, Starbucks, and Chipotle, notes one labor reporter, and "the way many employers treated workers during the pandemic has played an outsize role in the current unionizing surge." Mistreatment of frontline heroes, who were denied personal protective equipment even as they risked their lives for the rest of us, may also help explain why broader public opinion has shifted on issues of worker dignity. The percentage of Americans who approve of labor unions skyrocketed to 71 percent in 2022, the highest level in fifty-seven years.[96]

It is possible that the pandemic will help some people rethink exclusionary policies as well. It's hard to square the admiration Americans have expressed for these workers during the pandemic with exclusionary zoning policies that humiliate working-class people by saying they are unwelcome as neighbors and their children are unwelcome as public school classmates.

WINNING CROSS-PARTISAN SUPPORT WITH
APPEALS TO LIBERTY AND EQUALITY

The final piece of conventional wisdom is that bipartisan reform on a contentious issue like zoning is exceedingly difficult to achieve in today's highly polarized partisan environment. Yes, reform was possible in liberal cites, like Minneapolis and Charlotte, and liberal states like Oregon and California, but bipartisan reform in Congress is likely impossible, especially because parties are hesitant to be seen as granting a president in an opposing party any victory.

It is certainly true that cross-partisan reform on *any* issue faces an uphill battle today, but it's important to note three points: there was bipartisan support for zoning reform in both Oregon and California; some critical Republican-leading constituencies favor reform; and, philosophically, liberalization of zoning laws taps into deeply held American values surrounding both liberty and equality that cross party lines.

First, as a factual matter, both Republicans and Democrats supported zoning reform in California and Oregon, and in both places, the legislation would not have passed without Republican support.[97] Even in Washington, DC, bipartisan support has coalesced around the Yes in My Backyard (YIMBY) Act, a modest effort that requires recipients of Community Development Block Grants to report on their efforts to reduce exclusionary zoning.[98] The bill passed the House of Representatives in March 2020.[99] The legislation has not yet passed the Senate, but there, too, is bipartisan support. The YIMBY Act's lead sponsor is Senator Todd Young (R-IN).[100]

At an October 2021 House of Representatives hearing, chaired by Rep. Emanuel Cleaver, both Republicans and Democrats expressed support for the idea of reducing exclusionary zoning. House liberals championed zoning reform as a way to combat racial and economic segregation and improve opportunities, while conservatives supported reform as a way to use government deregulation to lower housing prices.[101]

Second, the "inside game" in politics is important, and recall from Chapter 6 that in Oregon key Republican-leaning constituencies, such as some developers and realtors, supported reform alongside left-leaning constituencies of civil rights activists, labor unions, and environmentalists. Broadly speaking, developers often want more freedom to build without government limitations, and realtors may see additional commissions from the existence of more housing in a region.[102] Developers often oppose inclusionary zoning, which is seen as a form of affirmative action in the marketplace, but they generally support reducing exclusionary zoning as a form of government deregulation that is more akin to antidiscrimination.

Finally, whereas democratic egalitarianism and the liberty to be free from government interference are values that are often in tension, in the case of exclusionary zoning, they are not. Curtailing exclusionary zoning honors both egalitarian (antidiscriminatory) and libertarian (small government) streams in the American belief system that cut across party lines.

Liberty, including the right to be left alone by government, is a fundamental American belief, which helps explain the staying power of the Republican Party over the years. Although Donald Trump came out hard against zoning reform, invoking fears about crime and reduced property values from the presence of low-income families, there is a second stream of Republican thought on zoning that taps into deeply held American beliefs about liberty, which may, over time, reemerge as dominant. (Indeed, the Trump administration itself created a commission to streamline zoning, before Trump saw a chance to demagogue the issue.)[103]

Scholars find that libertarians are part of an "emerging cross-ideological consensus on zoning." Indeed, more conservative western and southern communities tend to have less zoning regulation than the more liberal Northeast.[104] Libertarians see reducing exclusionary zoning as a "property rights issue."[105] One observer notes that zoning restrictions may be "the single biggest constraint in many parts of the country on people's ability to build what they want on their own property."[106] The property rights movement, meanwhile, has won a number of state ballot initiatives in the past fifteen years.[107] In addition, conservatives such as the American Enterprise Institute's Ryan Streeter support zoning reform as a way to make housing more affordable and thereby reduce government costs for providing public housing.[108] Given Trump's failure to motivate suburban voters in 2020 with his attacks on zoning reform, Republicans may well return over time to supporting zoning deregulation.

At the same time, reducing exclusionary zoning is deeply egalitarian because it says people should not be discriminated against by local governments because of their race or income. Reducing exclusionary policies taps into the fundamental American idea that even if people don't make the same amount of money, they are social equals, which is why Americans readily call each other by their first names in a way that people in other countries simply don't. "Equality is the first truth of our founding document," one journalist notes, "the one that leads to all the others."[109] This egalitarian thread is itself bipartisan: it challenges the racist idea that white people are better than Black people and the elitist idea that highly educated coastal residents are more enlightened than everyone else.

Exclusionary zoning could prove to be a particularly strong candidate for a cross-party coalition because bipartisan efforts around the issue have not been the result of typical split-the-difference negotiations. Instead, fighting exclusionary zoning appears to be one of those situations where, in the words of one analyst, "different groups in our society can arrive at the same policy conclusion from distinctly different directions."[110]

The reform effort is anti-racist and anti-elitist. It honors the most basic democratic ideals of the nation: that each of us has the right to be treated with human dignity. Exclusionary zoning, which suggests that low-income and working-class people are so degraded that they have no place in exclusive communities, offends the very foundations of democratic society. As such, the question is not so much whether reform can ever happen but rather why it has taken so long.

EPILOGUE

Imagining a Better America

When Rep. Emanuel Cleaver told *Vox* in 2022 that passing an Economic Fair Housing Act would be "one of the greatest tributes we can make to Dr. King's legacy," he made a profound point.[1] Indeed, the Economic Fair Housing Act picks up on four related themes in King's life: his focus on housing segregation as a fountainhead of inequality; his call for addressing economic injustice as the next phase of the civil rights revolution; his emphasis on the dignity of all workers; and his commitment to forming a multiracial alliance of working people.

Fundamental to King's vision of creating a "Beloved Community" was taking steps to eradicate racial residential segregation. In King's fight for fair housing in Chicago—where he said he aroused more hatred than he did in his fights for voting rights or fair employment laws—he declared, "Segregation distorts the soul and damages the personality. It gives the segregator a false sense of superiority and the segregated a false sense of inferiority."[2] When the Fair Housing Act of 1968 was signed into law just days after King's assassination, it was universally recognized as an homage to King's vision.

King would appreciate the 30 percent decline in racial segregation in the years since passage of the Fair Housing Act, but he surely would be deeply dismayed that, though many middle-class African Americans have had the chance to flee slums, millions of low-income people remain trapped in areas that impede their chance to flourish. In asking the rhetorical question—"What does it profit a man to be able to eat at an integrated lunch counter if he doesn't have enough money to buy a hamburger?"—King recognized that the second phase of the civil rights movement had to address economic barriers to advancement.[3] Dismantling government-sponsored economic discrimination through an Economic Fair Housing Act is a natural follow-on to the 1968 housing legislation.

The Economic Fair Housing Act also taps into King's emphasis on the dignity of all work and of all workers. When he was shot in April 1968, King was visiting Memphis, after all, to support striking sanitation workers. He told them that "all labor has dignity" and that they were performing an essential service upon which society depends.[4] The Economic Fair Housing Act reinforces that message: that erecting government-sponsored walls to exclude hardworking people from entire communities is insulting, demeaning, and offensive.

Finally, the Economic Fair Housing Act takes up the mantle for King's vision of accomplishing social change, not through a coalition centered around highly educated upper-middle-class white people and people of color but through a multiracial coalition of society's more humble members. Before his death, King was assembling the Poor People's Campaign to include Native Americans, Mexican Americans, poor white people, Puerto Ricans, and Black people. He declared, "And we're going to bring them together and enlarge this campaign into something bigger than just a civil rights movement for Negroes."[5]

Imagine how life would be different if we began to tear down the invisible walls that local governments erect to keep people apart.

Imagine what would happen if more low-wage mothers like KiAra Cornelius, Patricia McGee, Samantha, and Tehani had a chance to raise their kids in safer neighborhoods with better schools; if more kids could benefit from the 31 percent average wage increase Raj Chetty found for children who moved to better neighborhoods before age thirteen.

Imagine if the supply of housing wasn't artificially capped by zoning rules, and people like Janet Johnson didn't have to worry so much about whether to pay rent or buy medicine. If more affordable housing prices meant less homelessness. If people who wanted to move to coastal areas for a wage boost could do so because housing prices were not astronomical.[6] If workers had less stress because they didn't have to live on the outskirts of metropolitan areas and take two buses to work. If housing was built where people needed it so that auto emissions declined and we had fewer severe weather events.

Imagine if, because walls were coming down, metropolitan areas were less racially segregated and people met more neighbors who came from different racial and ethnic backgrounds—and as a result (according to 94 percent of studies) this interracial contact resulted in less racial prejudice.[7] Imagine also what life would be like if more African Americans experienced the higher employment and higher wages that result from reduced segregation.

Imagine, too, an America in which low-wage workers of all races had the legal tools to fight government-sponsored economic discrimination in zoning; if people could fight back against humiliating policies that tell them they are unwanted in entire communities. If, as Richard Reeves observes, "a geography gap can become an empathy gap," imagine a reversal of that reality: that as barriers came down, and we returned to an earlier time when people of different classes rubbed shoulders more often, understanding and empathy slowly grew and feelings of superiority began to ebb.[8] In this type of society, tearing down the walls of separation is a form of patriotism because it helps us see other Americans as fellow citizens to be honored and cherished.[9]

Imagine if an Economic Fair Housing Act helped blunt right-wing divide-and-conquer racial politics, showing working-class people of all races that Democrats have their back and are willing to stand up to wealthy interests on the right and on the left. Imagine, further, that in this America, a robust multiracial working-class coalition that came together around housing was inspired also to create laws to make union organizing easier and to make investments in education and health care possible, as the incessant pressure to reduce taxes for the wealthy subsided. In this America, working-class people would enjoy what Heather McGhee calls the "solidarity dividend"—higher wages from the ability to unionize and more investments in schooling for children.[10]

Imagine, finally, the possibility of a more cohesive, less polarized democracy. As state-sponsored walls that divide Americans by race and class began to come down, imagine that people of different backgrounds—who currently live apart and easily demonize one another as political enemies—were more likely to converse and come to know one another as more than just members of an opposing political party.[11] In this world, strong political differences would likely endure, as they do between extended family members, but if people had the chance to talk about sports, or their kids, it would become more difficult to see people from different political parties as just antagonists, and the chances of political compromise would increase.

America, as McGhee notes, is "the world's most radical experiment in democracy," because we are "a nation of ancestral strangers that has to work to find connection even as we grow more diverse every day."[12] The government-sponsored walls that divide us do enormous harm—blunting opportunity, making housing unaffordable, damaging the environment, segregating us by race and class, and doing significant injury to our fragile democracy. It is time to recognize the walls that separate us, and then proceed to tear them down.

Acknowledgments

THE IDEA FOR THIS BOOK DATES BACK TO APRIL 2014, WHEN
Paul Jargowsky, a longtime friend and colleague, raised an intriguing
question at an Economic Policy Institute panel discussion: Why don't
we make income discrimination in housing illegal?

Of the many people I wish to thank for help with this book, I want
to highlight the inspiring low-wage mothers who shared their stories
with me: KiAra Cornelius, Janet Williams (pseudonym), and Tehani in
the Columbus, Ohio, region; Patricia McGee in the Dallas, Texas, area;
and Samantha in the Springfield, Massachusetts, metropolitan area.
They were generous with their time, and open about their lives, in part
because they told me they want other low-wage families to have better
opportunities. They are an inspiration to me.

Thanks also to the local government officials, activists, and political
leaders from Ohio, Texas, Massachusetts, Minnesota, Oregon, and California who spoke to me about exclusionary obstacles in these states and
what people are trying to do about them: Michael Kelley, Amy Klaben,
and Jason Reece (Ohio); Mike Koprowski, Demetria McCain, Myriam

Acknowledgments

Igoufe, Jim Schutze, Miguel Solis, Mohammed Choudhury, Tyronda Minter, and Ann Lott (Texas); Kristin Haas, Dana LeWinter, and Chris Kluchman (Massachusetts); Denise Butler, Janne Flisrand, Kyrra Rankine, and Rick Varco (Minnesota); Taylor Smiley Wolfe (who spoke with my colleague Emma Vadehra) (Oregon); Brian Hanlon, Scott Wiener, and Don Falk (California). Thanks also to developers Matt Hoffman and Matt Murphy who spoke with me about development nationally and in the Washington, DC, area, and to Senator Cory Booker, who spoke to me about his legislation to curb exclusionary zoning.

In this book, I drew upon superb research from a number of important scholars and writers. Among those most influential to my thinking are Kendra Bischoff, Sara Bronin, Sheryll Cashin, Raj Chetty, Jerusalem Demsas, Matthew Desmond, Peter Dreier, Katherine Levine Einstein, Ingrid Gould Ellen, William Fischel, Richard Florida, Lance Freeman, Peter Ganong, Edward Glaeser, David Glick, M. Nolan Gray, Nancy Isenberg, Paul Jargowsky, Noah Kazis, Michael Lens, Diana Lind, Douglas Massey, Heather McGhee, Maxwell Palmer, Andre Perry, John Powell, Robert Putnam, Sean Reardon, Richard Reeves, Richard Rothstein, Jonathan Rothwell, David Rusk, Michael Sandel, Richard Sander, Jenny Schuetz, Heather Schwartz, Patrick Sharkey, Daniel Shoag, Ilya Somin, Matthew Stewart, Omar Wasow, William Julius Wilson, and Matt Yglesias.

I also want to acknowledge my former colleagues at the Century Foundation. To begin with, some of the stories and research in this book are adapted from a series of Century Foundation reports, and I am grateful to Mark Zuckerman and Jason Renker for their willingness to allow me to use material from those reports in this book. In addition, at the Century Foundation, a number of colleagues provided superb research assistance on housing issues, including Lara Adekeye, Michelle Burris, Yvette Chen, Tabitha Cortes, Emma Miller, Kimberly Quick, Elliott Rigsby, and Emma Vadehra. A special shout-out to Michelle, who worked tirelessly to identify voices not normally included in policy debates and who joined me in interviewing low-wage mothers in the Columbus, Ohio; Dallas, Texas; and Springfield, Massachusetts, regions.

I also want to thank my colleagues Stefan Lallinger, Halley Potter, Michelle Burris, and Lara Adekeye, who are involved in the Century Foundation's Bridges Collaborative, which brings together fifty-seven school districts, housing organizations, and charter schools that are committed to integration. I've learned a lot from Bridges members, and especially Karen DuBois Walton of New Haven, with whom I led a Bridges session, "Integrating Neighborhood Schools via Housing."

In December 2020, the Century Foundation and the Bridges Collaborative assembled more than twenty of the nation's leading thinkers from across the country to discuss a federal path forward on exclusionary zoning. I want to thank the participants, who included elected officials, civil rights activists, libertarians, and housing researchers, for shaping my thinking: Xavier de Souza Briggs, Sheryll Cashin, Ingrid Gould Ellen, William Fischel, Brandon Fuller, Salin Geevarghese, Solomon Greene, Megan Haberle, Olatunde C. Johnson, Noah Kazis, Tom Loftus, Demetria McCain, Tyronda Minter, Rolf Pendall, Lisa Rice, Cassandra Robertson, Ibraheem Samirah, Jenny Schuetz, Ilya Somin, Philip Tegeler, Scott Wiener, and Pablo Zevallos (as well as Century Foundation colleagues Casey Berkovitz, Michelle Burris, Stefan Lallinger, and Halley Potter, who participated in the discussion).

Thanks also to a number of colleagues who provided important editorial feedback and advice at one point or another in my writing and thinking about this topic, including Lara Adekeye, Greg Anrig, Casey Berkovitz, William Fischel, Paul Jargowsky, Stefan Lallinger, Tom Loftus, Lucy Muirhead, Halley Potter, Jason Renker, Elliot Rigsby, David Rusk, Richard Sander, Philip Tegeler, Brooke Williams, Jonathan Zabala, and Mark Zuckerman. Thanks as well to Century's communications team for their support, including Alex Edwards, Abby Grimshaw, Jonnea Herman, and McKenzie Maxson. And appreciation to Danny Weiss and Juan Diego Mazuera Arias, who helped me approach members of Congress with housing reform ideas. Special shout-out to

William Fischel, Thomas Loftus, and Conor Williams, who provided valuable feedback on the manuscript.

Thanks, too, to my students in a class I teach at George Washington University's Trachtenberg School of Public Policy and Public Administration called "Civil Rights and Economic Inequality," who have offered me fresh perspectives on housing segregation issues.

A huge thanks to my agent, Lisa Adams at the Garamond Agency, who helped shape my book proposal and negotiated the contract. Thanks to John Mahaney at PublicAffairs, whose editorial advice has been invaluable, and to Christina Palaia, whose copyediting was meticulous.

Finally, I want to thank my wonderful family—my mother, Jeannette Kahlenberg; my sisters, Joy Fallon and Trudi Picciano (and their husbands, Bob and Joe); my brilliant daughters, Cindy, Jessica, Caroline, and Amanda (and sons-in-law, Matt, Jason, and Will), and my incredible wife, Rebecca—for their love and support. Rebecca, who works with people experiencing homelessness, is the most generous person I know and opens her heart to people of all walks of life. She lives the values I write about in this book. During the writing of this volume, Rebecca and I were delighted by the birth of our first three grandchildren, Adam, Hailey, and David, who give us immeasurable amounts of pleasure. May they see a future in which the walls that divide us begin to come down.

Notes

INTRODUCTION: THE WALLS WE DON'T SEE

1. KiAra Cornelius, interview with Michelle Burris and author, February 12, 2020 (hereafter, Cornelius interview), 5, and 1–3; and KiAra Cornelius, interview with Michelle Burris and author, April 7, 2020 (hereafter, Cornelius interview II), 1–2.

2. "Siebert Elementary School," Great Schools, last accessed July 2020, https://www.greatschools.org/ohio/columbus/619-Siebert-Elementary-School/.

3. Cornelius interview, 2 and 5. "Columbus Arts and Technology Academy," Great Schools, last accessed July 2020, https://www.greatschools.org/ohio/columbus/5947-Columbus-Arts—Technology-Academy/.

4. See Richard Rothstein, *The Color of Law: A Forgotten History of How Our Government Segregated America* (New York: Liveright Publishing, 2017); and Ta-Nehisi Coates, "The Case for Reparations," *Atlantic*, June 2014, https://www.theatlantic.com/magazine/archive/2014/06/the-case-for-reparations/361631/.

5. Alex Baca, Patrick McAnaney, and Jenny Schuetz, "'Gentle' Density Can Save Our Neighborhoods," Brookings Institution, December 4, 2019, https://www.brookings.edu/research/gentle-density-can-save-our-neighborhoods/.

6. M. Nolan Gray, *Arbitrary Lines: How Zoning Broke the American City and How to Fix It* (Washington, DC: Island Press, 2022), 111.

7. Lee Anne Fennell, "Homes Rule (reviewing William A. Fischel, *The Home-Voter Hypothesis: How Home Values Influence Local Government Taxation, School

Finance, and Land-Use Policies)," *Yale Law Journal* 112 (2002): 617–664, https://chicagounbound.uchicago.edu/cgi/viewcontent.cgi?article=8029&context=journal_articles.

8. William Fischel, *Zoning Rules! The Economics of Land Use Regulation* (Cambridge, MA: Lincoln Institute of Land Policy, 2015), 201.

9. See John R. Logan and Brian Stults, "The Persistence of Segregation in the Metropolis: New Findings from the 2020 Census," Diversity and Disparities Project, Brown University, August 12, 2021, 2, https://s4.ad.brown.edu/Projects/Diversity/Data/Report/report08122021.pdf. See also William H. Frey, "Census Shows Modest Declines in Black-White Segregation," Brookings Institution, December 8, 2015, https://www.brookings.edu/blog/the-avenue/2015/12/08/census-shows-modest-declines-in-black-white-segregation/ (finding Black–white segregation declined in 45 of 52 metropolitan areas between 2000 and 2010–2014).

10. Maria Krysan, Kyle Crowder, and Michael D. M. Bader, "Pathways to Residential Segregation," in *Choosing Homes, Choosing Schools*, ed. Annette Lareau and Kimberly Goyette (New York: Russell Sage Foundation, 2014), 28.

11. Robert Putnam, *Our Kids: The American Dream in Crisis* (New York: Simon & Schuster, 2015), 38–39. See also Douglas S. Massey, Len Albright, Rebecca Casciano, Elizabeth Derickson, and David N. Kinsey, *Climbing Mount Laurel: The Struggle for Affordable Housing and Social Mobility in an American Suburb* (Princeton, NJ: Princeton University Press, 2013), 16. ("As class segregation increased and spatial concentration of both affluence and poverty rose in recent decades, the degree of black–white segregation steadily fell.")

12. Juliet Eilperin and Michelle Boorstein, "In Frank Language, Obama Tackles Poverty's Roots," *Washington Post*, May 13, 2015, A2, https://www.washingtonpost.com/local/in-frank-language-obama-addresses-povertys-roots/2015/05/12; and "Why Obama Is Worried About 'Class Segregation,'" *National Journal*, May 12, 2015, https://www.nationaljournal.com/s/27186. Racial segregation does contribute to income segregation, but the problems are also independent. If racial segregation were eliminated, two-thirds of economic segregation would remain. See Paul Jargowsky, "Segregation, Neighborhoods, and Schools," in Lareau and Goyette, *Choosing Homes, Choosing Schools*, 98 ("racial segregation by itself contributes about a third of the total economic segregation").

13. Sean Reardon and Kendra Bischoff, "The Continuing Increase in Income Segregation, 2007–2012," Stanford Center for Education Policy Analysis, 2016, https://cepa.stanford.edu/sites/default/files/the%20continuing%20increase%20in%20income%20segregation%20march2016.pdf.

14. Michael J. Sandel, *The Tyranny of Merit: What's Become of the Common Good?* (New York: Farrar, Straus & Giroux, 2020), 95.

15. Raj Chetty, Nathaniel Hendren, and Lawrence F. Katz, "The Effects of Exposure to Better Neighborhoods on Children: New Evidence from the

Moving to Opportunity Experiment" (NBER Working Paper no. 21156, National Bureau of Economic Research, May 2015), 2–3, www.nber.org/papers/w21156.

16. See Jason Reece and Jee Young Lee, "Move to PROSPER: Interim Program Evaluation 1.0," Ohio State University, January 2019, 8, 11, 13, 18, https://static1.squarespace.com/static/589c7c3ba5790a3587715ef5/t/5c64737ec83025c7da381a13/1550087058793/Final+MTP+Interim+Report+1.0+February+12+2019.pdf; Amy Klaben, interview with Michelle Burris and author, January 24, 2020 (hereafter, Klaben interview), 3.

17. Sheryll Cashin, *White Space, Black Hood: Opportunity Hoarding and Segregation in the Age of Inequality* (Boston: Beacon Press, 2021), 151.

18. "Goshen Lane Elementary School," Great Schools, last accessed July 2020, https://www.greatschools.org/ohio/gahanna/2312-Goshen-Lane-Elementary-School/.

19. "Gahanna South Middle School," Great Schools, last accessed July 2020, https://www.greatschools.org/ohio/columbus/2307-Gahanna-South-Middle-School/.

20. Cornelius interview, 5. Subsequent quotations and citations from Cornelius are from Cornelius interview, 3–5, and Cornelius interview II, 1.

21. Cornelius interview, 3–4; "Columbus Arts" and "Gahanna South Middle," Great Schools.

22. Jonathan Rothwell and Douglas Massey, "Density Zoning and Class Segregation in U.S. Metropolitan Areas," *Social Science Quarterly* 91, no. 5 (December 2010): 1123–1143, http://www.ncbi.nlm.nih.gov/pmc/articles/PMC3632084/.

23. Editorial Board, "Americans Need More Neighbors," editorial, *New York Times*, June 15, 2019, https://www.nytimes.com/2019/06/15/opinion/sunday/minneapolis-ends-single-family-zoning.html.

24. Susan J. Popkin, Samantha Batko, and Corianne Scally, "Why We Need to Expand, Not Restrict, Access to Housing Assistance," Urban Institute, January 4, 2018, https://www.urban.org/urban-wire/why-we-need-expand-not-restrict-access-housing-assistance.

25. Joint Center for Housing Studies at Harvard, *The State of the Nation's Housing 2021* (Cambridge, MA: Joint Center for Housing Studies of Harvard University, 2021), 4, https://www.jchs.harvard.edu/sites/default/files/reports/files/Harvard_JCHS_State_Nations_Housing_2021.pdf (46 percent of renters paid more than 30 percent of incomes); and Equitable Housing Institute, "Toward a Comprehensive Ban on Exclusionary Zoning Practices" (memorandum, Equitable Housing Institute, December 2019), 2, https://www.equitablehousing.org/images/PDFs/PDFs--2021-/EHI_Toward-comprehensive-ban-tech-edits_1-2022.pdf (in the 1960s, the proportion was half of what it is today).

26. Nicole Friedman, "U.S. Housing Affordability in June Was the Worst Since 1989," *Wall Street Journal*, August 12, 2022, https://www.wsj.com/articles/u-s-housing-affordability-in-june-was-the-worst-since-1989-11660312801.

27. "Is the Rent Too High? Way More Than 525,600 Minutes of Rent Data," FRED Blog, April 15, 2019, https://fredblog.stlouisfed.org/2019/04/the -climbing-cost-of-renting/.

28. Janet Williams is a pseudonym. See Richard D. Kahlenberg, "Hearing from Low-Wage Working Mothers: How a Housing Program in Ohio Connects Children to Better Schools," Century Foundation, August 4, 2020, https://tcf .org/content/report/hearing-from-low-wage-working-mothers-how-a-housing -program-in-ohio-connects-children-to-better-schools/.

29. Richard D. Kahlenberg, "Updating the Fair Housing Act to Make Housing More Affordable," Century Foundation, April 9, 2018, https://tcf.org /content/report/updating-fair-housing-act-make-housing-affordable/.

30. Gray, *Arbitrary Lines*, 74.

31. Chang-Tai Hsieh and Enrico Moretti, "Housing Constraints and Spatial Misallocation," *American Economic Journal: Macroeconomics* 11, no. 2 (2019): 1–39 (at 25–26), https://pubs.aeaweb.org/doi/pdfplus/10.1257/mac.20170388.

32. See discussion, Chapter 2.

33. Martin Luther King Jr., Remarks at Mason Temple, March 1968, quoted in Terry Gross and Michael Honey, "Martin Luther King's Last Campaign for Equality," National Public Radio, April 4, 2008, https://www.npr.org /templates/story/story.php?storyId=89372561.

34. See Kyle K. Moore and Valerie Wilson, "Pandemic-Related Economic Insecurity Among Black and Hispanic Households Would Have Been Worse Without a Swift Policy Response," Economic Policy Institute, September 16, 2021, https://www.epi.org/blog/pandemic-related-economic-insecurity -among-black-and-hispanic-households-would-have-been-worse-without-a-swift -policy-response/ (white median family income in 2020 was $74,912 and Black median household income was $46,600); and Neil Bhutta, Andrew C. Chang, Lisa J. Dettling, and Joanne W. Hsu, "Disparities in Wealth by Race and Ethnicity in the 2019 Survey of Consumer Finances," Board of Governors of Federal Reserve, FEDS Notes, September 28, 2020, https://www.federalreserve.gov /econres/notes/feds-notes/disparities-in-wealth-by-race-and-ethnicity-in-the -2019-survey-of-consumer-finances-20200928.html (white median family wealth was $188,200 and Black median family wealth was $36,100).

35. John R. Logan, "Separate and Unequal: The Neighborhood Gap for Blacks, Hispanics and Asians in Metropolitan America," US2010 Project, July 2011, 5, https://www.researchgate.net/publication/266355895_Separate_and _Unequal_The_Neighborhood_Gap_for_Blacks_Hispanics_and_Asians_in _Metropolitan_America.

36. *Buchanan v. Warley*, 245 US 60 (1917).

37. Alexander Sahn, "Racial Diversity and Exclusionary Zoning: Evidence from the Great Migration" (unpublished manuscript, January 26, 2022), pdf, https://drive.google.com/file/d/10_-WcJe4v6GfxVDfJ2h-R3pvjK4yjig0/view.

38. Rothstein, *The Color of Law*, 9–10.

39. Cashin, *White Space, Black Hood*, 60–61.

40. Rothstein, *The Color of Law*, 177.

41. Orlando Patterson, "The Long Reach of Racism in the U.S.," *Wall Street Journal*, June 5, 2020, https://www.wsj.com/articles/the-long-reach-of-racism-in -the-u-s-11591372542.

42. See Kimberly Quick and Richard D. Kahlenberg, "The Government Created Housing Segregation. Here's How the Government Can End It," *American Prospect*, July 2, 2019, https://prospect.org/civil-rights/government-created -housing-segregation.-government-can-end-it./.

43. See discussion, Chapter 4.

44. See, e.g., Ilya Somin, "Why More Liberal Cities Have Less Affordable Housing," *Washington Post*, November 2, 2014, https://www.washingtonpost .com/news/volokh-conspiracy/wp/2014/11/02/more-liberal-cities-have -less-affordable-housing/.

45. Sandel, *The Tyranny of Merit*, 95.

46. Sandel, *The Tyranny of Merit*, 25.

47. Sandel, *The Tyranny of Merit*, 96.

48. Sandel, *The Tyranny of Merit*, 95 (quoting Toon Kuppens, Russell Spears, Antony S. R. Manstead, Bram Spruyt, and Matthew J. Easterbrook, "Educationalism and the Irony of Meritocracy: Negative Attitudes of Higher Educated People Towards the Less Educated," *Journal of Experimental Social Psychology* 76 [May 2018]: 429–447, at 441–442, http://sro.sussex.ac.uk/id/eprint/71335/1 /__smbhome.uscs.susx.ac.uk_ellenaj_Desktop_SRO_after%20august_Kuppens %20Educationism%20and%20the%20irony%20of%20meritocracy.pdf).

49. See Richard D. Kahlenberg, "The 'New Redlining' Is Deciding Who Lives in Your Neighborhood," opinion, *New York Times*, April 19, 2021, https:// www.nytimes.com/2021/04/19/opinion/biden-zoning-social-justice.html.

50. See discussion, Chapter 5.

51. Cashin, *White Space, Black Hood*, 161.

52. Michael Lens, "Incorporating Data on Crime and Violence into the Assessment of Fair Housing," in *Furthering Fair Housing: Prospects for Racial Justice in America's Neighborhoods*, ed. Justin P. Steil, Nicholas F. Kelly, Lawrence J. Vale, and Maia S. Woluchem (Philadelphia: Temple University Press, 2021), 205.

53. See Jerusalem Demsas in Ezra Klein, "How Blue Cities Became So Outrageously Unaffordable: How the Party of Big Government Became the Party of Paralysis," *Ezra Klein Show* (podcast), *New York Times*, July 23, 2021, https://www.nytimes.com/2021/07/23/opinion/ezra-klein-podcast-jerusalem -demsas.html?showTranscript=1.

54. Nikole Hannah-Jones, "Living Apart: How the Government Betrayed a Landmark Civil Rights Law," *ProPublica*, June 25, 2015, https:// www.propublica.org/article/living-apart-how-the-government-betrayed -a-landmark-civil-rights-law.

55. Michael A. Fletcher, "Mikulski, Champion of Liberal Causes, Led Fight to Kill MTO," *Baltimore Sun*, September 25, 1994, https://www .baltimoresun.com/news/bs-xpm-1994-09-25-1994268041-story.html.

56. Janne Flisrand, "Minneapolis' Secret 2040 Sauce Was Engagement," *Streets MN*, December 10, 2018, https://streets.mn/2018/12/10/minneapolis -secret-2040-sauce-was-engagement/; and Richard D. Kahlenberg, "How Minneapolis Ended Single-Family Zoning," Century Foundation, October 24, 2019, https://tcf.org/content/report/minneapolis-ended-single-family-zoning/.

57. See Laura Bliss, "Oregon's Single-Family Zoning Ban Was a 'Long Time Coming,'" CityLab, Bloomberg, July 2, 2019, https://www.bloomberg.com/news /articles/2019-07-02/upzoning-rising-oregon-bans-single-family-zoning.

58. See Christian Britschgi, "Oregon Becomes First State to Ditch Single-Family Zoning: State Lawmakers End the Legislative Sessions by Passing a Bill That Will Allow for Denser Housing Construction Across the State," *Reason*, July 1, 2019, https://reason.com/2019/07/01/oregon-becomes-first-state -to-ditch-single-family-zoning/.

59. Henry Grabar, "The Most Important Housing Reform in America Has Come to the South," *Slate*, June 28, 2021, https://slate.com/business/2021/06 /charlotte-single-family-zoning-segregation-housing.html.

60. See Conor Dougherty, "Where the Suburbs End: A Single-Family Home from the 1950s Is Now a Rental Complex and a Vision of California's Future," *New York Times*, October 8, 2021, https://www.nytimes.com/2021/10/08 /business/economy/california-housing.html.

61. See Ben Fritz and Zusha Elinson, "California Limits Single-Family Home Zoning," *Wall Street Journal*, September 16, 2021, https://www.wsj.com /articles/california-limits-single-family-home-zoning-11631840086.

62. Evan Popp, "Mills Signs Bill Reforming Zoning Laws as Maine Grapples with Affordable Housing Crisis," *Maine Beacon*, April 28, 2022, https:// mainebeacon.com/mills-signs-bill-reforming-zoning-laws-as-maine-grapples -with-affordable-housing-crisis/.

63. Richard D. Kahlenberg, "Taking on Class and Racial Discrimination in Housing: Cory Booker's Big Idea to Rein In Exclusionary Zoning," *American Prospect*, August 2, 2018, https://prospect.org/civil-rights/taking-class-racial -discrimination-housing/.

64. Kahlenberg, "Taking on Class and Racial Discrimination."

65. Kahlenberg, "Taking on Class and Racial Discrimination."

66. "The Biden Plan for Investing in Our Communities Through Housing," Biden/Harris 2020 Campaign, https://joebiden.com/housing/.

67. See *Zoned Out: Examining the Impact of Exclusionary Zoning on People, Resources, and Opportunity, Hearing Before Subcommittee on Housing, Community Development and Insurance, U.S. House Financial Services Committee*, 117th Cong. (October 15, 2021) (testimony of Richard D. Kahlenberg, Senior Fellow, the Century Foundation), https://financialservices.house.gov/events/eventsingle .aspx?EventID=408494.

68. Trump quoted in Richard D. Kahlenberg, "The Low-Wage Mothers of Color Who Want to Become Suburban Moms," *American Prospect*, August 4,

2020, https://prospect.org/infrastructure/housing/the-low-wage-mothers-of
-color-who-want-to-become-suburban-mo/.

69. Trump quoted in Kahlenberg, "The Low-Wage Mothers of Color."

70. See Peter Dreier, "Not Your Granddad's Suburb: Trump's Racist Appeals Fall Flat in Diversified Suburbs," *Shelterforce*, August 17, 2020, https:// shelterforce.org/2020/08/17/trump_racist_appeal_suburbs/.

71. See William A. Galston, "Which Voters Made Joe Biden President?," *Wall Street Journal*, August 11, 2021. See also Geoffrey Skelley, Elena Mejía, Amelia Thomson-DeVeaux, and Laura Bronner, "Why the Suburbs Have Shifted Blue," *FiveThirtyEight*, December 16, 2020, https://fivethirtyeight.com /features/why-the-suburbs-have-shifted-blue/.

72. Peter Harrison and Henry Kraemer, *Homes for All: The Progressive 2020 Agenda for Housing* (Data for Progress, May 2019), 35, http://filesforprogress .org/reports/homes_for_all.pdf.

CHAPTER 1: THE WALLS THAT BLOCK OPPORTUNITY

1. Patricia McGee, interview with Kay Butler, Inclusive Communities Project, December 26, 2018, "'Voices of Vision': Voucher Holders Seeking Opportunity Moves Speak," Story Corps Archive, https://archive.storycorps.org /interviews/voices-of-vision-voucher-holders-seeking-opportunity-moves-speak -8/; Patricia McGee, interview with Michelle Burris and author, January 22, 2020 (hereafter, McGee interview), 22, and 6–7.

2. McGee interview, 4; Patricia McGee, interview with Michelle Burris and author, July 9, 2020 (hereafter, McGee interview II), 1, 5; and *Encyclopaedia Britannica Online*, s.v. "Longview, Texas, United States," accessed November 1, 2022, https://www.britannica.com/place/Longview-Texas; "About Longview," City of Longview, https://www.longviewtexas.gov/2443/About-Longview.

3. McGee interview, 1. (In January 2020, when this interview was conducted, the children were in tenth, eighth, fifth, and first grades, respectively.) See also McGee interview, 4, 8–9, 15. Subsequent citations and quotes from Ms. McGee are from McGee interview II, 2, and McGee interview, 15, 22, 11, 13, 25, 26, and 2.

4. "T. W. Browne Middle School," Great Schools, last accessed December 2021, https://www.greatschools.org/texas/dallas/1781-T-W-Browne-Middle -School/. Subsequent quotations are from McGee interview, 7–8.

5. "Ronald E. McNair Elementary School," Great Schools, last accessed December 2021, https://www.greatschools.org/texas/dallas/1950-Ronald-E -Mcnair-Elementary-School/. Subsequent quotations are from McGee interview, 7, 9, and 13.

6. McGee interview, 9 and 7.

7. "KIPP Destiny Middle," Great Schools, last accessed December 2021, https://www.greatschools.org/texas/dallas/25388-KIPP-Destiny-Middle/.

8. Emily Ekins, "Poll: What Americans Think Cause Wealth and Poverty," Cato Institute, September 27, 2019, https://www.cato.org/blog/poll-what -americans-think-cause-wealth-poverty. See also Economic Mobility Project, "Findings from a National Survey & Focus Groups on Economic Mobility," Pew Charitable Trusts, March 12, 2009, 3 ("By a 71 to 21 percent margin, Americans believe that personal attributes, like hard work and drive, are more important to economic mobility than external conditions, like the economy and economic circumstances growing up"), https://www.pewtrusts.org/~/media /legacy/uploadedfiles/wwwpewtrustsorg/reports/economic_mobility/emp 20200920survey20on20economic20mobility20for20print2031209pdf.pdf.

9. Cashin, *White Space, Black Hood*, 6.

10. Cashin, *White Space, Black Hood*, 6, 41, 89. See also Ibram X. Kendi, *How to Be an Anti-Racist* (New York: One World, 2019), 152, 156.

11. Massey et al., *Climbing Mount Laurel*, 18.

12. Lisa Prevost, "Town After Town, Residents Are Fighting Affordable Housing in Connecticut," *New York Times*, September 4, 2022, https://www .nytimes.com/2022/09/04/realestate/connecticut-affordable-housing-apartments .html.

13. Diana Lind, *Brave New Home: Our Future in Smarter, Simpler, Happier Housing* (New York: Bold Type Books, 2020), 94.

14. See Matthew Stewart, *The 9.9 Percent: The New Aristocracy That Is Entrenching Inequality and Warping Our Culture* (New York: Simon & Schuster, 2021), 6.

15. Paul Jargowsky, "Architecture of Segregation: Civil Unrest, the Concentration of Poverty, and Public Policy," Century Foundation, August 7, 2015, 14, https://tcf.org/content/report/architecture-of-segregation/.

16. See discussion, Chapter 5.

17. Jonathan Rothwell and Douglas Massey, "Density Zoning and Class Segregation in U.S. Metropolitan Areas," *Social Science Quarterly* 91, no. 5 (December 2010): 1123–1143, http://www.ncbi.nlm.nih.gov/pmc/articles/PMC3632084/.

18. Michael C. Lens and Paavo Monkkonen, "Do Strict Land Use Regulations Make Metropolitan Areas More Segregated by Income?," *Journal of the American Planning Association* 82, no. 1 (2016): 6–21, https://www.ncbi.nlm.nih .gov/pmc/articles/PMC5800413/ (referencing Massey and Rothman's analysis).

19. Lens and Monkkonen, "Do Strict Land Use Regulations."

20. See Douglas Massey and Jacob S. Rugh, "Segregation in Post–Civil Rights America: Stalled Integration or End of the Segregated Century," *Du Bois Review* 11, no. 2 (Fall 2014): 205–232, https://www.ncbi.nlm.nih.gov/pmc /articles/PMC4782806/. One researcher tried to challenge the idea that restrictive zoning promotes segregation, noting that Houston famously has less restrictive zoning than Dallas and yet Houston has high levels of segregation. See Christopher R. Berry, "Land Use Regulation and Residential Segregation: Does Zoning Matter?," *American Law and Economics Review* 3, no. 2 (2001):

251–274, https://papers.ssrn.com/sol3/papers.cfm?abstract_id=874185#. But as discussed in Chapter 3, Houston in fact employs a wide range of state-sponsored tools to exclude.

21. Rothstein, *The Color of Law*, 47.

22. Rothstein, *The Color of Law*, 50. See also id., 53.

23. Mike Koprowski, interview with Michelle Burris and author, June 9, 2020 (hereafter, Koprowski interview), 7. See also Heather Way, "Texas Must Do More to Create Inclusive Affordable Housing," *UT News*, April 9, 2015, https://news.utexas.edu/2015/04/09/texas-must-do-more-to-create-inclusive-affordable-housing/.

24. Jon Anderson, "Losing Amazon HQ2 Gave Dallas Time to Figure Out Zoning Policy," *DallasDirt*, July 23, 2019 (citing UrbanFootprint), https://candysdirt.com/2019/07/23/losing-amazon-hq2-gave-dallas-time-to-figure-out-zoning-policy/.

25. Miguel Solis, interview with Michelle Burris, Stefan Lallinger, and author, June 1, 2020, 2.

26. Koprowski interview. Originally, the district was on the outside of Dallas's city limits, but over time, Dallas came to surround it. See *Tasby v. Estes*, 572 F.2d 1010, 1015 (5th Cir., 1978).

27. "Early Development," Town of Highland Park, Texas, https://www.hptx.org/624/Early-Development.

28. "Highland Park Independent School District," Great Schools, last accessed December 2021, https://www.greatschools.org/texas/dallas/highland-park-independent-school-district/.

29. "Dallas Independent School District," Great Schools, last accessed December 2021, https://www.greatschools.org/texas/dallas/dallas-independent-school-district/.

30. Koprowski interview, 18.

31. *Tasby v. Estes*, 572 F.2d 1010, at 1015 (1978).

32. See "Zoning," Town of Highland Park, Texas, https://www.hptx.org/237/Zoning, and "Zoning Map with Addresses," Town of Highland Park, Texas, https://www.hptx.org/DocumentCenter/View/1448/ZONEMap-w-ADDRESSES-Model-Website-Upload-9-10-2020?bidId (showing virtually the entire town is dedicated to zones A, B, C, D, and E for single-family homes only. Tiny slivers on the periphery—F, G, and H—are open for duplexes and other multifamily units).

33. See *Dews v. Town of Sunnydale Tex.*, 109 F. Supp. 2d 526 (N.D. Tex. 2000), https://law.justia.com/cases/federal/district-courts/FSupp2/109/526/2522883/.

34. 109 F. Supp. 2d at 529. See also Alice M. Burr, "The Problem of Sunnyvale, Texas and Exclusionary Zoning Practices," *Journal of Affordable Housing & Community Development Law* 11, no. 2 (Winter 2002): 203–225, 203; and Demetria McCain, interview with Michelle Burris and author, June 12, 2020, 4–5.

35. "QuickFacts: Sunnyvale Town, Texas," US Census Bureau, https:// www.census.gov/quickfacts/fact/table/sunnyvaletowntexas/PST045219; and "QuickFacts: Texas," US Census Bureau, https://www.census.gov/quickfacts /TX (median household income in 2019 was $61,874).

36. 109 F. Supp. 2d at 529 and 540, 541–542, 547, and 539. See also Burr, "The Problem of Sunnyvale," 203 and 220n3. After years of lawsuits, Sunnyvale's population is still 51 percent white, 23 percent Asian, 12 percent Hispanic, and 9 percent Black. "QuickFacts: Sunnyvale Town, Texas," US Census Bureau, https://www.census.gov/quickfacts/fact/table/sunnyvaletowntexas /PST045219.

37. 109 F. Supp. 2d at 534, 537, 530, and 566. See also Burr, "The Problem of Sunnyvale," 203.

38. 109 F. Supp. 2d at 568, 569, and 573.

39. See "Exclusionary Zoning," Daniel & Beshara, https://www.daniel besharalawfirm.com/exclusionary-zoning; Daniel & Beshara is a Dallas-based civil rights law firm that works with ICP.

40. McCain interview, 4–5.

41. McCain interview, 6.

42. "QuickFacts: Sunnyvale, Texas," US Census Bureau, https://www .census.gov/quickfacts/fact/table/sunnyvaletowntexas/PST120221.

43. Fischel, *Zoning Rules!*, 201. See discussion of the difficulty of bringing "disparate impact" lawsuits against exclusionary zoning in Chapter 7.

44. Dallas Housing Authority, *Annual Report* (Dallas: Dallas Housing Authority, 2018), 16, https://dhantx.com/wp-content/uploads/2019/09/DHA -Annual-Report_Final_For-Web.pdf.

45. *Walker v. HUD*, 734 F. Supp. 1231, 1233 (N.D. Tex. 1989).

46. Philip Tegeler and Micah Herskind, *Coordination of Community Systems and Institutions to Promote Housing and School Integration* (Washington, DC: Poverty & Race Research Action Council, November 2018), 19, https://prrac .org/pdf/housing_education_report_november2018.pdf.

47. *Texas Dept. of Housing & Community Affairs v. Inclusive Communities Project*, 135 S. Ct. 2507, 2514 (2015).

48. 135 S. Ct., at 2526; US District Court, N.D. Tex., *Inclusive Community Project v. Texas Dept. of Housing & Community Affairs*, "Memorandum Opinion," August 16, 2016, at 15–16, 32, https://www.clearinghouse.net/chDocs/public /PH-TX-0004-0020.pdf.

49. Jim Schutze, interview with Michelle Burris and author, June 23, 2020 (hereafter, Schutze interview), 1–3.

50. Brian Knudsen, "Expanded Protections for Families with Housing Choice Vouchers," Poverty & Race Research Action Council, September 2022, 1, https://prrac.org/pdf/soi-voucher-data-brief.pdf.

51. Scott et al., "Appendix B" in *Expanding Choice*, 141. See also Schutze interview, 2; McCain interview, 8–9; Koprowski interview, 6; and Heather Way, "Texas Must Do More."

52. "Source of Income Laws by State, County and City," National Multifamily Housing Council, September 30, 2021, last modified April 5, 2022, https://www.nmhc.org/research-insight/analysis-and-guidance/source-of -income-laws-by-state-county-and-city/.

53. "ICP's Second Apartment Survey Shows Abysmal Results as Rampant Discrimination Against Housing Choice Voucher Holders Continues to Segregate North Texas Households," Inclusive Communities Project, https:// inclusivecommunities.net/northtexasvoucherdiscriminationincreases/.

54. University of Texas at Arlington, *North Texas Regional Housing Assessment: City of Dallas* (Dallas: City of Dallas, November 2018), 82, https:// dallascityhall.com/departments/fairhousing/PublishingImages/Pages/North -Texas-Regional-Assessment-of-Fair-Housing/North%20Texas%20Regional %20Assessment%20of%20Fair%20Housing.pdf.

55. Koprowski interview, 11.

56. Patricia McGee, interview II, 8; Inclusive Communities Project, https:// inclusivecommunities.net/; and Tegeler and Herskind, *Coordination of Community Systems*, 19.

57. Tegeler and Herskind, *Coordination of Community Systems*, 19–20.

58. See Demetria McCain, "The Legacy of Accessing Opportunity," in *Ten Years and Counting: Housing Mobility, Engagement and Advocacy: A Journey Towards Fair Housing in the Dallas Area* (Dallas: Inclusive Communities Project, n.d.), 2, https://lawsdocbox.com/Immigration/97239544-Ten-years-and -counting-housing-mobility-engagement-and-advocacy-a-journey-towards -fair-housing-in-the-dallas-area.html.

59. McGee interview, 1, 12,14–15, and 2–3.

60. "Brown Middle School," Great Schools, last accessed December 2021, https://www.greatschools.org/texas/forney/10311-Brown-Middle-School/.

61. McGee interview, 5, 8, 9, 11, 16, 21, 18, 6, and McGee interview II, 12.

62. McGee interview, 3–5, 28, 23, 20, and 24.

63. McGee interview, with Michelle Burris and Richard Kahlenberg, September 15, 2021 (hereafter, McGee interview III), 6, 4, 1, 2, and 5.

64. McGee interview III, 3–4; and "Rockwall High School," Great Schools, last accessed December 2021, https://www.greatschools.org/texas/rockwall /5825-Rockwall-High-School/.

65. Tegeler and Herskind, *Coordination of Community Systems*, 19–20; and Children's Health, *Beyond ABC: Assessing the Well-Being of Children in North Texas: 2019–2020* (Dallas: Children's Health, 2020), 57, https://www .childrens.com/wps/wcm/connect/childrenspublic/7e6c1960-8780-4e2e -8ba5-0550fea7c61f/2019+BABC+Online+FA.pdf?MOD=AJPERES &CVID=mVHiLAq&CONVERT_TO=url.

66. John Egan, "This Is Just How Much Dallas–Fort Worth's Population Exploded in the Last Decade," Dallas Culture Map, August 13, 2021, https:// dallas.culturemap.com/news/city-life/08-13-21-dallas-census-population -ranking-of-largest-metro-areas/ (7.6 million residents).

67. Richard Florida, "America's Most Economically Segregated Cities," CityLab, Bloomberg, February 23, 2015, https://www.citylab.com/life/2015/02/americas-most-economically-segregated-cities/385709/. Large metro regions were those with more than one million people.

68. "Inclusive Recovery in US Cities: Dallas, TX" (dashboard), Urban Institute, September 15, 2020, https://apps.urban.org/features/inclusion/index.html?city=dallas_TX.

69. Erika Poethig, Solomon Greene, Christina Stacy, Tanaya Srini, and Brady Meixell, *Inclusive Recovery in US Cities* (Washington, DC: Urban Institute, April 2018), Appendix B, 51. https://www.urban.org/sites/default/files/publication/97981/inclusive_recovery_in_us_cities_0.pdf.

70. University of Texas at Arlington, *North Texas Regional Housing Assessment*, 15, 102.

71. Tehani, interview with Michelle Burris and author, February 10, 2020 (hereafter, Tehani interview), 2, 6, and 8. Tehani requested I use only first names for her and her children.

72. Tehani interview, 2, 8.

73. "Columbus City School District," Ohio School Report Cards, https://reportcard.education.ohio.gov/district/overview/043802.

74. "Forest Park Elementary School," Great Schools, last accessed July 2020, https://www.greatschools.org/ohio/columbus/648-Forest-Park-Elementary-School/.

75. Tehani interview, 3, 5.

76. Joel Oliphint, "The Roots of Columbus' Ongoing Color Divide," *Columbus Alive*, June 27, 2018.

77. Patricia Burgess, *Planning for the Private Interest: Land Use Controls and Residential Patterns in Columbus, Ohio 1900–1970* (Columbus: Ohio State University Press, 1994), 113–114, 125.

78. Burgess, *Planning for the Private Interest*, 1–2, 59.

79. Burgess, *Planning for the Private Interest*, 6, 9, 198, and 203.

80. Joel Oliphint, "Move to Prosper's Forgotten Families," *Columbus Alive*, May 15, 2019.

81. Michael Kelley, interview with Michelle Burris and author, January 21, 2020, 2; Klaben interview, 11, 12; "Amy Klaben, Esq., Project Facilitator," Move to PROSPER, https://www.movetoprosper.org/amy-klaben.

82. Washington, DC, developer Matt Murphy cites the example of Washington, DC, area developer EYA. EYA got wealthier communities to agree to townhomes because they were upscale and built in walkable communities, Murphy says. EYA argued such development "will only increase the value of everyone else's homes because we're going to price these luxury townhome units at a higher price than these little cape cods and split level units right in Bethesda," Murphy says. Matt Murphy, interview with author, December 1, 2021 (hereafter, Murphy interview).

83. Klaben interview, 9, 11.

84. Klaben interview, 9.

85. Katherine Levine Einstein, David M. Glick, and Maxwell Palmer, *Neighborhood Defenders: Participatory Politics and America's Housing Crisis* (New York: Cambridge University Press, 2020), 18.

86. Murphy interview.

87. Oliphint, "Move to Prosper's Forgotten Families"; Klaben interview, 2, 9.

88. These districts received overall grades of A and B. See Ohio State Report Cards, "Dublin City," 2020, https://tinyurl.com/55sb7k6s; "Hilliard City," 2020, https://tinyurl.com/mr3c8j4t; "Gahanna–Jefferson City," 2020, https://tinyurl.com/4c2rdbre; and "Olentangy Local," 2020, https://tinyurl.com/2p8d3thy.

89. Oliphint, "Move to Prosper's Forgotten Families."

90. "School Report Cards: Dublin City District Overview," Ohio State Department of Education, https://reportcard.education.ohio.gov/district/overview/047027.

91. Tehani interview, 4; "Ann Simpson Davis Middle School," Great Schools, last accessed July 2020, https://www.greatschools.org/ohio/dublin/2366-Ann-Simpson-Davis-Middle-School/.

92. Tehani interview, 6, 7, 2, and 8.

93. Florida, "America's Most Economically Segregated Cities." Large metro regions were those with more than one million people.

94. Raj Chetty, Nathaniel Hendren, Patrick Kline, and Emmanuel Saez, "Economic Mobility: State of States," in *Pathways: The Poverty and Inequality Report* (Stanford, CA: Stanford Center on Poverty and Inequality, 2015), 59, Table 1, https://inequality.stanford.edu/sites/default/files/SOTU_2015_economic-mobility.pdf.

95. Alicia Mazzara and Brian Knudsen, *Where Families with Children Use Housing Vouchers: A Comparative Look at the 50 Largest Metropolitan Areas* (Washington, DC: Center for Budget and Policy Priorities and Poverty & Race Research Action Council, January 3, 2019), 2, https://prrac.org/pdf/where_families_use_vouchers_2019.pdf.

96. Ingrid Gould Ellen and Keren Mertens Horn, *Do Federally Assisted Households Have Access to High Performing Schools?* (New York: Poverty and Race Research Action Council, November 2012), 4, Table 1, http://www.prrac.org/pdf/PRRACHousingLocation&Schools.pdf.

97. Moving to Work North Texas, *MTW [Moving to Work] Cohort #2 Rent Reform* (Dallas: Dallas Housing Authority, December 15, 2020), 4, 11, and 29–30, https://dhantx.com/wp-content/uploads/2020/12/MTW-Plan-Application-20201216.pdf; and Myriam Igoufe, interview with author, November 17, 2021 (hereafter, Igoufe interview), 8 and 4.

98. Igoufe interview, 5 and 6.

99. See discussion, Chapter 4.

100. Jenny Schuetz, "To Improve Housing Affordability, We Need Better Alignment of Zoning, Taxes and Subsidies," Brookings Institution, January 7, 2020, https://www.brookings.edu/policy2020/bigideas/to-improve-housing -affordability-we-need-better-alignment-of-zoning-taxes-and-subsidies/. See also Emily Badger and Quoctrung Bui, "Cities Start to Question an American Ideal: A House with a Yard on Every Lot," *New York Times*, June 18, 2019, https://www.nytimes.com/interactive/2019/06/18/upshot/cities-across-america -question-single-family-zoning.html.

101. Brent Toderian, "The Link Between Density and Affordability," *Planetizen*, April 22, 2008, https://www.planetizen.com/node/30877. See also California Planning Roundtable and California Department of Housing & Community Development, *Myths and Facts About Affordable & High Density Housing* (Pasadena: California Planning Roundtable and California Department of Housing & Community Development, 2002), https://www.losgatosca.gov /DocumentCenter/View/2716/Myths—Facts-about-Afford—Hi-Density -Housing.

102. "American Housing Survey (AHS) Table Creator," US Census Bureau, https://www.census.gov/programs-surveys/ahs/data/interactive/ahstablecreator .html?s_areas=00000&s_year=2019&s_tablename=TABLE1&s_bygroup1 =1&s_bygroup2=1&s_filtergroup1=1&s_filtergroup2=1. The median monthly housing costs were as follows: detached single-family ($1,479); attached single-family ($1,400); 2–4 units ($1,179), and mobile homes ($832).

103. Jane Lyons, "Montgomery County Considers Allowing More Housing Types," Greater Greater Washington, August 9, 2021, https://ggwash.org /view/82183/montgomery-county-considers-allowing-more-housing-types.

104. Teo Armus, "As Housing Prices Soar, a Wealthy County Rethinks the Idea of Suburbia," *Washington Post*, October 14, 2022, https://www.washington post.com/dc-md-va/2022/10/14/missing-middle-housing-arlington-affordable/.

105. Elizabeth Kneebone, "Trump Is Clinging to Outdated Vision of America's Suburbs," Brookings Institution, August 20, 2020, https://www .brookings.edu/blog/the-avenue/2020/08/20/trump-is-clinging-to-an-outdated -vision-of-americas-suburbs/ (noting that suburban single-family homes had a median home value of $223,600 in the 2013–2018 Census data when they were in a neighborhood where less than 90 percent of neighbors were detached single-family homes, but that figure jumps to $297,200 when they were in 90 percent or more single-family-home neighborhoods).

106. "Small Lots in Smart Places," Desegregate Connecticut, https://www .desegregatect.org/lots.

107. Amrita Kulka, "Sorting into Neighborhoods: The Role of Minimum Lot Sizes" (job market paper), December 30, 2019, https://drive.google.com /file/d/1Wr8T687wz-jVVMEVWoZCQXB53pxCM5hK/view.

108. Desegregate Connecticut, *Issue Brief: Small Lots in Smart Places: a Right-Sized Solution for CT* (Desegregate Connecticut, 2022), 7, https://static1

.squarespace.com/static/5ee8c6c9681b6f2799a4883a/t/61ea028879710056b2a90fe9 /1642726053008/Issue+Brief+-+Minimum+Lot+Sizes.pdf.

109. Christian Britschgi, "George City Sued over Ban on Tiny Homes, Small Cottages," *Reason*, October 27, 2021.

110. Nancy Isenberg, *White Trash: The 400-Year Untold History of Class in America* (New York: Penguin Books, 2017), 236. Technically mobile homes are those built before June 15, 1976, and manufactured homes are those built after. See US Department of Housing and Urban Development, "Frequently Asked Questions," https://www.hud.gov/program_offices/housing/rmra/mhs/faqs.

111. Ben Eisen and Nicole Friedman, "Market Expands for Factory-Built Homes," *Wall Street Journal*, November 22, 2021, A1. See also Beth DeCarbo, "A Different Kind of Affordable Housing: Manufactured Homes Are Garnering Interest but Caveats Exist," *Washington Post*, September 11, 2021, T11 (citing Urban Institute study that "manufactured housing is 35 to 47 percent less expensive per square foot than new or existing site-built homes").

112. Kriston Capps, "Biden's New Housing Plan: Fire Up the Housing Factories," CityLab, Bloomberg, May 20, 2022, https://www.bloomberg.com/news /articles/2022-05-20/mobile-homes-might-make-biden-s-housing-plan-work.

113. *Vickers v. Township Comm of Gloucester Township*, 37 N.J. 232, 365, 181 A.2s 129 (1962), cited in Isenberg, *White Trash*, 244–245.

114. Eisen and Friedman, "Market Expands for Factory-Built Homes."

115. Gray, *Arbitrary Lines*, 56.

116. Will Parker and Nicole Friedman, "Homeowner Groups Fight Investors' Push into Suburbs," *Wall Street Journal*, April 18, 2022, https:// www.wsj.com/articles/homeowner-groups-seek-to-stop-investors-from -buying-houses-to-rent-11650274203. See also Anika Singh Lemar, "How Owner-Occupancy Regulations Are Contributing to the Housing Crisis," Brookings Institution, October 27, 2022, https://www.brookings.edu/blog /the-avenue/2022/10/27/how-owner-occupancy-regulations-are-contributing -to-the-housing-crisis/.

117. See Casey Berkovitz, "Testimony: Why New York State Must Legalize Accessory Homes," Century Foundation, October 13, 2021, https://tcf.org /content/commentary/testimony-new-york-state-must-legalize-accessory -homes/.

118. Lind, *Brave New Home*, 75, 122–124.

119. Dougherty, "Where the Suburbs End."

120. M. Nolan Gray, "The Housing Revolution Is Coming," *Atlantic*, October 5, 2022, https://www.theatlantic.com/ideas/archive/2022/10/california -accessory-dwelling-units-legalization-yimby/671648/.

121. Sara Bronin, "Zoning and Equity: Rappaport Center for Law & Public Policy Webinar Co-sponsors: Harvard Joint Center for Housing Studies; BC Black Law Students Association," YouTube video, 1:28:20 at 1:15, BC Law, October 21, 2021, https://www.youtube.com/watch?v=l-CjFtLwmsc.

122. Patrick Sisson, "Can Minneapolis's Radical Rezoning Be a National Model?," *Curbed*, November 27, 2018, https://www.curbed.com/2018/11/27 /18113208/minneapolis-real-estate-rent-development-2040-zoning; Jenny Schuetz, "Minneapolis 2040: The Most Wonderful Plan of the Year," Brookings Institution, December 12, 2018, https://www.brookings.edu/blog/the-avenue/2018/12/12 /minneapolis-2040-the-most-wonderful-plan-of-the-year/.

123. Linda Poon, "Buffalo Becomes First City to Bid Minimum Parking Goodbye," CityLab, Bloomberg, January 9, 2017, https://www.bloomberg.com /news/articles/2017-01-09/buffalo-is-the-first-to-abandon-minimum -parking-requirements-citywide. See also James Brasuell, "How Parking Reform Changed Development in Buffalo: New Research Quantifies the Effect of Parking Reforms Implemented by the City of Buffalo in 2017," *Planetizen*, April 8, 2021, https://www.planetizen.com/news/2021/04/112901-how-parking -reform-changed-development-buffalo#:~:text=A%20new%20study%20 of%20Buffalo,parking%20if%20given%20the%20chance; Bronin, "Zoning and Equity" video; and Kea Wilson, "How the Twin Cities Abolished Parking Minimums (and How Your City Can, Too)," Streets Blog USA, September 2, 2021, https://usa.streetsblog.org/2021/09/02/how-the-twin-cities-abolished -parking-minimums-and-how-your-city-can-too/.

124. Matt Hoffman, interview with author, September 8, 2021, 14–15.

125. Einstein, Glick, and Palmer, *Neighborhood Defenders*, 11 (citing research studies in 2005, 2009, and 2013).

126. See discussion in Chapter 3 centered around the work of William Fischel.

127. Richard Reeves and Dimitrios Halikias, "How Land Use Regulations Are Zoning Out Low-Income Families," *Social Mobility Memos* (blog), Brookings Institution, August 16, 2016, https://www.brookings.edu/blog/social -mobility-memos/2016/08/16/zoning-as-opportunity-hoarding/ (citing research by Peter Ganong and Daniel Shoag).

128. Einstein, Glick, and Palmer, *Neighborhood Defenders*, 81 (citing research from 2016).

129. Richard Reeves, *Dream Hoarders: How the American Upper-Middle Class Is Leaving Everyone Else in the Dust, Why That Is a Problem, and What to Do About It* (Washington, DC: Brookings Institution Press, 2017), 140.

130. Douglas S. Massey and Nancy A. Denton, *American Apartheid: Segregation and the Making of the Underclass* (Cambridge, MA: Harvard University Press, 1998), 149, 169, and 178–179.

131. Sherrilyn Ifill, "FHEO Speaker Series: The Problem We All Live With: Residential Segregation and Urban Policy," YouTube video, 1:01:12, HUDchannel, June 5, 2015, https://www.youtube.com/watch?v=3dB2vGW mIvg.

132. See Charis E. Kubrin and Gregory D. Squires, "Privileged Places: Race, Opportunity and Uneven Development in Urban America," *NHI Shelterforce*

Online 147 (Fall 2006), https://www.academia.edu/2769587/Privileged_Places _Race_Uneven_Development_and_the_Geography_of_Opportunity_in_Urban _America.

133. Johnny Harris and Binyamin Appelbaum, "Why Do States with Democratic Majorities Fail to Live Up to Their Values?," opinion, *New York Times* video, 14:20, November 9, 2021 https://www.nytimes.com/video/opinion /100000007886969/democrats-blue-states-legislation.html.

134. Douglas S. Massey and Jacob S. Rugh, "The Intersections of Race and Class: Zoning, Affordable Housing and Segregation in US Metropolitan Areas," in *The Fight for Fair Housing: Causes, Consequences, and Future Implications of the 1968 Federal Fair Housing Act*, ed. Gregory D. Squires (New York: Routledge, 2018), 246–247 (summarizing Jonathan Rothwell and Douglas S. Massey, "Geographic Effects on Intergenerational Income Mobility," *Economic Geography* 91, no. 1 [2014]: 83–106).

135. For a summary, see Richard D. Kahlenberg and Halley Potter, *A Smarter Charter: Finding What Works for Charter Schools and Public Education* (New York: Teachers College Press, 2014), 58–63; Richard D. Kahlenberg, *All Together Now: Creating Middle-Class Schools Through Public School Choice* (Washington, DC: Brookings Institution Press, 2001), 32–34; and Putnam, *Our Kids*, 217.

136. Tomas E. Monarrez, "School Attendance Boundaries and the Segregation of Public Schools in the U.S.," *American Economic Journal* (forthcoming), https://www.aeaweb.org/articles?id=10.1257/app.20200498#:~:text=Residential %20segregation%20alone%20explains%20more,small%20compared%20to%20 residential%20choice.

137. "Fast Facts: Public School Choice Programs," National Center for Education Statistics, accessed November 1, 2022, https://nces.ed.gov/fastfacts /display.asp?id=6 (indicating that 71 percent of students attended an assigned public school in 2015, while 20 percent attended public schools chosen by parents and 9 percent used private school).

138. David Rusk, "Housing Policy Is School Policy" (paper presented to Housing Mobility and Education Forum, Baltimore, MD, December 3, 2017), http://www.prrac.org/pdf/Rusk.pdf. See also National Coalition on School Diversity, "Linking Housing and School Integration Policy: What Federal, State, and Local Governments Can Do" (Issue Brief no. 5, National Coalition on School Diversity and Poverty & Race Research Action Council, March 2015), https://files.eric.ed.gov/fulltext/ED556323.pdf.

139. Richard D. Kahlenberg, "Turnaround Schools and Charter Schools That Work: Moving Beyond Separate but Equal," in *The Future of School Integration: Socioeconomic Diversity as an Education Reform Strategy*, ed. Richard D. Kahlenberg (New York: Century Foundation, 2012), 283–308.

140. Douglas N. Harris, *Ending the Blame Game on Educational Inequity: A Study of "High Flying" Schools and NCLB* (Tempe, AZ: Education Policy Research Unit, Arizona State University, March 2006).

141. See Richard D. Kahlenberg, Halley Potter, and Kimberly Quick, "A Bold Agenda for School Integration," Century Foundation, April 8, 2019, fig. 1, https://tcf.org/content/report/bold-agenda-school-integration/.

142. Robert J. Sampson, Patrick Sharkey, and Stephen W. Raudenbush, "Durable Effects of Concentrated Disadvantage on Verbal Ability Among African-American Children," *Proceedings of the National Academy of Sciences* 105, no. 3 (January 22, 2008): 845–852.

143. Gregory Palardy, "Differential School Effects Among Low, Middle, and High Social Class Composition Schools," *School Effectiveness and School Improvement* 19, no. 1 (2008): 37.

144. Raj Chetty, Matthew O. Jackson, Theresa Kuchler, and Johannes Stoebel, Abigail Hiller, Sarah Oppenheimer, and Opportunity Insights Team, *Social Capital and Economic Mobility* (Cambridge, MA: Opportunity Insights, August 2022), https://opportunityinsights.org/wp-content/uploads/2022/07/socialcapital_nontech.pdf.

145. Carl Chancellor and Richard D. Kahlenberg, "The New Segregation," *Washington Monthly*, November/December 2014; Heather Schwartz, "Housing Policy Is School Policy," in Kahlenberg, *The Future of School Integration*.

146. Schwartz, "Housing Policy Is School Policy."

147. *Southern Burlington County NAACP v. Mount Laurel*, 67 N.J. 151 (1975), 174, 189, 190, and 212.

148. Jake Blumgart, "The Fight for the Mount Laurel Doctrine," Next City, February 4, 2013, https://nextcity.org/urbanist-news/the-fight-for-the-mount-laurel-doctrine.

149. See Massey et al., *Climbing Mount Laurel*, 5, 72 (that comparing public housing residents in Mount Laurel with a control group of those who applied but could not be accommodated).

150. Massey et al., *Climbing Mount Laurel*, 6.

151. Massey and Rugh, "The Intersections of Race and Class," 259.

152. David L. Kirp, "Here Comes the Neighborhood," opinion, *New York Times*, October 20, 2013, http://www.nytimes.com/2013/10/20/opinion/Sunday/here-comes-the-neighborhood.html?mcubz=0.

153. Massey et al., *Climbing Mount Laurel*, 178.

154. "The Gautreaux Lawsuit," Business and Professional People for the Public Interest, n.d., http://www.bpichicago.org/programs/housing-community-development/public-housing/gautreaux-lawsuit/.

155. See Kahlenberg, *All Together Now*, 33 (citing James Rosenbaum and others, "Social Integration of Low-Income Black Adults in Middle-Class White Suburbs," *Social Problems* 38 [November 1992]: 48–61; and Susan J. Popkin, James E. Rosenbaum, and Patricia M. Meaden, "Labor Market Experience of Low-Income Black Women in Middle-Class Suburbs," *Journal of Policy Analysis and Management* 12 [1993]: 556, 558).

156. Raj Chetty, Nathaniel Hendren, and Lawrence F. Katz, "The Effects of Exposure to Better Neighborhoods on Children: New Evidence from the Mov-

ing to Opportunity Experiment" (NBER Working Paper no. 21156, National Bureau of Economic Research, May 2015), 2, www.nber.org/papers/w21156.

157. Chetty, Hendren, and Katz, "The Effects of Exposure to Better Neighborhoods on Children," 2–3.

158. Raj Chetty, Nathaniel Hendren, and Lawrence Katz, "The Effects of Exposure to Better Neighborhoods on Children: New Evidence from the Moving to Opportunity Experiment," *American Economic Review* 106, no. 4 (2016): 855–902, https://opportunityinsights.org/paper/newmto/.

159. See discussion, Chapter 5.

160. Gregory Arcs, Rolf Pendall, Mark Treskon, and Amy Khare, *The Cost of Segregation: National Trends and the Case of Chicago, 1990–2010* (Washington, DC: Urban Institute and Metropolitan Planning Council of Chicago, March 2017), 2, 4–5, and 8, https://www.metroplanning.org/uploads/cms/documents/cost-of-segregation.pdf.

161. Tomas Monarrez, Brian Kisida, and Matthew Chingos, *When Is a School Segregated?* (Washington, DC: Urban Institute, September 2019), 2–3, https://www.urban.org/sites/default/files/publication/101101/when_is_a_school_segregated_making_sense_of_segregation_65_years_after_brown_v._board_of_education_0.pdf. See also Tim DeRoche, *A Fine Line: How Most American Kids Are Kept Out of the Best Public Schools* (Los Angeles: Redtail Press, 2020), 74, citing Genevieve Siegel Hawley (60–70 percent of racial segregation is between districts rather than within them).

162. Under the Supreme Court's decision in *Milliken v. Bradley*, 418 U.S. 717 (1974), school desegregation orders rarely reach across school district lines to include urban-suburban boundaries.

163. These data are for those without a child under eighteen. For those with children under eighteen, the generic support is 42–27 percent for racially diverse schools, but that turns to 25 percent support and 33 percent opposition if the racially diverse school is farther away. See Halley Potter, Stefan Lallinger, Michelle Burris, Richard D. Kahlenberg, Alex Edwards, and Topos Partnership, "School Integration Is Popular. We Can Make It More So," Century Foundation, June 3, 3021, fig. 5, https://tcf.org/content/commentary/school-integration-is-popular-we-can-make-it-more-so/.

164. Stewart, *The 9.9 Percent*, 112.

165. Jeff St. Clair, "Ohio Case: The 'Rosa Parks Moment' for Education?," *All Things Considered*, National Public Radio, January 28, 2011, https://www.npr.org/2011/01/28/133307552/ohio-case-the-rosa-parks-moment-for-education.

CHAPTER 2: KEEPING HOUSING UNAFFORDABLE

1. Janet Williams (pseudonym), interview with Michelle Burris and author, January 27, 2021 (hereafter, Williams interview II), 2.

2. Janet Williams (pseudonym), interview with Michelle Burris and author, March 30, 2020 (hereafter, Williams interview).

3. Williams interview, 1.

4. Williams interview, 2.

5. Williams interview, 8.

6. Williams interview II.

7. Wages need to be higher in America. See, for example, Richard D. Kahlenberg and Moshe Z. Marvit, *Why Labor Organizing Should Be a Civil Right* (New York: Century Foundation Press, 2012).

8. Fischel, *Zoning Rules!*, 212.

9. Fischel, *Zoning Rules!*, 214.

10. Matthew Rognlie, "Deciphering the Fall and Rise in Net Capital Shares" (Brookings Papers on Economic Activity, Brookings Institution, Washington, DC, March 2015), 12–13, https://www.brookings.edu/wp-content/uploads/2016/07/2015a_rognlie.pdf. See also Richard Florida, *The New Urban Crisis: How Our Cities Are Increasing Inequality, Deepening Segregation, and Failing the Middle Class—and What We Can Do About It* (New York: Basic Books, 2017), 32.

11. Fischel, *Zoning Rules!*, xii, 163, 201, 212–214.

12. Mitchell Hartman, "Home Prices Rise Much Faster Than Wages and Consumer Prices," *Marketplace*, National Public Radio, November 28, 2017, https://www.marketplace.org/2017/11/28/home-prices-rise-much-faster-wages-and-consumer-prices/.

13. See "2022 Housing Underproduction in the U.S.," Up for Growth, July 2022, https://upforgrowth.org/apply-the-vision/housing-underproduction/; and Emily Badger and Eve Washington, "The Housing Shortage Isn't Just a Coastal Crisis Anymore," *New York Times*, July 14, 2022, https://www.nytimes.com/2022/07/14/upshot/housing-shortage-us.html.

14. Sam Khater, Len Kiefer, and Venkataramana Yanamandra, "Housing Supply: A Growing Deficit," Freddie Mac Research Note, May 7, 2021, https://www.freddiemac.com/research/insight/20210507-housing-supply.

15. See, for example, Joseph Gyourko and Raven Molloy, "Regulation and Housing Supply" (NBER Working Paper no. 20536, National Bureau of Economic Research, October 2014), http://www.nber.org/papers/w20536.

16. Daniel Hertz, "One of the Best Ways to Fight Inequality in Cities: Zoning," *Washington Post*, August 13, 2014, https://www.washingtonpost.com/posteverything/wp/2014/08/13/the-best-way-to-fight-inequality-in-cities-is-through-zoning/.

17. Jenny Schuetz, *Fixer-Upper: How to Repair America's Broken Housing System* (Washington, DC: Brookings Institution Press, 2022), 5.

18. Edward L. Glaeser and Joseph Gyourko, "Why Is Manhattan So Expensive?" (Civic Report no. 39, Center for Civic Innovation, Manhattan Institute, November 2003), 17, Table 1, https://media4.manhattan-institute.org/pdf/cr_39.pdf.

19. Dan Bertolet, "Exclusionary Zoning Robs Our Cities of Their Best Qualities: Eight Ways It Makes Our Communities More Expensive and Less

Just," Sightline Institute, April 20, 2016, https://www.sightline.org/2016/04/20/how-exclusionary-zoning-robs-our-cities-of-their-best-qualities/.

20. Joseph Gyourko and Jacob Krimmel, "The Impact of Local Residential Land Use Restrictions on Land Values Across and Within Single Family Housing Markets" (NBER Working Paper no. 28993, National Bureau of Economic Research, July 2021), 20–21, https://www.nber.org/papers/w28993.

21. Susan J. Popkin, Samantha Batko, and Corianne Scally, "Why We Need to Expand, Not Restrict, Access to Housing Assistance," Urban Institute, January 4, 2018, https://www.urban.org/urban-wire/why-we-need-expand-not-restrict-access-housing-assistance.

22. Joint Center for Housing Studies at Harvard University, *The State of the Nation's Housing 2021* (Cambridge, MA: President and Fellows of Harvard College, 2021), 4, https://www.jchs.harvard.edu/sites/default/files/reports/files/Harvard_JCHS_State_Nations_Housing_2021.pdf.

23. Booker, quoted in Kahlenberg, "Taking on Class and Racial Discrimination in Housing." See also Anna Bahney, "Minimum Wage Workers Can't Afford Rent Anywhere in America," CNN, July 15, 2021 (citing report of the National Low Income Housing Coalition).

24. Abha Bhattarai, "Millions Feel the Pinch of Rising Rents," *Washington Post*, January 31, 2022, A1; and M. Nolan Gray, "Cancel Zoning," *Atlantic*, June 21, 2022, https://www.theatlantic.com/ideas/archive/2022/06/zoning-housing-affordability-nimby-parking-houston/661289/.

25. Hartman, "Home Prices Rise Much Faster Than Wages and Consumer Prices."

26. Hartman, "Home Prices Rise Much Faster Than Wages and Consumer Prices."

27. Heather McGhee, *The Sum of Us: What Racism Costs Everyone and How We Can Prosper Together* (New York: One World, 2021), 172 (re: 1970 ratio); and Joint Center for Housing Studies at Harvard, *The State of the Nation's Housing 2021*, 2 (price to income ratio in 2020 was 4.4).

28. Orla McCaffrey, "Home Affordability Hits Lowest Point in Years," *Wall Street Journal*, October 4, 2021, A3.

29. Lind, *Brave New Home*, 3.

30. See Lind, *Brave New Home*, 222; and Maurie Backman, "8 Expenses that Account for 87% of the Average Household Budget," *Motley Fool*, August 14, 2017 ("housing continues to be most Americans' greatest monthly expense").

31. Matthew Desmond, *Evicted: Poverty and Profit in the American City* (New York: Crown Publishers, 2016), 41–43.

32. Michael Karpman, Stephen Zuckerman, and Dulce Gonzalez, "Despite Labor Market Gains in 2018, There Were Only Modest Improvements in Families' Ability to Meet Basic Needs," Urban Institute, May 13, 2019, https://www.urban.org/research/publication/despite-labor-market-gains-2018-there-were-only-modest-improvements-families-ability-meet-basic-needs.

33. Steven Brown and Breno Braga, "Financial Distress Among American Families: Evidence from the Well-Being and Basic Needs Survey," Urban Institute, February 14, 2019, https://www.urban.org/research/publication/financial -distress-among-american-families-evidence-well-being-and-basic-needs-survey.

34. National Public Radio, Robert Wood Johnson Foundation, and Harvard T. H. Chan School of Public Affairs, *The Impact of Coronavirus on Households Across America* (Cambridge, MA: National Public Radio, Robert Wood Johnson Foundation, and Harvard T. H. Chan School of Public Affairs, September 2020), 6 (Table 1) and 14 (Table 2), https://drive.google.com /file/d/1Bd6dcGSke4fm8TyEjAz__UFXl1k1z8oP/view.

35. Whitney Airgood-Obrycki, Alexander Hermann, and Sophia Wedeen, "The Rent Eats First: Rental Housing Unaffordability in the US," Joint Center for Housing Studies at Harvard, January 13, 2021, https://www.jchs .harvard.edu/research-areas/working-papers/rent-eats-first-rental-housing -unaffordability-us.

36. Joseph Llobrera, Alicia Mazzara, Catlin Nchako, Arloc Sherman, and Claire Zippel, "New Data: Millions Struggling to Eat and Pay Rent," Center for Budget and Policy Priorities, September 23, 2020, https://www.cbpp.org /research/poverty-and-inequality/new-data-millions-struggling-to-eat-and -pay-rent.

37. Lind, *Brave New Home*, 180.

38. Desmond, *Evicted*, 3–4 and 295.

39. Desmond, *Evicted*, 98, 5, 32–43, and 131.

40. Desmond, *Evicted*, 5, 295 ("When people have a place to live, they become better parents, workers, and citizens").

41. Desmond, *Evicted*, 293.

42. Dan Bertolet, "Nine Reasons to End Exclusionary Zoning," Sightline Institute, September 29, 2021, https://www.sightline.org/2021/09/29/nine -reasons-to-end-exclusionary-zoning/ (citing Thomas Byrne, Ellen A. Munley, Jamison D. Fargo, Anne E. Montgomery, and Dennis P. Culhane, "New Perspectives on Community-Level Determinants of Homelessness," *Journal of Urban Affairs*, November 4, 2012, https://doi.org/10.1111/j.1467-9906.2012.00643.x).

43. Joint Center for Housing Studies of Harvard University, *America's Rental Housing 2017* (Cambridge, MA: President and Fellows of Harvard College, December 14, 2017), 34, https://www.jchs.harvard.edu/sites/default/files /media/imp/harvard_jchs_americas_rental_housing_2017_0.pdf.

44. Peter Dreier, "Homelessness Meets Cluelessness," *American Prospect*, March 18, 2022, https://prospect.org/culture/books/homelessness-meets -cluelessness-shellenberger-review/

45. Jerusalem Demsas in Ezra Klein, "How Blue Cities Became So Outrageously Unaffordable" podcast.

46. Demsas in Klein, "How Blue Cities Became So Outrageously Unaffordable" podcast.

47. Stewart, *The 9.9 Percent*, 100.

48. Conor Dougherty, "After Years of Failure, California Lawmakers Pave the Way for More Housing," *New York Times*, August 26, 2021.

49. Jonathan Edwards, "School District in Bay Area Asks Parents to Let Teachers Move In as Rent Soars," *Washington Post*, September 2, 2022, https://www.washingtonpost.com/nation/2022/09/02/teacher-housing-california-bay-area/.

50. Julia Carpenter, "For Some Millennials, a Starter Home Is Hard to Find," *Wall Street Journal*, July 4, 2021, https://www.wsj.com/articles/for-some-millennials-a-starter-home-is-hard-to-find-11625391002?mod=e2tw.

51. Emily Badger, "Whatever Happened to the Starter Home?," *New York Times*, September 25, 2022, https://www.nytimes.com/2022/09/25/upshot/starter-home-prices.html.

52. Ronda Kaysen, "Older, White, and Wealthy Homebuyers Are Pushing Others Out of the Market," *New York Times*, November 3, 2022, https://www.nytimes.com/2022/11/03/realestate/housing-market-buyer-wealth-race.html.

53. See "Spotlight on Home Ownership," Sightlines Project, Stanford Center on Longevity, https://longevity.stanford.edu/home-ownership/. See also Annie Nova, "Waiting Longer to Buy a House Could Hurt Millennials in Retirement," CNBC, October 25, 2018, https://www.cnbc.com/2018/10/25/the-homeownership-rate-is-falling-among-millennials-heres-why.html.

54. Kaysen, "Older, White and Wealthy Homebuyers."

55. Carpenter, "For Some Millennials."

56. Einstein, Glick, and Palmer, *Neighborhood Defenders*, 7.

57. Marco della Cava, "San Francisco Is Losing Residents Because It's Too Expensive for Nearly Everyone," *USA Today*, October 19, 2019, https://www.usatoday.com/story/news/nation/2019/10/19/california-housing-crisis-residents-flee-san-francisco-because-costs/3985196002/.

58. Einstein, Glick, and Palmer, *Neighborhood Defenders*, 7.

59. Einstein, Glick, and Palmer, *Neighborhood Defenders*, 111–112.

60. Maya Brennan, Emily Peiffer, and Kimberly Burrowes, "How Zoning Shapes Our Lives," Urban Institute, June 12, 2019, https://housingmatters.urban.org/articles/how-zoning-shapes-our-lives.

61. See Samuel Kling, "Is the City Itself the Problem? There's a Long History of Blaming Urban Areas Rather Than Economic Factors for Physical and Moral Ills. But Density Can Be an Asset for Fighting Coronavirus," CityLab, Bloomberg, April 20, 2020, https://www.bloomberg.com/news/articles/2020-04-20/the-long-history-of-demonizing-urban-density; and Harold Meyerson, "Why COVID-19 Has Run Amok in Los Angeles: The Jam-Packed Living Arrangements of Frontline Workers in an Unaffordable Housing Market Are Partly to Blame," *American Prospect*, January 25, 2021, https://prospect.org/coronavirus/why-covid-19-has-run-amok-in-los-angeles/.

62. Equitable Housing Institute, "Economic Fair Housing Act of 2021: Partial Draft Bill and Comments," 6–7 (citing several studies), https://

www.equitablehousing.org/images/pdfs/pdfs--2018-/EHI_Economic
_FHA_of_2021_draft-rev_11-30-20.pdf; Scott Wiener, "Paths for the New
Administration to Reduce Exclusionary Zoning" (transcript of the Century
Foundation/Bridges Collaborative Roundtable Discussion videoconference,
December 11, 2020), 82–83 (hereinafter referred to as Roundtable Discussion
transcript); and Lind, *Brave New Home*, 201–202.

63. Fischel, *Zoning Rules!*, 165.

64. "Historical Census of Housing Tables—Home Values," State of Wyoming, http://eadiv.state.wy.us/housing/Home_Value_ST.htm.

65. Fischel, *Zoning Rules!*, 164.

66. Robert D. Putnam and Shaylyn Romney Garrett, *The Upswing: How
America Came Together a Century Ago and How We Can Do It Again* (New York:
Simon & Schuster, 2020), 222.

67. Isabel Wilkerson, *The Warmth of Other Suns: The Epic Story of America's
Great Migration* (New York: Random House, 2010).

68. Putnam and Garrett, *The Upswing*, 221.

69. Florida, *The New Urban Crisis*, 9.

70. Florida, *The New Urban Crisis*, 19.

71. Edward Glaeser and David Cutler, "The American Housing Market Is
Stifling Mobility," *Wall Street Journal*, September 4, 2021, C3 (citing research by
Peter Ganong and Daniel Shoag).

72. "2010 Census: Gains and Losses in Congressional Seats," National
Conference of State Legislatures, https://www.ncsl.org/research/redistricting
/spotlight-census-2010.aspx.

73. John Mangin, "The New Exclusionary Zoning," *Stanford Law & Policy
Review* 25 (2014): 92–93.

74. Paul Krugman, "The Gentrification of Blue America," *New York Times*,
August 27, 2021.

75. Debra Kamin, "Californians Are on the Move," *New York Times*, May
30, 2021, 10.

76. Glaeser and Cutler, "The American Housing Market."

77. Kathleen Ronayne, "California Losing Congressional Seat for First
Time," Associated Press, April 26, 2021, https://apnews.com/article/census-2020
-government-and-politics-california-dd4a4f3ce3070231b0aecdc1cac3e97b.

78. David Schleicher, "Stuck! The Law and Economics of Residential Stability," *Yale Law Journal* 127 (2017).

79. Ezra Klein, "Why Housing Is So Expensive—Particularly in Blue
States" (transcript: Ezra Klein interviews Jenny Schuetz), *New York Times*,
July 19, 2022, https://www.nytimes.com/2022/07/19/podcasts/transcript-ezra
-klein-interviews-jenny-schuetz.html.

80. Demsas in Klein, "How Blue Cities Became So Outrageously Unaffordable" podcast.

81. Florida, *The New Urban Crisis*, xii, 4–7.

82. Florida, *The New Urban Crisis*, 191–192.

83. See Andrew Van Dam, "The Remote Work Revolution Is Already Reshaping America," *Washington Post*, August 19, 2022, https://www.washingtonpost.com/business/2022/08/19/remote-work-hybrid-employment-revolution/.

84. Florida, *The New Urban Crisis*, 25.

85. Florida, *The New Urban Crisis*, 25.

86. Florida, *The New Urban Crisis*, 32.

87. Chang-Tai Hsieh and Enrico Moretti, "Housing Constraints and Spatial Misallocation," *American Economic Journal: Macroeconomics* 11, no. 2 (2019): 1–39 (at 25–26), https://pubs.aeaweb.org/doi/pdfplus/10.1257/mac.20170388. See also Florida, *The New Urban Crisis*, 27 (describing an earlier 2015 version of the paper); Bryan Caplan, "Hsieh-Moretti on Housing Regulation: A Gracious Admission of Error," Econlib, April 5, 2021, https://www.econlib.org/a-correction-on-housing-regulation/; Ilya Somin, "Exclusionary Zoning Is Even Worse Than Previously Thought," *Reason*, April 10, 2021; and Matthew Yglesias, "Who Is the Racial Justice Case for Zoning Reform For?," Slow Boring (newsletter), April 22, 2021, https://www.slowboring.com/p/race-and-zoning.

88. Edward Glaeser and Joseph Gyourko, "The Economic Implications of Housing Supply," *Journal of Economic Perspectives* 2, no. 1 (Winter 2018): 3–30 (at 5), https://pubs.aeaweb.org/doi/pdf/10.1257/jep.32.1.3.

89. Susan Rice, "White House Event on Making It Easier to Build Accessory Dwelling Units (ADUs)," YouTube video, 1:10:25, February 1, 2022, https://www.youtube.com/watch?v=C-vzPIHUTts. The GDP in 2021 was an estimated $23 trillion. See US Department of Commerce, Bureau of Economic Analysis, "Gross Domestic Product, Fourth Quarter and Year 2021 (Advance Estimate) January 27, 2022," https://www.bea.gov/news/2022/gross-domestic-product-fourth-quarter-and-year-2021-advance-estimate#:~:text=Current%2Ddollar%20GDP%20increased%2010.0,(tables%201%20and%203.

90. Florida, *The New Urban Crisis*, 47.

91. Dexter Roberts, "The Myth of Chinese Capitalism: Challenges to China's Future as a Superpower," Chautauqua Institution lecture, July 1, 2021, https://assembly.chq.org/videos/dexter-roberts-2021. See also Dexter Roberts, *The Myth of Chinese Capitalism: The Worker, the Factory, and the Future of the World* (New York: Macmillan, 2020).

92. Florida, *The Urban Crisis*, 6–7.

93. Michael Kolomatsky, "Where Are Workers Making the Longest Commutes?," *New York Times*, August 26, 2021.

94. John Egan, "This Is Just How Much Dallas-Fort Worth's Population Exploded."

95. Theodore Kim, Jessica Meyers, and Michael E. Young, "North Texas' Sprawl Sprang from Pro-growth Policies," *Dallas Morning News*, February 4, 2012, https://www.dallasnews.com/news/2012/02/05/north-texas-sprawl-sprang-from-pro-growth-policies/.

96. Annette Schaefer, "Commuting Takes Its Toll," *Scientific American*, October 1, 2005, https://www.scientificamerican.com/article/commuting-takes-its-toll/.

97. Stewart, *The 9.9 Percent*, 111.

98. See, for example, Oregon governor Tom McCall's support for smart growth. Carl Abbott and Deborah Howe, "The Politics of Land-Use Law in Oregon: Senate Bill 100, Twenty Years After," *Oregon Historical Quarterly* 94, no. 1 (1993), http://pdxscholar.library.pdx.edu/cgi/viewcontent.cgi?article=1029 &context=usp_fac.

99. US Environmental Protection Agency, "Sources of Greenhouse Gas Emissions: Transportation Sector Emissions," https://www.epa.gov/ghgemissions /sources-greenhouse-gas-emissions#transportation.

100. US Environmental Protection Agency, "Sources of Greenhouse Gas Emissions."

101. US Environmental Protection Agency, *Our Built and Natural Environments*, EPA 231-R-01-002 (Washington, DC: EPA, January 2001), 12–13, https://archive.epa.gov/greenbuilding/web/pdf/built.pdf.

102. See Equitable Housing Institute, "Economic Fair Housing Act," 8–10, https://www.equitablehousing.org/images/PDFs/PDFs--2018-/EHI _Economic_FHA_of_2021_draft-rev_11-30-20.pdf (citing several studies on the negative effects of exclusionary zoning and resulting sprawl on the environment).

103. See Edward L. Glaeser, "Green Cities, Brown Suburbs: To Save the Planet, Build More Skyscrapers—Especially in California," *City Journal*, Winter 2009, https://www.city-journal.org/html/green-cities-brown-suburbs-13143 .html; and Conor Dougherty and Brad Plumer, "A Bold, Divisive Plan to Wean Californians from Cars," *New York Times*, March 16, 2018, https:// www.nytimes.com/2018/03/16/business/energy-environment/climate-density .html.

104. See Devin Edwards, "Green Houses and Greenhouse Gases: Why Exclusionary Zoning Is a Climate Catastrophe," *Georgetown Public Policy Review*, November 5, 2019, http://gppreview.com/2019/11/05/green-houses-greenhouse -gases-exclusionary-zoning-climate-catastrophe/ (noting direct emissions from residences create 6 percent of greenhouse gases, and when indirect emissions from offsite electricity are included, the total is 16 percent).

105. Robert Sanders, "Suburban Sprawl Cancels Carbon-Footprint Savings of Dense Urban Cores," *Berkeley News*, January 6, 2014, https://news .berkeley.edu/2014/01/06/suburban-sprawl-cancels-carbon-footprint-savings -of-dense-urban-cores/.

106. J. Norman, H. L. MacLean, and C. A. Kennedy, "Comparing High and Low Residential Density: Life-Cycle Analysis of Energy Use and Greenhouse Gas Emissions," *Journal of Urban Planning and Development* 132, no. 1 (2006): 10–21, cited in Maanvi Singh and Oliver Milman, "Denser Cities Could Be a Climate Boon—but Nimbyism Stands in the Way," *Guardian*, August 22,

2021, https://www.theguardian.com/us-news/2021/aug/22/cities-climate
-change-dense-sprawl-yimby-nimby.

107. See University of Michigan Center for Sustainable Systems, "U.S. Cities Fact Sheet," https://css.umich.edu/publications/factsheets/built-environment
/us-cities-factsheet (citing S. Lee and B. Lee, "The Influence of Urban Form on GHG Emissions in the U.S. Household Sector," *Journal of Energy Policy* 68 [2014]: 534–549). See also Singh and Milman, "Denser Cities Could Be a Climate Boon."

108. See Singh and Milman, "Denser Cities Could Be a Climate Boon"; and Burak Güneralp, Yuyu Zhou, Diana Ürge-Vorsatz, Mukesh Gupta, Sha Yu, Pralit L. Patel, Michail Fragkias, Xiaoma Li, and Karen C. Seto, "Global Scenarios of Urban Density and Its Impacts on Building Energy Use Through 2050," *Proceedings of the National Academy of Sciences*, August 22, 2017, https://www.pnas.org/content/114/34/8945.full.

CHAPTER 3: HOW CLASS BIAS BECAME THE PRIMARY OBSTACLE TO HOUSING ADVANCEMENT FOR BLACK PEOPLE

1. Cashin, *White Space, Black Hood*, 9–10, 40.

2. Paige Glotzer, *How the Suburbs Were Segregated: Developers and the Business of Exclusionary Housing, 1890–1960* (New York: Columbia University Press, 2021), 59. Today Roland Park is a part of Baltimore City.

3. Rothstein, *The Color of Law*, 41. For a contrary reading, see Douglas Massey, "The Legacy of the 1968 Fair Housing Act," *Sociological Forum* 30 (Suppl. 1, 2015): 571–588, https://www.ncbi.nlm.nih.gov/pmc/articles/PMC4808815/ (that the Black–white dissimilarity index was just 36 in 1860 [in 19 Northern and Southern cities] but rose to 69 in 1900 [in 64 cities] and 78 in 1970 [in 287 metropolitan areas]).

4. Putnam and Garrett, *The Upswing*, 219 (citing Trevon D. Logan and John M. Parman, "The National Rise in Residential Segregation," *Journal of Economic History* 77, no. 1 [March 2017]: 127–170). See also Steil et al., "Introduction," in Steil et al., *Furthering Fair Housing*, 17.

5. Rothstein, *The Color of Law*, 46–47.

6. *Buchanan v. Warley*, 245 U.S. 60, 79 (1917).

7. Fischel, *Zoning Rules!*, 79.

8. Henry Louis Gates, cited in Thomas B. Edsall, "Voters Seem to Think Biden Is the 'Law and Order' Candidate," opinion, *New York Times*, September 9, 2020, https://www.nytimes.com/2020/09/09/opinion/trump-portland-kenosha.html.

9. Cashin, *White Space, Black Hood*, 56.

10. William Julius Wilson, "Don't Ignore Class When Addressing Racial Gaps in Intergenerational Mobility," *Social Mobility Memos* (blog), Brookings Institution, April 12, 2018, https://www.brookings.edu/blog/social-mobility
-memos/2018/04/12/dont-ignore-class-when-addressing-racial-gaps-in

-intergenerational-mobility/ ("Although the absolute level of black income is well below that of whites, blacks nonetheless display the most intra-group income inequality, with a household Gini index of 0.50 in 2016, followed by whites and Hispanics at 0.47, and Asians at 0.46"). A Gini index of 0 represents perfect equality, and 1 is maximum inequality.

11. Gregory Squires, "Fair Housing Yesterday," in Squires, *The Fight for Fair Housing*, 3; and Richard H. Sander, Yana A. Kucheva, and Jonathan M. Zasloff, *Moving Toward Integration: The Past and Future of Fair Housing* (Cambridge, MA: Harvard University Press, 2018), 8.

12. Jonathan Zasloff, "The Price of Equality: Fair Housing, Land Use and Disparate Impact," *Columbia Human Rights Law Review* 48, no. 3 (2017): 109.

13. Margery Austin Turner, Rob Santos, Diane K. Levy, Doug Wissoker, Claudia Aranda, Rob Pitingolo, and the Urban Institute, *Housing Discrimination Against Ethnic and Racial Minorities 2012* (Washington, DC: US Department of Housing and Urban Development, June 2013), 39, cited in Zasloff, "The Price of Equality," 109.

14. William Julius Wilson, *The Truly Disadvantaged: The Inner City, the Underclass, and Public Policy*, 2nd ed. (Chicago: University of Chicago Press, 2012), 268.

15. Sam Fulwood III, "The Costs of Segregation and the Benefits of the Fair Housing Act," in Squires, *The Fight for Fair Housing*, 51.

16. Sheryll Cashin, "Middle-Class Black Suburbs and the State of Integration: A Post-Integrationist Vision of Metropolitan America," *Cornell Law Review* 86, no. 729 (2001): 735–736, cited in Fulwood, "The Costs of Segregation," 51.

17. Sophie Tareen, "Why Black Residents Are Leaving US Cities for Suburbs," *Christian Science Monitor*, March 14, 2022, https://www.csmonitor.com/USA/2022/0314/Why-Black-residents-are-leaving-US-cities-for-suburbs.

18. Myron Orfield and Will Stancil, "Fair Housing and Stable Suburban Integration," in Squires, *The Fight for Fair Housing*, 228–230, 234.

19. Ted Mellnik and Andrew Van Dam, "How Mixed-Race Neighborhoods Quietly Became the Norm in the U.S.," *Washington Post*, November 4, 2022, https://www.washingtonpost.com/business/2022/11/04/mixed-race-neighborhoods/.

20. See "QuickFacts: Winnetka Village, Illinois," US Census, https://www.census.gov/quickfacts/fact/table/winnetkavillageillinois/PST045221.

21. Walter F. Mondale, "Afterword: Ending Segregation—the Fair Housing Act's Unfinished Business," in Squires, *The Fight for Fair Housing*, 294.

22. Steil et al., "Introduction," in Steil et al., *Furthering Fair Housing*, 23 (citing Turner et al., *Housing Discrimination Against Racial and Ethnic Minorities 2012*).

23. Cashin, *White Space, Black Hood*, 72. See also Douglas Massey and Jonathan Tannen, "A Research Note on Trends in Black Hypersegregation," *Demography*, June 2015, fig. 2.

24. Cashin, *White Space, Black Hood*, 73.

25. Jargowsky, "Segregation, Neighborhoods and Schools," in Lareau and Goyette, *Choosing Homes, Choosing Schools*, 103–104.

26. Mike Maciag, "Residential Segregation Data for U.S. Metro Areas," *Governing*, January 10, 2019, https://www.governing.com/gov-data/education-data /residential-racial-segregation-metro-areas.html.

27. John R. Logan and Brian J. Stults, "Metropolitan Segregation: No Breakthrough in Sight" (Working Paper Number CES-22-14, Center for Economic Studies, August 12, 2021), 2, https://www.census.gov/library/working -papers/2022/adrm/CES-WP-22-14.html ("At the rate of decline that now seems firmly entrenched, one can project that segregation of African Americans could converge with that of Hispanics and Asians in the year 2050").

28. Patrick Sharkey, "Spatial Segmentation and the Black Middle Class," *American Journal of Sociology* 119, no. 4 (2014): 903–954, http://www.ncbi.nlm .nih.gov/pubmed/25032266.

29. John R. Logan, Brian D. Stults, and Rachel McKane, "Less Separate, No Less Unequal," Brown University Data Reports (draft report, September 27, 2022), 7, Table 2, https://s4.ad.brown.edu/Projects/Diversity/data/report /report0727.pdf.

30. Lens, "Incorporating Data on Crime," in Steil et al., *Furthering Fair Housing*, 202 (citing 2014 research).

31. David Leonhardt, "Middle-Class Black Families, in Low-Income Neighborhoods," *New York Times*, June 24, 2015, https://www.nytimes.com /2015/06/25/upshot/middle-class-black-families-in-low-income-neighborhoods .html.

32. Florida, *The New Urban Crisis*, 117.

33. See, for example, Maria Kryson, Kyle Crowder, and Michael Bader, "Pathways to Residential Segregation," in Lareau and Goyette, *Choosing Homes, Choosing Schools*, 36–39.

34. Kryson, Crowder, and Bader, "Pathways to Residential Segregation," in Lareau and Goyette, *Choosing Homes, Choosing Schools*, 39.

35. Olivia Winslow, "Poll: LI Blacks Prefer Integrated Housing," *Newsday*, February 29, 2012, http://eraseracismny.org/storage/documents/Olivia _Winslows_article_about_Housing_Survey_Report.pdf (citing Erase Racism, "Housing and Neighborhood Preferences of African Americans on Long Island, 2012 survey research report; integrated neighborhoods were defined at 50 percent Black and 50 percent white).

36. Olivia Winslow, "Dividing Lines, Visible and Invisible," *Newsday*, November 17, 2019, https://projects.newsday.com/long-island/segregation-real-estate -history/#nd-promo.

37. "Americans See Advantages and Challenges in Country's Growing Racial and Ethnic Diversity," Pew Research Center, May 8, 2019, https://www .pewsocialtrends.org/2019/05/08/americans-see-advantages-and-challenges -in-countrys-growing-racial-and-ethnic-diversity/.

38. See, for example, Megan Haberle and Jorge Soto, *Discrimination and Segregation in Housing: Continuing Lack of Progress in United States Compliance with the International Convention on the Elimination of All Forms of Racial Discrimination* (report to the UN Committee on the Elimination of Racial Discrimination, Poverty and Race Research Action Council, July 2014), http://www.prrac.org/pdf/CERD_Shadow_Report_Housing_Segregation_July_2014.pdf; and "Fair Housing Testing in Chicago Finds Discrimination Based on Race and Source of Income," National Low Income Housing Coalition, January 28, 2019, https://nlihc.org/resource/fair-housing-testing-chicago-finds-discrimination-based-race-and-source-income; source-of-income discrimination is defined as discrimination based on a renter's alternative means to pay for the rental property, such as a housing choice voucher.

39. Sander et al., *Moving Toward Integration*, 8 (citing Stephen L. Ross, "Understanding Racial Segregation: What Is Known About the Effect of Housing Discrimination" [paper presented at the Penn IUR and Federal Reserve Conference "Reinventing Older Communities: How Does Place Matter?," Penn Institute for Urban Research, 2008]).

40. Massey and Rugh, "The Intersections of Race and Class," 246 and 257. See also Matthew Resseger, "The Impact of Land Use Regulation on Racial Segregation: Evidence from Massachusetts Zoning Borders" (unpublished manuscript), November 26, 2013, https://scholar.harvard.edu/files/resseger/files/resseger_jmp_11_25.pdf (finding that in Massachusetts, Census blocks "zoned for multi-family housing have black population shares 3.36 percentage points higher and Hispanic population shares 5.77 percentage points higher than single-family zoned blocks directly across a border from them"); and Salim Furth, "New Research Shows How Zoning Slows Racial Integration," Mercatus Center, George Mason University, October 11, 2022, https://www.mercatus.org/publications/urban-economics/new-research-shows-how-zoning-slows-racial-integration (finding that in the Twin Cities area, allowing multifamily zoning is associated with a 21 percentage point increase in the nonwhite population share).

41. Massey et al., *Climbing Mount Laurel*, 19 and 20–21.

42. Massey and Rugh, "The Intersections of Race and Class," 250. See also Massey et al., *Climbing Mount Laurel*, 19; Jonathan Rothwell, "Racial Enclaves and Density Zoning: The Institutionalized Segregation of Racial Minorities in the United States," *American Law and Economics Review* 13 (2011): 290–358, https://academic.oup.com/aler/article-abstract/13/1/290/182611/Racial-Enclaves-and-Density-Zoning-The; and Douglas Massey and Jacob S. Rugh, "Segregation in Post–Civil Rights America: Stalled Integration or End of the Segregated Century?," *Du Bois Review* 11, no. 2 (Fall 2014): 205–232, https://www.ncbi.nlm.nih.gov/pmc/articles/PMC4782806/.

43. Rothstein, *The Color of Law*, 50.

44. Rothstein, *The Color of Law*, 53.

45. Rothstein, quoted in Einstein, Glick, and Palmer, *Neighborhood Defenders*, 41; and Rothstein, *The Color of Law*, 53.

46. Fischel, *Zoning Rules!*, 137.

47. William A. Fischel, "An Economic History of Zoning and a Cure for Its Exclusionary Effects," *Urban Studies* 41, no. 2 (February 2004), http://journals.sagepub.com/doi/abs/10.1080/0042098032000165271; and Fischel, *Zoning Rules!*, 171.

48. Fischel, "An Economic History of Zoning"; and Fischel, *Zoning Rules!*, 307.

49. See Bill Fulton, "Houston Doesn't Have Zoning, but There Are Work-arounds," Kinder Institute of Urban Research, Rice University, January 12, 2020, https://kinder.rice.edu/urbanedge/2020/01/09/no-zoning-in-Houston-there-are-workarounds; Cashin, *White Space, Black Hood*, 112–113; Einstein, Glick, and Palmer, *Neighborhood Defenders*, 12; and Schuetz, *Fixer-Upper*, 19. At the same time, because exclusionary policies such as deed restrictions are limited to about a quarter of residential communities in Houston, overall growth is greater there than in cities with strict zoning across the board. Gray, *Arbitrary Lines*, 144.

50. Fischel, "An Economic History of Zoning."

51. Alexander Sahn, "Racial Diversity and Exclusionary Zoning"; and Rothstein, *The Color of Law*, 9.

52. Rothstein, *The Color of Law*, 53.

53. 272 U.S. 365 (1926). See also discussion in Chapter 4.

54. Fischel, *Zoning Rules!*, 201. See also Massey et al., *Climbing Mount Laurel*, 19 (on the increase in density zoning since the 1970s).

55. Fischel, *Zoning Rules!*, 201. Fischel also says "general exclusion" (that is, stopping growth altogether) was part of the response to calls to "open up the suburbs." Fischel, *Zoning Rules!*, 216.

56. John A. Powell and Stephen Menendian, "Opportunity Communities: Overcoming the Debate over Mobility Versus Place-Based Strategies," in Squires, *The Fight for Fair Housing*, 208 (citing David D. Troutt, *The Price of Paradise: The Costs of Inequality and a Vision for a More Equitable America* [New York: New York University Press, 2013], 81–86).

57. Bhutta et al., "Disparities in Wealth by Race and Ethnicity" (white median family wealth was $188,200 and Black median family wealth was $36,100).

58. William Darity Jr., *A New Agenda for Eliminating Racial Inequality in the United States: The Research We Need* (New York: William T. Grant Foundation, 2019), 1, https://wtgrantfoundation.org/library/uploads/2019/01/A-New-Agenda-for-Eliminating-Racial-Inequality-in-the-United-States_WTG-Digest-2018.pdf.

59. See Tracy Jan, "HUD Nominee Lays Out Priorities at Confirmation Hearing," *Washington Post*, January 29, 2021, A12, https://www.washingtonpost.com/business/2021/01/28/hud-fudge-confirmation-hearing/.

60. Rothstein, *The Color of Law*, 66.

61. McGhee, *The Sum of Us*, 80.

62. Lisa Rice, "The Fair Housing Act: A Tool for Expanding Access to Quality Credit," in Squires, *The Fight for Fair Housing*, 78 and 81.

63. Rothstein, *The Color of Law*, 67.

64. Ta-Nehisi Coates, "The Case for Reparations," *Atlantic*, June 2014.

65. Rothstein, *The Color of Law*, 76.

66. Rothstein, *The Color of Law*, 76.

67. Thomas J. Sugrue, "From Jim Crow to Fair Housing," in Squires, *The Fight for Fair Housing*, 16.

68. George Lipsitz, "Living Downstream: The Fair Housing Act at Fifty," in Squires, *The Fight for Fair Housing*, 269 (describing percentage of funds going to nonwhite people between 1934 and 1978).

69. Hoffman interview, 8.

70. McGhee, *The Sum of Us*, 171 (citing Daniel Aaronson, Daniel Hartley, and Bhash Mazumder, "The Effects of the 1930s HOLC 'Redlining' Maps" [Working Paper no. 2017-12, Federal Reserve Bank of Chicago, revised August 2020], at 31, https://www.chicagofed.org/publications/working-papers/2017/wp2017-12. "Overall, we conclude that the maps account for between 15 to 30 percent of the overall gap in share African American and home ownership over the 1950 to 1980 period and 40 percent of the gap in house values. If we focus just on the C versus B neighborhoods over the 1950–1980 period, the maps account for roughly half of the homeownership and house value gaps. After 1980, our estimates decline in magnitude and therefore account for 0 to 20 percent of the D-C and C-B gap in each of our outcomes").

71. Michela Zonta, "Racial Disparities in Home Appreciation," Center for American Progress, July 15, 2019, https://americanprogress.org/article/racial-disparities-home-appreciation/ (citing Chenoa Flippen, "Unequal Returns to Housing Investments? A Study of Real Housing Appreciation Among Black, White, and Hispanic Households," *Social Forces* 82, no. 4 [2004]: 1523–1551; and Sunwoong Kim, "Race and Home Price Appreciation in Urban Neighborhoods: Evidence from Milwaukee, Wisconsin," *Review of Black Political Economy* 28, no. 2 [2000]: 9–28).

72. See Vanessa Gregory, "How the Real Estate Boom Left Black Neighborhoods Behind," *New York Times*, November 18, 2021, https://www.nytimes.com/2021/11/18/magazine/real-estate-memphis-black-neighborhoods.html; "Race Determines Home Values More Today Than It Did in 1980," Rice University Kinder Institute for Urban Research, September 24, 2020. https://kinder.rice.edu/urbanedge/2020/09/24/housing-racial-disparities-race-still-determines-home-values-America; and Junia Howell and Elizabeth Korver-Glenn, "The Increasing Effect of Neighborhood Racial Composition on Housing Values, 1980–2015," *Social Problems* 68, no. 4 (November 2021): 1051–1071, https://doi.org/10.1093/socpro/spaa033.

73. Gregory, "How the Real Estate Boom Left Black Neighborhoods Behind."

74. In Chapter 4, we also explore the possibilities of class bias that disproportionately affects Black people, a hypothesis advanced by researchers at the American Enterprise Institute.

75. See Andre M. Perry, Jonathan Rothwell, and David Harshbarger, "The Devaluation of Assets in Black Neighborhoods: The Case of Residential Property," Brookings Institution, November 27, 2018, https://www.brookings.edu/research/devaluation-of-assets-in-black-neighborhoods/.

76. Stewart, *The 9.9 Percent*, 219.

77. Margery Turner, remarks at the Roots of Structural Racism: Residential Segregation in the US Conference, YouTube video, 2:54:06, Othering and Belonging Institute, June 22, 2021, https://www.youtube.com/watch?v=7Q1eUrpbnzU.

78. Rothstein, *The Color of Law*, 80.

79. *Corrigan v. Buckley*, 271 U.S. 323 (1926).

80. Rothstein, *The Color of Law*, 82–83.

81. *Shelley v. Kraemer*, 334 U.S. 1 (1948).

82. Rothstein, *The Color of Law*, 93.

83. National Association of Real Estate Boards, *Code of Ethics* (Chicago: National Association of Real Estate Boards, June 6, 1924), 7, Article 34, https://www.nar.realtor/sites/default/files/documents/COE1924.pdf.

84. Jim Schutze, "*The Accommodation* Tanked 30 Years Ago. It's Time to Try Again." *D Magazine*, September 2021, https://www.dmagazine.com/publications/d-magazine/2021/september/the-accommodation-tanked-30-years-ago-its-time-to-try-again/; Jim Schutze, *The Accommodation: The Politics of Race in an American City* (Secaucus, NJ: Citadel Press, 1987), 5, 13.

85. "Background Information: DISD Desegregation Litigation," Southern Methodist University, https://www.smu.edu/Law/Library/Collections/DISD-Desegregation-Litigation-Archives/Background-Info.

86. Schutze, *The Accommodation*, 86.

87. *Tasby v. Estes*, 342 F. Supp. 945, 947–950 (1971).

88. See Gerald S. McCorkle, "Busing Comes to Dallas," *Southwestern Historical Quarterly* 111, no. 3 (January 2008): 304–333, at 313, https:doi.org/10.1353/swh.2008.0094.

89. McCorkle, "Busing Comes to Dallas," 321.

90. McCorkle, "Busing Comes to Dallas," 305.

91. Marvin E. Edwards, "Equity and Choice: Issues and Answers in the Dallas Schools, Address Before the National Committee for School Desegregation 17" (March 1990), cited in John A. Powell, "Living and Learning: Linking Housing and Education," *Minnesota Law Review* 80 (1996), at 789n132, https://scholarship.law.umn.edu/cgi/viewcontent.cgi?article=2666&context=mlr.

92. See Kahlenberg, *All Together Now*, 92.

93. "Dallas Independent School District," Great Schools, last accessed December 2021, https://www.greatschools.org/texas/dallas/dallas-independent-school-district/.

94. Dana Goldstein, "Dallas Schools, Long Segregated, Charge Forward on Diversity," *New York Times*, June 19, 2017, https://www.nytimes.com/2017/06/19/us/dallas-schools-desegregation.html.

95. See Kahlenberg, "Hearing from Low-Wage Working Mothers."

96. "Quarterly Residential Vacancies and Homeownership, Third Quarter 2021," US Census Bureau, November 2, 2021, 10, table 7, https://www.census .gov/housing/hvs/files/currenthvspress.pdf.

97. Cashin, *White Space, Black Hood*, 121, 201.

98. Sander et al., *Moving Toward Integration*, 1.

99. Sander et al., *Moving Toward Integration*, 1–4.

100. Sander et al., *Moving Toward Integration*, 2, table 0.1.

101. Sander et al., *Moving Toward Integration*, 12 (citing David M. Cutler and Edward L. Glaeser, "Are Ghettoes Good or Bad?," *Quarterly Journal of Economics* 112, no. 3 [1997]: 827).

102. Sander et al., *Moving Toward Integration*, 4, table 0.2.

103. Jargowsky, "Architecture of Segregation," 2.

104. Patrick Sharkey, *Neighborhoods and the Black-White Mobility Gap* (New York: Economic Mobility Project of the Pew Charitable Trusts, 2009), 2. See also Sharkey, *Stuck in Place*, 27, fig. 2.1.

105. Emma Garcia, "Poor Black Children Are Much More Likely to Attend High-Poverty Schools Than Poor White Children," Economic Policy Institute, January 13, 2017, https://www.epi.org/publication/poor-black -children-are-much-more-likely-to-attend-high-poverty-schools-than-poor-white -children/.

106. Kahlenberg, Potter, and Quick, "A Bold Agenda for School Integration," fig. 1 (NAEP Fourth Grade Math Scores for Students Eligible for the National School Lunch Program, 2017).

CHAPTER 4: HOW MERITOCRATIC ELITISM SUSTAINS THE WALLS

1. Samantha, interview with Michelle Burris and author, August 3, 3021 (hereafter, Samantha interview).

2. "QuickFacts: Springfield City, Massachusetts," US Census Bureau, https://www.census.gov/quickfacts/fact/table/springfieldcitymassachusetts, US/PST045219; and "QuickFacts: Massachusetts," US Census Bureau, https:// www.census.gov/quickfacts/fact/table/MA/INC110219 (state median income is more than $81,000).

3. Jeanette DeForge, "War on Poverty: Poor Schoolchildren Face Hunger, Limited Vocabulary, Host of Problems," MassLive, March 24, 2019, https:// www.masslive.com/news/2015/01/springfield_holyoke_schools_am.html.

4. Samantha, interview with Michelle Burris and author, September 2, 2021 (hereafter, Samantha interview II), 4.

5. "2019 Crime in the United States: Massachusetts Offenses Known to Law Enforcement by City," Federal Bureau of Investigation, Uniform Crime Report, table 8, https://ucr.fbi.gov/crime-in-the-u.s/2019/crime-in-the-u.s.-2019/tables /table-8/table-8-state-cuts/massachusetts.xls.

6. Samantha interview, 6.

7. "Top 235 Cities in Massachusetts by Population," World Population Review, https://worldpopulationreview.com/states/cities/massachusetts; Samantha interview, 1.

8. Samantha interview, 1, 2, 6, 7; Samantha interview II, 1–3.

9. "Frank H. Freedman," Great Schools, last accessed November 2021, https://www.greatschools.org/massachusetts/springfield/1537-Frank-H-Freedman/.

10. "Elias Brookings," Great Schools, last accessed November 2021, https://www.greatschools.org/massachusetts/springfield/1536-Elias-Brookings/.

11. "Springfield Public Day Middle School," Great Schools, last accessed November 2021, https://www.greatschools.org/massachusetts/springfield/5408-Springfield-Public-Day-Middle-School/; Samantha interview, 3.

12. Samantha interview, 3.

13. Kristin Haas, interview with Michelle Burris and author, September 1, 2021 (hereafter, Haas interview), 1. For a very comprehensive analysis, see also Amy Dain, "The State of Zoning for Multi-Family Housing in Greater Boston," Massachusetts Smart Growth Alliance, June 2019, https://ma-smartgrowth.org/resources/resourcesreports-books/.

14. Haas interview, 1.

15. Renée Loth, "Zoning Reform Offers a Path to Economic Equality and Social Integration," *Boston Globe*, January 16, 2018 ("According to the Metropolitan Area Planning Council, 200 of the state's 351 cities and towns haven't built any new multifamily housing in the past 10 years").

16. Samantha interview, 4, 7.

17. See Cashin, *White Space, Black Hood*, 102 (over the last several years, white people have constituted 36 percent of SNAP food aid recipients on average, while Black people have constituted 25 percent of recipients); and National Low Income Housing Coalition, "Who Lives in Federally Assisted Housing?," Housing Spotlight, November 2012, 3, chart 2 (In project-based Section 8 housing, which is private housing that is publicly subsidized based on long-term agreements, 49 percent of residents are white, 33 percent are Black, 13 percent are Hispanic, and 5 percent are "other").

18. Donald Trump, quoted in Isenberg, *White Trash*, xvi.

19. Isenberg, *White Trash*, xxv–xxvi.

20. See Richard D. Kahlenberg, "Harvard's Class Gap: Can the Academy Understand Donald Trump's 'Forgotten' Americans?," *Harvard Magazine*, May–June 2017.

21. See, for example, Robert Coles, "In the South These Children Prophesy," *Atlantic*, March 1963, 111–116; Jennie Rothenberg Gritz, "How Kids Dealt with the Stress of Desegregation," *Atlantic*, January 19, 2014, https://www.theatlantic.com/education/archive/2014/01/how-kids-dealt-with-the-stress-of-desegregation/283146/; and Robert Coles, *The Story of Ruby Bridges* (New York: Scholastic Press, 1995).

22. A very small number of Black students were permitted to attend the school's affluent suburbs such as Wellesley as part of the METCO program,

but these students and their families were not permitted to actually live in the neighborhoods. Instead, they had to take long bus rides each day to commute back and forth.

23. See J. Anthony Lukas, *Common Ground: A Turbulent Decade in the Lives of Three American Families* (New York: Alfred A. Knopf, 1985), 244–245. For 2019 demographic data, see US Census Bureau, "QuickFacts: Wellesley, CDP, Massachusetts," https://www.census.gov/quickfacts/wellesleycdpmassachusetts.

24. Mike Barnicle, interview with Robert Coles, "Busing Puts Burdens on Working Class, Black and White," *Boston Globe*, October 15, 1974, 23.

25. Barnicle interview with Coles, "Busing Puts Burdens."

26. Rolf Pendall, Robert Puentes, and Jonathan Martin, "From Traditional to Reformed: A Review of Land Use Regulations in the Nation's 50 Largest Metropolitan Areas," Brookings Institution, August 1, 2006, https://www.brookings.edu/research/from-traditional-to-reformed-a-review-of-the-land-use-regulations-in-the-nations-50-largest-metropolitan-areas/.

27. Einstein, Glick, and Palmer, *Neighborhood Defenders*, 58–59, 64.

28. "QuickFacts: Weston Town, Middlesex County, Massachusetts," US Census Bureau, https://www.census.gov/quickfacts/fact/table/westontownmiddlesexcountymassachusetts,MA,US/PST045219; and "QuickFacts: Cambridge City, Massachusetts," US Census Bureau, https://www.census.gov/quickfacts/fact/table/cambridgecitymassachusetts/PST045219.

29. Einstein, Glick, and Palmer, *Neighborhood Defenders*, 62.

30. Einstein, Glick, and Palmer, *Neighborhood Defenders*, 103–105.

31. Einstein, Glick, and Palmer, *Neighborhood Defenders*, 16.

32. Dana LeWinter, interview with author, September 14, 2021.

33. Einstein, Glick, and Palmer, *Neighborhood Defenders*, 3.

34. Massachusetts outlawed source-of-income discrimination in 1971 and strengthened the law in 1989. See Scott et al., "Appendix B: State, Local, and Federal Laws Barring Source-of-Income Discrimination," in *Expanding Choice*, August 2021, 20–22, https://www.prrac.org/pdf/AppendixB.pdf.

35. Alison Bell, Barbara Sard, and Becky Koepnick, "Prohibiting Discrimination Against Renters Using Housing Vouchers Improves Results," Center on Budget and Policy Priorities, December 20, 2018, https://www.cbpp.org/research/housing/prohibiting-discrimination-against-renters-using-housing-vouchers-improves-results#:~:text=Voucher%20holders%20have%20incentives%20to,and%20not%20pay%20rent%20reliably.

36. Jamie Langowski, William Berman, Grace Brittan, Catherine LaRaia, Jee-Yeon Lehmann, and Judson Woods, *Qualified Renters Need Not Apply: Race and Voucher Discrimination in the Metro Boston Rental Housing Market* (Boston: Boston Foundation, Suffolk University Law School, and Analysis Group, July 2020), 13, 12, 52, 7, 11, 28, and 27, https://www.suffolk.edu/-/media/suffolk/documents/news/2020/law-news/rental_housing_study_july2020.pdf?la=en&hash=B0FFF5916ECA23DFD054170DA223780EDA571241; and "Qualified Renters Need Not Apply" (study summary), Suffolk University Boston, June 26,

2020, https://www.suffolk.edu/news-features/news/2020/06/27/01/03/qualified
-renters-need-not-apply.

37. "Fair Housing Testing in Chicago Finds Discrimination Based on Race and Source of Income," National Low Income Housing Coalition, January 28, 2019, https://nlihc.org/resource/fair-housing-testing-chicago-finds -discrimination-based-race-and-source-income (racial discrimination occurred 20 percent of the time and source-of-income discrimination 49 percent of the time).

38. Haas interview, 2.

39. Haas interview, 2.

40. Haas interview, 3.

41. Haas interview, 3. See also Langowski et al., *Qualified Renters*, 25.

42. Haas interview, 3.

43. Dana LeWinter, interview with author, September 14, 2021. See also Jerusalem Demsas, "The Housing Shortage Makes Housing Discrimination Much Easier," *Vox*, May 26, 2021, https://www.vox.com/2021/5/26/22453293 /housing-supply-shortage-discrimination-real-estate-cover-letters.

44. David Scharfenberg, "Boston's Struggle with Income Segregation," *Boston Globe*, March 5, 2016, https://www.bostonglobe.com/metro/2016/03/05 /segregation/NiQBy000TzsGgLnAT0tHsL/story.html. The *Boston Globe* article was based on an analysis conducted for the *Globe* by Kendra Bischoff and Sean F. Reardon, which included six neighborhood categories: affluent, high income, upper middle income, lower middle income, low income, and poor.

45. Haas interview, 13.

46. Haas interview, 12.

47. "QuickFacts: Longmeadow CDP, Massachusetts," US Census Bureau, https://www.census.gov/quickfacts/fact/table/longmeadowcdpmassachusetts /BZA010219.

48. Samantha interview, 3, 6.

49. "Wolf Swamp Road," Great Schools, last accessed November 2021, https:// www.greatschools.org/massachusetts/longmeadow/927-Wolf-Swamp-Road/.

50. Samantha interview, 2. "Longmeadow High School," Great Schools, last accessed November 2021, https://www.greatschools.org/massachusetts /longmeadow/926-Longmeadow-High-School/.

51. Samantha interview, 3–4, 7–8.

52. Haas interview, 14, 16.

53. Haas interview, 8–10.

54. Haas interview, 8.

55. Haas interview, 8.

56. Dolly Parton, "Coat of Many Colors," YouTube video, 3:19, Gussie5555, December 23, 3008, https://www.youtube.com/watch?v=w_-YbWHs6DE (ten million views on YouTube).

57. Vernell Hackett, "New Statistics About Country Music Fans Revealed at Billboard Country Summit," Billboard News, June 8, 2011, https://www .billboard.com/music/music-news/new-statistics-about-country-music-fans

-revealed-at-billboard-country-1177554/; and Lee Mizell with Brett Crawford and Caryn Anderson, *Musical Preferences in the U.S., 1982–2002* (Washington, DC: National Endowment for the Arts, June 2005), 26, tables 9 and 15, table 5, https://files.eric.ed.gov/fulltext/ED511715.pdf (45 percent of those with a bachelor's degree or higher liked classical/chamber music in 2002 compared with 12 percent of those with less than a high school degree. In contrast country/western music was more popular among those with less than a high school degree or high school degree/some college than those with a bachelor's degree or higher).

58. Lauren Rivera and András Tilcsik, "Research: How Subtle Class Cues Can Backfire on Your Resume," *Harvard Business Review*, December 21, 2016, https://hbr.org/2016/12/research-how-subtle-class-cues-can-backfire-on-your-resume; and Lauren A. Rivera and András Tilcsik, "Class Advantage, Commitment Penalty: The Gendered Effect of Social Class Signals in an Elite Labor Market," *American Sociological Review*, October 12, 2016, https://doi.org/10.1177/0003122416668154 (of those from identical law schools and with identical GPAs, 16.25 percent of those who signaled high class status received interviews vs. 1.28 percent of those who signaled low class status).

59. Rothstein, *The Color of Law*, 67 (emphasis added).

60. Rothstein, *The Color of Law*, 67.

61. Rothstein, *The Color of Law*, 68.

62. Isenberg, *White Trash*, 239.

63. Glotzer, *How the Suburbs Were Segregated*, 158–159.

64. See Kahlenberg, *All Together Now*, 228–251; and Richard D. Kahlenberg, *Rescuing* Brown v. Board of Education*: Profiles of Twelve School Districts Pursuing Socioeconomic School Integration* (New York: Century Foundation, June 28, 2007), 13–28, https://production-tcf.imgix.net/assets/downloads/tcf-districtprofiles.pdf.

65. See Kahlenberg, *All Together Now*, 228–251; and Kahlenberg, *Rescuing* Brown v. Board of Education, 13–28.

66. Mickey Kaus, *The End of Equality* (New York: Basic Books, 1992), 275n28.

67. Isenberg, *White Trash*, 240–241.

68. See *Vickers v. Township Comm of Gloucester Township*, 37 N.J. 232, 365, 181 A.2s 129 (1962), cited in Isenberg, *White Trash*, 244–245.

69. Isenberg, *White Trash*, 236.

70. Steven T. Anderson, "Trailer Park Residents: Are They Worthy of Society and Respect?," *Social Thought and Research* 35 (2019): 113–140, at 129–130, table 2.

71. Jargowsky, "Architecture of Segregation," 4.

72. Chris McGreal, "America's Poorest White Town: Abandoned by Coal, Swallowed by Drugs," *Guardian*, November 12, 2015, https://www.theguardian.com/us-news/2015/nov/12/beattyville-kentucky-and-americas-poorest-towns.

73. See, for example, Roger Starr, "The Lesson of Forest Hills," *Commentary*, June 1972, https://www.commentarymagazine.com/articles/roger-starr-2/the-lesson-of-forest-hills/ (re: Baisley Park).

74. Cashin, *White Space, Black Hood*, 88.

75. Howard Husock, "Affirmatively Furthering Fair Housing: Are There Reasons for Skepticism?" in Steil et al., *Furthering Fair Housing*, 132–133 (noting Black middle-class resistance to economic integration in Westchester County, New York, and Chicago).

76. Einstein et al., *Neighborhood Defenders*, 110. Having said that, the authors also found that Black support for new housing was higher than among other racial groups (id.).

77. See D. W. Rowlands, "Prince George's County's Belt of High-Income Majority Black Census Tracts Really Is Unique," *Greater Greater Washington*, November 6, 2020, https://ggwash.org/view/79489/prince-georges-countys-belt-of-high-income-majority-black-census-tracts-really-is-unique.

78. Hoffman interview, 19.

79. Murphy interview.

80. Murphy interview.

81. Murphy interview.

82. Jargowsky, "Segregation, Neighborhoods and Schools," in Lareau and Goyette, *Choosing Neighborhoods, Choosing Schools*, 108.

83. Jargowsky, "Segregation, Neighborhoods and Schools," in Lareau and Goyette, *Choosing Homes, Choosing Schools*, 109, tables 4.4 and 104, table 4.1. The highest segregation rates can be found when race and class combine. The dissimilarity index between poor Black people and affluent white people is an astounding .79. See also Paul Jargowsky, "What Would a New Kerner Commission Conclude Today?," *Pathways*, Winter 2019, 45, table 1, https://inequality.stanford.edu/sites/default/files/Pathways_Winter2019_Kerner.pdf (finding the dissimilarity index between poor Black people and wealthy Black people is .50).

84. Cashin, *White Space, Black Hood*, 56.

85. Wilson, quoted in Cashin, *White Space, Black Hood*, 69.

86. Sharkey, *Stuck in Place*, 24 (citing Wilson).

87. Christopher Ingraham, "The Most Racist Places in America, According to Google," *Washington Post*, April 28, 2015, https://www.washingtonpost.com/news/wonk/wp/2015/04/28/the-most-racist-places-in-america-according-to-google/ (citing the South and rural areas).

88. See, for example, Ilya Somin, "Why More Liberal Cities Have Less Affordable Housing," *Washington Post*, November 2, 2014, https://www.washingtonpost.com/news/olokh-conspiracy/wp/2014/11/02/more-liberal-cities-have-less-affordable-housing/; Michael Hobbes, "Progressive Boomers Are Making It Impossible for Cities to Fix the Housing Crisis: Residents of Wealthy Neighborhoods Are Taking Extreme Measures to Block Much-Needed Housing and

Transportation Projects," *Huffington Post*, July 8, 2019, https://www.huffpost
.com/entry/cities-fight-baby-boomers-to-address-housing-crisis_n_5d1bcf0
ee4b07f6ca58598a9 (citing examples in Seattle, Los Angeles, San Francisco,
and elsewhere); Edward Glaeser and Joseph Gyourko, "Zoning's Steep Price,"
Regulation, Fall 2002, 26, https://www.researchgate.net/publication/228180251
_Zoning%27s_Steep_Price (noting that although it is true that there is more
demand for housing in coastal states, it is also true that there is plenty of land
available, but its use is restricted by zoning regulations); and Johnny Harris and
Binyamin Appelbaum, "Blue States, You're the Problem: Why Do States with
Democratic Majorities Fail to Live Up to Their Values?," opinion, *New York
Times* video, November 9, 2021, https://www.nytimes.com/2021/11/09/opinion
/democrats-blue-states-legislation.html (Binyamin Appelbaum notes that exclusionary zoning is particularly problematic in places like California; "Blue states
is where the housing crisis is located," he said). In a 2018 study, Massey and
Rugh do find that anti-Black prejudice is positively correlated with increase
restrictions in zoning. But the correlation (0.176) is modest. See Massey and
Rugh, "The Intersections of Race and Class," 251.

    89. See Pendall, Puentes, and Martin, "From Traditional to Reformed";
and Joseph Gyourko, Albert Saiz, and Anita Summers, "A New Measure of the
Local Regulatory Environment for Housing Markets: The Wharton Residential
Land Use Regulatory Index," *Urban Studies* 45, no. 3 (March 2008): 693–729,
http://journals.sagepub.com/doi/abs/10.1177/0042098007087341.

    90. Schuetz, *Fixer-Upper*, 23–24 (citing research from 2014, 2018, and
2019). See also Einstein, Glick, and Palmer, *Neighborhood Defenders*, 11 (citing
research from 2011 and 2013).

    91. Schuetz, *Fixer-Upper*, 152.

    92. Mathew Kahn, "Do Liberal Cities Limit New Housing Development?
Evidence from California," *Journal of Urban Economics*, March 2011, https://
www.sciencedirect.com/science/article/abs/pii/S0094119010000720.

    93. Harris and Appelbaum, "Blue States, You're the Problem." See also "City
of Palo Alto Rezoning of Maybell Avenue, Measure D (November 2013)," Bal-
lotpedia, from the November 5, 2013, election ballot, https://ballotpedia.org
/City_of_Palo_Alto_Rezoning_of_Maybell_Avenue,_Measure_D_(November
_2013).

    94. Sam Griffin, Erin Boggs, Roger Maldonado, and Peter Haberlandt,
*Zoning for Equity: Examining Planning and Zoning Impediments to Housing and
School Diversity*, vol. 2 (Hartford, CT: Open Communities Alliance, March
2022), 31, https://assets.nationbuilder.com/opencommunitiesalliance/pages/823
/attachments/original/1649280490/Zoning_for_Equity_Vol_2_FINAL_-
_Reduced_Size.pdf?1649280490.

    95. See Davis Dunavin, "Report: The Vast Majority of Connecticut Zoning
Blocks Affordable Housing," WSHU Public Radio, January 28, 2021, https://
www.wshu.org/news/2021-01-28/report-the-vast-majority-of-connecticut

-zoning-blocks-affordable-housing; Lisa Prevost, "A Push for Zoning Reform in Connecticut," *New York Times*, February 26, 2021, https://www.nytimes.com/2021/02/26/realestate/connecticut-zoning-reform.html; and "Connecticut Zoning Atlas," Desegregate Connecticut, https://www.desegregatect.org/atlas.

96. Don Falk, interview with author, December 6, 2021 (hereafter, Falk interview), 15–17.

97. Falk interview, 19.

98. Falk interview, 19–21. See also J. K. Dineen, "Supervisor Mar Pushes Compromise for Contested Sunset District Affordable Housing Project," *San Francisco Chronicle*, November 23, 2021.

99. Falk interview, 26–30.

100. Florida, *The New Urban Crisis*, 112.

101. Florida, *The New Urban Crisis*, 109. See also 99–100.

102. See, for example, Ezra Klein, "Government Is Flailing, in Part Because Liberals Hobbled It," opinion, *New York Times*, March 13, 2022, https://www.nytimes.com/2022/03/13/opinion/berkeley-enrollment-climate-crisis.html?.

103. William Marble and Clayton Nail, "Where Self-Interest Trumps Ideology: Liberal Homeowners and Local Opposition to Housing Development," *Journal of Politics* 83, no. 4 (October 2021).

104. Fareed Zakaria, "The Two Sins That Defined the Election," opinion, *Washington Post*, November 10, 2016, https://www.washingtonpost.com/opinions/the-two-sins-that-defined-this-election/2016/11/10/97fdfcf2-a78b-11e6-ba59-a7d93165c6d4_story.html.

105. See David Leonhardt, "What's the Matter with Scarsdale? Democrats' Struggles with Working-Class Voters Seem to Be Getting Worse," *New York Times*, November 4, 2021, https://www.nytimes.com/2021/11/04/briefing/democrats-election-working-class-voters.html; and David Brooks, "Democrats Need to Confront Their Privilege," opinion, *New York Times*, November 4, 2021, https://www.nytimes.com/2021/11/04/opinion/democrats-culture-wars.html.

106. Nate Cohn, "How Educational Differences Are Widening America's Political Rift," *New York Times*, September 8, 2021.

107. Stewart, *The 9.9 Percent*, 249 (citing Thomas Piketty, "Brahmin Left v. Merchant Right," World Inequality Database, 2018).

108. Stewart, *The 9.9 Percent*, 249.

109. Brooks, "Democrats Need to Confront Their Privilege."

110. Ruy Teixeira, "The Democrats' Shifting Coalition: Unlike Trump, They Love the Highly Educated," *Liberal Patriot* (newsletter), August 25, 2022, https://theliberalpatriot.substack.com/p/the-democrats-shifting-coalition?utm_source=email.

111. Astead W. Herndon and Shane Goldmacher, "In Rural Areas, Prospects Sink for Democrats," *New York Times*, November 7, 2021, 1, 16.

112. Nate Cohn, "Poll Shows Tight Race for Control of Congress as Class Divide Widens," *New York Times*, July 13, 2022, https://www.nytimes.com/2022/07/13/upshot/poll-2022-midterms-congress.html.

113. Toon Kuppens, Russell Spears, Antony S. R. Manstead, Bram Spruyt, and Matthew J. Easterbrook, "Educationism and the Irony of Meritocracy: Negative Attitudes of Higher Educated People Towards the Less Educated," *Journal of Experimental Social Psychology* 76 (2018): 429–447, http://sro.sussex.ac.uk/id/eprint/71335/1/__smbhome.uscs.susx.ac.uk_ellenaj_Desktop_SRO_after%20august_Kuppens%20Educationism%20and%20the%20irony%20of%20meritocracy.pdf.

114. Kuppens et al., "Educationalism and the Irony of Meritocracy," 61.

115. Kuppens et al., "Educationalism and the Irony of Meritocracy," 27, 29, and 63.

116. Kuppens et al., "Educationalism and the Irony of Meritocracy," 32.

117. Kuppens et al., "Educationalism and the Irony of Meritocracy," 34.

118. Daniel T. Lichter and Martha L. Crowley, "Poverty in America: Beyond Welfare Reform," *Population Bulletin* 57, no. 2 (June 2002): 18, https://www.prb.org/wp-content/uploads/2021/02/06052002_57.2PovertyInAmerica.pdf.

119. Isenberg, *White Trash*, xxviii.

120. See James Gordon, "Move Over Alec Baldwin! SNL Unveils It's [*sic*] New Trump Character Played by James Austin Johnson as Show Sends Youngkin's Virginia Gubernatorial Win," *Daily Mail*, November 7, 2021, https://www.dailymail.co.uk/news/article-10173803/SNL-mocks-Glenn-Youngkins-Virginia-Governor-win-struggling-explain-critical-race-theory.html.

121. Cashin, *White Space, Black Hood*, 106.

122. Katie Rogers, "Obamas Pay $8.1 Million for Home Just Miles from White House," *New York Times*, May 31, 2017, https://www.nytimes.com/2017/05/31/us/obama-buys-house-washington-kalorama.html.

123. "Beautiful Home in Exclusive Neighborhood 4br/4.5ba," Airbnb, https://www.airbnb.com/rooms/32676078?source_impression_id=p3_1657134748_%2Ba7XayoDxqgmUNx2.

124. Edward J. Blakely and Mary Gail Snyder, *Fortress America: Gated Communities in the United States* (Washington, DC: Brookings Institution Press, 1997).

125. Robert Reich, "Secession of the Successful," *New York Times*, January 20, 1991, http://www.nytimes.com/1991/01/20/magazine/secession-of-the-successful.html.

126. John Blake, "How 'Good White People' Derail Racial Progress," CNN, August 2, 2020, https://amp.cnn.com/cnn/2020/08/01/us/white-liberals-hypocrisy-race-blake/index.html?__twitter_impression=true.

127. Stewart, *The 9.9 Percent*, 7.

128. Hanlon, quoted in Farhad Manjoo, "America's Cities Are Unlivable. Blame Wealthy Liberals," opinion, *New York Times*, May 22, 2019, https://www.nytimes.com/2019/05/22/opinion/california-housing-nimby.html.

129. Richard Reeves, "Everyday Equality," op-ed, Brookings Institution, September 3, 2020, https://www.brookings.edu/opinions/everyday-equality/.

130. William Smith, "Map: See How Your Town or City Voted in the 2020 Election," WBUR, November 3, 2020, https://www.wbur.org/news/2020/11/03/2020-massachusetts-election-map.

131. See, for example, David Leonhardt and Ian Prasad Philbrick, "Donald Trump's Racism: The Definitive List, Updated," opinion, *New York Times*, January 15, 2018, https://www.nytimes.com/interactive/2018/01/15/opinion/leonhardt-trump-racist.html.

132. The President's News Conference (transcript), Administration of Donald J. Trump, August 12, 2020, 14, https://www.govinfo.gov/content/pkg/DCPD-202000598/pdf/DCPD-202000598.pdf.

133. See discussion, Chapter 5.

134. US Constitution, Amendment XIV.

135. 272 U.S. 365 (1926).

136. See Richard D. Kahlenberg, "The Walls We Won't Tear Down," opinion, *New York Times*, August 3, 2017, https://www.nytimes.com/2017/08/03/opinion/sunday/zoning-laws-segregation-income.html.

137. 272 U.S. 365, at 394–395.

138. 272 U.S. 365 at 388.

139. *Hunter v. Erickson*, 393 U.S. 385 (1969).

140. *James v. Valtierra*, 402 U.S. 137, 141 (1971).

141. Today, through amendment, the Fair Housing Act outlaws discrimination on the basis of "race, color, religion, sex, familial status, national origin, or disability." See Steil et al., "Introduction," in Steil et al., *Furthering Fair Housing*, 21, 27.

142. Douglas S. Massey, "The Legacy of the 1968 Fair Housing Act," *Sociological Forum* 30 (Suppl. 1, June 2015): 571–588, https://www.ncbi.nlm.nih.gov/pmc/articles/PMC4808815/.

143. Burr, "The Problem of Sunnyvale," 205. See also 109 F. Supp. 2d at 563 ("The Act has been interpreted to prohibit municipalities from using their zoning powers in a discriminatory manner, that is in a manner which excludes housing for a group of people on the basis of one of the enumerated classifications").

144. Alexander von Hoffman, "The Origins of the Fair Housing Act of 1968," in Steil et al., *Furthering Fair Housing*, 62.

145. Von Hoffman, "The Origins," in Steil et al., *Furthering Fair Housing*, 61.

146. Von Hoffman, "The Origins," in Steil et al., *Furthering Fair Housing*, 62 (citing Fair Housing Act of 1967, Hearings, Testimony of Proxmire, 73, 177–178, 417; and Mara S. Sidney, "Images of Race, Class and Markets: Rethinking the Origins of the U.S. Fair Housing Policy," *Journal of Policy History* 13, no. 2 [2001]: 181–214).

147. Von Hoffman, "The Origins," in Steil et al., *Furthering Fair Housing*, 62.

148. Brian Knudsen, "Expanded Protections for Families with Housing Choice Vouchers," Poverty & Race Research Action Council, September 2022, https://prrac.org/pdf/soi-voucher-data-brief.pdf.

149. As discussed further in Chapter 7, under the Fair Housing Act, plaintiffs can challenge zoning laws that have a "disparate impact" on protected racial groups. See *Texas Department of Housing and Community Affairs v. Inclusive Communities Project*. But there is no comparable federal protection against zoning laws that discriminate on the basis of income alone. The handful of states that provide some remedies for municipalities whose zoning laws discriminate on the basis of income include New Jersey, Pennsylvania, California, and New Hampshire. But these are the outliers. See Brian W. Blaeser et al., "Advocating Affordable Housing in New Hampshire: The Amicus Brief of American Planning Association in *Wayne Britton v. Town of Chester*," *Washington University Journal of Urban and Contemporary Law* 40, no. 3 (1991): 3, 23–28, http://openscholarship .wustl.edu/cgi/viewcontent.cgi?article=1211&context=law_urbanlaw.

150. Catharina Germaine, Isabelle Chopin, and Directorate-General for Justice and Consumers (European Commission), *A Comparative Analysis of Non-discrimination Law in Europe* (Brussels: European Commission, 2016), table 1, 11–14, https://op.europa.eu/en/publication-detail/-/publication/54a944d6 -dc81-11e6-ad7c-01aa75ed71a1/language-en/format-PDF/source-275075356.

151. For discussion of the specialized bodies and commissions that enforce antidiscrimination provisions, including those based on economic status, see European Commission, *A Comparative Analysis of Non-discrimination*, table 12, 108–112.

152. See, for example, Mario L. Barnes and Erwin Chemerinsky, "The Disparate Treatment of Race and Class in Constitutional Jurisprudence," *Law and Contemporary Problems* 72, no. 4 (Fall 2009): 109–130, https://scholarship.law .duke.edu/cgi/viewcontent.cgi?article=1547&context=lcp.

153. See Constitution of Austria, Article 7 (emphasis added). See also Constitution of Portugal, Article 13; Constitution of Cyprus, Article 28; and European Commission Directorate-General for Justice and Consumers, *A Comparative Analysis of Non-discrimination*, 11–14, and Annex 1, 130–140.

154. Cass Sunstein, "Why Does the American Constitution Lack Social and Economic Guarantees?," *Syracuse Law Review* 56, no. 1 (2005): 2–5, https://chicagounbound.uchicago.edu/cgi/viewcontent.cgi?article=12526 &context=journal_articles. See also Richard D. Kahlenberg, "The Impact of Class, Legacy, Status, and Wealth in Higher Education Law and Policy: Combatting Disadvantages in a Culture That Celebrates Advancement and Merit," in *Oxford Handbook of U.S. Higher Education Law*, ed. Peter F. Lake (forthcoming, Oxford University Press).

155. Isenberg, *White Trash*, 1.

156. Isenberg, *White Trash*, 85.

157. Isenberg, *White Trash*, 197.

158. McGhee, *The Sum of Us*, 7.

159. Kendi, *How to Be an Anti-Racist*, 238.

160. Sandel, *The Tyranny of Merit*, 13.

161. Stewart, *The 9.9 Percent*, 7.

162. Ray Fisman and Daniel Markovits, "Why Income Inequality Isn't Going Anywhere: Rich Elites—Even Liberal Rich Elites—Don't Believe in Redistributing Wealth," *Slate*, September 18, 2015, https://slate.com/news-and-politics/2015/09/income-inequality-rich-democrats-dont-care-about-the-problem-any-more-than-rich-republicans-do.html; and Raymond Fisman, Pamela Jakiela, Shachar Kariv, and Daniel Markovits, "The Distributional Preferences of an Elite," *Science* 349, no. 6254 (September 18, 2015), https://science.sciencemag.org/content/349/6254/aab0096.abstract?sid=121580e9-c559-4974-883c-7b278eeb0c07. The phenomenon extends to the Silicon Valley liberal donors, who are more opposed to labor unions than are Republican voters. See Jacob S. Hacker and Paul Pierson, *Let Them Eat Tweets: How the Right Rules in an Age of Extreme Inequality* (New York: W. W. Norton, 2020), 59.

163. Sandel, *The Tyranny of Merit*, 59.

164. Stewart, *The 9.9 Percent*, 124.

165. Pablo A. Mitnik and David B. Grusky, *Economic Mobility in the United States* (Pew Charitable Trusts/Russell Sage Foundation, July 2015), http://www.pewtrusts.org/~/media/assets/2015/07/fsm-irs-report_artfinal.pdf.

166. Steil et al., "Introduction," in Steil et al., *Furthering Fair Housing*, 7, citing Raj Chetty, Nathaniel Hendren, Patrick Kline, Emmanuel Saez, and Nicholas Turner, "Is the United States Still a Land of Opportunity? Recent Trends in Intergenerational Mobility," *American Economic Review* 104, no. 5 (2014): 141–147.

167. Sandel, *The Tyranny of Merit*, 122.

168. Sandel, *The Tyranny of Merit*, 122.

169. See, for example, David U. Himmelstein, Deborah Thorne, Elizabeth Warren, and Steffie Woolhandler, "Medical Bankruptcy in the United States, 2007: Results of a National Study," *American Journal of Medicine* 122, no. 8 (August 2009): 741–746, https://www.amjmed.com/article/S0002-9343(09)00404-5/fulltext.

170. Sandel, *The Tyranny of Merit*, 210.

171. David Rusk, "Inclusionary Zoning—Gautreaux by Another Pathway by David Rusk (January–February 2005 P&R Issue)," Poverty & Race Research Action Council, February 1, 2005, https://www.prrac.org/inclusionary-zoning-gautreaux-by-another-pathway/.

172. McGhee, *The Sum of Us*, 122.

173. Stewart, *The 9.9 Percent*, 99.

174. Richard Reeves, *Dream Hoarders*, 48, fig. 3.2 (examining likelihood of living near a school in the top 10 percent of performers).

175. Leslie Lenkowsky, "Getting Ahead, Falling Behind" (review of Adrian Wooldridge, *The Aristocracy of Talent*), *Wall Street Journal*, July 8, 2021, A15. See also Sheryll Cashin, *White Space, Black Hood*, 111, 118–119, 127.

176. Reihan Salam, "Should We Care About Relative Mobility?," *National Review*, November 29, 2011, https://www.nationalreview.com/the-agenda/should-we-care-about-relative-mobility-reihan-salam/.

177. See John R. Logan and Brian Stults, "The Persistence of Segregation in the Metropolis: New Findings from the 2020 Census," Diversity and Disparities Project, Brown University, August 12, 2021, 2, https://s4.ad.brown.edu/Projects/Diversity/Data/Report/report08122021.pdf. One contrary study from the Othering and Belonging Institute, from June 2021, found that "most metros in the US have become more segregated since 1990 using a new measure called the 'divergence index'" ("Most Metros in the US Have Become More Segregated Since 1990" [press release], Othering & Belonging Institute, June 21, 2021, https://belonging.berkeley.edu/press-release-most-metros-us-have-become-more-segregated-1990). But the report has come under fire. See, for example, Judge Glock, "An Advocacy Group Spins Diversity as Evidence of 'Segregation,'" *Wall Street Journal*, June 30, 2021 (arguing that the "divergence index" penalizes cities that have become more diverse. "If a city had no Asian or Hispanic residents 30 years ago, but some moved in and didn't perfectly scatter in every neighborhood, the statistics would show a sudden increase in 'racial divergence.'" Glock notes that because the measure focuses on census tract divergence, the cities of Chicago, Cleveland, and Detroit are seen as integration success stories in the new measure).

178. Putnam, *Our Kids*, 38.

179. Sean F. Reardon and Kendra Bischoff, "Residential Segregation by Income, 1970–2000" (report prepared for the Russell Sage Foundation US2010 Project, October 16, 2013), http://www.s4.brown.edu/us2010/Data/Report/report10162013.pdf.

180. Reardon and Bischoff, "The Continuing Increase in Income Segregation, 2007–2012."

181. Jargowsky, "Architecture of Segregation," 1.

182. Ann Owens, "Inequality in Children's Contexts: The Economic Segregation of Households with and Without Children," *American Sociological Review* 81, no. 3 (2016): 549–574.

183. Josh Leung Gagne and Sean F. Reardon, "It Is Surprisingly Difficult to Measure Income Segregation" (CEPA Working Paper no. 22-01, Stanford Center for Education and Policy Analysis, May 2022), 36 (table 2), and 22, https://cepa.stanford.edu/sites/default/files/wp22-01-v052022.pdf.

184. Sophie Kasakove and Robert Gebeloff, "The Shrinking Middle-Class Neighborhood," *New York Times*, July 6, 2022, https://www.nytimes.com/2022/07/06/us/economic-segregation-income.html.

185. David Rusk, quoted in Kahlenberg, *All Together Now*, 22.

186. See Paul Jargowsky, "Segregation, Neighborhoods and Schools," in Lareau and Goyette, *Choosing Homes, Choosing Schools*, 107–108. See also Richard Fry and Paul Taylor, "The Rise of Residential Segregation by Income," Pew

Research Center, August 1, 2012, http://www.pewsocialtrends.org/2012/08/01/the-rise-of-residential-segregation-by-income/.

187. Paul Jargowsky, email to Richard Kahlenberg, June 12, 2019.

188. Paul Jargowsky, "What Would a New Kerner Commission Conclude Today?," *Pathways*, Winter 2019, 44.

189. See earlier discussion; and Fischel, *Zoning Rules!*, 201.

CHAPTER 5: RECOGNIZING AND RESPONDING TO EIGHT CONCERNS

1. See comments on Richard D. Kahlenberg, "The 'New Redlining' Is Deciding Who Lives in Your Neighborhood," opinion, *New York Times*, April 19, 2021, https://www.nytimes.com/2021/04/19/opinion/biden-zoning-social-justice.html#commentsContainer.

2. Einstein, Glick, and Palmer, *Neighborhood Defenders*, 33, 87, 162.

3. See Melvin Maddocks, "There Goes the Neighborhood," *Christian Science Monitor*, March 17, 1983, https://www.csmonitor.com/1983/0317/031725.html (describing River Edge, New Jersey, ordinance suggesting such vehicles "depreciate property values").

4. "Larry from Richmond" received 847 recommendations for his comment. See https://www.nytimes.com/2021/04/19/opinion/biden-zoning-social-justice.html#commentsContainer. (All subsequent comments cited in the text can be found here.)

5. Sherry and Rohit Khanna, "The Impact of Thrive and Other Housing Interventions on Our Town," Somerset listserv, Chevy Chase, Maryland, October 29, 2021.

6. Helen Eriksen, "School District, Residents Oppose Plans for Low-Income Apartments," *Houston Chronicle*, November 14, 2016, https://www.chron.com/neighborhood/katy-news/article/School-district-residents-oppose-plans-for-1504314.php.

7. See "Preventing Overcrowding & Other School Impacts of Poorly Planned Growth," Community & Environmental Defense Services, https://ceds.org/school/. The site helpfully offers: "If you're concerned about how growth may affect schools anywhere in the USA then contact CEDS at 410-654-3021 (call-text) or Help@ceds.org for an initial no-cost discussion of strategy options."

8. Sam Khater, Len Kiefer, and Venkataramana Yanamandra, "Housing Supply: A Growing Deficit," Freddie Mac Research Note, May 7, 2021, https://www.freddiemac.com/research/insight/20210507-housing-supply.

9. Wilmington City planner Glenn Harbeck, quoted in Kelly Kenoyer, Mattie Holloway, and Benjamin Schachtman, "The Newsroom Special Edition: The Northside Story—Segregation, Gentrification, and Zoning in Wilmington," WHQR, July 16, 2021, https://www.whqr.org/show/the-newsroom/2021-07-16/the-newsroom-special-edition-the-northside-story-segregation-gentrification-and-zoning-in-wilmington.

10. See Emily Badger and Christopher Ingraham, "The Most Popular Type of Home in Every Major American City, Charted," *Washington Post*, September 21, 2015, https://www.washingtonpost.com/news/wonk/wp/2015/09/21/the-most-popular-type-of-home-in-every-major-american-city-charted/ (re: Chicago); and Daniel Herriges, "Where the Missing Middle Isn't Missing," Strong Towns, August 5, 2020, https://www.strongtowns.org/journal/2020/8/5/where-the-missing-middle-isnt-missing (re: Madison).

11. "About Controlled Choice," Cambridge Public Schools, https://www.cpsd.us/departments/src/making_your_choices/about_controlled_choice.

12. See *New York Times* reader "Ampleforth from Airstrip One," https://www.nytimes.com/2021/04/19/opinion/biden-zoning-social-justice.html #commentsContainer.

13. Hanna Rosin, "American Murder Mystery: Why Is Crime Rising in So Many American Cities?," *Atlantic*, July/August 2008, https://www.theatlantic.com/magazine/archive/2008/07/american-murder-mystery/306872/.

14. See Nikole Hannah-Jones, "The Problem We All Live With" (transcript), *This American Life*, National Public Radio, July 31, 2015, https://www.thisamericanlife.org/562/transcript (quoting parent Beth Cirami).

15. McGhee, *The Sum of Us*, 387.

16. Cashin, *White Space, Black Hood*, 161.

17. Cashin, *White Space, Black Hood*, 161

18. Cashin, *White Space, Black Hood*, 191. See also "QuickFacts: Richmond City, California," US Census Bureau, https://www.census.gov/quickfacts/richmondcitycalifornia.

19. Cashin, *White Space, Black Hood*, 158.

20. Michael C. Lens, "Subsidized Housing and Crime: Theory, Mechanisms, and Evidence," *Journal of Planning Literature* 28, no. 4 (January 2013): 352–363, https://doi.org/10.1177/0885412213500992. See also Michael Lens, "Incorporating Data on Crime and Violence in the Assessment of Fair Housing," in Steil et al., *Furthering Fair Housing*, 205 (citing a number of studies).

21. Massey et al., *Climbing Mount Laurel*, xiii–xiv, 82.

22. Ingrid Gould Ellen, Michael C. Lens, and Katherine M. O'Regan, "American Murder Mystery Revisited: Do Housing Voucher Households Cause Crime?" (NYU Wagner Research Paper no. 2012-02, December 14, 2011), 10, 19, 2, 4, https://papers.ssrn.com/sol3/papers.cfm?abstract_id=2016444.

23. Michael C. Lens, "Incorporating Data on Crime and Violence into the Assessment of Fair Housing," in Steil et al., *Furthering Fair Housing*, 193, 195–196.

24. Cashin, *White Space, Black Hood*, 7.

25. Jesse Jackson, remarks at the 1988 Democratic National Convention, Atlanta, Georgia, https://www.americanrhetoric.com/speeches/jessejackson1988dnc.htm.

26. Special thanks to my Century Foundation colleagues Conor Williams, Halley Potter, Stefan Lallinger, Lara Adekeye, and Jonathan Zabala for sharing their personal observations with me.

27. Richard Florida, "Kids Raised in Walkable Cities Earn More Money as Adults," CityLab, Bloomberg, October 24, 2019, https://www.bloomberg.com /news/articles/2019-10-24/kids-from-walkable-cities-gain-economic-mobility.

28. See Richard Florida, "The Particular Creativity of Dense Urban Neighborhoods," CityLab, Bloomberg, November 1, 2019, https://www.bloomberg .com/news/articles/2019-11-01/how-density-and-innovation-are-linked-in-cities. The study, by Maria P. Roche of the Georgia Institute of Technology, finds the number of patents produced increases with street density after controlling for factors such as concentration of college graduates or the presence of universities.

29. Jane Jacobs, *The Death and Life of Great American Cities* (New York: Random House, 1961).

30. Cecilie Rohwedder, "Many House Hunters Are Choosing Diverse Neighborhoods That Reflect a Changing Population," *Wall Street Journal*, October 14, 2021, https://www.wsj.com/articles/more-house-hunters-are-choosing -diverse-neighborhoods-that-reflect-a-changing-population-11634157174.

31. Amy Stuart Wells, Lauren Fox, and Diana Cordova-Cobo, "How Racially Diverse Schools and Classrooms Can Benefit All Students," Century Foundation, February 9, 2016, https://tcf.org/content/report/how-racially -diverse-schools-and-classrooms-can-benefit-all-students/.

32. Wells, Fox, and Cordova-Cobo, "How Racially Diverse Schools."

33. Kahlenberg, *All Together Now*, 235.

34. Kahlenberg and Potter, *A Smarter Charter*, 59–63, 120; Kahlenberg, *All Together Now*, 39–42.

35. Robert Crain and Rita Mahard, *Desegregation and Black Achievement* (Santa Monica, CA: Rand Corporation, 1977); and David Armor, *Forced Justice: School Desegregation and the Law* (New York: Oxford University Press, 1995).

36. See Matt Barnum, "Did Busing for School Desegregation Succeed? Here's What Research Says," Chalkbeat, July 1, 2019, https://tinyurl.com/y4u4wvb7.

37. Nicole Friedman, "Housing Wealth Flowed to Affluent in Past Decade," *Wall Street Journal*, March 10, 2022.

38. "How to Close the Wealth Gap from the Bottom Up," editorial, *New York Times*, July 27, 2021, A22.

39. Fischel, *Zoning Rules!*, 213; and "Topic No. 701 Sale of Home," Internal Revenue Service, https://www.irs.gov/taxtopics/tc701.

40. "Topic No. 505 Interest Expense," Internal Revenue Service, https:// www.irs.gov/taxtopics/tc505.

41. See earlier discussion. Fischel, *Zoning Rules!*, 201, and 212–214.

42. William Fischel, email to Richard Kahlenberg, February 6, 2022.

43. "QuickFacts: Mount Laurel Township, Burlington County, New Jersey," US Census Bureau, https://www.census.gov/quickfacts/mountlaureltownship burlingtoncountynewjersey.

44. Len Albright, Elizabeth S. Derickson, and Douglas S. Massey, "Do Affordable Housing Projects Harm Suburban Communities? Crime, Property Values, and Taxes in Mount Laurel, NJ," *City and Community* 12, no. 2 (June

2013): 89–112, http://onlinelibrary.wiley.com/doi/10.1111/cico.12015/abstract. See also Massey et al., *Climbing Mount Laurel*, xiii–xiv, 4–5, 85, and 98; and Massey and Rugh, "The Intersections of Race and Class," 258 (that 90 percent of the families were Black or Hispanic).

45. Mai Thi Nguyen, "Does Affordable Housing Detrimentally Affect Property Values? A Review of the Literature," *Journal of Planning Literature* 20, no. 1 (August 2005): 15–26, http://journals.sagepub.com/doi/abs/10.1177/08854122 05277069. See also Lance Freeman and Hilary Botein, "Subsidized Housing and Neighborhood Impacts: A Theoretical Discussion and Review of the Evidence," *Journal of Planning Literature* 16, no. 3 (2002): 359–378, http://journals.sagepub .com/doi/abs/10.1177/088541420222093419 (literature review suggesting fears that affordable housing reduces property values are overblown).

46. Stewart, *The 9.9 Percent*, 103.

47. Stewart, *The 9.9 Percent*, 99.

48. Stewart, *The 9.9 Percent*, 106.

49. Friedman, "Housing Wealth Flowed to Affluent in Past Decade."

50. Stewart, *The 9.9 Percent*, 111.

51. See Andre M. Perry, Jonathan Rothwell, and David Harshbarger, "The Devaluation of Assets in Black Neighborhoods: The Case of Residential Property," Brookings Institution, November 27, 2018, https://www.brookings.edu /research/devaluation-of-assets-in-black-neighborhoods/; Stewart, *The 9.9 Percent*, 219. See also Maria Krysan, Reynolds Farley, and Mick P. Couper, "In the Eye of the Beholder: Racial Beliefs and Residential Segregation," *Du Bois Review* 5, no. 1 (2008): 5–26, https://www.cambridge.org/core/journals/du-bois -review-social-science-research-on-race/article/abs/in-the-eye-of-the-beholder /156668060E33B58AE863B9C96F3C5BC3; and Robert Cervero and Michael Duncan, "Neighbourhood Composition and Residential Land Prices: Does Exclusion Raise or Lower Values?," *Urban Studies* 41, no. 2 (February 2004), http:// usj.sagepub.com/content/41/2/299.

52. See Edward Pinto and Tobias Peter, "The Impact of Race and Socio-Economic Status on the Value of Homes by Neighborhood: A Critique of the Brookings Institution's 'The Devaluation of Assets in Black Neighborhoods,'" American Enterprise Institute Housing Center, August 5, 2021, https://tinyurl .com/ncw5me66; and Jonathan Rothwell and Andre Perry, "Biased Appraisals and the Devaluation of Housing in Black Neighborhoods," Brookings Institution, November 17, 2021, https://www.brookings.edu/research/biased-appraisals -and-the-devaluation-of-housing-in-black-neighborhoods/.

53. See discussion, Chapter 3.

54. Cashin, *White Space, Black Hood*, 10.

55. National Association of Real Estate Boards, *Code of Ethics*, 7, Article 34.

56. Rothstein, *The Color of Law*, 54.

57. Rothstein, *The Color of Law*, 85 (quoting a 1928 federally sponsored report).

58. Lisa Rice, "The Fair Housing Act: A Tool for Expanding Access to Quality Credit," in Squires, *The Fight for Fair Housing*, 78 and 81.

59. Judith Shulevitz, "Co-Housing Makes Parents Happier," *New York Times*, October 24, 2021, 4.

60. D. J. Taylor, "A Man for All Seasons," *Wall Street Journal*, October 29, 2021, https://www.wsj.com/articles/orwells-roses-book-review-george-orwell-rebecca-solnit-the-nature-of-truth-11635520757.

61. Lind, *Brave New Home*, 143.

62. Quoctrung Bui, Matt A. V. Chaban, and Jeremy White, "40 Percent of Buildings in Manhattan Could Not Be Built Today," *New York Times*, May 20, 2016, https://www.nytimes.com/interactive/2016/05/19/upshot/forty-percent-of-manhattans-buildings-could-not-be-built-today.html. See also Einstein, Glick, and Palmer, *Neighborhood Defenders*, 81.

63. See Joe Cortright, *America's Most Diverse Mixed Income Neighborhoods*, City Reports (Portland, OR: City Observatory, June 18, 2018), 5, https://cityobservatory.org/wp-content/uploads/2018/06/ADMIN_Report_18June.pdf; "City Observatory Map: America's Most Diverse, Mixed Income Neighborhoods," City Observatory, https://cityobservatory.org/maps/admin/; and Alissa Walker, "Why U.S. Cities Need More Multi-Racial, Mixed-Income Neighborhoods," *Curbed*, August 21, 2018, https://archive.curbed.com/2018/8/21/17759380/segregation-diversity-neighborhoods-mixed-income.

64. Sharkey, *Stuck in Place*, 60–61 (citing Anthony Downs, *New Visions for Metropolitan America* [Washington, DC: Brookings Institution Press, 1994]). See also Fischel, *Zoning Rules!*, 32 ("The United States is unusual among nations of the world for the decentralized nature of its planning and zoning").

65. Nico Calavita and Alan Mallach, "An International Perspective on Inclusionary Housing," in *Inclusionary Housing in International Perspective: Affordable Housing, Social Inclusion, and Land Value Recapture*, ed. Nico Calavita and Alan Mallach (Cambridge, MA: Lincoln Institute of Land Policy, 2010), 11.

66. Byron Shibata, "Land-Use Law in the United States and Japan: A Fundamental Overview and Comparative Analysis," *Washington University Journal of Law and Public Policy* 10 (2002): 161, 166, and 168, https://openscholarship.wustl.edu/law_journal_law_policy/vol10/iss1/7. See also Alan Durning, "Yes, Other Countries Do Housing Better, Case 1: Japan," Sightline Institute, May 25, 2021, https://www.sightline.org/2021/03/25/yes-other-countries-do-housing-better-case-1-japan/.

67. Durning, "Yes, Other Countries Do Housing Better, Case 1: Japan." See also Jiro Yoshida, "Land Scarcity, High Construction Volume, and Distinctive Leases Characterize Japan's Rental Housing Markets (Case Study: Japan)," Brookings Institution, April 20, 2021, https://www.brookings.edu/essay/Japan-rental-housing-markets/ ("The Japanese housing market is characterized by a large construction volume").

68. Gray, *Arbitrary Lines*, 123.

69. Christopher S. Elmendorf and Darien Shanske, "Auctioning the Up-zone," *Case Western Reserve Law Review* 70 (2020): 540–541, https://scholarly commons.law.case.edu/cgi/viewcontent.cgi?article=4859&context=caselrev (re: Japan).

70. Maarten van Ham, Tiit Tammaru, Rūta Ubarevičienė, and Heleen Janssen, eds., *Urban Socio-economic Segregation and Income Inequality: A Global Perspective* (New York: Springer, 2021), 13, fig. 1.3, and 14, https://link.springer .com/content/pdf/10.1007%2F978-3-030-64569-4.pdf; and Masaya Uesugi, "Changes in Occupational Structure and Residential Segregation in Tokyo," in van Ham et al., *Urban Socio-economic Segregation and Income Inequality*, 210.

71. Alan Durning, "Yes, Other Countries Do Housing Better, Case 2: Germany," Sightline Institute, May 27, 2021, https://www.sightline.org/2021/05 /27/yes-other-countries-do-housing-better-case-2-germany/.

72. Durning, "Yes, Other Countries Do Housing Better, Case 2: Germany."

73. See Sonia Hirt, "To Zone or Not to Zone? Comparing European and American Land-Use Regulation," *PND Online*, 2010, 1, 6, https://vtechworks .lib.vt.edu/bitstream/handle/10919/48185/hirt_to_zone_or_not_to_zone.pdf ?sequence=4.

74. Carolin Schmidt, "Strong Tenant Protections and Subsidies Support Germany's Majority-Renter Housing Market (Case Study: Germany)," Brook-ings Institution, April 20, 2021, https://www.brookings.edu/essay/Germany -rental-housing-markets/; and Jenny Schuetz and Sarah Crump, "What the US Can Learn from Rental Housing Markets Across the Globe," Brookings Insti-tution, April 20, 2021, https://www.brookings.edu/essay/intro-rental-housing -markets/ ("Germany's tax policy is the inverse of the U.S. mortgage interest deduction: Property owners can deduct the interest paid on a mortgage from income taxes only if the owners do not occupy the property").

75. Durning, "Yes, Other Countries Do Housing Better, Case 2: Germany."

76. Talja Blokland and Robert Vief, "Making Sense of Segregation in a Well-Connected City: The Case of Berlin," in van Ham et al., *Urban Socio-economic Segregation and Income Inequality*, 267.

77. During, "Yes, Other Countries: Japan." ("France has long trailed its German-speaking neighbors in housing abundance.")

78. Andre Comandon and Paolo Veneri, "Residential Segregation Between Income Groups in International Perspective," in van Ham et al., *Urban Socio-economic Segregation and Income Inequality*, 41.

79. See Nico Calavita and Alan Mallach, "National Differences and Commonalities: Comparative Analysis and Future Prospects," in Calavita and Mallach, *Inclusionary Housing in International Perspective*, 379.

80. Yonah Freemark, "Lessons from France for Creating Inclusionary Housing by Mandating Citywide Affordability," Urban Institute, September 14, 2021, https://www.urban.org/urban-wire/lessons-france-creating-inclusionary -housing-mandating-citywide-affordability.

81. Arthur Acolin, "The Public Sector Plays an Important Role in Supporting French Renters," Brookings Institution, April 20, 2021, https://www.brookings.edu/essay/France-rental-housing-markets/. See also Alan Mallach, "France: Social Inclusion, Fair Share Goals, and Inclusionary Housing," in Calavita and Mallach, *Inclusionary Housing in International Perspective*, 203 and 212 (noting the initial goal was 20 percent affordable housing, and when the law was adopted, 750 French communities needed to take action in order to comply with the fair share goal).

82. Anna K. Chmielewski and Sean F. Reardon, "Education," in "State of the Union: Policy and Inequality Report 2016," special issue, *Pathways* (Stanford Center of Poverty and Inequality) 2016 (2016): 48, fig. 4, https://inequality.stanford.edu/sites/default/files/Pathways-SOTU-2016.pdf. Of the countries discussed below, Germany had moderate levels of income segregation among schools; France and Japan were not included in the analysis.

83. Daniel T. Lichter, Domenico Parisi, and Helga De Valk, "Residential Segregation," in "State of the Union: Policy and Inequality Report 2016," 72–73.

84. Hoffman interview, 16.

85. Desmond, *Evicted*, 59.

86. Will Fischer, Sonya Acosta, and Erik Gartland, "More Housing Vouchers: Most Important Step to Help More People Afford Stable Homes," Center for Budget and Policy Priorities, May 13, 2021, https://www.cbpp.org/research/housing/more-housing-vouchers-most-important-step-to-help-more-people-afford-stable-homes. Some get other forms of housing assistance, but even counting those, 67 percent of poor renting families receive no assistance. Desmond, *Evicted*, 302–303.

87. "Federal Rental Assistance Fact Sheets," Center on Budget and Policy Priorities, updated January 19, 2022, https://www.cbpp.org/research/housing/federal-rental-assistance-fact-sheets#US.

88. Desmond, *Evicted*, 303.

89. "Federal Rental Assistance Fact Sheets."

90. Bret Stephens, "New York's Superstar Progressive Isn't A.O.C.," *New York Times*, September 21, 2021.

91. Rachel M. Cohen, "Elizabeth Warren Introduces Plan to Expand Affordable Housing and Dismantle Racist Zoning Practices," *Intercept*, September 28, 2018, https//theintercept.com/2018/09/28/elizabeth-warren-affordable-housing-bill.

92. Brian R. Lerman, "Mandatory Inclusionary Zoning—the Answer to the Affordable Housing Problem," *Boston College Environmental Affairs Law Review* 33 (2006): 383–416, https://www.semanticscholar.org/paper/Mandatory-Inclusionary-Zoning--The-Answer-to-Lerman/19cfd1b27528b6ddeaea58cd1042479931777330.

93. US Department of Housing and Urban Development Office of Policy Development and Research, "Exploring Inclusionary Zoning's Effect on Af-

fordable Housing," *PD&R Edge*, https://www.huduser.gov/portal/pdredge/pdr
_edge_research_012513.html.

94. David Rusk, cited in Nicholas Brunick and Patrick Maier, "Renewing
the Land of Opportunity," *Journal of Affordable Housing* 19, no. 2 (2010): 161–
190, https://www.jstor.org/stable/25782870.

95. "Americans Need More Neighbors," editorial, *New York Times*, June 15,
2019, 10, https://www.nytimes.com/2019/06/15/opinion/sunday/minneapolis
-ends-single-family-zoning.html, citing Stuart S. Rosenthal, "Are Private
Markets and Filtering a Viable Source of Low-Income Housing? Estimates
from a 'Repeat Income' Model," *American Economic Review* 104, no. 2 (2014):
687–706.

96. Daniel Herriges, "Here's Why Developers Seem to Only Build Luxury
Housing," *Greater Greater Washington*, July 30, 2018, https://ggwash.org/view
/68496/why-are-developers-only-building-luxury-housing.

97. Konrad Putzier, "The U.S. Is Running Short of Land for Housing," *Wall
Street Journal*, September 25, 2022, https://www.wsj.com/articles/the-u-s-is
-running-short-of-land-for-housing-11664125841.

98. Murphy interview.

99. Emily Badger, "If America Needs Starter Homes, Why Are Perfectly
Good Ones Being Torn Down?," *New York Times*, October 9, 2022, https://www
.nytimes.com/2022/10/09/upshot/housing-home-prices-analysis.html.

100. Michael Andersen, "We Ran the Rent Numbers in Portland's 7 Newly
Legal Home Options," Sightline, August 1, 2021, https://www.sightline.org
/2021/08/01/we-ran-the-rent-numbers-on-portlands-7-newly-legal-home
-options/. As discussed in Chapter 1, it was rising rents in Greenwich, Connecticut, that made it profitable for developers to create multifamily housing even
when they must set aside 30 percent of units for low-income families.

101. Hoffman interview, 2. See also Jill Rosenfeld, "The Art of Business
Judo," *Fast Company*, July 31, 2001, https://www.fastcompany.com/43353/art
-business-judo#:~:text=Judo%20(Japanese%20for%20%E2%80%9Cthe
%20gentle,own%20mental%20and%20physical%20energy.

102. Sara Bronin, "Zoning and Equity" video, at 1:01.

103. Falk interview, 45.

104. Einstein, Glick, and Palmer, *Neighborhood Defenders*, 149.

105. See Lance Freeman, "Five Myths About Gentrification," opinion, *Washington Post*, June 3, 2016, https://www.washingtonpost.com/opinions/five-myths
-about-gentrification/2016/06/03/b6c80e56-1ba5-11e6-8c7b-6931e66333e7
_story.html.

106. Freeman, "Five Myths About Gentrification."

107. Cashin, *White Space, Black Hood*, 158–159, citing Quentin Brummet
and David Reed, "The Effects of Gentrification on the Well-Being and Opportunity of Original Resident Adults and Children," Federal Reserve Bank
of Philadelphia, July 2019, https://cdn.theatlantic.com/assets/media/files
/gentrification_final.pdf.

108. Sharkey, *Stuck in Place*, 158.

109. Sharkey, *Stuck in Place*, 162, fig. 6.4.

110. Sharkey, *Stuck in Place*, 159–160, 164.

111. Jerusalem Demsas, "What We Talk About When We Talk About Gentrification. The Worst Problems Are in the Neighborhoods That Aren't Gentrifying," *Vox*, September 5, 2021, https://www.vox.com/22629826/gentrification-definition-housing-racism-segregation-cities.

112. Cashin, *White Space, Black Hood*, 122.

113. Sheryll Cashin, "How Larry Hogan Kept Blacks in Baltimore Segregated and Poor," *Politico*, July 18, 2020, https://www.politico.com/news/magazine/2020/07/18/how-larry-hogan-kept-black-baltimore-segregated-and-poor-367930.

114. Sam Levin, "'Largest-Ever' Silicon Valley Eviction to Displace Hundreds of Tenants," *Guardian*, July 7, 2016, https://www.theguardian.com/technology/2016/jul/07/silicon-valley-largest-eviction-rent-controlled-tenants-income-inequality.

115. See *Approaches to Resolving Displacement Concerns in Gentrifying, Urban Neighborhoods* (Vienna, VA: Equitable Housing Institute, June 29, 2021, updated July 6, 2021), 9, https://www.equitablehousing.org/images/PDFs/PDFs—2021-/EHIResolving-city-displacement-concerns-7-6-21.pdf.

116. Sam Tepperman-Gelfant, "Local Preferences Require Local Analysis," Furman Center Discussion, November 2015, https://furmancenter.org/research/iri/essay/local-preferences-require-local-analysis.

117. Tepperman-Gelfant, "Local Preferences Require Local Analysis."

118. Marissa J. Lang, "Gentrification in D.C. Means Widespread Displacement, Study Finds," *Washington Post*, April 26, 2019, https://www.washingtonpost.com/local/in-the-district-gentrification-means-widespread-displacement-report-says/2019/04/26/950a0c00-6775-11e9-8985-4cf30147bdca_story.html.

119. Freeman, "Five Myths About Gentrification."

120. Richard Florida, "The Closest Look Yet at Gentrification and Displacement," City Lab, Bloomberg, November 2, 2015, https://www.bloomberg.com/news/articles/2015-11-02/study-a-close-look-at-gentrification-and-displacement-in-philadelphia.

121. Kacie Dragon, Ingrid Ellen, and Sherry A. Glied, "Does Gentrification Displace Poor Children?" (NBER Working Paper, National Bureau of Economic Research, May 2019).

122. Ingrid Ellen and Gerard Torrats-Espinosa, "Gentrification and Fair Housing: Does Gentrification Further Integration?," *Housing Policy Debate*, December 10, 2018, 846–847. See also Sander et al., *Moving Toward Integration*, 372.

123. John Mangin, "The New Exclusionary Zoning," *Stanford Law Review* 25: 91–120, cited in Einstein, Glick, and Palmer, *Neighborhood Defenders*, 150.

124. Einstein, Glick, and Palmer, *Neighborhood Defenders*, 9.

125. Demsas in Klein, "How Blue Cities Became So Outrageously Unaffordable" podcast.

126. Jerusalem Demsas, "In Defense of the 'Gentrification Building': The New Multifamily Buildings in Your Neighborhood Actually Slow Displacement," *Vox*, September 10, 2021, https://www.vox.com/22650806/gentrification-affordable-housing-low-income-housing.

127. See Mac Taylor, "Perspectives on Helping Low-Income Californians Afford Housing," *Legislative Analyst*, February 9, 2016, 9–10, fig. 3, https://lao.ca.gov/Reports/2016/3345/Low-Income-Housing-020816.pdf.

128. See Taylor, "Perspectives on Helping Low-Income Californians Afford Housing," 1.

129. Freeman, "Five Myths About Gentrification."

130. Jared Brey, "Who's Paying for Public Services in a Changing City?," *Next City*, July 2, 2018, https://nextcity.org/daily/entry/who-paying-for-public-services-in-a-changing-city.

131. Lei Ding and Jackelyn Hwang, "Effects of Gentrification on Homeowners: Evidence from a Natural Experiment" (working paper, Federal Reserve Bank of Philadelphia, April 2018), https://www.philadelphiafed.org/-/media/community-development/publications/discussion-papers/discussionpaper-effects-of-gentrification-on-homeowners.pdf?la=en.

132. "Cambridge Affordable Housing Trust: Celebrating 30 Years," Cambridge Community Development Department, May 31, 2019, https://www.cambridgema.gov/CDD/News/2019/5/cambridgeaffordablehousingtrust celebrates30years.aspx. See also Hoffman interview, 5–6.

133. Sander et al., *Moving Toward Integration*, 432.

134. Vicki Been, "Gentrification, Displacement and Fair Housing," in Steil et al., *Furthering Fair Housing*, 185.

135. Heather Schwartz, *Housing Policy Is School Policy: Economically Integrative Housing Promotes Academic Success in Montgomery County, Maryland* (New York: Century Foundation, 2010), https://production-tcf.imgix.net/app/uploads/2010/10/16005437/tcf-Schwartz-2.pdf.

136. Equitable Housing Institute, *Approaches to Resolving Displacement Concerns*, 35.

137. Sheryll Cashin, "'Cashin: A Reply to Kahlenberg' by Sheryll Cashin (July–September 2017 P&R Issue)," Poverty and Race Research Action Council, September 15, 2017, 5–6, https://prrac.org/a-reply-to-kahlenberg/.

138. Cashin, "'Cashin: A Reply to Kahlenberg,'" 5–6.

139. See Rigel C. Oliveri, "The Legislative Battle for the Fair Housing Act (1966–1968)," in Squires, *The Fight for Fair Housing*, 37–38; and Michael Allen and Jamie Crook, "More Than Just Race: Proliferation of Protected Groups and the Increasing Influence of the Act," in Squires, *The Fight for Fair Housing*, 57–58.

140. Henderson, "Foreword," in Squires, *The Fight for Fair Housing*, xxi.

141. Douglas Massey and Jacob S. Rugh, "Segregation in Post–Civil Rights America: Stalled Integration or End of the Segregated Century," *Du Bois Review* 11, no. 2 (Fall 2014): 205–232, https://www.ncbi.nlm.nih.gov/pmc/articles /PMC4782806/.

CHAPTER 6: TEARING DOWN THE WALLS IN LOCAL COMMUNITIES

1. Janne Flisrand, interview with author, February 3, 3022 (hereafter, Flisrand interview II), 3–4.

2. Jessica Lee, "How Much Will Minneapolis' 2040 Plan Actually Help with Housing Affordability in the City?," *Minnpost*, May 31, 2019, https://www .minnpost.com/metro/2019/05/how-much-will-minneapolis-2040-plan-actually -help-with-housing-affordability-in-the-city/; John Edwards, "The Whole Story on Minneapolis 2040," *Wedge-Times Picayune*, December 13, 2018, https:// wedgelive.com/the-whole-story-on-minneapolis-2040/.

3. John Edwards, "The Whole Story on Minneapolis 2040"; and John Edwards, "Minneapolis City Council President Barb Johnson Predicts Doom over ADUs in 2014," YouTube video, 1:35, Wedge Live, March 10, 2017, https:// www.youtube.com/watch?v=I-CrltFkiow.

4. Jessica Lee, "How Much Will Minneapolis' 2040 Plan Actually Help?" (140 ADUs); and Bender's thoughts, paraphrased in Henry Grabar, "Minneapolis Confronts Its History of Housing Segregation," *Slate*, December 7, 2018, https://slate.com/business/2018/12/minneapolis-single-family-zoning-housing -racism.html.

5. Henry Grabar, "'Talk to Your Friends About Zoning': A PSA Campaign for the NIMBY in Your Life," *Slate*, February 13, 2017, https://slate.com /business/2017/02/talk-to-your-friends-about-zoning-a-psa-campaign-for-your -nimby-neighbors.html; and @MoreNeighbors, "Neighbors for More Neighbors," Twitter, https://twitter.com/MoreNeighbors?ref_src=twsrc%5Egoogle %7Ctwcamp%5Eserp%7Ctwgr%5Eauthor.

6. Peter Callaghan, "Inclusionary Zoning: Will Minneapolis See It This Year?," *Minnpost*, February 19, 2018, https://www.minnpost.com/metro/2019/08 /minneapolis-inclusionary-zoning-policy-takes-shape-even-as-developers -cry-foul/; and Grabar, "Minneapolis Confronts Its History of Housing Segregation." (Frey may be the city's "first tenant mayor.")

7. Grabar, "Minneapolis Confronts Its History of Housing Segregation"; Janne Flisrand, telephone interview with author and Tabby Cortes, July 8, 2019; Rick Varco, telephone interview with author and Tabby Cortes, July 9, 2019; and Edwards, "The Whole Story on Minneapolis 2040."

8. Janne Flisrand, telephone interview with author and Tabby Cortes, July 8, 2019.

9. Flisrand interview II, 9.

10. Patrick Sisson, "Can Minneapolis's Radical Rezoning Be a National Model?," *Curbed*, November 27, 2018, https://www.curbed.com/2018/11/27 /18113208/minneapolis-real-estate-rent-development-2040-zoning.

11. Edwards, "The Whole Story on Minneapolis 2040."

12. Flisrand interview II, 18.

13. Edwards, "The Whole Story on Minneapolis 2040"; Flisrand interview II, 5.

14. Flisrand interview II, 10.

15. Flisrand interview II, 13.

16. Flisrand interview II, 12, 14.

17. Badger and Bui, "Cities Start to Question an American Ideal."

18. Badger and Bui, "Cities Start to Question an American Ideal."

19. Demsas in Klein, "How Blue Cities Became So Outrageously Unaffordable" podcast.

20. William A. Fischel, *The Homevoter Hypothesis: How Home Values Influence Local Government Taxation, School Finance, and Land-Use Policies* (Cambridge, MA: Harvard University Press, 2005).

21. Einstein, Palmer, and Glick, *Neighborhood Defenders*, 103–105. See also Sarah Holder and Kriston Capps, "The Push for Denser Zoning Is Here to Stay," CityLab, Bloomberg, May 21, 2019, https://www.bloomberg.com/news /articles/2019-05-21/to-tackle-housing-inequality-try-upzoning.

22. Von Hoffman, "The Origins," in Steil et al., *Furthering Fair Housing*, 60.

23. See Nikole Hannah-Jones, "Living Apart"; and Mark Santow and Richard Rothstein, "A Different Kind of Choice: Educational Inequality and the Continuing Significance of Racial Segregation," *Economic Policy Institute*, August 22, 2012, http://www.epi.org/publication/educational-inequality -racial-segregation-significance/.

24. Rothstein, *The Color of Law*, 201.

25. Alvin S. Felzenberg, *Governor Tom Kean from the New Jersey Statehouse to the 9-11 Commission* (New Brunswick, NJ: Rivergate Books/Rutgers University Press, 2006), 352.

26. Claire Heininger, "Christie, Lonegan Make Campaign Promises Experts Say a Governor Can't Keep," *NJ.com*, May 25, 2009.

27. Salvador Rizzo, "N.J. Supreme Court Blocks Christie's Plan to Abolish Affordable-Housing Agency," *Star-Ledger* (Trenton, NJ), July 10, 2013, http://www.nj.com/politics/index.ssf/2013/07/nj_supreme_court_blocks _christies_plan_to_abolish_affordable-housing_agency.html.

28. Brent Johnson, "N.J. Supreme Court Rebukes Christie Administration, Puts Courts in Charge of Affordable Housing," *NJ.com*, March 10, 2015, https://www.nj.com/politics/2015/03/nj_supreme_court_rebukes_christie _administration_puts_courts_in_charge_of_affordable_housing.html. See also Editorial Board, "Chris Christie's Fair Housing Problem," editorial, *New York Times*, March 20, 2015, https://www.nytimes.com/2015/03

/21/opinion/chris-christies-fair-housing-problem.html. One exception to the resistance, interestingly, is the wealthy suburb of Bedminster, New Jersey, where 20 percent of the housing stock is now available to moderate and low-income families. See Calavita and Mallach, "National Differences and Commonalities," in Calavita and Mallach, *Inclusionary Housing in International Perspective*, 380.

29. Massey et al., *Climbing Mount Laurel*, xiii, 3–4, and 35 (affordable housing project was proposed in late 1960s, and the final project did not open until 2000).

30. Sheryll Cashin, *White Space, Black Hood*, 19. See also Fletcher, "Mikulski, Champion of Liberal Causes."

31. Conor Dougherty and Brad Plumer, "A Bold, Divisive Plan to Wean Californians from Cars," *New York Times*, March 16, 2018.

32. See Jonathan Woetzel, Jan Mischke, Shannon Peloquin, and Daniel Weisfield, "Closing California's Housing Gap," McKinsey Global Institute, October 2016, https://www.mckinsey.com/featured-insights/urbanization/closing -californias-housing-gap. See also Liam Dillon, "Get Ready for a Lot More Housing Near the Expo Line and Other California Transit Stations If New Legislation Passes," *Los Angeles Times*, January 4, 2018.

33. Dante Ramos, "Go On, California—Blow Up Your Lousy Zoning Laws," *Boston Globe*, January 14, 2018.

34. Einstein, Glick, and Palmer, *Neighborhood Defenders*, 158.

35. Dougherty and Plumer, "A Bold, Divisive Plan to Wean Californians." See also Roberts, "A Sweeping New Bill."

36. Einstein, Glick, and Palmer, *Neighborhood Defenders*, 154.

37. City Council News Service, "LA City Council Opposes State Housing Bill," *Los Angeles Daily News*, March 27, 2018, https://www.dailynews .com/2018/03/27/la-city-council-opposes-state-housing-bill/.

38. Einstein, Glick, and Palmer, *Neighborhood Defenders*, 152.

39. Einstein, Glick, and Palmer, *Neighborhood Defenders*, 156 (quoting Randy Shaw, editor of Beyond Chron and director of San Francisco's Tenderloin Housing Clinic).

40. Einstein, Glick, and Palmer, *Neighborhood Defenders*, 155, citing Rodriguez, "SB 827 Rallies End with YIMBYs Shouting Down Protesters of Color," *San Francisco Chronicle*, April 5, 2018.

41. See "The YIMBY Guide to Bullying and Its Results: SB 827 Goes Down in Committee," *City Watch*, April 19, 2018.

42. Einstein, Glick, and Palmer, *Neighborhood Defenders*, 44, citing Dillon, "A Major California Housing Bill Failed After Opposition from the Low-Income Families It Aimed to Help," *Los Angeles Times*, May 2, 2018.

43. Fischel, *Zoning Rules!*, 150. See also Einstein, Glick, and Palmer, *Neighborhood Defenders*, 106–107.

44. See Chapter 4.

45. Jessica Lee, "How Much Will Minneapolis' 2040 Plan Actually Help." Kriston Capps, "2018 Was the Year of the YIMBY," CityLab, Bloomberg, December 28, 2018, https://www.citylab.com/equity/2018/12/single-family -housing-zoning-nimby-yimby-minneapolis/577750/ (Minneapolis follows Buffalo, Hartford, and San Francisco); Henry Grabar, "Minneapolis Confronts Its History of Housing Segregation"; John Edwards, "The Whole Story on Minneapolis 2040." Nelima Sitati Munene and Aaron Berc, "Minneapolis Inclusionary Housing Policy Framework Is Needed Throughout the Region," *Minnpost*, December 13, 2018, https://www.minnpost.com/community-voices/2018/12 /minneapolis-inclusionary-housing-policy-framework-is-needed-throughout -the-region/; Erick Trickey, "How Minneapolis Freed Itself from the Stranglehold of Single-Family Homes," *Politico*, July 11, 2019, https://www.politico.com /magazine/story/2019/07/11/housing-crisis-single-family-homes-policy-227265; J. Brian Charles, "Will Up-Zoning Make Housing More Affordable?," *Governing*, July 2019, https://www.governing.com/topics/urban/gov-zoning-density.html; and Patrick Sisson, "Can Minneapolis's Radical Rezoning Be a National Model?," *Curbed*, November 27, 2018, https://www.curbed.com/2018/11/27/18113208 /minneapolis-real-estate-rent-development-2040-zoning.

46. See, for example, Yonah Freemark and Lydia Lo, "Effective Zoning Reform Isn't as Simple as It Seems," CityLab, Bloomberg, May 24, 2022, https://www.bloomberg.com/news/articles/2022-05-24/the-limits-of-ending -single-family-zoning; and Jake Blumgart, "How Important Was the Single-Family Zoning Ban in Minneapolis?," *Governing*, May 26, 2022, https://www .governing.com/community/how-important-was-the-single-family-housing -ban-in-minneapolis.

47. Sisson, "Can Minneapolis's Radical Rezoning Be a National Model?"

48. Sisson, "Can Minneapolis's Radical Rezoning Be a National Model?"

49. Trickey, "How Minneapolis Freed Itself from the Stranglehold of Single-Family Homes."

50. Christian Britschgi, "Progressive Minneapolis Just Passed One of the Most Deregulatory Housing Reforms in the Country," *Reason*, December 10, 2018, https://reason.com/2018/12/10/progressive-minneapolis-just-passed-one.

51. Sisson, "Can Minneapolis's Radical Rezoning Be a National Model?"; and Lee, "How Much Will Minneapolis' 2040 Plan Actually Help."

52. Lee, "How Much Will Minneapolis' 2040 Plan Actually Help."

53. Grabar, "Minneapolis Confronts Its History of Housing Segregation."

54. "QuickFacts: Minneapolis City, Minnesota," US Census Bureau, https://www.census.gov/quickfacts/minneapoliscityminnesota (income data are from 2013–2017).

55. John Eligon, "Minneapolis's Less Visible, and More Troubled, Side," *New York Times*, January 10, 2016, https://www.nytimes.com/2016/01/11/us /minneapoliss-less-visible-and-more-troubled-side.html; and Burl Gilyard, "Why North Minneapolis Struggles to Attract Businesses—and Why That May Be Changing," *Minnpost*, March 21, 2016, https://www.minnpost.com/twin-cities

-business/2016/03/why-north-minneapolis-struggles-attract-businesses-and
-why-may-be-chang/.

56. *Welcome to Minneapolis 2040: The City's Comprehensive Plan* (Minne-apolis: Minneapolis City Council, 2019), 8–13, https://minneapolis2040.com
/media/1488/pdf_minneapolis2040.pdf.

57. Trickey, "How Minneapolis Freed Itself from the Stranglehold of Single-Family Homes."

58. Sisson, "Can Minneapolis's Radical Rezoning Be a National Model?"

59. Lisa Bender, "How U.S. Cities Are Tackling the Affordable Hous-ing Crisis," *1A with Joshua Johnson*, WAMU, August 28, 2019, https://the1a
.org/shows/2019-08-28/1a-across-america-yimby-can-density-increase
-affordable-housing.

60. Grabar, "Minneapolis Confronts Its History of Housing Segregation."

61. Grabar, "Minneapolis Confronts Its History of Housing Segregation."

62. Quoted in Richard D. Kahlenberg, "Minneapolis Saw That NIMBYism Has Victims," *Atlantic*, October 24, 2019.

63. *Welcome to Minneapolis 2040*, 11, https://minneapolis2040.com/media
/1488/pdf_minneapolis2040.pdf.

64. "Americans Need More Neighbors," editorial, *New York Times*, June 15, 2019, 10, https://www.nytimes.com/2019/06/15/opinion/sunday/minneapolis
-ends-single-family-zoning.html.

65. See *Welcome to Minneapolis 2040*, 107, https://minneapolis2040.com
/media/1488/pdf_minneapolis2040.pdf; Badger and Bui, "Cities Start to Ques-tion an American Ideal"; and "Best Schools in Minneapolis Public School District," SchoolDigger.com, https://www.schooldigger.com/go/MN/district
/21240/search.aspx.

66. Kyrra Rankine, telephone interview with author and Michelle Burris, October 7, 2019. See also "Integration and School Choice in MPS," Minneapo-lis Public Schools, September 2019, https://mpls.k12.mn.us/uploads/integration
_and_choice_in_mps.pdf.

67. "Integration and School Choice in MPS"; Kyrra Rankine, telephone interview with author and Michelle Burris, October 7, 2019.

68. "Integration and School Choice in MPS."

69. See "Questions and Answers," Minneapolis Public Schools, https://
exploremps.org/FAQ.

70. See, for example, Heather Schwartz, "Housing Policy Is School Policy," Century Foundation, 2010, https://tcf.org/content/commentary/housing-policy
-is-school-policy/.

71. Grabar, "Minneapolis Confronts Its History of Housing Segregation."

72. "Minneapolis, Tackling Housing Crisis and Inequity, Votes to End Single-Family Zoning," One World News, December 14, 2018, https://theone
worldnews.com/americas/minneapolis-tackling-housing-crisis-and-inequity
-votes-to-end-single-family-zoning/; and Edwards, "The Whole Story on Min-neapolis 2040."

73. Janne Flisrand, "Minneapolis' Secret 2040 Sauce Was Engagement," *Streets.mn*, December 10, 2018, https://streets.mn/2018/12/10/minneapolis -secret-2040-sauce-was-engagement/.

74. Sisson, "Can Minneapolis's Radical Rezoning Be a National Model?"

75. Miguel Otarola, "Judge Hears Lawsuit over Minneapolis 2040 Plan," *Minneapolis Star Tribune*, January 31, 2019, http://www.startribune.com/judge -to-rule-on-lawsuit-over-minneapolis-2040-plan/505156872/.

76. Einstein, Glick, and Palmer, *Neighborhood Defenders*, 166, citing Miguel Otarola, "Minneapolis City Council Approves 2040 Comprehensive Plan on 12–1 Vote," *Minneapolis Star Tribune*, December 7, 2018, https://www .startribune.com/minneapolis-city-council-approves-2040-comprehensive-plan -on-12-1-vote/502178121/.

77. Janne Flisrand, telephone interview with author and Tabby Cortes, July 8, 2019. See also Brian Hanlon, interview with author, April 20, 2018.

78. Grabar, "Minneapolis Confronts Its History of Housing Segregation"; and Edwards, "The Whole Story on Minneapolis 2040."

79. Edwards, "The Whole Story on Minneapolis 2040."

80. "Americans Need More Neighbors," editorial, *New York Times*, June 15, 2019, citing Rosenthal, "Are Private Markets and Filtering a Viable Source," 687–706.

81. Sisson, "Can Minneapolis's Radical Rezoning Be a National Model?"

82. Grabar, "Minneapolis Confronts Its History of Housing Segregation"; and Britschgi, "Progressive Minneapolis Just Passed One of the Most Deregulatory Housing Reforms in the Country."

83. Philip Kiefer, "Here Comes the Neighborhood," *Grist*, May 21, 2019, https://grist.org/article/seattle-zoning-density-minneapolis-2040/; and Flisrand interview.

84. Flisrand interview.

85. Trickey, "How Minneapolis Freed Itself from the Stranglehold of Single-Family Homes."

86. "Disparate Impact," NAACP Legal Defense and Educational Fund, http://www.naacpldf.org/case-issue/disparate-impact.

87. Denise Butler, telephone interview with author and Tabby Cortes, July 12, 2019.

88. Einstein, Glick, and Palmer, *Neighborhood Defenders*, 103–105. See also Holder and Capps, "The Push for Denser Zoning Is Here to Stay."

89. Flisrand interview. See also Casey Berkovitz, "Is a Better Community Meeting Possible?," Century Foundation, August 20, 2019, https://tcf.org /content/commentary/better-community-meeting-possible/.

90. Flisrand, "Minneapolis' Secret 2040 Sauce Was Engagement."

91. Grabar, "Minneapolis Confronts Its History of Housing Segregation."

92. *Welcome to Minneapolis 2040*, 177, https://minneapolis2040.com/media /1488/pdf_minneapolis2040.pdf.

93. Berkovitz, "Is a Better Community Meeting Possible?"

94. Flisrand interview.

95. Flisrand, "Minneapolis' Secret 2040 Sauce Was Engagement."

96. Desmond, *Evicted*, 180.

97. "Tenant Protections," Policy 41, Minneapolis 2040 Plan, https://minneapolis2040.com/policies/tenant-protections/.

98. Flisrand interview.

99. Rick Varco, interview with author and Tabby Cortes, July 9, 2019.

100. Rick Varco, "#Mpls2040: Pro-Worker" (testimony before City Planning Commission), YouTube video, 1:48, WEDGE Live!, October 29, 2018, https://www.youtube.com/watch?v=ZJHyHOkCG9U.

101. "Minneapolis 2040 Comprehensive Plan Public Comments," in SEIU MN State Council Resolution in Support of Increased Housing Density, adopted April 26, 2018, https://lims.minneapolismn.gov/Download/File/1784/Online%20Comments%20on%20Revised%20Draft%20Plan%20Pt%203%20Oct%2029-Nov%201%202018.pdf. See also "Americans Need More Neighbors," editorial, *New York Times*, June 15, 2019.

102. Edwards, "The Whole Story on Minneapolis 2040"; Flisrand interview.

103. See, for example, Oregon governor Tom McCall's support for smart growth. Carl Abbott and Deborah Howe, "The Politics of Land-Use Law in Oregon: Senate Bill 100, Twenty Years After," *Oregon Historical Quarterly* 94, no. 1 (1993), http://pdxscholar.library.pdx.edu/cgi/viewcontent.cgi?article=1029&context=usp_fac.

104. Glaeser, "Green Cities, Brown Suburbs."

105. "Americans Need More Neighbors," editorial, *New York Times*, June 15, 2019.

106. Lind, *Brave New Home*, 88.

107. Shulevitz, "Co-Housing Makes Parents Happier."

108. Pawan Naidu, "What Do Millennials Want? More Trains and Buses, Fewer Automobiles," The Observatory, April 17, 2018, https://observatory.journalism.wisc.edu/2018/03/21/what-do-millennials-want-more-trains-and-buses-fewer-automobiles/ (citing 2014 Nielson survey).

109. Powell and Menendian, "Opportunity Communities," in Squires, *The Fight for Fair Housing*, 213 (citing 2016 research).

110. Lind, *Brave New Home*, 119–120, 134–139.

111. See, for example, the New York City student group championing integration, known as IntegrateNYC4me, http://www.integratenyc4me.com/about-us/.

112. Trickey, "How Minneapolis Freed Itself from the Stranglehold of Single-Family Homes"; and Grabar, "Minneapolis Confronts Its History of Housing Segregation."

113. Lind, *Brave New Home*, 171.

114. "Americans Need More Neighbors," editorial, *New York Times*, June 15, 2019.

115. "Minneapolis, Tackling Housing Crisis and Inequity"; and Schuetz, "Minneapolis 2040: The Most Wonderful Plan."

116. Flisrand interview.

117. Lee, "How Much Will Minneapolis' 2040 Plan Actually Help?"

118. Badger and Bui, "Cities Start to Question an American Ideal."

119. Badger and Bui, "Cities Start to Question an American Ideal" (citing Salim Furth of the conservative Mercatus Center). In June 2022, a judge temporarily suspended 2040 on the basis that it had not gone through proper environmental review, but in July 2022, the court allowed implementation, at least for the time being. Matt Sepic, "Minneapolis 2040 Plan Back in Play as Lawsuit Grinds On," Minnesota Public Radio, July 26, 2022, https://www .mprnews.org/story/2022/07/26/minneapolis-2040-plan-back-in-play-as-lawsuit -grinds-on.

120. "Forbes Votes Minneapolis 6th Most Liberal City," WCCO Radio, July 16, 2015, https://minnesota.cbslocal.com/2015/07/16/forbes-votes -minneapolis-6th-most-liberal-city/.

121. "Minneapolis, Tackling Housing Crisis and Inequity."

122. See, for example, "Ben Carson vs. the Fair Housing Act," editorial, *New York Times*, May 13, 2018, https://www.nytimes.com/2018/05/13/opinion /ben-carson-hud-fair-housing-act.html.

123. "Across America: How Cities Are Tackling the Affordable Housing Crisis," *1A*, WAMU National Public Radio, August 28, 2019, https://the1a.org /shows/2019-08-28/1a-across-america-yimby-can-density-increase-affordable -housing; and Trickey, "How Minneapolis Freed Itself from the Stranglehold of Single-Family Homes."

124. "Executive Order Establishing a White House Council on Eliminating Regulatory Barriers to Affordable Housing," White House, June 25, 2019, https://trumpwhitehouse.archives.gov/presidential-actions/executive-order -establishing-white-house-council-eliminating-regulatory-barriers-affordable -housing/.

125. As we shall discuss further in Chapters 7 and 8, once President Trump saw the possibility of appealing to "Suburban House Wives of America" by opposing zoning reform, Carson and Trump teamed up in an August 2020 *Wall Street Journal* op-ed to *oppose* Minneapolis's decision to legalize duplexes and triplexes citywide. The duo condemned "a relentless push for more high-density housing in single-family residential neighborhoods." Donald J. Trump and Ben Carson, "We'll Protect America's Suburbs," op-ed, *Wall Street Journal*, August 16, 2020, https://www.wsj.com/articles/well-protect-americas-suburbs -11597608133?st=sugm9qikzzzxyx0&reflink=article_email_share.

126. Christian Britschgi, "Progressive Minneapolis Just Passed One of the Most Deregulatory Housing Reforms in the Country."

127. Rick Varco, interview with author and Tabby Cortes, July 9, 2019.

128. See Angela Ruggiero, "Berkeley to End Single Family Residential Zoning, Citing Racist Ties," *Mercury News*, February 24, 2021 ("resolution calls for change by December 2022"); Patrick Spauster, "Gainesville, Florida, Moves to End Single-Family Zoning," CityLab, Bloomberg, August 9, 2022,

https://www.bloomberg.com/news/articles/2022-08-09/gainesville-florida
-moves-to-end-single-family-zoning; Katherine Shaver, "Montgomery Council Approves 30-Year Plan for Denser Development," *Washington Post*, October
25, 2022, https://www.washingtonpost.com/transportation/2022/10/25/thrive
-2050-montgomery-county/ (noting the Thrive 2050 plan recommends allowing
duplexes, triplexes, and small apartments in certain areas that have been zoned
only for single-family homes); "Zoning Reform Is Creating Opportunities for
More Housing Types," Raleigh, North Carolina, June 8, 2022, https://raleighnc
.gov/planning/zoning-reform-creating-opportunities-more-housing-types (regarding reforms allowing accessory dwelling units, missing middle housing, and
reduced parking requirements); Lisa Prevost, "The A.D.U. Experiment: Accessory Dwelling Units, Long Popular on the West Coast, Are Coming to the
Northeast. And Princeton, N.J., Is the 'Guinea Pig,'" *New York Times*, December
10, 2021 (Connecticut passed ADU law); Lisa Prevost, "A Push for Zoning
Reform in Connecticut: Momentum Is Growing for Multifamily Housing to
Be Built in a State Full of Detached Single-Family Houses," *New York Times*,
February 6, 2021, https://www.nytimes.com/2021/02/26/realestate/connecticut
-zoning-reform.html; Gray, *Arbitrary Lines*, 119 (in 2019, Arkansas overrode
local community efforts to impose a minimum floor area on single-family
homes); Popp, "Mills Signs Bill Reforming Zoning Laws"; and Katie McKellar,
"What's the Answer to the U.S. Housing Crisis? Why National Experts Have
Eyes on Utah," *Deseret News* (Salt Lake City, UT), September 1, 2022, https://
www.deseret.com/utah/2022/9/1/23331816/housing-market-crisis-shortage
-home-prices-recession-bubble-solutions (in 2022, Utah passed legislation "requiring cities to zone for some moderate-income housing").

129. See Gray, *Arbitrary Lines*, 118.

130. Einstein, Glick, and Palmer, *Neighborhood Defenders*, 166, citing Andy
Mannix, "In Minneapolis, a Test Case for Cities Looking to Solve Affordable
Housing Crisis," *Minneapolis Star Tribune*, April 27, 2019; and Lauren Dake,
"Tina Kotek Is Oregon's New Governor, Continuing Democrats' Rule," Na-
tional Public Radio, November 10, 2022, https://www.npr.org/2022/11/10
/1134206147/oregon-governor-results-drazan-kotek-johnson.

131. A special thanks to Emma Vadehra, who provided critical research on
Oregon.

132. Laura Bliss, "Oregon's Single-Family Zoning Ban Was a 'Long Time
Coming,'" CityLab, Bloomberg, July 2, 2019, https://www.citylab.com/equity
/2019/07/oregon-single-family-zoning-reform-yimby-affordable-housing
/593137/ (legislation passed on June 30, 2019).

133. Michael Andersen, "Eight Ingredients for a State-Level Zoning
Reform: Lessons from Oregon's Landmark Legalization of Fourplexes and
Townhouses," Sightline Institute, August 13, 2021, https://www.sightline.org
/2021/08/13/eight-ingredients-for-a-state-level-zoning-reform/.

134. "HB 2001 Signed into Law," 1000 Friends of Oregon, August 8, 2019,
https://friends.org/news/2019/8/hb-2001-signed-law (governor signed legislation);

and Badger and Bui, "Cities Start to Question an American Ideal" (77 percent of residential land in Portland zoned for single-family homes).

135. Bliss, "Oregon's Single-Family Zoning Ban Was a 'Long Time Coming'"; and Christian Britschgi, "Oregon Becomes First State to Ditch Single-Family Zoning," *Reason*, July 1, 2019, https://reason.com/2019/07/01/oregon -becomes-first-state-to-ditch-single-family-zoning/.

136. See, for example, "Oregonians Worry New Zoning Law May Change Neighborhoods," Oregon Live, July 22, 2019, updated July 28, 2022, https://www.oregonlive.com/teens/2019/07/oregonians-worry-new-zoning -law-may-change-neighborhoods.html (quoting Corvallis, Oregon, neighborhood association president); and Taylor Griggs, "HB 2001: A Eugene Odyssey," *Eugene Weekly*, July 24, 2020, https://www.eugeneweekly.com/2020/07/24/hb -2001-a-eugene-odyssey/ (that Eugene City Council "hated" HB 2001).

137. "Meet Tina," Tina for Oregon, https://www.tinafororegon.com/.

138. Bliss, "Oregon's Single Family Zoning Ban Was a 'Long Time Coming.'"

139. Jane Eastman, "Put a Spare Home or Two in Your Backyard: Oregon's ADU Rules Allow for More Income-Producing Rentals," *Oregonian*, September 10, 2021, https://tinyurl.com/mrxn3fb2.

140. "HB 2001 Signed into Law," 1000 Friends of Oregon, August 8, 2019, https://friends.org/news/2019/8/hb-2001-signed-law.

141. Fahey, quoted in Laura Wamsley, "Oregon Legislature Votes to Essentially Ban Single-Family Zoning," NPR, July 1, 2019, https://www.npr .org/2019/07/01/737798440/oregon-legislature-votes-to-essentially-ban -single-family-zoning.

142. Michael Andersen and Anna Fahey, "Lessons from Oregon's Missing Middle Success," Sightline Institute, November 4, 2019, https://www.sightline .org/2019/11/04/lessons-from-oregons-missing-middle-success/; and Fahey and Andersen, "Message Memo: OR Missing Middle Bill."

143. Kotek, quoted in Wamsley, "Oregon Legislature Votes to Essentially Ban Single-Family Zoning."

144. Fahey and Andersen, "Message Memo: OR Missing Middle Bill."

145. Michael C. Lens and Paavo Monkkonen, "Do Strict Land Use Regulations Make Metropolitan Areas More Segregated by Income?," *Journal of the American Planning Association* 82, no. 1 (2016): 6–21, https://www.ncbi.nlm.nih .gov/pmc/articles/PMC5800413/.

146. Taylor Smiley Wolfe (former policy director to Speaker Tina Kotek), interview with Emma Vadehra, September 13, 2021.

147. See Andersen and Fahey, "Lessons from Oregon's Missing Middle Success."

148. "HB 2001 Signed into Law," 1000 Friends of Oregon, August 8, 2019, https://friends.org/news/2019/8/hb-2001-signed-law.

149. Taylor Smiley Wolfe, interview with Emma Vadehra, September 13, 2021.

150. Einstein, Glick, and Palmer, *Neighborhood Defenders*, 161.

151. Einstein, Glick, and Palmer, *Neighborhood Defenders*, 6.

152. See Britschgi, "Oregon Becomes First State to Ditch Single-Family Zoning."

153. Andersen, "Eight Ingredients." ("HB 2001 did have staunch opponents in the Democratic Party, mainly from representatives of some suburban districts.")

154. Andersen, "Eight Ingredients."

155. Britschgi, "Oregon Becomes First State to Ditch Single-Family Zoning."

156. "2019 Session: House Bill 2001," *Oregonian*, https://gov.oregonlive.com /bill/2019/hb2001/.

157. Andersen, "Eight Ingredients."

158. Michael Andersen, "Housing Is Popular, Actually," Sightline Institute, February 8, 2022, https://www.sightline.org/2022/02/08/housing-is-popular/.

159. Everton Bailey Jr., "Portland Changes Zoning Rules to Allow Duplexes, Triplexes, Fourplexes in Areas Previously Reserved for Single-Family Homes," *Oregonian*, August 13, 2020, https://www.oregonlive.com/portland /2020/08/portland-changes-zoning-code-to-allow-duplexes-triplexes-fourplexes -in-areas-previously-reserved-for-single-family-homes.html. See also Michael Andersen, "Portland Just Passed the Best Low-Density Zoning Reform in US History," Sightline Institute, August 11, 2020.

160. Andersen, "Portland Just Passed the Best Low-Density Zoning Reform in US History."

161. Henry Grabar, "The Most Important Housing Reform in America Has Come to the South," *Slate*, June 28, 2021, https://slate.com/business/2021/06/ charlotte-single-family-zoning-segregation-housing.html.

162. Grabar, "The Most Important Housing Reform."

163. Grabar, "The Most Important Housing Reform."

164. Dougherty, "Where the Suburbs End"; Grace Hase, "Law Takes Aim at Calif. Housing Crisis," *Washington Post*, October 10, 2010, A11; and Stephen Eide, "Homelessness Is Behind the Anger at Gavin Newsom," *Wall Street Journal*, September 4, 2021.

165. Dougherty, "After Years of Failure, California Lawmakers Pave the Way"; and Ilya Somin, "California Enacts Two Important New Zoning Reform Laws," *Reason*, September 17, 2021. The bill was passed in August but signed by the governor in September.

166. Conor Dougherty, "Where the Suburbs End" (quoting Ben Metcalf of the University of California at Berkeley's Turner Center).

167. Somin, "California Enacts Two Important New Zoning Reform Laws"; and Shulevitz, "Co-Housing Makes Parents Happier."

168. See Ben Fritz and Zusha Elinson, "California Limits Single-Family Home Zoning," *Wall Street Journal*, September 16, 2021, https://www.wsj.com /articles/california-limits-single-family-home-zoning-11631840086.

169. Michael Andersen, "Five Lessons from California's Big Zoning Reform: A Pattern Is Emerging Here," Sightline Institute, August 26, 2021, https://www.sightline.org/2021/08/26/four-lessons-from-californias-big-zoning-reform/.

170. Hanlon in David Roberts, "The Future of Housing Policy Is Being Decided in California," *Vox*, April 4, 2018, https://www.vox.com/cities-and-urbanism/2018/2/23/17011154/sb827-california-housing-crisis.

171. Schuetz, *Fixer-Upper*, 150.

172. Dougherty, "After Years of Failure, California Lawmakers Pave the Way."

173. Scott Wiener, Roundtable Discussion transcript, 68.

174. Scott Wiener, Roundtable Discussion transcript, 82.

175. Scott Wiener, Roundtable Discussion transcript, 77.

176. Scott Wiener, Roundtable Discussion transcript, 64.

177. Scott Wiener, Roundtable Discussion transcript, 77.

178. James Brasuell, "California Makes Planning History, Resets the Housing Status Quo," *Planetizen*, September 1, 2022, https://www.planetizen.com/news/2022/09/118560-california-makes-planning-history-resets-housing-status-quo; and Darrell Owens, "YIMBYs Triumph in California," Discourse Lounge (newsletter), September 3, 2022, https://darrellowens.substack.com/p/yimby-triumph-in-california.

179. Conor Dougherty and Soumya Karlamangla, "California Fights Its NIMBYs," *New York Times*, September 1, 2022, https://www.nytimes.com/2022/09/01/business/economy/california-nimbys-housing.html.

180. Noah Smith, "The Long March of the YIMBYs," *Noahpinion* (newsletter), September 20, 2022, https://noahpinion.substack.com/p/the-long-march-of-the-yimbys.

181. Scott Wiener, Roundtable Discussion transcript, 77–78.

182. Equitable Housing Institute, "Toward a Comprehensive Ban," 13–31.

CHAPTER 7: MAKING ECONOMIC DISCRIMINATION VISIBLE NATIONALLY

1. Marc Peyser, "Taking It to the Streets," *Stanford Magazine*, March/April 2000, https://stanfordmag.org/contents/taking-it-to-the-streets.

2. Kahlenberg, "Taking on Class and Racial Discrimination in Housing."

3. Kahlenberg, "Taking on Class and Racial Discrimination in Housing."

4. "Booker, Clyburn Take Innovative Two-Pronged Approach to Tackling Affordable Housing Crisis," Cory Booker, October 23, 2019, https://www.booker.senate.gov/news/press/booker-clyburn-take-innovative-two-pronged-approach-to-tackling-affordable-housing-crisis.

5. "Booker, Clyburn Take Innovative."

6. Cassandra Robertson, Roundtable Commentary. (The Roundtable Commentary notation here and below cites unpublished commentaries that various individuals who participated in the Roundtable Discussion provided in advance of the discussion.)

7. Kahlenberg, "Taking on Class and Racial Discrimination."

8. Kahlenberg, "Taking on Class and Racial Discrimination."

9. Kahlenberg, "Taking on Class and Racial Discrimination."

10. Steil et al., "Introduction," in Steil et al., *Furthering Fair Housing*, 9–10.

11. Richard D. Kahlenberg, "Homes for Us All: Rethinking the American Dream in Cities and Suburbs," *American Prospect*, November 13, 2020; and Shane Reiner-Roth, "YIMBY Act Passes House of Representatives, Could Pave the Way for More Affordable Housing," *Architect's Newspaper*, March 5, 2020, https://www.archpaper.com/2020/03/yimby-act-passes-house-of-representatives/; and Yes in My Backyard Act, H.R. 4351, 116th Cong. (2019–2020), https://www.congress.gov/bill/116th-congress/house-bill/4351/cosponsors?search ResultViewType=expanded.

12. Fischel, *Zoning Rules!*, 52–53.

13. *Heart of Atlanta Motel, Inc. v. U.S.*, 379 U.S. 241 (1964); *Katzenbach v. McClung*, 379 U.S. 294 (1964); and US Constitution, Article I, Section 8 (Commerce Clause). See also Congressional Research Service, "The Power to Regulate Commerce: Limits on Congressional Power," May 16, 2014, https://www.everycrsreport.com/reports/RL32844.html.

14. See Brian T. Yeh, "The Federal Government's Authority to Impose Conditions on Grant Funds," Congressional Research Service, March 23, 2017, https://fas.org/sgp/crs/misc/R44797.pdf, citing among other Supreme Court decisions *South Dakota v. Dole*, 483 U.S. 203, 205–208 (1987) and *Nat'l Fed'n of Indep. Bus. (NFIB) v. Sibelius*, 567 U.S. 519, 132 S. Ct. 2566, 2605 (2012).

15. Ryan Streeter, "When the Culture War Comes for Affordable Housing," *Real Clear Policy*, July 29, 2020, https://www.realclearpolicy.com/articles/2020 /07/29/when_the_culture_war_comes_for_affordable_housing_500380.html.

16. *Buchanan v. Warley*, 245 U.S. 60 (1917).

17. See *Texas Dept. of Housing and Community Affairs v. Inclusive Communities Project, Inc.* (2015) noting that challenges to exclusionary zoning policies under the Fair Housing Act "reside at the heartland of disparate-impact liability."

18. Fischel, *Zoning Rules!*, 52.

19. Solomon Greene and Ingrid Gould Ellen, *Breaking Barriers, Boosting Supply: How the Federal Government Can Help Eliminate Exclusionary Zoning* (Washington, DC: Urban Institute, September 2020), 6, https://www.urban.org /sites/default/files/publication/102963/breaking-barriers-boosting-supply_0.pdf.

20. Religious Land Use and Institutionalized Persons Act of 2000, 42 U.S.C. §§ 2000cc, et seq., https://www.justice.gov/crt/religious-land-use-and -institutionalized-persons-act.

21. Fischel, *Zoning Rules!*, 52.

22. "HUD Rule on Affirmatively Furthering Fair Housing," US Department of Housing and Urban Development, July 16, 2015, https://archives .huduser.gov/affh/affh.html.

23. Megan Haberle, "Furthering Fair Housing: Lessons for the Road Ahead," in Steil et al., *Furthering Fair Housing*, 213.

24. Megan Haberle and Philip Tegeler, "Coordinated Action on School and Housing Integration: The Role of State Government," *University of Richmond Law Review* 53 (2019): 949–976, https://prrac.org/pdf/housing_and_school _integration_univ_of_richmond_1_rev_2019.pdf: 962; and Megan Haberle, Peter Kye, and Brian Knudsen, "Reviving and Improving HUD's Affirmatively Furthering Fair Housing Regulation: A Practice-Based Roadmap" (policy brief, Poverty and Race Research Action Council, December 2020), https://prrac.org /pdf/improving-affh-roadmap.pdf.

25. Megan Haberle, Roundtable Commentary.

26. Lens, "Incorporating Data," in Steil et al., *Furthering Fair Housing*, 194 (noting the creating of "the School Proficiency Index, the Jobs Proximity Index, the Labor Market Engagement Index, the Low Transportation Cost Index, the Transit Trips Index, and the Environmental Health Index").

27. Steil et al., "Introduction," in Steil et al., *Furthering Fair Housing*, 5; and Lens, "Incorporating Data on Crime," in Steil et al., *Furthering Fair Housing*, 194. Note, in addition to the 40 percent poverty threshold, a community can be defined as a R/ECAP if it has a poverty rate three times the poverty rate of the metro area. Lens, "Incorporating Data," 194.

28. "The Biden Plan for Investing in Our Communities Through Housing," Biden–Harris 2020 Campaign, https://joebiden.com/housing/ (endorsing Clyburn HOME Act, https://www.congress.gov/bill/116th-congress/house-bill /4808).

29. Kriston Capps, "The Trump Administration Just Derailed a Key Obama Rule on Housing Segregation," CityLab, Bloomberg, January 4, 2018, https://www.bloomberg.com/news/articles/2018-01-05/trump-s-hud-delays -affirmatively-furthering-fair-housing.

30. Justin P. Steil, Nicholas F. Kelly, Lawrence J. Vale, and Maia S. Woluchem, "Introduction," in Steil et al., *Furthering Fair Housing*, 11.

31. Steil et al., "Introduction," in Steil et al., *Furthering Fair Housing*, 36.

32. Zack Budryk, "Booker Hits Back at Trump Tweet, Mocks Misspelling of Name," *The Hill*, August 12, 2020, https://thehill.com/homenews /senate/511691-booker-hits-back-at-trump-tweet-mocks-misspelling-of-name.

33. Stanley Kurtz, "Biden and Dems Are Set to Abolish the Suburbs," *National Review*, June 30, 2020, https://www.nationalreview.com/corner /biden-and-dems-are-set-to-abolish-the-suburbs/.

34. "Trump Falsely Claims Joe Biden Would 'Abolish the Suburbs,'" MSNBC, July 17, 2020, https://www.msnbc.com/morning-joe/watch/trump -falsely-claims-joe-biden-would-abolish-the-suburbs-87869509821.

35. Trump and Carson, "We'll Protect America's Suburbs."

36. Matthew Yglesias, "Trump's Tweets About Saving the 'Suburban Lifestyle Dream,' Explained: White Identity Politics Trump Free Market Regulatory Reform," *Vox*, August 3, 2020, https://www.vox.com/2020/8/3 /21347565/suburban-lifestyle-dream-trump-tweets-fair-housing.

37. See "St. Louis Couple Famous for Pointing Guns at Protesters Speak at RNC," CBS News, August 24, 2020, https://www.cbsnews.com/video /st-louis-couple-famous-for-pointing-guns-at-protesters-speak-at-rnc/.

38. See Richard D. Kahlenberg, "The Ugly History of Single-Family Zoning Resurfaces," Century Foundation, September 16, 2020, https://tcf.org/content /commentary/ugly-history-single-family-zoning-resurfaces/.

39. William A. Galston, "Which Voters Made Joe Biden President?," *Wall Street Journal*, August 11, 2021. See also Geoffrey Skelley, Elena Mejía, Amelia Thomson-DeVeaux, and Laura Bronner, "Why the Suburbs Have Shifted Blue," *FiveThirtyEight*, December 16, 2020, https://fivethirtyeight.com/features/why -the-suburbs-have-shifted-blue/.

40. See National Fair Housing Alliance, "Business Roundtable's Call to Support Fair Housing and Civil Rights Earns Praise from National Fair Housing Alliance, Center for Responsible Lending" (press release), National Fair Housing Alliance, October 16, 2020, https://nationalfairhousing.org/business -roundtables-call-to-support-fair-housing-and-civil-rights-earns-praise-from -national-fair-housing-alliance-center-for-responsible-lending/.

41. See "Memorandum on Redressing Our Nation's and the Federal Government's History of Discriminatory Housing Practices and Policies," White House, January 26, 2021, Section 2, https://www.whitehouse.gov /briefing-room/presidential-actions/2021/01/26/memorandum-on-redressing -our-nations-and-the-federal-governments-history-of-discriminatory-housing -practices-and-policies/; and Rachel M. Cohen, "Your Segregated Town Might Finally Be in Trouble," *Vox*, January 23, 2023.

42. See "Implementation of the Fair Housing Act's Discriminatory Effects Standard," 78 Fed. Reg. 11460 (February 15, 2013), https://www.federal register.gov/citation/78-FR-11460 (Obama rule); https://www.federalregister .gov/documents/2020/09/24/2020-19887/huds-implementation-of-the-fair -housing-acts-disparate-impact-standard#footnote-2-p60288 (Trump's repeal); "Memorandum on Redressing Our Nation's and the Federal Government's History of Discriminatory Housing Practices and Policies" (Biden's intent to reinstate); and Department of Housing and Urban Development, "Reinstatement of HUD's Discriminatory Effects Standard: A Proposed Rule by the Housing and Urban Development Department," 86 Fed. Reg. 33590 (June 25, 2021), https://www.federalregister.gov/documents/2021/06/25/2021-13240 /reinstatement-of-huds-discriminatory-effects-standard.

43. Morgan Williams and Stacy Seicshnaydre, "The Legacy and Promise of Disparate Impact," in Squires, *The Fight for Fair Housing*, 175–176, citing Section 100.500(c)1.

44. Williams and Seicshnaydre, "The Legacy," citing Section 100.500(c)(2).

45. Williams and Seicshnaydre, "The Legacy," citing Section 100.500(c)(3).

46. *Texas Department of Housing and Community Affairs v. The Inclusive Communities Project*, 135 S. Ct., 2507, 2521–2522 (2015).

47. *United States v. City of Black Jack,* 508 F.2d 1179, 1183 (8th Cir. 1974).

48. *Huntington Branch, NAACP v. Huntington,* 844 F.2d 926, 928 (2d. Cir. 1988). See also Jerusalem Demsas, "America's Racist Housing Rules Really Can Be Fixed: More Than 50 Years After Passage of the Fair Housing Act, It's Time to Sue the Suburbs," *Vox,* February 17, 2021, https://www.vox.com/22252625/america-racist-housing-rules-how-to-fix.

49. *Inclusive Communities Project,* slip opinion, 18.

50. See Philip Tegeler, Roundtable Commentary.

51. See "Fact Sheet: The American Jobs Plan," White House, March 31, 2021, https://www.whitehouse.gov/briefing-room/statements-releases/2021/03/31/fact-sheet-the-american-jobs-plan/. See also Andy Sullivan and Jarrett Renshaw, "Biden Seeks to Ease Housing Shortage with $5 Billion 'Carrot, Not Stick' Approach," Reuters, April 8, 2021, https://www.reuters.com/article/us-usa-biden-infrastructure-zoning-idUSKBN2BV1CX.

52. "Fact Sheet: The American Jobs Plan."

53. Brian Deese, "White House Event on Reducing and Use and Zoning Restrictions," YouTube video, 1:15:33, October 29, 2021, https://www.youtube.com/watch?v=8UwSZeNSi00; see also Yonah Freemark and Eleanor Noble, "Reconciliation Bill Could Help Localities Fight Exclusionary Zoning," Urban Institute, October 27, 2021, https://www.urban.org/urban-wire/reconciliation-bill-funding-could-help-localities-fight-exclusionary-zoning.

54. See Richard D. Kahlenberg, "Polite, Legal and Unacknowledged: The Devastating Biases of Well-Heeled Suburbia," *American Prospect,* December 2, 2021.

55. "President Biden Announces New Actions to Ease the Burden of Housing Costs" (press release), White House, May 16, 2022, https://www.whitehouse.gov/briefing-room/statements-releases/2022/05/16/president-biden-announces-new-actions-to-ease-the-burden-of-housing-costs/; and Joseph R. Biden Jr., "My Plan for Fighting Inflation," opinion, *Wall Street Journal,* May 31, 2022, https://www.wsj.com/articles/my-plan-for-fighting-inflation-joe-biden-gas-prices-economy-unemployment-jobs-covid-11653940654.

56. See Richard D. Kahlenberg, "The 'New Redlining' Is Deciding Who Lives in Your Neighborhood," *New York Times,* April 19, 2021.

57. See Richard D. Kahlenberg, "An Economic Fair Housing Act," Century Foundation, August 3, 2017, https://tcf.org/content/report/economic-fair-housing-act/.

58. Richard D. Kahlenberg, "The Walls We Won't Tear Down," opinion, *New York Times,* August 3, 2017, https://www.nytimes.com/2017/08/03/opinion/sunday/zoning-laws-segregation-income.html.

59. Kahlenberg, "An Economic Fair Housing Act." See also Equitable Housing Institute, "Economic Fair Housing Act of 2021: Partial Draft Bill and Comments," revised November 30, 2020, 12, https://www.equitablehousing.org/images/PDFs/PDFs--2018-/EHI_Economic_FHA_of_2021_draft-rev

_11-30-20.pdf. ("This section does not independently require the provision of housing at public expense.")

60. Equitable Housing Institute, "Economic Fair Housing Act of 2021," 1. For an earlier version, see Equitable Housing Institute, "Toward a Comprehensive Ban on Exclusionary Housing Practices" (memorandum, Equitable Housing Institute, December 2019), https://www.equitablehousing.org/images /PDFs/PDFs--2021-/EHI_Toward-comprehensive-ban-tech-edits_1-2022.pdf.

61. Tom Loftus, interview with author, January 14, 2022 (hereafter, Loftus interview), 15–16.

62. Thomas A. Loftus III, "That Baby: Justice Jackson's Writings About a Grandchild, and Vice Versa," *Albany Law Review* 68 (2004): 37, 38, and 40.

63. Loftus interview, 5–6.

64. Loftus interview, 8–9, 11.

65. For a list of participants, see Richard D. Kahlenberg, "Tearing Down the Walls: How the Biden Administration and Congress Can Reduce Exclusionary Zoning," Century Foundation, April 18, 2021, https://tcf.org/content/report /tearing-walls-biden-administration-congress-can-reduce-exclusionary-zoning/.

66. Equitable Housing Institute, "Economic Fair Housing Act," 2.

67. Equitable Housing Institute, "Economic Fair Housing Act," 1 and 2n3.

68. *Texas Dept. of Housing and Community Affairs v. Inclusive Communities Project*, 135 S. Ct. 2507 (2015), slip opinion, 19, https://www.justice.gov/sites /default/files/crt/legacy/2015/06/25/tdhcainclusiveopinion.pdf.

69. Equitable Housing Institute, "Economic Fair Housing Act," 3.

70. Equitable Housing Institute, "Economic Fair Housing Act," 10–22. Even in states that have adopted source-of-income discrimination laws, violations can be common, so resources for enforcement are important. See, for example, Matthew Haag, "'She Wants Well-Qualified People': 88 Landlords Accused of Housing Bias," *New York Times*, March 15, 2021, https://www .nytimes.com/2021/03/15/nyregion/real-estate-lawsuit-section-8-discrimination .html.

71. Wade Henderson, "Foreword," in Squires, *The Fight for Fair Housing*, xx.

72. Cashin, *White Space, Black Hood*, 64 (citing Michael S. Schill and Samantha Friedman, "The Fair Housing Act of 1988: First Decade," *Cityscape* 4, no. 3 (1999), https://www.huduser.gov/periodicals/cityscpe/vol4num3/schill .pdf); and Von Hoffman, "Origins," in Steil et al., *Furthering Fair Housing*, 64–65.

73. Kendi, *How to Be an Anti-Racist*, 208 (pointing to "soaring White support for interracial marriage decades after the policy changed in 1967").

74. Sander et al., *Moving Toward Integration*, 121.

75. Sander at al., *Moving Toward Integration*, 120–121.

76. Sander et al., *Moving Toward Integration*, 125.

77. Sander et al., *Moving Toward Integration*, 461. See also University of Illinois, "Principles of Racial Equality," fig. 2, https://igpa.uillinois.edu/racial -attitude/principles-of-racial-equality/ (In the 1960s, a majority of white people

said white people should have a right to keep Black people out of their neighborhoods, but today virtually no one would say that); Squires, "Fair Housing Yesterday, Today, and Tomorrow," in Squires, *The Fight for Fair Housing*, 3 (The percentage of white people who view public fair housing laws favorably has increased from 37 percent in 1972 to 69 percent in 2008); and Putnam and Garrett, *The Upswing*, 234, fig. 6.9 (whereas a majority of white Americans in the 1960s did not support free residential choice for Black people, today racial discrimination in housing is thoroughly delegitimized).

78. Oliveri, "The Legislative Battle," in Squires, *The Fight for Fair Housing*, 37–38.

79. Sander et al., *Moving Toward Integration*, 140.

80. Squires, "Fair Housing Yesterday," in Squires, *The Fight for Fair Housing*, 3.

81. John R. Logan and Brian J. Stults, "The Persistence of Segregation in the Metropolis: New Findings from the 2010 Census" (census brief prepared for Russell Sage Foundation US2010 Project, March 24, 2011), http://www.s4.brown.edu/us2010/Data/Report/report2.pdf (national 1970 dissimilarity index); and John R. Logan and Brian J. Stults, "Metropolitan Segregation: No Breakthrough in Sight," Brown University, August 12, 2021, 2, https://s4.ad.brown.edu/Projects/Diversity/Data/Report/report08122021.pdf (finding the Black–White dissimilarity index was 55 in 2020).

82. Having said that, an Economic Fair Housing Act would be less far-reaching than the Fair Housing Act in other respects. The Fair Housing Act prohibits private-sector landlords from discriminating on the basis of race, whereas the Economic Fair Housing Act would limit its antidiscrimination protection in the private sector to source-of-income discrimination, not to income per se. In a market system, a landlord remains free to discriminate on the basis of ability to pay.

83. Tom Loftus, memorandum to author, June 8, 2020, 1.

84. Loftus, memorandum to author, June 8, 2020, 1.

85. 104 F.3d 300, at 306–307 (9th Cir. 1997).

86. Stacy Seicshnaydre, "Is Disparate Impact Having Any Impact? An Appellate Analysis of Forty Years of Disparate Impact Claims Under the Fair Housing Act," *American University Law Review* 63, no. 2 (2013), https://digitalcommons.wcl.american.edu/cgi/viewcontent.cgi?article=1906&context=aulr.

87. *Texas Dept. of Housing and Community Affairs v. Inclusive Communities Project*, 135 S. Ct. 2507 (2015), slip opinion, 19, https://www.justice.gov/sites/default/files/crt/legacy/2015/06/25/tdhcainclusiveopinion.pdf.

88. Zasloff, "The Price of Equality," at 117 (citing slip opinion, 4, which quotes the 2013 HUD regulation).

89. Brandon Fuller, Roundtable Commentary.

90. Noah Kazis, Roundtable Commentary. See also Jenny Schuetz, Roundtable Commentary (the major challenge of the ban on exclusionary zoning is

"the difficulty in defining what constitutes problematic zoning"); and Noah Kazis, Roundtable Discussion transcript, 18.

91. Greene and Ellen, "Breaking Barriers," 9 (suggesting that "states could create a goal that at least 20 percent of all new construction in any region should be affordable to households with 80 percent of the region's median income and that at least half of these affordable units should be built in neighborhoods where median income is above the region's median income"); and Greene and Ellen, "Breaking Barriers," 10 (elimination of single-family exclusive zoning would allow a state to automatically qualify for housing production goal).

92. See, for example, Brandon Fuller, Roundtable Commentary (noting the attractiveness of setting goals, but then giving jurisdictions the flexibility to get there); and Salin Geevarghese, Roundtable Commentary (same).

93. Jenny Schuetz, Roundtable Discussion transcript, 65.

94. Jenny Schuetz, Roundtable Commentary. See also Jenny Schuetz, "Is Zoning a Useful Tool or a Regulator Barrier?," Brookings Institution, October 31, 2019, https://www.brookings.edu/research/is-zoning-a-useful-tool-or-a -regulatory-barrier/.

95. Einstein, Glick, and Palmer, *Neighborhood Defenders*, 80.

96. Equitable Housing Institute, "Economic Fair Housing Act of 2021," 1.

97. Fischel, *Zoning Rules!*, 361 (New Jersey's proportion is higher than Massachusetts's); Gray, *Arbitrary Lines*, 225n12 (explaining that New Jersey does not have a flat percentage requirement but instead uses a formula to determine fair share for particular communities); Nico Calavita and Alan Mallach, "National Differences and Commonalities: Comparative Analysis and Future Prospects," in Calavita and Mallach, *Inclusionary Housing in International Perspective*, 379 (Spain's Catalonia region has a goal that every municipality include social housing as at least 15 percent of its overall housing stock); and Yonah Freemark, "Lessons from France for Creating Inclusionary Housing by Mandating Citywide Affordability" (by 2025, most urban municipalities in France are supposed to ensure that 25 percent of their housing is publicly supported).

98. Chris Elmendorf (@CSElmendorf), Twitter thread, January 21, 2022, https://twitter.com/CSElmendorf/status/1484559230736633857.

99. Fischel, *Zoning Rules!*, 202, and 360–361.

100. Under the Fair Housing Act, reverse discrimination cases are not permissible in the cases of disability or familial status. Although the act refers to some protected classes broadly (race, color, religion, national origin, and sex), for other protected classes it employs more specific terms—such as "disability" (as opposed to ability status), and the act specifically defines "family status" to include having "at least one child under 18 years old." See Ron Leshnower and Ann O'Connell, "The Fair Housing Act's Protected Classes: What Landlords Need to Know," NOLO.com, https://www.nolo.com/legal-encyclopedia/the -fair-housing-acts-protected-classes-what-landlords-need-know.html.

101. Demetria McCain, Roundtable Discussion transcript, 17.

102. Jenny Schuetz, "HUD Can't Fix Exclusionary Zoning by Withholding CDBG Funds," Brookings Institution, October 15, 2018, https://www.brookings.edu/research/hud-cant-fix-exclusionary-zoning-by-withholding-cdbg-funds/.

103. Katy O'Donnell, "Biden Allies Push Back on Sweeping Plan to Promote Fair Housing," *Politico*, December 25, 2020, https://www.politico.com/news/2020/12/25/biden-allies-push-back-fair-housing-450352.

104. Nikole Hannah-Jones, "Living Apart."

105. Noah Kazis, Roundtable Discussion transcript, 16.

106. Noah Kazis, Roundtable Discussion transcript, 18.

107. Equitable Housing Institute, "Economic Fair Housing Act," 4.

108. Equitable Housing Institute, "Economic Fair Housing Act," 3–4.

109. Scott Wiener, Roundtable Discussion transcript, 72.

110. Scott Wiener, Roundtable Discussion transcript, 79.

111. Ilya Somin, Roundtable Discussion transcript, 75; Ilya Somin, Roundtable Commentary.

112. Noah Kazis, Roundtable Commentary.

113. See Equitable Housing Institute, "Economic Fair Housing Act," 7–8 (citing Peter Ganong and Daniel Shoag, "Why Has Regional Income Convergence in the U.S. Declined?," *Journal of Urban Economics* 102 (2017): 76–90 (finding "hyperinflation in housing costs in the wealthier states since 1980 has had adverse effects on the upward mobility of American workers in other states, and on the American economy overall"). See also Noah Kazis, "Ending Exclusionary Zoning in New York City's Suburbs," Furman Center, November 9, 2020, 6 (citing Ganong and Shoag study); and Chang-Tai Hsieh and Enrico Moretti, "Housing Constraints and Spatial Misallocation," *American Economic Journal: Macroeconomics* 11 (2019): 1–39 (finding that "exclusionary housing practices at the local level are a significant drag on American economic growth").

114. See Equitable Housing Institute, "Economic Fair Housing Act," 5 and 8 (citing *Shapiro v. Thompson*, 394 U.S. 618, 629, 631 [1969]: "freedom to travel throughout the United States has long been recognized as a basic right under the Constitution," and that right has been applied to an "indigent who desires to migrate, resettle, find a new job, and start a new life").

115. Phil Tegeler, Roundtable Discussion transcript, 60.

116. Olatunde Johnson, Roundtable Discussion transcript, 76.

117. See Brian T. Yeh, "The Federal Government's Authority to Impose Conditions on Grant Funds," Congressional Research Service, March 23, 2017, https://fas.org/sgp/crs/misc/R44797.pdf. *South Dakota v. Dole*, 483 U.S. 203, 205–208 (1987) and *Nat'l Fed'n of Indep. Bus. (NFIB) v. Sibelius*, 567 U.S. 519, 132 S. Ct. 2566, 2605 (2012).

118. *Nat'l Fed'n of Indep. Bus. (NFIB) v. Sibelius*, 567 U.S. 519, 132 S. Ct. 2566, 2605 (2012). See also Pablo Zevallos, Roundtable Commentary.

119. See Jerusalem Demsas, "America's Racist Housing Rules"; and "HUD Awards Over $47 Million to Fight Housing Discrimination: Grants to Sup-

port and Promote Fair Housing Nationwide" (press release), US Department of Housing and Urban Development, September 2, 2021, https://www.hud.gov /press/press_releases_media_advisories/HUD_No_21_132 (describing the Fair Housing Initiatives Program).

120. See discussion, Chapter 4.

121. See Meir Rinde, "Could This Supreme Court Ruling Affect Fair Housing?," Shelterforce, August 25, 2022, https://shelterforce.org/2022/08/25 /could-this-supreme-court-ruling-affect-fair-housing/ (asking "could disparate impact be at risk?").

122. "Full Biography," Congressman Emanuel Cleaver, https://cleaver.house .gov/about/full-biography.

123. *Zoned Out: Examining the Impact of Exclusionary Zoning on People, Resources, and Opportunity, Hearing Before Subcommittee on Housing, Community Development and Insurance, U.S. House Financial Services Committee*, 117th Cong. (October 15, 2021), https://financialservices.house.gov/events/eventsingle .aspx?EventID=408494.

124. See discussion, Chapter 8.

125. Jerusalem Demsas, "Could a 54-Year-Old Civil Rights Law Be Revived?," *Vox*, January 17, 2022, https://www.vox.com/22883459/martin-luther -king-jr-fair-housing-act-housing-crisis.

126. "Housing Mobility—Coming to a PHA Near You?," Poverty and Race Research Action Council, February 21, 2019, https://prrac.org/prrac-update -housing-mobility-coming-to-a-pha-near-you/.

127. Ingrid Gould Ellen, Keren Horn, Yiwen Kuai, Roman Pazuniak, and Michael David Williams, *Effect of QAP Incentives on the Location of LIHTC Properties* (Washington, DC: US Department of Housing and Urban Development Office of Policy Development and Research, April 2015), https://www .novoco.com/sites/default/files/atoms/files/pdr_qap_incentive_location_lihtc _properties_050615.pdf (finding that 40 percent of Nevada housing tax credit units were in high-opportunity, low-poverty neighborhoods, compared with only 2.3 percent of housing tax credit units in nearby Arizona).

CHAPTER 8: THE POLITICAL POSSIBILITIES OF A BRIGHTER FUTURE

1. King, quoted in UPI, "Dr. King's Group Maps Civil Disobedience Strategy," *New York Times*, November 27, 1967, 53; Stephen B. Oates, *Let the Trumpet Sound: The Life of Martin Luther King, Jr.* (New York: New American Library, 1982), 434–435.

2. Bayard Rustin, "The Blacks and the Unions," *Harper's*, May 1971, 81.

3. See Martin Luther King Jr., *Why We Can't Wait* (New York: New American Library, 1964), 138.

4. David Halberstam, *The Unfinished Odyssey of Robert Kennedy* (New York: Random House, 1968), 91; Jean Stein and George Plimpton, *American Journey: The Times of Robert Kennedy* (New York: Harcourt Brace Jovanovich, 1970), 261.

5. May 1968 Harris Poll, cited in Richard M. Scammon and Ben J. Wattenberg, *The Real Majority* (New York: Coward-McCann, 1970), 98.

6. Jeff Greenfield, interview with author, January 30, 1985.

7. Evan Thomas, *Robert Kennedy: His Life* (New York: Simon & Schuster, 2000), 376 (citing "Analysis of Indiana Primary Results," May 8, 1968, Schlesinger Papers, John F. Kennedy Library, Boston).

8. See Richard D. Kahlenberg, "The Inclusive Populism of Robert F. Kennedy," Century Foundation, March 16, 2018, https://tcf.org/content/report/inclusive-populism-robert-f-kennedy/; Richard D. Kahlenberg, "The Bobby Kennedy Pathway," *New York Times*, March 16, 2018; and Simon Greer and Richard D. Kahlenberg, "How Progressives Can Recapture Seven Deeply Held American Values," Century Foundation, February 26, 2020, https://tcf.orgcontent/report/progressives-can-recapture-seven-deeply-held-american-values/.

9. See, for example, Leonhardt and Philbrick, "Donald Trump's Racism," https://www.nytimes.com/interactive/2018/01/15/opinion/leonhardt-trump-racist.html.

10. Kathy Orton and Aaron Gregg, "Tax Law to Shift Housing Markets," *Washington Post*, December 30, 2017, A1.

11. Jerusalem Demsas, "The Housing Crisis Is the Top Concern for Urban Residents," *Vox*, September 16, 2021, https://www.vox.com/2021/9/16/22674410/housing-crisis-homelessness-poll.

12. Kyle Swenson, Emily Guskin, and Scott Clement, "Majority of D.C. Residents Support Clearing of Homeless Encampments, Post Poll Finds," *Washington Post*, February 24, 2022, https://www.washingtonpost.com/dc-md-va/2022/02/24/dc-poll-housing-homeless-bowser/.

13. "Seattle Housing and Livability Agenda: Final Advisory Recommendations to Mayor Edward R. Murray and the Seattle City Council," Seattle Housing and Livability Agenda, July 13, 2015, app. C, http://www.seattle.gov/documents/departments/hala/policy/hala_report_2015.pdf.

14. Conor Dougherty, "Twilight of the NIMBY," *New York Times*, June 5, 2022, https://www.nytimes.com/2022/06/05/business/economy/california-housing-crisis-nimby.html.

15. Brian Hanlon, interview with author, April 20, 2018.

16. Dougherty and Plumer, "A Bold, Divisive Plan to Wean Californians from Cars."

17. Conor Dougherty, "Getting to Yes on Nimby Street," *New York Times*, December 3, 2017.

18. "Let's End California's Housing Shortage—Support SB 827," technology industry leaders' letter in support of SB 827, January 24, 2018, https://www.cayimby.org/technetwork/.

19. "SB 827," California Yes in My Backyard (YIMBY), https://www.cayimby.org/sb827.

20. Brian Hanlon, interview with author, April 20, 2018.

21. Eva Corlett and Caitlin Cassidy, "New Zealand Has Adopted a Radical Rezoning Plan to Cut House Prices—Could It Work in Australia?," *Guardian*, December 15, 2021, https://www.theguardian.com/world/2021/dec/15/new -zealand-has-adopted-a-radical-rezoning-plan-to-cut-house-prices-could-it -work-in-australia.

22. Emily Badger and Eve Washington, "The Housing Shortage Isn't Just a Coastal Crisis Anymore," *New York Times*, July 14, 2022, https://www.nytimes .com/2022/07/14/upshot/housing-shortage-us.html.

23. Up for Growth, *2022 Housing Underproduction in the U.S.* (Washington, DC: Up for Growth, 2022), 5, https://upforgrowth.org/apply-the-vision /housing-underproduction/.

24. Peter Harrison and Henry Kraemer, *Homes for All: The Progressive 2020 Agenda for Housing* (Data for Progress, May 2019), 35, http://filesforprogress .org/reports/homes_for_all.pdf.

25. Manny Garcia, "Across 26 Metro Areas, Residents Largely Support Allowing Missing Middle Homes in Residential Neighborhoods," Zillow Research, April 11, 2022, https://www.zillow.com/research/modest-densification -zhar-30934/.

26. See Fischel, "An Economic History of Zoning"; and Fischel, *Zoning Rules!*, 357–358.

27. Fischel, *Zoning Rules!*, 354.

28. Fischel, *Zoning Rules!*, 354–355.

29. Fischel, *Zoning Rules!*, 355.

30. Jean Folger, "Best Countries for Pensions and Retirement: How the U.S. Compares May (or May Not) Be a Surprise," Investopedia, June 4, 2021, https:// www.investopedia.com/articles/personal-finance/042914/top-pension-systems -world.asp.

31. See Putnam and Garrett, *The Upswing*, 234, fig. 6.9.

32. See Inae Oh, "Trump Ramps Up the Racism and Sexism After Harris Makes History," *Mother Jones*, August 12, 2020, https://www.motherjones .com/politics/2020/08/trump-suburban-housewife-racist-housing/; Peter Dreier, "Not Your Granddad's Suburb: Trump's Racist Appeals Fall Flat in Diversified Suburbs," *Shelterforce*, August 17, 2020, https://shelterforce.org/2020/08 /17/trump_racist_appeal_suburbs/; Geoffrey Skelley, Elena Mejía, Amelia Thomson-DeVeaux, and Laura Bronner, "Why the Suburbs Have Shifted Blue," *FiveThirtyEight*, December 18, 2020, https://fivethirtyeight.com/features/why -the-suburbs-have-shifted-blue/; and Ilya Somin, Roundtable Discussion transcript, 49.

33. Cashin, *White Space, Black Hood*, 8, 100–101.

34. Booker, quoted in Kahlenberg, "Taking on Class and Racial Discrimination."

35. Cassandra Robertson, Roundtable Discussion transcript, 33.

36. See Glenn Thrush, "Trump Attacks a Suburban Housing Program. Critics See a Ploy for White Votes," *New York Times*, July 1, 2020; and Stanley

Kurtz, "Biden and Dems Are Set to Abolish the Suburbs," *National Review*, June 30, 2020.

37. Cassandra Robertson, Roundtable Discussion transcript, 33.

38. Jenny Schuetz, Roundtable Discussion transcript, 66.

39. Scott Wiener, Roundtable Discussion transcript, 77.

40. Raphael W. Bostic, Katherine O'Regan, and Patrick Pontius, with Nicholas F. Kelly, "Fair Housing from the Inside Out: A Behind the Scenes Look at the Creation of the Affirmatively Furthering Fair Housing Rule," in Steil et al., *Furthering Fair Housing*, 77.

41. Edward G. Goetz, "The Fair Housing Challenge to Community Development," in Steil et al., *Furthering Fair Housing*, 156–158.

42. Goetz, "The Fair Housing Challenge to Community Development," in Steil et al., *Furthering Fair Housing*, 149–150.

43. Chris Elmendorf (@CSElmendorf), Twitter thread, January 21, 2022, https://twitter.com/CSElmendorf/status/1484559230736633857.

44. Jamelle Bouie, "What 'Structural Racism' Really Means," *New York Times*, November 9, 2021.

45. McGhee, *The Sum of Us*, 10. See also Isenberg, *White Trash*, 37–39.

46. Calhoun, quoted in Ta-Nehisi Coates, "The Case for Reparations," *Atlantic*, June 2014, https://www.theatlantic.com/magazine/archive/2014/06/the-case-for-reparations/361631/.

47. McGhee, *The Sum of Us*, 108–109.

48. W. E. B. Du Bois, *Black Reconstruction in America: 1860–1880*, quoted in McGhee, *The Sum of Us*, 121.

49. McGhee, *The Sum of Us*, 118.

50. See, for example, Leonhardt and Philbrick, "Donald Trump's Racism," https://www.nytimes.com/interactive/2018/01/15/opinion/leonhardt-trump-racist.html.

51. See Jared Bernstein, "The Trump Tax Cuts in Action: Socialism for the Rich," *Washington Post*, January 2, 2020, https://www.washingtonpost.com/outlook/2020/01/02/trump-tax-cuts-action-socialism-rich/.

52. Elie Mystal, "Democrats Are Ready to Abandon Black Voters, Again," *Nation*, October 13, 2021, https://www.thenation.com/article/politics/democrats-election-shor/.

53. Richard D. Kahlenberg, "The 'New Redlining' Is Deciding Who Lives in Your Neighborhood," *New York Times*, April 19, 2021.

54. McGhee, *The Sum of Us*, 170.

55. Dolly Parton's America, "Dixie Disappearance," December 17, 2019, WNYC, https://www.wnycstudios.org/podcasts/dolly-partons-america/episodes/dixie-disappearance (for original meaning of "Hillbilly"); and *Oxford English Dictionary* (for contemporary meaning).

56. McGhee, *The Sum of Us*, 170.

57. See Richard D. Kahlenberg, "Achieving Better Diversity: Reforming Affirmative Action in Higher Education," Century Foundation, December 3,

2015, https://tcf.org/content/report/achieving-better-diversity/. See also Matthew Watkins and Neena Satija, "The Price of Admission: How an Attempt to Boost Diversity at Texas Colleges Could Kill Affirmative Action," pt. 1, *Texas Tribune*, March 29, 2016, https://apps.texastribune.org/price-of-admission/.

58. Conor Dougherty, "The Rent Revolution Is Coming," *New York Times*, October 15, 2022, https://www.nytimes.com/2022/10/15/business/economy/rent-tenant-activism.html.

59. William Fischel, *Zoning Rules!*, 150.

60. Fischel, *Zoning Rules!*, 150 (calling the legislation "tit for tat").

61. Sharon P. Krefetz, "The Impact and Evolution of the Massachusetts Comprehensive Permit and Zoning Appeals Act," *Western New England Law Review* 22 (2001): 381–430 at 385–386.

62. Fischel, *Zoning Rules!*, 150. See also Einstein, Glick, and Palmer, *Neighborhood Defenders*, 106–107.

63. Gray, *Arbitrary Lines*, 145–146.

64. Andersen, "Eight Ingredients." ("HB 2001 did have staunch opponents in the Democratic Party, mainly from representatives of some suburban districts.")

65. Scott Wiener, Roundtable Discussion transcript, 64.

66. Scott Wiener, Roundtable Discussion transcript, 69; see also Scott Wiener, Roundtable Discussion transcript, 78.

67. Kahlenberg, "Updating the Fair Housing Act to Make Housing More Affordable."

68. McGhee, *The Sum of Us*, 25.

69. McGhee, *The Sum of Us*, 28.

70. Isenberg, *White Trash*, 47, 60 (that James Oglethorpe, founder of the colony of Georgia, argued that slavery should be opposed because legalizing slavery would "starve the poor white laborer"); McGhee, *The Sum of Us*, 144 (that poor white voters were also hurt by poll tax); McGhee, *The Sum of Us*, 145 (majority of felons banned from voting in Florida before reform had been white); Isenberg, *White Trash*, 239, and Cashin, *White Space, Black Hood*, 14–15 (on redlining by class as well as race); and McGhee, *The Sum of Us*, 108–109 (unions).

71. McGhee, *The Sum of Us*, 172, citing the impact of the Supreme Court's decision in *Village of Arlington Heights v. Metropolitan Housing Development Corp.*, 429 U.S. 252 (1977).

72. Cashin, *White Space, Black Hood*, 160.

73. McGhee, *The Sum of Us*, 103.

74. McGhee, *The Sum of Us*, 132–133.

75. McGhee, *The Sum of Us*, 135–136.

76. Anne Kim, "The Wrong Way to Build Black Wealth: Maxine Waters Has a Well-Intentioned but Bad Idea for Promoting Homeownership and Wealth for Black Americans," *Washington Monthly*, June 8, 2021.

77. Micah English and Joshua Kalla, "Racial Equality Frames and Public Policy Support: Survey Experimental Evidence," OSF Preprints, April 26, 2021, https://osf.io/tdkf3/.

78. Jerusalem Demsas, "How to Convince a NIMBY to Build More Housing," *Vox*, February 24, 2021, https://www.vox.com/22297328/affordable-housing -nimby-housing-prices-rising-poll-data-for-progress.

79. See Jason Sorens, *The New Hampshire Statewide Housing Poll and Survey Experiments: Lessons for Advocates* (Manchester, NH: Center for Ethics in Business and Governance, Saint Anselm College, January 1, 2021), 11–12, https:// www.anselm.edu/sites/default/files/CEBG/20843-CEBG-IssueBrief-P2.pdf (finding that arguments against exclusionary zoning that emphasized basic issues of fairness were particularly appealing).

80. Ashley Jardina, *White Identity Politics* (New York: Cambridge University Press, 2019), 81–82 and 241.

81. Guy Molyneux, "Mapping the White Working Class," *American Prospect*, December 20, 2016, https://prospect.org/economy/mapping-white-working -class/.

82. Jamelle Bouie, "How a Still Segregated Country Holds Us All Back," opinion, *New York Times*, October 8, 2022, https://www.nytimes.com/2022 /10/08/opinion/segregation-progress-america.html.

83. See Paul Frymer and Jacob M. Grumbach, "Labor Unions and White Racial Politics," *American Journal of Political Science* 65, no. 1 (2021): 225–240, published ahead of print, June 29, 2020, https://scholar.princeton.edu/sites /default/files/pfrymer/files/ajps12537_rev.pdf; and Matthew Rozsa, "Why Labor Unions Make People Less Racist," *Salon*, July 1, 2020, https://www.salon .com/2020/07/01/why-labor-unions-make-people-less-racist/.

84. See Adam Kelsey, "Behind Hillary Clinton's 'Basket of Deplorables' Line," ABC News, September 13, 2016, http://abcnews.go.com/Politics/hillary -clintons-basket-deplorables-line/story?id=42069200.

85. See Amy Chozick, *Chasing Hillary: Ten Years, Two Presidential Campaigns, and One Intact Glass Ceiling* (New York: Harper, 2018), cited in Gideon Resnick, "Hillary Clinton on Election Night," *Daily Beast*, April 20, 2018, https://www .thedailybeast.com/hillary-clinton-they-were-never-going-to-let-me-be-president.

86. Harold Meyerson, "The Democrats in Opposition: They Not Only Need to Resist Trump. They Need to Build Power Wherever They Can," *American Prospect*, Winter 2017, 26, https://issuu.com/americanprospect/docs/tap_winter_2017.

87. Sandel, *The Tyranny of Merit*, 72.

88. Sandel, *The Tyranny of Merit*, 27.

89. Sandel, *The Tyranny of Merit*, 26 and 101; and Richard D. Kahlenberg, "The Politics of Pretension," *Washington Monthly*, August 30, 2020, https:// washingtonmonthly.com/2020/08/30/the-politics-of-pretension/ (re: seven-point margin).

90. Sandel, *The Tyranny of Merit*, 26–27. See also Stewart, *The 9.9 Percent*, 234 (citing Mark Munro et al., "Biden Counties Equal 70 Percent of America's Economy," Brookings Institution, November 10, 2020, that in 2016, Trump-supporting counties represented just 36 percent of US GDP).

91. George Packer, *Last Best Hope: America in Crisis and Renewal* (New York: Picador, 2021), 86.

92. J. Anthony Lukas, interview with author, January 3, 1995; quoted in Richard D. Kahlenberg, *The Remedy: Race, Class, and Affirmative Action* (New York: Basic Books, 1996), 191.

93. Chris Elmendorf (@CSElmendorf), Twitter thread, January 21, 2022, https://twitter.com/CSElmendorf/status/1484559230736633857.

94. Cashin, *White Space, Black Hood*, 5.

95. McGhee, *The Sum of Us*, 222.

96. Steven Greenhouse, "Younger Workers Are Organizing. Can Their Fervor Save Unions?," *Washington Post*, September 2, 2022, https://www.washington post.com/outlook/2022/09/02/young-workers-unions-starbucks-amazon/.

97. See discussion, Chapter 6.

98. Noah Kazis, Roundtable Commentary; and Trey Hollingsworth, "Rep. Hollingsworth Introduces YIMBY Act" (press release), September 17, 2019, https://hollingsworth.house.gov/news/documentsingle.aspx?DocumentID=904.

99. Lind, *Brave New Home*, 221.

100. Pablo Zevallos, Roundtable Commentary.

101. *Zoned Out: Examining the Impact of Exclusionary Zoning on People, Resources, and Opportunity, Hearing Before Subcommittee on Housing, Community Development and Insurance, U.S. House Financial Services Committee*, 117th Cong. (October 15, 2021), https://financialservices.house.gov/calendar/eventsingle .aspx?EventID=408494.

102. See discussion, Chapter 6.

103. Ilya Somin, "Expanding Housing and Job Opportunities by Cutting Back on Zoning," *Washington Post*, June 10, 2017, https://www.washingtonpost .com/news/volokh-conspiracy/wp/2017/06/20/expanding-housing -and-job-opportunities-by-cutting-back-on-zoning/.

104. Ilya Somin, "The Emerging Cross-Ideological Consensus on Zoning," opinion, *Washington Post*, December 5, 2015, https://www.washingtonpost .com/news/volokh-conspiracy/wp/2015/12/05/the-emerging-cross-ideological -consensus-on-zoning/.

105. Ilya Somin, Roundtable Discussion transcript, 48.

106. Ilya Somin, Roundtable Discussion transcript, 76.

107. Ilya Somin, Roundtable Commentary. See also Ilya Somin, Roundtable Discussion transcript, 48.

108. Streeter, "When the Culture War Comes for Affordable Housing."

109. Packer, *Last Best Hope*, 156–157.

110. Yuval Levin, "Against All Odds, the Possibility of New Coalitions in Education," in *The Opportunity to Rise: Rethinking K–12 Pathways to Social and Economic Mobility*, ed. Bruno Manno (Bentonville, AR: Walton Family Foundation, 2022), 239 (describing the general concept of what constitutes a powerful cross-party coalition).

EPILOGUE: IMAGINING A BETTER AMERICA

1. Demsas, "Could a 54-Year-Old Civil Rights Law Be Revived?"

2. Walter F. Mondale, "Afterword," in Squires, *The Fight for Fair Housing*, 291, citing Martin Luther King Jr., *The Essential Writings and Speeches of Martin Luther King*, ed. James Washington (New York: HarperCollins, 1986), 85.

3. Martin Luther King Jr., remarks at Mason Temple, March 1968, quoted in Terry Gross and Michael Honey, "Martin Luther King's Last Campaign for Equality," National Public Radio, April 4, 2008, https://www.npr.org/templates /story/story.php?storyId=89372561.

4. Sandel, *The Tyranny of Merit*, 210.

5. King, quoted in Kahlenberg, *The Remedy: Class, Race, and Affirmative Action*, xiii.

6. See discussion, Chapter 1, of $8,775 boost in wages across the board.

7. Linda R. Tropp, *Benefits of Contact Between Racial and Ethnic Groups: A Summary of Research Findings: Testimony in Support of New York City School Diversity Bills, Hearings on Diversity in New York City Schools* (Washington, DC: National Coalition on School Diversity, December 11, 2014), 1–2, http:// school-diversity.org/wp-content/uploads/2014/09/Tropp-written-testimony -for-New-York-City-Schools-12-2014.pdf (Of 515 studies from thirty-eight countries between the 1940s and 2000, 94 percent found greater interracial contact is associated with reduced racial prejudice).

8. Richard Reeves, *Dream Hoarders*, 106.

9. See Packer, *Last Best Hope*, 175 (invoking the concept of Francis Perkins, Franklin Roosevelt's labor secretary, that "patriotism" was "based upon the love of men and who were fellow citizens").

10. McGhee, *The Sum of Us*, xxii.

11. More racially segregated cities tend to have higher levels of political polarization. Rachael Dottle, "Where Democrats and Republicans Live in Your City," *Five Thirty-Eight*, May 20, 2019, https://projects.fivethirtyeight.com /republicans-democrats-cities/. See also Jeremy Engle, "Do You Think You Live in a Political Bubble?," *New York Times*, May 7, 2021, https://www.nytimes .com/2021/05/07/learning/do-you-think-you-live-in-a-political-bubble.html.

12. McGhee, *The Sum of Us*, 288.

Index

accessory dwelling units (ADUs)
elderly and, 172, 175
exclusionary zoning and, 14, 39–42,
126, 143, 158–159, 184
"missing middle" housing and, 11,
126, 140, 158–159
single-family homes and, 14, 39–42,
126, 158, 172, 175, 212
affirmative action, xi, 47, 187, 230
Affirmatively Furthering Fair
Housing (AFFH), 85, 154,
186–189, 199, 204, 216
Affordable Care Act, 202
Affordable Housing Trust, 153
AFL-CIO, 219
African Career, Education, and
Resource, 169
Akron, Ohio, 50, 111
Alabama, 68, 220, 222–223
Alves, Michael, ix–x
Amazon, 31–32, 131, 228
American Apartheid (book), 43
American Association of Retired
Persons (AARP), 172, 177

American Dream, 4, 17, 43, 63, 138,
224
American Enterprise Institute, 230
American Housing Survey, 39–40
American Prospect (magazine), 123
Americans with Disabilities Act, 186
Amherst College, 193
Andersen, Michael, 176, 178
Ann Simpson Davis Middle School,
37
anti-snob zoning law, 163, 221
Appleton, Wisconsin, 212
Arizona, 58, 83–84
Arkansas, 174
Arlington, Virginia, 40
Assembly Bill 2011, 180
Assembly Bill 2097, 180
Atlanta, Georgia, 68
Atlantic, The (magazine), 90, 123, 128,
130
Audubon Chapter of Minneapolis,
167
Austin, Texas, 29, 32, 37, 105,
220–221

Richard D. Kahlenberg is a researcher and writer on education and housing policy. He is a senior fellow at the Progressive Policy Institute and a nonresident scholar at Georgetown University's McCourt School of Public Policy. He is known as "the intellectual father of the economic integration movement" in K–12 schooling and "the nation's chief proponent of class-based affirmative action in higher education admissions." His articles have been published in the *New York Times*, the *Washington Post*, the *Wall Street Journal*, the *New Republic*, and the *Atlantic*, and he has appeared on ABC, CBS, CNN, FOX, C-SPAN, MSNBC, PBS, and NPR. A graduate of Harvard College and Harvard Law, he has been a senior fellow at the Century Foundation, a fellow at the Center for National Policy, a visiting associate professor of constitutional law at George Washington University, and a legislative assistant to Senator Charles S. Robb (D-VA).